1994

Social Studies in the Elementary Schools

Social Studies in the Elementary School

Francis P. Hunkins
University of Washington

Jan Jeter
St. Mary's Dominican College

Phyllis F. Maxey
University of California at Los Angeles

Charles E. Merrill Publishing Company
A Bell & Howell Company
Columbus   Toronto   London   Sydney

Published by
Charles E. Merrill Publishing Co.
A Bell & Howell Company
Columbus, Ohio 43216

This book was set in Bembo.
Production Coordination: Martha Morss

Photographs:

p. 1 (Strix Pix), p. 5 (Celia Drake), p. 10 (Strix Pix), p. 13 (Paul Conklin), p. 15 (Printed with permission of the *Northshore Citizen*, Bothell, Washington), p. 22 (Richard Khanlian), p. 26 (Paul Conklin), p. 31 (Strix Pix), p. 34 (Printed with permission of the *Northshore Citizen*, Bothell, Washington), p. 37 (Michael Hayman), p. 40, 45 (Strix Pix), p. 50, 54 (Printed with permission of the *Northshore Citizen*, Bothell, Washington), p. 83 (© C. Quinlan 1983), p. 94 (*The Columbus Ohio Dispatch*/Charles Hay), p. 96 (Rohn Engh), p. 97 (McDonald's Corporation), p. 99, 113 (Strix Pix), p. 118 (Tennessee Valley Authority), p. 120 (Jean-Claude Lejeune), p. 123 (Paul Conklin), p. 125 (Jean-Claude Lejeune), p. 128 (Strix Pix), p. 129 (Dan Unkefer), p. 131 (© 1982 Anne Schullstrom), p. 132 (Strix Pix), p. 137 (Printed with permission of the *Northshore Citizen*, Bothell, Washington), p. 140 (Strix Pix), p. 144 (Paul Conklin), p. 150 (Dan Unkefer), p. 155 (Larry Hamill), p. 160 (Phillips Photo Illustrators), p. 162 (Printed with permission of the *Northshore Citizen*, Bothell, Washington), p. 168, 183 (Strix Pix), p. 186 (*Values in the Classroom*, Charles E. Merrill, 1977), p. 188 (Barbara Lagomarsino), p. 189 (Dan Unkefer), p. 203 (Printed with permission of the *Northshore Citizen*, Bothell, Washington), p. 211 (Constance Brown), p. 217 (Rohn Engh), p. 226 (Dan Unkefer), p. 227 (Barbara Lagomarsino), p. 230, 231 (Dan Unkefer), p. 235, 253 (Strix Pix), p. 259 (Paul Conklin), p. 271 (Constance Brown), p. 277 (Paul Conklin), p. 293 (Strix Pix), p. 307 (Constance Brown), p. 342, 344 (Strix Pix), p. 347 (Paul Conklin), p. 352 (Strix Pix), p. 356 (*Resource Teaching*), p. 372 (Tom McGuire), p. 375 (Mercedes-Benz of North America, Inc.), p. 377 (Strix Pix), p. 378 (Paul Conklin), p. 383 (Printed with permission of the *Northshore Citizen*, Bothell, Washington).

Library of Congress Catalog Card Number: 81-84316
International Standard Book Number: 0–675–09835–1

Printed in the United States of America
1 2 3 4 5 6 7 8 9 10–86 85 84 83 82

Contents

1 Social Studies: The Current Scene

2 The Teacher of Social Studies

3 Social Studies Foundations

4 Other Foundations for the Social Studies

5 New Sources of Social Studies Content

6 Social Studies Content

7 Decision Making in Planning Social Studies

8 Effective Instruction in the Social Studies

9 Teaching Social Studies Skills

10 Questions and Questioning for Teaching and Learning

11 Environments for Social Studies Learning

12 Technological and Material Supports for Social Studies Teaching

13 Managing the Social Studies Program

14 Evaluating Social Studies Learning

15 The Future and Social Studies Education

Preface

The world of the 1980s and beyond will present unique challenges to its citizens—international tensions and conflicts, inflation, poverty, world hunger, illiteracy, disease, and energy consumption. The citizens who best meet these challenges will be well-informed thinkers and decision makers, those with a broad understanding of human nature and human problems.

But how is this understanding gained? If social studies is defined as the overall study of humanity, then it falls to the teachers of social studies to help prepare future citizens in the understanding and cooperation that their world will demand. These teachers must, themselves, be planners and decision makers well versed in all social science foundations, the traditional areas as well as psychology, anthropology, and other emerging fields. Further, since social studies is still only a portion of the elementary curriculum, teachers must be prepared to incorporate this discipline equally and at all levels with other areas of the curriculum.

The teacher, then, also has skills to master and understanding to gain. This book takes the teacher through the processes of planning, decision making, and classroom instruction. It describes the role of the social studies teacher as a questioner, a manager, and a futurist, as well as the social studies disciplines. Both the traditional and the somewhat newer social studies foundations, and the effective application of these bases in teaching social studies are discussed. Attention is given to the types of decisions teachers make in chapter 7, and to the nature of instruction with both gifted and learning disabled children in chapter 8. Other decision-making areas—questioning, in chapter 10, and environments for social studies, in chapter 11—are also considered. Our emphasis on questioning reflects our belief that the question is both central to learning and a powerful teaching tool. Although all teachers work in a specialized environment designed to facilitate learning, most educators are unaware of the nature of classroom and other learning environments and how individuals function in such spaces. The detailed treatment of environment in chapter 11 provides information for deciding how to develop, arrange, and utilize educational spaces to optimize social studies learnings. We also believe that those who understand the future will have a hand in influencing it; we discuss the place of social studies in the future in chapter 15.

This book is designed for individuals who are preparing to teach or are already teaching social studies in the elementary and middle-school grades. Although the book's organization is somewhat traditional, the information reflects the latest thinking regarding social studies education.

Textbooks are rarely individual undertakings. In the development of this textbook, Jan Jeter assumed initial responsibility for writing early drafts of chapters 2, 7, 8 and 9, and Phyllis Maxey for chapters 3, 4, 5, 12 and 13. At Charles E. Merrill Gil Imholz worked with the authors in the early phases of the book, and Julie Estadt contributed her editorial talents as the manuscript was revised. To them we extend our special appreciation. Thanks also to all the persons who reviewed the manuscript and contributed helpful comments, especially John R. Adams of Georgia Southern College, David Boyd of Towson State University, John Cogan of the University of Minnesota, and Dan A. White of West Texas State University.

Each member of this writing team recognizes the contributions made by family members; no book can be written without their support. Thanks go to Doreen Hunkins and to Leah and Francis, Jr., and to Jimmy Jeter and Charles Maxey for their understanding.

Social Studies:
The Current Scene

Each society wants its young people to gain those skills, attitudes, values, and knowledge that will prepare them for effective participation in that society. The hope is that these youth will acquire learnings to enable them to improve society. Toward this task, modern societies have created institutions to help families and communities educate children in the ways of the local, national and world communities.

While the entire educational curriculum helps prepare youth for this participation, the social studies curriculum plays a special role. This area of the curriculum has the particular mission of helping students develop the skills for dealing with and, to some extent, managing the varied forces that make up the world.

Social Studies Defined

The social studies curriculum draws on all those fields that deal with the investigation of humankind. Its content derives from the social sciences—history, geography, economics, political science, sociology, anthropology—and from the everyday experiences of the human family. Philosophy, religion, art, and other subjects in the humanities also contribute to the social studies curriculum. Social studies thus enables people to understand their past and their present, and to have some comprehension of their emerging futures. The focus is local, national, and international.

Social Studies or Social Sciences?

When someone reads the list of subjects that make up social studies, he is likely to react by saying, "But those are the social *sciences*." Perhaps you have made the statement yourself. But what are the differences, if any, between the social studies and the social sciences? Certainly, the social studies and the social sciences share much of the same content—focusing on the behavior of

2

human beings. Beyond that, however, we can gain further insight by investigating the objectives of each field.

The primary objective of the social sciences is to generate new knowledge and to refine existing knowledge about ourselves as humans. Social scientists strive for objectivity. They ask questions in particular ways to expand the information base of their subject. They make *hypotheses,* special statements that require investigation to determine their truth, then test them to discover how we function in our world. The testing of these hypotheses results in theories, which are statements that explain, describe, or predict how certain phenomena, in our case human behaviors, occur or will occur. For example, the geographer may be interested in how land use affects people's behavior. The economist may want to know why people use and value certain resources. Historians like to explore people's actions in both past and present.

Clearly, educators draw much of the content of social studies from the social sciences. But social studies educators are not concerned with generating new social science knowledge. Rather, their objective is to provide students with the attitudes, skills, and knowledge necessary for participation in local, national, and world society.

Social studies really involve learning about ourselves and others and how we interact with people and places. For instance, to get a good understanding of yourself, you need to know your background (history), the social group or groups to which you belong (anthropology, sociology), the values you consider essential (philosophy, religion), where you live and how you relate to your environment (geography), how others influence you and how you influence others (political science), and how you satisfy your basic needs and wants (economics).

Getting to know ourselves and others is a complex process. Because it takes time, most schools introduce social studies in the primary grades, usually beginning with "ourselves and our families." Such a topic draws heavily on sociology and anthropology. History and the other social sciences are usually introduced in the intermediate grades, with a focus on the study of other people, the role of technology, nations of the world, and international commerce.

Goals and Objectives

Questions for Educators

Why should we take time to teach social studies? What are the benefits to students? Is what they learn applicable in society? How much more effectively will students contribute to society as a result of their social studies courses?

These are difficult questions, but they are legitimate and must be answered. The opening paragraph of this chapter offers a general response to these questions. The following statements provide a more specific but still only partial answer to our queries. Essentially, social studies should:

1. Help students acquire behaviors that will enable them to be effective members of social groups.
2. Help students become skilled in using decision-making processes when considering social concerns. Social studies can contribute to students' thinking abilities by stressing problem solving, critical and creative thinking, and the procedures necessary for processing specific information. These skills grow from opportunities to work independently and to observe, classify, interpret, synthesize, and evaluate data.
3. Help students understand events and people of the past, and how they have influenced the present.
4. Enable students to develop a sense of identity. They should be able to describe their values and why they have them.
5. Help students become effective citizens. It should encourage them to use effectively the processes of a representative democracy. Students should be aware of and committed to their responsibilities as citizens of particular communities, starting with the classroom and the school community and extending to the state, the nation, and the world.
6. Promote an appreciation and understanding of diversity. The aim is to encourage students to gain true acceptance of, rather than just a tolerance for, those who are different.
7. Enable students to develop a "future view," a view of alternative futures and the possible roles they might play in creating and managing those futures.
8. Enable students to appreciate the creative genius of the human race and to value the products of such creativity in both the arts and technology.
9. Provide students with questioning attitudes and skills in order to carry out independent and cooperative investigations, with the hope of motivating continued learning beyond formal schooling.
10. Provide students with an understanding of and skill in group dynamics—working with others in both small and large groups.
11. Enable students to understand the dynamic interactions between their nation and their world. They should understand the workings of government, economics, and culture.
12. Heighten sensitivity by helping students see people's commonalities as well as their uniquenesses.
13. Motivate students to continue to be students of the human family and to apply such learnings to the betterment of the human race.

This list is not exhaustive. Before continuing, jot down some of your own reasons for including social studies in the school curriculum.

General Objectives

Objectives are statements that denote end points to be achieved. Such statements are intended to communicate to teachers, students, and sometimes to the lay public, the reason for a particular action or series of actions. Many educators divide objectives into two categories: *cognitive objectives*, which focus on intellectual development, and *affective objectives*, which deal with feelings, sensitivities, and attitudes.

Cognitive Objectives

Cognitive objectives in social studies focus on developing learners' knowledge and capabilities in the realms of content, process, and skills. These three realms receive attention at all levels of the elementary school.

Content Objectives

Content objectives refer to the learning of information specific to each discipline of the social sciences and to information drawn from outside experiences. Content objectives deal with specific facts, such as the major battles of

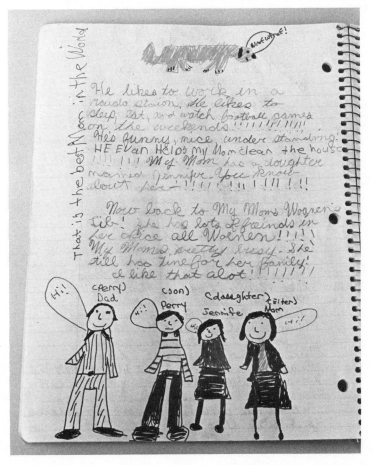

Students can begin their study of social groups by writing about themselves and their families.

the American Revolution, or the production rate of wheat in the United States, or the branches of government. Content objectives also deal with major generalizations and with theories that explain some particular phenomenon. We can divide content objectives by the *specificity* of the content to which the objectives refer. Thus, one might show objectives ordered on a continuum.

Objectives

←————————————————————————————————→

Specific facts   Concepts   Generalizations
or rules

Concepts and generalizations are discussed in some detail later in this book. For now, however, you can see that the content of objectives ranges from the very specific, such as "Boston is the capital of Massachusetts," to the rather general, such as "the cultures in which people are raised influence the values and attitudes the people hold." *Concepts* are midway between the two extremes. Concepts are names given to groups of objects or events that share common characteristics. Concepts are organizers of our reality. One concept addressed in social studies is *culture*. This concept refers to a grouping of people who share a common language, a common set of values, a common history, and common goals for the future. One might write content objectives with a general content emphasis as follows:

Students will identify the functions of the family as an institution, education as an institution, and other institutions in the United States.

Students will list environmental problems that are currently receiving attention, the causes and effects of the problems on the environment, and the steps necessary to correct the problems.

Students will identify the contributions of women to the growth of the culture of the United States.

Process Objectives
Processes are all the random or ordered methods used in social science inquiry. They are the means by which people not only gain knowledge but also use and communicate it. For example, social scientists use the process of organization to put information into various classifications—they analyze the information and ask questions to determine what might be the most meaningful way to categorize it. If a geographer were gathering data on waterways in New York, for example, he would need to decide on one or more ways to group the data. Waterways might be grouped as artificial or natural, in use or defunct, and so on. Once information is organized, the social scientist can begin to make inferences and to apply these inferences to other investigations. If you were trying to make some sense out of a social studies classroom you

were observing, you might make a data chart on which to organize and record your observations. Such a chart might look like this:

Classroom # _____

Children's Actions		Teacher's Actions		Inference
Alone	With Others	Alone	With Others	

Data are organized on this chart according to who is performing the action and how (alone or with others) it is performed. Allow space to record any ideas or inferences you may come up with after observing this classroom.

A teacher wishing to emphasize process might write the following objectives:

> *In studying a unit on energy, students will be able to use the processes of observing, comparing/contrasting, and classifying different types of energy.*

> *In investigating the roles of government, students will use questions at the analysis and synthesis levels to create a general statement relating to roles of government.*

Skills Objectives

Skills are performance abilities—intellectual, social, and motor—that people use in doing something. Skills emphasized in social studies are reading, viewing, listening, outlining, note-taking, and asking questions, as well as particular thinking skills. Such skills are common to all of the social sciences as well as to the other studies concerned with learning about ourselves. Some skills, of course, are unique to a particular social science. In geography, for example, mapping and map interpretation skills sometimes receive attention in the upper elementary grades, and when dealing with historical content, students may be taught content analysis skills.

Students can also have ample opportunities in social studies for perfecting the study skills that are not unique to the discipline. The skills for locating and gathering information from primary and secondary sources (documents and books) can be developed within the social studies. Reading skills—interpreting, applying, analyzing, synthesizing, and evaluating—and critical listening skills can also be enhanced in this curricular area.

7

Of course, effective social studies teachers do more than foster the perfection of study skills. They also arrange curricular experiences so that students can perfect their intellectual skills—defining and identifying problems, generating hypotheses for testing, mapping plans for testing key questions, analyzing relationships among information, synthesizing conclusions into additional novel combinations, and evaluating the accuracy and usefulness of conclusions.

Citizenship is central to social studies. Effective citizens work well with each other, and the social studies program addresses the development of skills relating to this goal. Group skills range from those necessary to group leadership to those required of an effective member and listener.

Although it is easy to list these skills objectives separately, the reality of the classroom usually blurs their distinctions. One skills objective may direct that students critically read a passage in a book, but also that they use communication skills in relating their findings to other children. In addition, in such a situation, children will have opportunities to perfect their listening skills. Samples of skills objectives might be:

> *Students will develop competence in locating, gathering, evaluating and summarizing information related to the unit's focus.*

> *Students will, as a result of this lesson, organize material from several sources and present it in graphic form to the whole class.*

Affective Objectives

Learning encompasses more than just gathering facts and repeating them. Indeed, we all react to learning with feelings, with emotions. Our response to certain information is based on our value system. Such reactions fall within the affective domain. Skilled teachers of social studies include in their lesson plans objectives that foster values and feelings. Their goal is for students to gain those attitudes, values, and feelings that sensitize them to the feelings and ideas of others, as well as to enhance their self-awareness.

Many of the affective objectives that teachers develop deal with values traditionally honored by society, such as respect for the individual, and belief in the rule of the majority with responsibility for the minority. Most schools stress the value of rational thought and scientific inquiry as well. Teachers might word these affective objectives as follows:

> *Individuals, as a result of experiencing this unit on human diversity, will have self-respect and will show respect for others regardless of race, creed, or social and economic status.*

> *Students, as a result of social studies, will value democratic beliefs, human freedom, civic responsibilities, and intelligent loyalty to the nation-state.*

A good social studies program addresses these objectives concurrently. One does not work on understandings one day, values on another, and process on another. Cognitive and affective objectives are integrated into the same lessons. Often, they cannot be separated, and are even found in the same objective, such as:

> *Students, after studying three major cultures in the United States, will understand the primary beliefs of these cultures and appreciate the diversity found in each.*

This objective is both cognitive (addressing understanding of the cultures) and affective (addressing appreciation of cultural diversity).

Activity 1:1

Looking Back

Recall the way you were taught social studies. Did your experience closely resemble the definition of the overall study of humanity or the social sciences designed for educational purposes? Or was it just history?

Activity 1:2

Self-Check on Objectives of Social Studies

How do you feel about emphasizing both the cognitive and affective domains in social studies? Jot down your impressions. After you read the other chapters in this book, recheck your views. Have they changed?

Major Trends in Social Studies

It would be helpful now to take a brief look at what has been and is happening in the field of social studies, to get some clear notions of current and possible future directions of the field. Such an overview can trigger ideas for organizing units, teaching lessons, using educational resources, and interacting with students.

Emphasizing Concepts

An established trend in social studies is emphasis on the conceptual structure of the curriculum. Most, if not all, social studies programs are organized around major ideas to be developed either as concepts, generalizations, basic ideas, main ideas, or major understandings. Such key ideas serve as organizers for the basic units and, at the same time, suggest a sequence for teaching the content.

These are concepts common to most social studies programs:

Region	Social class	Power
Resource	Freedom	Culture
Market	Urban	Needs and wants
Production	Responsibility	Values
Conflict	Justice	Institution

Almost all social studies programs deal with *generalizations,* statements that note the relationship of two or more concepts. Some examples of generalizations that have been used as points of focus in social studies (Jarolimek, 1977, pp. 10-11) are, from history:

History is one of the core disciplines of social studies in the primary grades.

The affairs of human societies have historical antecedents and consequences; events of the past influence those of the present.

Several civilizations have risen and fallen during the history of human societies; many past civilizations have contributed to current civilizations.

The early history of a country has a definite bearing on the culture, relations, beliefs, attitudes, and ways of living of its people.

From geography:

Geographic facts influence where and how people live and what they do; people adapt, shape, utilize, and exploit the earth to their ends.

The global location of a nation or a region contributes to its importance in international affairs.

Every place on the earth has a distinctiveness about it which differentiates it from all other places.

From political science:

Every known society has some kind of authority structure that may be called its government; such a government is granted coercive power.

All societies have made policies or laws about how groups of people should live together.

A stable government facilitates the social and economic development of a nation.

From economics:

The economy of a country (or region) is related to its available resources, investment capital, and its people's educational development.

In any society, the number of consumers outnumbers the producers of goods and services.

The interdependence of peoples of the world makes exchange and trade a necessity in the modern world.

From sociology:

In most cultures, the family is the basic social unit and the source of some of the most fundamental and necessary learnings in a culture.

11

> *Every society develops a system of roles, norms, values, and sanctions that guide the behavior of its individuals and groups.*
>
> *The satisfaction of social needs is a strong motivating force in determining individual behavior.*

And from anthropology:

> *Every society, however primitive, has formed its own system of beliefs, knowledge, values, traditions, and skills that may be called its culture.*
>
> *The art, music, architecture, foods, clothing, sports, and customs of a people help to produce a national identity.*
>
> *Nearly all human beings, regardless of racial or ethnic background, are capable of participating in and contributing to any culture.*

(Specific suggestions for involving students in learning concepts and generalizations are discussed primarily in chapters 6, 7, and 8)

Stimulating Intellectual Growth

We want students to do more than remember facts. To accomplish this, teachers must motivate pupils to use the processes of explaining, analyzing, and evaluating. Teachers must encourage pupils to engage in hypothetical thought. The teachers who are most effective in stimulating intellectual growth and development in children usually ask questions at the upper cognitive levels and assign activities that require investigating and analyzing relationships among social phenomena.

A teacher who wishes to stress intellectual functioning would not just ask how much corn is grown in Iowa. Rather, he would ask questions that stimulate an understanding of the relationships among soil type, climate, market, level of technology, and cultural values. For instance, a fifth-grade teacher might use maps showing the various soil types in Iowa and the regions where corn is grown, and charts showing the number of sunny and rainy days. He might say, "Here we have some maps that tell us some things about corn production in Iowa." Then he could ask:

1. Where are the major corn-growing regions in Iowa?
2. What types of soil are present in these regions?
3. Tell me what you think might explain what soil type has to do with the cultivation of corn.
4. What types of weather do the corn-producing regions of Iowa have?
5. After looking at these maps, make a statement that explains the relationship of soil, climate, and corn production.

This sequence begins by requiring pupils to interpret or read a map to answer the first questions. The subsequent questions involve students at increasingly higher levels of thinking so that eventually, in response to the last question, they have to synthesize the information and ideas they have gathered. The lesson assumes that children have had some experience with soil types, perhaps in a science lesson. Of course, one most likely will not ask all these questions in one class period, since the children will need time to process higher-order questions.

The teacher's attention to intellectual skills will engage students more actively in learning social studies content. Teachers who want to make students active learners use various procedures to get pupils to identify problems and organize them into manageable parts. Students learn the steps of problem identification and the ways of analyzing, synthesizing, and evaluating data.

An emphasis on active learning assumes that thinking skills improve and maximum learning occurs during a student's active involvement in the classroom. By taking on the roles of searcher and investigator, a student will see the materials of the classroom—the textbooks, maps, pictures, and films—as sources to utilize in processing questions, in researching hypotheses, in determining the value of conclusions, and in formulating generalizations.

Portraying Reality

Most new social studies materials reflect attempts to depict accurately the world and the human family. This stress on realism has, for example,

The ability to carry out cooperative investigations is one skill developed through social studies.

13

brought about new treatment of ethnic minorities and women in the United States. Materials no longer assume that minorities have been totally assimilated into a common culture. Rather, our national culture is presented as a pluralistic one.

Also, as part of this stress on realism, social studies materials are dealing more accurately with *all* peoples of our nation and the world, and come closer to assuring that students will be aware of the many challenges facing this large urban nation.

Accurately portraying the peoples of the world is a major challenge both to teachers and to the creators of social studies materials. Part of their difficulty is due to the rate and amount of change taking place in the world; our printed materials are quickly dated. (Think, for example, of the changes that have occurred in Africa in the past few years—countries have changed their forms of government, their names, and in some instances made major modifications in their economic bases.) Teachers are doing a good job of transmitting current and accurate information to students, but the conscientious teacher must remain alert to ever-changing world events through continual study.

Expanding Learning Resources

If social studies was taught at all early in this century, the textbook was the sole resource. While the textbook is still our major resource, new technology has provided us with films, filmstrips, filmloops, slides, photographs, audio cassettes, videocassettes, videodisks, overhead transparencies, computers, teaching machines, maps, charts, globes, television, documents, artifacts, and a host of other materials. The new materials are designed to involve students in learning and to allow them to develop realistic and accurate perceptions of the human family.

Because of the wealth of available resources, teachers must know procedures for selecting materials. They must make special efforts to assure that the materials they select will meet the wide range of individual differences in their classrooms. Materials that deal with individual student differences are widely available. There are special books and media for minority students and students with learning difficulties, and the teaching guides and units of instruction suggest ways to use such materials with these special students.

Emphasizing Affective Learning

For the past two decades, educators have acknowledged that the cognitive and affective domains cannot be separated. Current social studies programs focus on attitudes, values, ideas, and appreciations. The programs suggest procedures to make students aware of their feelings and to come to a better understanding of themselves as individuals. Questions that draw on the affective domain (Krathwohl, 1964) are suggested and incorporated into teaching strategies. (More attention is given to questions in the affective domain in chapter 10.)

Expanding Content

Today, a greater number of disciplines and other areas of knowledge contribute to social studies curricula. History and geography are still the main content areas, but we now find economics, sociology, anthropology, and political science included in elementary school programs. In creating social studies

Social studies materials may be drawn from the arts, literature, drama, and music, as well as from the major content areas.

curriculum guides, schools also draw materials from the arts, literature, drama, and music, and sometimes from philosophy and religion as well. Educators realize that children often gain a better understanding of people by studying their poetry, literature, and art rather than by merely reading their history.

In addition to content from these sources, many social studies teachers include units on modern social problems—drug use, human relations, environmental problems, law-related subjects, and death. The content for these varied topics is drawn from many disciplines.

Personalizing Education

One challenge teachers face is to make decisions regarding curriculum content, materials, teaching methods, and educational activities that will address classroom diversity—the intellectual, social, emotional, experiential, and developmental characteristics of individuals.

Our currently available diagnostic instruments do not provide all the information needed for responding to this diversity. Even if they did, we would not always be able to make the right "mix" of content, materials, and activities to enable each student to learn according to his personal style and interests. We can, however, make a major attempt to address the individuality of our students by becoming as well acquainted with each one as possible. If we realize that students have unique needs and interests and individualized ways of learning, we will be able to set the stage for addressing such diversity. For instance, a unit on communities should have relevant films, photographs, and books available for students to use. Lesson plans can include opportunities for students to view films, to make field trips, or to have panel discussions on this topic. Some children may wish to write letters to important community leaders. We may even have pupils study different aspects of the topic of community. Planning for variety in social studies units affords a greater chance of addressing the diversity of the class members.

Curriculum Designs and Organization

Besides selecting content and activities that address student diversity, we have a variety of ways in which we can structure the social studies program. Many educators believe the best approach for elementary students is an interdisciplinary or multidisciplinary structure. A multidisciplinary plan incorporates content from more than one discipline, but maintains the identity and integrity of the disciplines involved. For instance, one unit might include history, geography, and political science, but the student would recognize each as a separate subject. As an example, a lesson on "Your Community" might have students deal first with past community events (history), followed by a lesson or lessons dealing with the location of the community and its physical features (geography). This geography segment might include the size of the community, the number of people, and the location of schools and businesses. The political science segment would deal with community government and its various power groups.

An interdisciplinary arrangement also includes content from more than one discipline, but in this instance, the identity of the disciplines is of no particular consequence. Using our above example, with the focus on "our community," its history, geography, and political science would not be introduced in sequence. Rather, one might talk of the important events of the community, making sure to locate the events in space (geography) as well as in time (history). One could also deal with the people involved in the events (political science). The point is that the students learn about the community without necessarily realizing they are discussing history or geography or political science at any particular time.

The design most common at the elementary school level is the *broad fields* or *fused design*. In employing this design, the teacher groups logically related subjects around some organizer, such as the United States. This design allows students to consider the interrelationships among various topics and to relate school content to their everyday world. The design can be either multidisciplinary or interdisciplinary. It frequently focuses on human activities fundamental to all people. For example, units might be organized around the topics of industrial production, defense, child rearing, education, communication, food production, and making rules and regulations.

The social studies curriculum occasionally follows the design of a separate subject, though this procedure is more common at the secondary level. Here we might find a course in history, one in geography, one in economics, and one in political science, all presented separately but in some definite sequence. Students might be counseled to take history first, then geography, then economics, and so on. Sometimes we have units at the elementary level that are like separate mini-courses contained within year-long, interdisciplinary courses.

Activity 1:3

Observing Educational Trends

Drawing from either your own school experiences or from your observations of the school where you are to do your student teaching, list the educational trends that are evident. Try to determine the reasons that these trends, rather than others, are apparent.

Although the content and sequence of social studies programs vary from one school district to another, there are two common viewpoints for the arrangement of social studies content. First, we can view it from the standpoint of *scope*—what is to be taught and in how much detail; second, we can look at it from a *sequence* viewpoint—when it is to be taught. All teachers are challenged to be specific in determining design and in dealing with the scope and sequence of content. These decisions are complicated by the various opinions as to what constitute optimal scope and sequence. We are not, however, without some guidance.

For many years, social studies programs have been organized and topics sequenced according to the *widening horizons format,* of which Paul Hanna (1963) was an advocate. This organization is shown graphically in Figure 1.1.

This content arrangement is based on the rationale that children need to start with the familiar and work toward the less familiar. In this design, children start with the world with which they have immediate contact and move toward other, more distant, topics. Each level is an outgrowth of those that precede it; the principle is that of moving from the simple to the complex.

This widening horizons format came under some criticism in the late 1950s. Children were no longer unfamiliar with distant places. They could sit in their homes and watch television programs about far off societies. Many children were also traveling throughout the country on family vacations. It made little sense to focus students' attention exclusively on their immediate communities. Another basis for criticism was that the materials following this scheme tended to stereotype communities, states, and nations. Children were also treated as passive learners. They were not encouraged to compare their

Figure 1.1
The Widening
Horizons Format

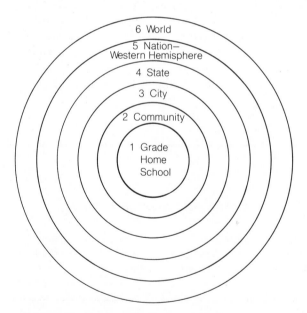

6 World
5 Nation—
Western Hemisphere
4 State
3 City
2 Community
1 Grade
Home
School

From "The expanding community of men" from *The social studies program in the elementary school in the Twentieth Century* by Paul R. Hanna in THE SOCIAL STUDIES edited by G. Wesley Sowards. Copyright © 1963 by the Board of Trustees of the Leland Stanford Junior University. Reprinted by permission of Scott, Foresman and Company.

Activity 1:4

Situation Analysis—Program Design

Visit a school district of your own choosing and interview the social studies coordinator to determine what program design the district utilizes. Write a brief report of your findings, mentioning the rationale given for using the particular design.

Activity 1:5

Social Studies Goals

Assume you have your own classroom and that you are asked to develop a social studies program. Note what goals you would select and/or create to guide the direction of your program. Indicate why you think these goals important.

---

communities with more distant ones in order to formulate general conclusions about communities. For studying families, the usual model was that of the white middle class. Educators began to point out, largely in response to outside pressures, that there were other types of families, and that materials should reflect that fact. A third criticism of this design was that by delaying study of the world community until last, children found it more difficult to develop a world view; they had a tendency to become ethnocentric in their outlooks.

One might think that this curriculum design would be of only historical interest. Despite efforts to modify it, however, it is still quite commonplace in today's schools, although current treatment of the major topics does reflect many of the educational trends mentioned earlier.

An imaginative organizational concept that has interested educators for some time is the *spiral curriculum*. The central idea of this curriculum design is that each social science discipline carries a basic structure of concepts and processes that can be organized to make social studies learning meaningful. To follow this design, one must first identify all the major concepts of the disciplines and then incorporate them into the first year of the curriculum. The teacher must also note the various processes that will be introduced at the outset of the program.

For example, a social studies program following the spiral organization might introduce the concept of family. Kindergarten children would study their own families. The concept would be continued in the first grade

19

with attention to families in the community, followed by families in other lands in grade three. In the sixth grade, the spiral would be completed with attention to new types of families. Concurrently, children would study the concept of freedom, beginning with freedom in the family, freedoms in the community, and so on.

These concepts can be taught to children in a lecture, but the central notion of the spiral curriculum is that children should be active learners. As a result, the processes used in each discipline would be introduced in the early grades and continually developed throughout the curriculum spiral. Thus, when studying families in the community in grade one, children would be guided in asking questions to gather information. They might be involved in classifying pictures of various types of families. Ideally, by having children experience the same concepts at increasingly sophisticated levels and practice the use of particular methods with more difficult content, they will grasp social studies knowledge far beyond the level of memorization. More importantly, the pupils have opportunities to be inquirers. Several of the trends mentioned previously are incorporated in this organizational schema which is illustrated in Figure 1.2.

Figure 1.2
The Spiral Curriculum
Format

Discussion

A primary purpose of education is to prepare young people to participate in and help to improve society. The content of social studies is particularly vital to that participation, drawing as it does from the fields of the social sciences and the humanities, and from human experience.

Although both the social sciences and social studies focus on human behavior, it is the goal of the social sciences to generate new knowledge. The social studies concern the use of that knowledge for understanding human interaction.

Educational goals get translated into objectives. The social studies program seeks to attain cognitive objectives in the areas of content, process, and skills, as well as affective objectives, which refer to feelings, sensitivities, and attitudes. Content objectives revolve around specific facts, concepts, and major generalizations. Process objectives are those of organizing, classifying, and applying information. The skills objectives concern the intellectual, social, and motor abilities necessary to learn. Social studies teachers particularly emphasize study skills and group skills. In the affective domain, social studies teachers promote the attitudes, values, and feelings requisite to self-awareness and good citizenship.

The most established trend in the social studies curriculum is its organization around concepts, such as those of freedom, culture, values, and institutions, and their presentation through the use of generalizations, or statements that relate two or more concepts to each other. To frame these generalizations, the social studies educator draws from the fields of history, geography, political science, economics, sociology, and anthropology, as well as from the humanities.

The best social studies teachers are those who encourage active rather than passive learning. They promote the use of intellectual skills such as explaining, analyzing, and evaluating, rather than simple recall. These teachers also attempt to portray reality accurately, to expand their students' learning resources, to emphasize affective learning rather than the merely cognitive, to expand the content of social studies, and to personalize education by responding to their students' diverse backgrounds and abilities.

Of the various curriculum designs available for social studies, two common ones are the multidisciplinary and the interdisciplinary. The multidisciplinary approach treats content discretely; that is, the areas of history, geography, and political science are handled separately. In the interdisciplinary approach, the separate areas are mingled under one general topic. The broad fields or fused design is most common at the elementary level, wherein subjects are grouped around an organizing topic, such as food production, education, or communication.

We may consider social studies programs according to their scope (what will be taught and in what degree of detail) and their sequence (the order in which the material will be taught). The usual sequence has been the widening horizons format, in which children begin with material familiar to them—self and family—and move outward to material about their state, their country, and the world. Although still in use, this format has been criticized for treating children as passive learners, promoting stereotypes, and encouraging ethnocentricity. Educators are currently more enthusiastic about the spiral curriculum format, in which students deal with a topic, such as the family, on a personal level, then move on to new material about the same topic—families in the community, then families around the world. Other concepts, such as freedom, are treated in the same way, beginning with freedom in the family, freedom at the national level, etc. The spiral curriculum format is thus felt to promote more active learning by dealing with concepts at increasingly sophisticated levels and introducing scholarly methods earlier in the educational process.

References

Hanna, Paul. "The Social Studies Program in the Elementary School in the Twentieth Century." In *The Social Studies,* edited by G. Wesley Sowards. Glenview, Ill.: Scott, Foresman, 1963.

Jarolimek, John. *Social Studies in Elementary Education.* 5th ed. New York: Macmillan Co., 1977.

Krathwohl, David. *Taxonomy of Educational Objectives, Handbook II: Affective Domain.* New York: David McKay Co., 1964.

The Teacher of
Social Studies

2

So much is happening in the field of social studies that teachers must become increasingly skillful in dealing with critical issues. Schools are discarding traditions in their quest for more personalized, humanized, and individualized programs. Concurrently, they are moving "back to the basics" with increased emphasis on objectives, basic competency, and mastery learning. In this changing educational world, the effective social studies teacher assumes numerous roles, some traditional and some less so.

Traditional Roles

Information Source and Presenter

Teachers have always been expected to be knowledgeable in their subject matter and skillful in presenting it to their students. They have typically dispensed information to their pupils by lecturing or reading. Many educators realize that this teaching mode can no longer be primary—today's proliferation of knowledge makes it impossible for any one teacher to keep abreast of all that is happening in her field.

A more realistic teaching role, then, is that of facilitator—*assisting* students in learning. In this role, teachers involve students in interaction with both the social studies content and with their fellow students. For this teaching mode, the teacher cannot be less knowledgeable, but must convey the dynamic nature of social studies. The teacher must present facts and provide situations so that students become aware that learning is constant. Furthermore, questions about the meaning of social studies must also be raised. Skilled teachers have found that by being good models themselves, they can facilitate pupil learning. Students benefit greatly from seeing their teachers as curious questioners excited by the challenges of the study of humankind.

Organizer and Manager

Effective classrooms utilize planned as well as spontaneous activities. In fact, teachers should prepare for spontaneous activities by organizing the environment in such a way that students are comfortable in satisfying their curiosities about many topics in many ways.

Teacher preparation in the 1940s and the 1950s stressed classroom control. Education students were cautioned not to lose control, and to demand obedience. During the 1950s, education became more management oriented. Studies on discipline by social and behavioral scientists contributed to this shift. Drawing on this new information, teachers responded by setting the stage for democratic discipline. The teacher was no longer to be the primary authority, the one individual responsible for controlling her students. Rather, she was the person who provided plans and ways of carrying them out in a pleasant and productive learning atmosphere (Orlich et al., 1980).

Currently, classroom management encompasses much more than maintaining discipline. It extends to dealing with the visible and invisible characteristics of the classroom. The visible qualities relate to the physical arrangement of the room. How have the learning centers been placed and organized? What pupil materials are available and where are they located? How have work stations been arranged so that both individual work and group inquiry are facilitated? What displays are present to heighten student interest?

The invisible characteristics are the emotional and social climate or atmosphere. Is the classroom organized and managed so that hostility, stress, and aggression are avoided? Litwin and Stringer (1968) define climate as follows:

> Climate is made up of expectations and incentives which interact with a variety of psychological needs to produce aroused motivation and behavior directed toward need satisfaction. Climate is assumed to be influenced by a variety of factors such as the physical situation, nature of the activity, needs of the people, group norms, and behavior and leadership of formal and informal leaders. (p. 110)

The key words here are *expectations, incentives,* and *psychological needs.* In an environment organized and managed for optimal learning, students know what is expected of them. They know because the teacher identifies rules, regulations, and procedures, and even allows the students to participate in making these guidelines. Pupils understand their classroom responsibilities.

Incentives are the rewards of being involved. Ideally, the rewards will be intrinsic—learning for the joy of learning and for the positive feeling of doing a job well. *Psychological needs* are the various needs that must be met in individual children, ranging from achievement and recognition to security. In managing the environment, the teacher arranges for activities and materials that respond to her pupils' myriad needs. Meeting needs is a difficult task, for it requires the teacher to keep extensive data on the pupils. To begin, one assumes that most people have the same general needs. The differences lie in the manner in which they should be addressed, and the varying degrees of accomplishment and attention individuals require. For instance, all people require some support for their activities. But some pupils require only a "you can do it," while others need constant reassurance that what they are doing is correct. All people require some sense of security, but differ in the amount of

25

risk they are willing to assume. Some students balk at taking even the smallest risk; others delight in accepting risks when they feel they have the background to tackle the task.

Teachers who wish to address both the physical and invisible dimensions of the classroom should remember that:

> Individuals are attracted to climates which arouse their dominant needs.
> Climates are made up of incentives and experiences.
> Climates interact with needs to arouse motivation toward need satisfaction.
> Climates represent the most powerful level available to [teachers] in facilitating change, learning, in pupils. (Wiles & Bondi, 1980, p. 271)

But despite the general guidelines for making social studies learning possible, there are no fixed recipes. In fact, how a teacher approaches this task depends greatly on her personality, philosophy, teaching style, and competence.

What features of a successful learning environment are evident in the classroom shown here?

Jarolimek (1977a) explains that the teacher who is successful in achieving the role of facilitator is likely to have a classroom in which:

1. There is evidence of unity and cohesiveness; pupils willingly cooperate to achieve class goals.
2. There are pupils involved in decision making regarding the work and life of the classroom.
3. There is evidence of good interpersonal relations among pupils and teacher.
4. Pupils are interested in what they are doing.
5. Pupils have choices as to what types of assignments to do, what tasks to accomplish, and the amount of time they can spend working.
6. The visible dimensions of the classroom show flexibility of use and activities.
7. The materials provided are diverse and in adequate supply.
8. The children's work is well displayed, showing that the classroom is theirs. (p. 26)

The role of manager thus involves much more than maintaining discipline. Success includes making decisions about creating and selecting general goals and objectives, about content and experiences, about social studies materials, and about educational space and the types of groups within it (whole class, small group, one-to-one, independent study).

Evaluator

Teaching requires decisions about what, how, whom, and when to teach. The quality of those decisions depends upon the accuracy of the data at hand, and the evaluation of those data is used to decide which content or teacher action or pupil activity should be used, changed, or eliminated. Evaluation provides the answer to the question, "Are our actions and the curriculum producing the desired effects upon our pupils?"

Until recently, teachers' evaluation efforts centered almost solely on gathering information as to pupil achievement levels. Tests and experiences were designed to measure pupils' learning at the end of a unit. Such information allowed teachers to give their pupils grades. Today, evaluation activities have been expanded to furnish teachers with information at several points during their pupils' learning experiences. This type of evaluation is called *formative evaluation*, in contrast to summative assessment at the end of a unit or year. Chapter 14 presents a detailed discussion of these two types of evaluation. Formative evaluation provides both students and teachers with information critical to making decisions about instruction and curriculum. Essentially, it furnishes feedback as to the degree of mastery or understanding of specific material. With such involvement, students come to view evaluation not only as a concluding activity done only by the teacher for a mark, but rather as a way of discovering their own progress and making the changes necessary to insure understanding and success in social studies.

How teachers perform their roles as evaluators greatly affects how children view themselves and social studies. Overemphasis on grades causes students to view evaluation as a time when deficiencies and lack of understanding are exposed. For many, it is a time to dread. But if evaluation is used to furnish information that enables students and teachers to adjust actions and content, then students will see it as a means by which they can attain success.

Teachers occasionally give students responsibility for determining some of their objectives. In such cases, students are guided in self-evaluation to determine their initial level of understanding of their objectives. Discovering that they lack certain information should not discourage students; rather, they should see this as an opportunity to adjust their approach to certain content.

As an evaluator, the teacher is interested both in learner behavior and product. There will be times, however, when the teacher will allow student self-evaluation, to judge their understanding of a process and their skill in applying it. For example, the teacher may evaluate or allow the students to assess their own levels of map and chart interpretation. In this case, the teacher is not interested in map-production skills per se; at other times *products,* such as test papers and special reports, will be the goal.

A sensitive teacher realizes students are very concerned with success or failure. Therefore, the teacher's style of evaluation is often more critical than the evaluation itself. Educators who approach evaluation with a helping attitude contribute to their students' healthy psychological development. They plan ahead by providing experiences that allow children maximum opportunities for success, to receive evaluation data, and, often, to participate in their own assessment.

Emerging Roles

Coinquirer

Teaching is more than presenting, managing, and evaluating. Good teachers know the importance of being coinquirers with their students. In this role, they serve as models and assist pupils in identifying significant questions and interesting problems. They provide an atmosphere that allows freedom of exploration with sufficient materials for inquiry.

With the teacher as coinquirer, there is a high degree of interaction among teacher, learners, materials, and environment. Both teacher and students are persistent seekers, questioners, and thinkers. Questioning is a dominant behavior. As coinquirer, the teacher involves students in activities intended both to structure learning and to disrupt the structure of previous learnings. For example, the teacher might have a group of pupils investigate energy issues, ask guiding questions, and outline steps for obtaining answers to major energy issues. This is the structuring phase of the lesson. When some solutions have been suggested, however, the teacher raises concerns or situations that cause students to ask whether their energy findings or solutions are appropriate. The teacher may tell them there is really no way to evaluate their findings, and encourage the students to brainstorm other approaches to solving the problems.

At this point in the lesson, the students will realize there is no well-defined approach to the energy problems they are studying. They may conclude that answers that were appropriate in the past may now be dangerous. If the students conclude that the solution to oil dependency is to use coal reserves, the teacher can break the "structure" of this conclusion by pointing out the dangers of increased amounts of carbon dioxide in the atmosphere that would result from increased use of coal. The students face a dilemma—information learned earlier about the use of coal has to be "unlearned," or modified to some degree.

Teachers committed to the coinquirer role realize that behavior is a function of the interaction between the learner and any given factor in the environment. When students interact with people, materials, ideas, and situations, they learn that certain behaviors and uses of materials may have to be adjusted in new situations. Learning occurs around two poles; gaining and organizing information at the one, and at the other, discarding inappropriate information or modifying it so that it continues to have value. The coinquirer role, if performed well, helps students realize that unlearning or modifying views is just as important as learning or forming them in the first place. Teachers committed to the coinquirer concept expect students to gain from social studies the skills essential for critical thinking and effective problem solving.

Planner

We will discuss in chapter 7 the decision making involved in teaching social studies. This decision process takes place in three stages: planning, implementing, and assessing. Effective teaching requires planning, and planning involves not only deciding what to teach, but implementing and achieving success. Ideally, teachers would occupy a central position in curriculum planning and decision making; in reality, however, curriculum is most strongly influenced by the school district, state agencies, and organizations at the national, state, and local levels.

Social studies education is influenced at the national level by legislation, by special projects funded by the national government, by textbook authors and their publishers, and by national professional associations. The National Council for the Social Studies has given nationwide leadership and direction to social studies planning. At the state level, the office of education, through its curriculum guides, sets curricular requirements for social studies education. Local districts also usually have a curriculum guide for the social studies. The teacher must keep in mind these national, state, and local requirements when planning.

Good teaching requires both long-range and short-range planning. Long-range plans establish goals, contents, and learning experiences for units of work, semester courses, and year-long courses. Short-range plans itemize specific objectives, contents, experiences, materials, and procedures for lessons that can usually be completed in one or two periods.

Most teachers accept responsibility for instructional planning, but some reject their role in curriculum planning. Fortunately, more teachers are beginning to assume tasks they have previously neglected or which have been managed by others—developing curriculum packages, conceptualizing resource centers, assisting in piloting curriculum units, and communicating with the public about new curriculum projects. Even so, curricular planning is still an add-on activity for most teachers, coming after instructional planning and teaching, usually at the end of the day or on weekends. This situation should change.

Diagnostician

Planning does not occur in a vacuum. It requires gathering data through the general process of diagnosis. Social studies teachers must diagnose to determine what their pupils need, what society needs, and what the local community demands. Diagnosis reveals how much an individual, a small group, or a class of students knows. The data furnish the basis for determining what must be learned and possible methods for delivering content. Teachers look for data regarding students' skill levels, understanding of topics, and attitudes, to establish a starting point for instruction.

Numerous diagnostic tools and tests are available: observation of performance, checklists, anecdotal records, work samples, teacher-created tests, and standardized tests. Which ones are used depends upon the types of students being tested, how much information is available about them, the school policy, and local community expectations. For instance, observation is useful in providing a record of students' abilities. Can students read a map, give a report, or write down questions at various cognitive levels to guide their inquiry? Watching students provides information that will help determine behavior performance.

The teacher's objectives determine the focus of a lesson. For example, students might work together to create a relief map, but the real purpose of the activity may be to allow them to learn group cooperation. In this instance, the teacher may pay less attention to the quality of the map than to what did or did not happen in the group. Did each group member contribute suggestions? Listen to others? Accept group decisions? Accept a task and complete it? Other skill performances to observe include discussion, debate, social interaction, inquiry, and study. Observation might also be used to assess students' abilities to retain and use facts and concepts.

Examining work is useful when learners generate a tangible product. Testing is often fruitful, and utilizes inventories or preassessment tests to discover what students know. Using preassessment tests is not restricted to individual programs. Such tests can also be employed with whole-class instruction. The method the teacher selects will depend upon the nature of the unit of study, the time available, the amount of detail needed, and the teacher's preferred style of gathering data. No matter what method, diagnosis is crucial in planning. Accurate diagnosis provides information about student needs, problems, and interests. Through diagnosis, teachers come to know the characteristics of their individual students, and this information is essential for making social studies meaningful.

Materials Expert

Continual advancements in instructional technology provide us with systems and multimedia kits comprised of books, films, film loops, transparencies, cassettes, and sound filmstrips, in addition to numerous types of maps and charts. Teaching has become a multimedia process. Teachers no longer have a scarcity of materials; rather, they face the difficulty of choosing from among legions of materials. To make wise choices requires some degree of expertise.

Social studies materials should be geared to the students' developmental intellectual levels. Further, materials should be selected with a view

Important information about a student's level of understanding can be obtained through observation.

toward the objectives of the lesson or units. Will the materials allow students to achieve important objectives? The teacher may, for example, locate a social studies textbook that ranks high on accuracy of material and depth of topic treatment, but decide against using it if it lacks activities that will help students consider social studies from a social science perspective. The questions may stress levels of knowledge and understanding, but neglect questions designed to get students to think about the topics in the book.

When selecting materials, you must try to match the material to students' interests and abilities, community expectations, your own expertise and knowledge, and the overall goals and objectives of the social studies curriculum. It is a difficult task, but careful selection will enhance the quality of your students' social studies experiences.

Activity 2:1

An Instructional Materials Center

Visit your local curriculum library or instructional materials center and examine the social studies resources available. What types of materials are available? What topics are covered? Are the materials appropriate for the age-grade level? Are the materials valid? Do the materials involve the students' many senses?

Action Researcher

Good teachers have always tried out new ideas and assessed their effectiveness. But such experimentation with ideas, approaches, and materials usually took place in individual classrooms for individual benefit. Rarely did teachers record their results and communicate their findings to their colleagues, especially those outside the school system. Today, teachers are urged to continue to try out ideas, to develop and record the results, and to realize the importance of cooperation with other social studies teachers, curriculum specialists, administrators, and even with researchers outside the school or school system. Teachers are encouraged to consider themselves members of research teams.

Belonging to a research team does not mean the teacher will be the primary researcher, but it does require an understanding of research methods. Most classroom research will not be of the empirical type, with carefully controlled groups of subjects, but rather will fall in the category of *action research*. While such research raises questions about the effect of a particular teaching technique or the impact of particular materials, its thrust is not on the generalization of findings to other classrooms. Rather, action research allows teachers to determine whether or not certain content and ways of teaching are appropriate for their particular students. In experimenting with action research, teachers constantly monitor the way students deal with information and participate in activities. If materials, methods, or activities are inappropriate, they adjust and modify until they find appropriate content and approaches. Recording adjustments and modifications allows development of consistency when teaching the topic in the future. Diagnosis is thus clearly compatible with the action research mode.

In the role of action researcher, a teacher considers her classroom an educational laboratory. She realizes that classrooms are places not only for teaching social studies, but also for experimenting with different ways of teaching. When teachers perform this role well, students too may realize they can approach social studies as action researchers, experimenting with new ways to study and learn, and changing their approaches according to the data they gather themselves.

Activity 2:2

Teacher Roles

Observe several elementary social studies classes. Note the roles assumed by each teacher: information presenter, manager, evaluator, inquirer, curriculum planner, diagnostician, materials expert. Which roles are most common? What might explain the dominance of these roles?

Resource Persons

Teachers must often supplement their own general knowledge with the expertise of resource persons. No matter where you live, there are people in the school, the community, or in the state who can help you.

Of course, not everyone is suitable as a classroom resource. In addition to expertise, a person must have the ability to communicate with children and have an interest in doing so. The teacher should discuss ahead of time with the visitor the nature of the unit under study, the class activities that have occurred, and the specific points the resource person should address. Some potential classroom resource persons are authors, city officials, business leaders, dentists, physicians, lawyers, newspaper reporters, law enforcement officers, firefighters, legislators, judges, environmentalists, urban planners, longtime community residents, and travelers. The list is almost endless.

Resource persons need not always come to the class. Students can go into the community to interview people who have special interests or information. They can also interview neighbors, grandparents, and local business people, but the same careful planning used for classroom visits must be employed here as well.

Activity 2:3

Resource Persons

Begin to organize a file of resource persons who could contribute to the social studies program. A simple 3 × 5 card system can be used. Besides the obvious community members, do not overlook the possibility of using resource persons from among your classmates and personal friends. Some of your friends may have jobs, hobbies, or interests that could add an interesting dimension to your elementary classroom.

Issues Confronting Teachers

New developments in education and in fields affecting education have come faster than ever in recent years. Some have arisen from advances in scholarly research and psychological theory, some from the general knowledge explosion, and some from the dynamics of the times or from judicial decisions and laws. Today's educators are under intense pressure to show results, to be accountable. In addition, federal legislation passed late in 1975 directly affects "handicapped" students and virtually every classroom in the country. Public Law 94-142 prescribes full educational opportunity to all students—the

A firefighter from the local community describes equipment used in putting out fires.

learning disabled, emotionally disturbed, educable mentally retarded, and physically handicapped. To function effectively, teachers must understand these issues, and find ways to respond to the spirit of the law as well as its letter.

Accountability

The public is demanding that educational results be documented, that evidence be provided to show whether or not students have learned. In general, the push for accountability seems to have had beneficial effects on social studies education. Teachers have been prompted to question their actions and to refine old teaching techniques and experiment with new ones.

This public demand for evidence of educational accomplishment has forced teachers to list what they intend to accomplish in the form of instructional and behavioral objectives. Increasing numbers of teachers are voluntarily specifying objectives, and in some school districts, they are required to put objectives in writing. Pupil progress in attaining detailed objectives is used in many school districts as a basis for appraising teacher effectiveness.

Expanded Content

The increase in the amount of social studies information is reflected in the number of topics drawn from areas outside the social science disciplines. Societal issues and challenges such as population growth, the energy crisis, urban deterioration, and social inequality appear increasingly in social studies curricula. Law-related topics, careers and consumerism, multicultural and international events, environmental issues, and education for the future are now common in many social studies programs.

Law-related Education

Advocates of law-related education argue that students need to be knowledgeable about the legal institutions in the United States. This new content is not treated as a set of abstract concepts, but rather as knowledge essential for effective participation in modern society. Students are not asked to become lawyers, but simply to comprehend and respect the legal system. The curriculum emphasizes rights, responsibilities, rules, laws, and freedom, with teachers drawing on individuals in the legal system as resource persons.

Many institutions concerned with law-related education have created materials appropriate for classroom use, including:

Constitutional Rights Foundation
1510 Cotner Boulevard
Suite 402
Los Angeles, CA 90025

Street Law
Georgetown University Law Center
605 G. Street
Washington, DC 20001

Special Committee on Youth for Citizenship
American Bar Association
1155 East 60th Street
Chicago, IL 60637

Career Education

Career education stresses student awareness of the numerous careers available today. A variety of occupations receive attention, and care is taken to avoid stereotyping groups of workers. For example, women are no longer always portrayed as housewives, teachers, or secretaries.

As with many of the new content areas, teachers must decide whether to integrate the new material into existing social studies units or to develop special units on the topics. Both approaches have been used, but integration seems to be favored. With an integrated approach, the teacher can relate the new content to topics already established in the curriculum. For example, careers might be introduced in a unit on the community, thus enabling students to learn about the job opportunities in their own community.

Occasionally, people cannot see the value of offering career education in the elementary school, since elementary students obviously are not preparing for jobs. But its advocates point out that this subject is not aimed primarily at career counseling or vocational guidance; rather, the aim is to help students understand the world of work and the roles people play in society. Attention focuses on attitudes, appreciation, and feelings. Ideally, pupils will begin to appreciate the contributions people make to the general society through their work. As a bonus, the students develop an increased awareness of the careers available to them.

Consumer and Economics Education

Consumer education is another new topic that some schools offer. It is really an aspect of economics education, dealing with such concepts as wants, scarcity, opportunity, cost, resources, markets, consumption, supply, demand, money, and credit. The Joint Council on Economic Education (Hansen et al., 1977) feels this experience should enable students to make appropriate decisions and act as responsible citizens in their economic system. Again, this content can be integrated into existing curriculum units such as Our Community or America in the Twentieth Century.

Multicultural and International Education

Multicultural education is intended to acquaint students with the composition of our society, to develop a respect for the contributions of all groups to society, and to cultivate pride and understanding of one's own ethnic and cultural heritage. Ideally, multicultural education allows students to gain the understandings necessary for improving relations in this multiclass, multiracial, and multiethnic country.

The task is difficult because of the country's immense diversity. All groups want the course content to represent their group accurately. Adding to the difficulty is confusion over meanings of terms. Social class, for example, refers to grouping individuals on the basis of income, occupation, life styles, values, and family background. Racial groups are formed from innate and unalterable genetically transmitted physical characteristics, and are often identified by physical characteristics such as skin color, hair texture, and facial features. Ethnic groups differ from racial groups in that they are formed on the basis of common cultural variables such as customs, mores, language, religion, nationality, and history. Skillful teachers point out these differences so that students will acquire an accurate view of our national diversity. Pupils can study specific cultures or groups by participating in civic activities and conducting field interviews with members of various groups. Involving students in analyzing their own backgrounds also furnishes a vehicle for attaining greater understanding of their own cultures as well as those of others.

The greatest benefit of studying diverse peoples is not becoming skilled in recognizing differences, but rather in realizing commonalities. Jarolimek (1977) notes that, while emphasizing our national diversity, we must also recognize the commonality of all citizens as members of the human family and of the national community.

Most schools that offer multicultural education also include international education. This joint treatment is a natural outgrowth; focusing on cultural and ethnic groups in the United States leads automatically to discussions of the world community. All facets of technology, from communica-

By studying different ethnic groups students become aware of our national diversity as well as the cultures of other countries.

tions satellites to jet travel, make it imperative that students understand the world family. Scenes of the earth from space show dramatically that we are coinhabitors of one small planet. The resulting contact and interdependency make this new content area most important, and verify its aims of international goodwill and understanding of others. International education most likely will not be taught in separate units at the elementary level, but will probably be incorporated into existing programs and addressed through art, science, literature, and music.

The Future

A new and crucial area in social studies is the study of the future. At a time characterized by an accelerating pace of change in attitudes and values, technology, political and economic affairs, and social institutions, students need to be aware of future developments and become skilled in dealing with them. They must develop an awareness of and prepare to contribute to the solution of such problems as depletion of natural resources, environmental pollution, overpopulation, and starvation in underdeveloped nations. As Goodman (1976) points out, the real challenge of the future is not in developing the technology to solve these problems, but rather in nurturing the social understanding and conscience requisite for solving them.

The study of the future can be incorporated into existing social studies units. While studying present-day society, students can make projections by analyzing trends of technological growth, urbanization, cultural modifications, and changes in the environment. Children enjoy forecasting what the future elementary school will look like and how such a school will influence children and the community.

Environmental Education

With heightened consciousness of environmental problems, educators are drawing content from the sciences to create units or lessons on the environment. Two major subtopics in this area are ecology and conservation. Ecology focuses on the interrelationships among living systems and their environments; how humans use and misuse their environments is a frequent topic.

Environmental education frequently serves to tie social studies to other areas of investigation. The problems of pollution often combine social studies with health and climatology, while other topics integrate geography, sociology, economics, and political science.

Conservation receives increasing attention in elementary social studies as more people come to realize that our environment is being misused, not only to the detriment of today, but to tomorrow as well. Teachers create units that deal with soil use, water management, wildlife preservation and the use of mineral and natural products. These units are designed to emphasize the "wise use of resources." Conservation education furnishes a place for considering values and the valuing process. For example, should the resources be used or not? Many such topics can be presented to pupils in the form of value dilemmas that require solutions.

As with several other new content areas, teachers can incorporate ecology and conservation into existing social studies programs. This occurs easily in units on geography and economics. Children can also study the politics involved in ecological and conservation issues. In fact, it may be more difficult to avoid teaching this subject than to find ways to integrate it into the social studies curriculum.

Activity 2:4

Social Concerns

Examine one or two social studies textbooks and note examples of law-related education, career and consumer education, multicultural and international education, education for the future, and environmental education. Write a position paper on how you perceive the current use of these new content areas.

Expanded Range of Student Audience

Social studies teachers are confronted with teaching students who range from the mentally handicapped to the academically gifted. In response to Public Law 94-142, the Education for All Handicapped Children Act, teachers are striving to adapt or create curricula appropriate for these students. As Goodman (1976) reports, the major components of this law are:

> A free public education will made available to all handicapped children ... between 3 and 21 by September 1980 ...
> For each handicapped child there will be an "individualized educational program"— ...
> Handicapped and nonhandicapped children will be educated together to the maximum extent appropriate ...
> Tests and other evaluation material used in placing handicapped children will be prepared and administered in such a way as not to be racially or culturally discriminatory ...
> The states and localities will undertake comprehensive personnel development, including inservice training for regular as well as special education teachers and support personnel ...

Essentially, this law states that children previously placed in special classes are now to be instructed whenever possible in regular classrooms by regular classroom teachers. This placement is called *mainstreaming*.

Comparing the goals and instructional practices of desirable social studies programs with those identified by mainstreaming proponents reveals many similarities (Jarolimek, 1974). Both regular programs and special programs stress self-concept enhancement, tolerance of diversity, a curriculum that builds upon the reality of the immediate community, and full citizenship for every individual. When analyzing materials in both regular and special programs, one also finds similarities in practices characterized by informality and student-to-student interaction, multidisciplinary instruction, and individualization. With such similarities, the difficulties in mainstreaming special children may not be as overwhelming as many people first imagined.

In striving to provide the least restrictive environment to these children, Sanford's (1980) admonition may prove useful:

> The handicapped are not a homogeneous group, but are more like the nonhandicapped in terms of their heterogeneity. All have varying strengths,

Attention to handicapped children has made teachers more aware of the exceptionality of all children.

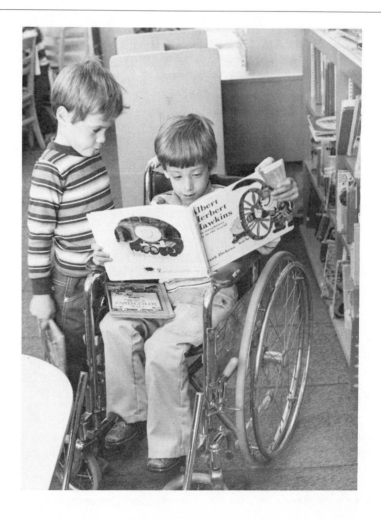

weaknesses, interests, and needs. Different handicapping conditions will require different instructional strategies.

Attention to handicapped children has made all of us more aware of the exceptionality of *all* children. All children should have a "least restrictive environment" in which to learn. Educators remind us that we need to attend to all children, children who represent the entire range of abilities. While concern for education of the gifted arose before the passage of Public Law 94–142, this law gave greater impetus to the move to provide programs and learning opportunities to those children classified as gifted and talented.

Who are the gifted? James J. Gallagher, a specialist in education for the gifted, provides a useful definition:

> Gifted and talented children are those identified by professionally qualified persons who by virtue of outstanding abilities are capable of high performance. These are children who require differentiated educational programs and services beyond those normally provided by the regular school program in order to realize their contribution to self and society.
>
> Children capable of high performance include those with demonstrated achievement and/or potential ability in any of the following areas.
>
> 1. General intellectual ability
> 2. Specific academic aptitude
> 3. Creative or productive thinking
> 4. Leadership ability
> 5. Visual and performing arts
> 6. Psychomotor ability (Reynolds and Birch, 1977)

Gallagher's definition considers high ability, social contribution, and personal development. It does hold that differentiated educational programs and services should be provided, an aspect of the definition that is currently receiving some debate. Some teachers believe such students need special programs, while others argue that the regular classroom should be the main arena for their learning, especially at a time when we are mainstreaming others into the "regular" classroom. Segregating the gifted and talented would make the classroom less "regular." Also, those who favor retaining the gifted in the regular classroom point out that gifted students will eventually have to work and live with persons of lesser talent. In addition, including gifted students in the regular classroom heightens the quality of learning by the other students.

While teachers have always been concerned with the gifted and the talented, these students are receiving more attention today in both talk and action. Teachers are now asked to develop individualized educational plans for these students; there are specialized staff and particularized instructional procedures to support the work of the regular classroom teacher; and parents are assuming a more active and visible role in their children's education (Reynolds and Birch, 1977).

The Teacher As Professional

A professional possesses specialized knowledge and is involved in decision making that influences the nature and development of her field of expertise. Some people argue about whether or not educators are in fact professionals. It certainly seems that educators have the potential to be professionals, and this potential rests upon how willing and able they are to assume responsibility for the direction of education. Professionalism is a state of mind, a realization that one has responsibilities to her chosen field and obligations to ensure that the field influences the greatest possible number of people. A teacher concerned only with teaching social studies tomorrow to her thirty pupils, with no attention to the general purpose of education, is not really a professional.

Professionalism does not come about suddenly. Educators begin their professional development when they realize they have a stake in determining the quality of educational practice in all schools. Teachers begin to become professionals when they see that education is designed to address certain social issues, and when they work for the optimal development of all children.

A hallmark of a professional is involvement in decision making. Teachers who are professionals are involved in all aspects of educational decision making. They have a say in determining program aims, goals, and objectives. They help identify and implement a level of quality for persons entering the field. They participate in plotting the nature and direction of the curricula offered to children, and in evaluating the effectiveness of programs and various means of instruction.

There is no standard model for professionalism; we can all be professionals in our unique ways. We must share the common desire for involvement and accept responsibility for making defensible educational decisions, but how we will look as professionals remains an individual task. Professionals must remain current in understanding both teaching and social studies education. They must keep up-to-date on developments that influence education. They need to volunteer for those special projects, such as curriculum development and workshops, aimed at making instruction more effective. They need to attend educational conferences and to schedule time for professional reading.

The path to professionalism begins in undergraduate preparation. Development is a continuous process, one that is never finished. This will not discourage the true educators, who will enjoy the constantly renewing challenges. The requirement for continued study and active involvement is what makes education dynamic and challenging. The responsibility for increased professionalism rests primarily with the individual teacher. It is her duty to continually upgrade skills and knowledge by taking university courses, reading journals, attending workshops, and becoming involved in educational associations.

The National Council for the Social Studies (NCSS) is the largest and most influential professional association for social studies educators. Headquartered in Washington, D.C., its official publication is the journal *Social Education;* it also publishes other material pertinent to social studies education. It also issues policy statements on curriculum issues, standards for teacher preparation, students' rights, and academic freedom. Through these publications, it keeps teachers apprised of trends and developments in the field.

NCSS holds a national convention at which classroom teachers, state and local social studies supervisors, and college and university professors discuss issues and share perceptions and findings about the social studies field. The Association also sponsors regional meetings that focus on current issues affecting social studies education. In each state, local councils meet to discuss ways to assure quality social studies education.

Another organization useful to social studies teachers, especially those interested in geography, is the National Council for Geographic Education (NCGE) in Houston, Texas. The Association's primary aim is to furnish useful information to teachers of geography. The NCGE also holds annual meetings that feature the latest information regarding geographic materials, instructional techniques, and issues affecting geographic education. The organization's major publication, *The Journal of Geography,* is most valuable to teachers seeking ways to make teaching geography dynamic.

A third organization that social studies teachers find fruitful in maintaining their professionalism is the Social Science Education Consortium (SSEC) located in Boulder, Colorado. This consortium offers diverse sources of information useful to educators who are responsible for developing social studies curricula. The *Social Studies Curriculum Materials Data Book* provides teachers with a most complete source of information; it should be available in a well-stocked school library or the social studies department. Teachers who have difficulty thinking of new materials to use or new activities to initiate will find the *Data Book* most valuable.

Professional teachers of social studies do more than carry out the ideas and commands of others. They create many of the ideas and are involved in formulating program directives for themselves and others. Professionalism does not come in the first year on the job; indeed, it is something that must be worked for and continually worked on to maintain.

Discussion

The social studies teacher currently confronts the challenge of changing educational attitudes. The teacher must fulfill traditional roles and prepare to assume new roles. She must continue to act as a source of information and to present information; to organize and manage the classroom; and to evaluate course content and student performance. At the same time, she must respond to new demands, instilling in her students a spirit of inquiry, taking a more active role in curriculum planning, diagnosing learning skills and needs, selecting materials from an evergrowing supply, and becoming an active researcher into the effects of contents and methods on her particular students.

The teacher must also cope with current educational issues, such as mainstreaming and accountability, and acquaint herself with contemporary additions to the social studies curriculum. Even elementary students frequently explore such areas as law, careers, consumerism and economics, multicultural and international topics, the future, and the environment. The expanded curriculum range calls for imaginative use of resource personnel; the expanded student audience brought about through mainstreaming demands even greater effort to individualize instruction for both handicapped and gifted students.

Professionalism is yet another concern for today's teachers. To be regarded as a professional, the teacher must be willing to assume responsibility, particularly in educational decision making, and to accept the necessity for continuing her own learning experiences. Finally, to achieve professionalism, today's social studies teacher must also dare to be creative and innovative, and to care about her and her students' contributions to society.

References

Goodman, Leroy V. "A Bill of Rights for the Handicapped." *American Education* 12 (1976); 6–8.

Hansen, W. Lee; Bach, B.L.; Calderwood, J.D.; and Saunders, P. Part I, *Master Curriculum Guide in Economics for the Nation's Schools; A Framework for Teaching Economics: Basic Concepts.* New York: Joint Council on Economic Education, 1977.

Jarolimek, John, ed. *Readings for Social Studies in Elementary Education.* New York: Macmillan Co., 1974.

Jarolimek, John. *Social Studies Competencies and Skills: Learning to Teach as An Intern.* New York: Macmillan Co., 1977a.

Jarolimek, John. *Social Studies in Elementary Education.* 5th ed. New York: Macmillan Co., 1977b.

Litwin, G. H., and Stringer, R. A. *Motivation and Organizational Climate.* Boston: Harvard University Press, 1968.

Orlich, Donald C. et al. *Teaching Strategies: A Guide to Better Instruction.* Lexington, Mass.: D. C. Heath & Co., 1980.

Reynolds, Maynard C. and Birch, Jack W. *Teaching Exceptional Children in All America's Schools.* Reston, Va.: Council for Exceptional Children, 1977.

Sanford, Howard. "Organizing and Presenting Social Studies Content in a Mainstreamed Class." In *Mainstreaming in the Social Studies,* edited by John G. Herlihy and Myra T. Herlihy. Washington, D. C.: National Council for the Social Studies, 1980.

Wiles, John, and Bondi, Joseph. *Supervision, A Guide to Practice.* Columbus, Oh.: Charles E. Merrill Publishing Co., 1980.

Social Studies Foundations

3

As we have mentioned, social studies draws much of its content from the scholarly disciplines that focus on humankind: history, geography, economics, sociology, anthropology, political science, psychology, and philosophy. In this chapter and the next, we will look at the contributions of these disciplines to human understanding. Each discipline offers a fresh perspective on the relationship between people and their environments. Ideally, the social sciences and the humanities help us understand how our lives are interwoven with historical and societal forces.

History: The Oldest Foundation

The study of history has been central to the American school curriculum from colonial times to the present. Why must students study the past? Why do people think such study is important? Why are we interested in comprehending what humans before us did, what they failed to do, what they considered important, what they loved, and what they hated? All of us have a past with roots or ties to those who lived before us; we know how we became what we are. Armed with such knowledge, we understand where we are going. Furthermore, such knowledge enhances our appreciation of who we are as members of the human family.

Defining History

Some students regard history as nothing more than a collection of facts, dates, or names to be memorized. All too frequently, they consider it boring. These viewpoints usually arise when history is poorly taught.

History offers a view of the past as reconstructed by the historian's analysis. Jacob Burckardt (1958) has defined history as "what one age finds worthy of note in another." This definition suggests the notion of interpretation, a vital aspect of historical inquiry. This attention to interpretation is crucial in understanding why historians sometimes disagree, and why the history of one time seems to be rewritten during another. The historian's task is to examine the story of the human family and to interpret portions of this drama. As observers of the past, historians do not escape the influences of their own times. They read diaries, newspaper accounts, and essays by others who also have been influenced by the values and beliefs of earlier times. We can even say that historians reinterpret interpretations.

Collingwood (1969) defines history as a "kind of research or inquiry" into the past through the process of interpreting available evidence. The evidence with which the historian works, however, is often fragmentary and biased and frequently, he can examine only a portion of the data based on particular research questions. Given the restriction of lifespan, a researcher can read and analyze only so much from the vast archives of past and present human activity. Fenton (1967) notes that the significant contributions of history to the social studies are the analytical questions generated by historians.

Centuries ago, Cicero warned that "to be ignorant of what happened before you is to be ever a child." History can help us understand the many dimensions of our humanity by offering opportunities to go beyond the present, to study human behavior as it has been affected by institutions, movements, and ideas from other times.

Because of its broad scope, covering all areas of human endeavor, history is really not a social science to some scholars. If we allow that one attribute of scientific endeavor is the ability to make predictions, then history certainly is outside the social sciences. Historical statements are not predictive in the same sense as economic or sociological statements. Because of its scope, history draws from numerous sources. How one organizes the study of history depends upon the focus desired. These are some of the many possible categories:

- Chronological history—European history between 1871 and 1914
- Geographical history—studies of the Near East, South America
- Intellectual history—history of science, diplomacy, economics
- Topical history—future history, oral history, psychohistory
- Biographical history—studies of prominent figures of a period
- Cultural history—history of the mind and character of a people

In reality, history shares characteristics of both the social sciences and the humanities. Along with the social sciences, history creates an information base and communicates this information to others, raises questions about people's actions, follows a rational systematic process, and attempts to provide evidence for conclusions. Additionally, history has been written with attention to style, dramatic presentation of events, and descriptions of actors. It is often presented in a story or narrative format to engage our imaginations about times and people in the past.

Historians can be categorized as either scientific or literary, depending upon their approach. Crane Brinton 1962 has been called a "scientific" historian because of the way he studied revolutions. He investigated the British, American, French, and Russian Revolutions in an attempt to identify characteristics of revolutions and to generalize about their nature. He looked for evidence to support or refute each conclusion or generalization he formed. Three of Brinton's conclusions were:

> *Revolutions are not started by starving, miserable people. The revolutions under study came at a time when the respective societies were on the upgrade.*

> *The pre-revolutionary governments were inefficient and unwilling or unable to make necessary reforms.*

> *All revolutions are led by a minority of dedicated followers who are conscious and very proud of their small numbers.*

Historical Concepts and Generalizations

Despite the fact that historians have not agreed that history has its own unique content, certain concepts are commonly used to organize this content realm, among them, time, event, period, theme, place, year, decade, generation, epoch, age, era, ancient, medieval, modern, interpretation, periodization, and criticism. Figure 3.1 shows one way to organize the content of history.

Historians strive to interpret, and thus to form general conclusions. Some of their major generalizations can provide a focus for children's learning, such as:

> *The affairs of human societies have historical antecedents and consequences; past events affect the present.*

Figure 3.1
Organizing Historical
Content

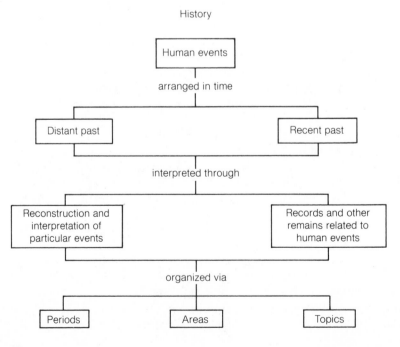

*Human societies have undergone and continue to undergo constant, though
perhaps gradual, changes as means of dealing with various physical, political,
and social forces.*

*The struggle for freedom and human dignity has occurred relatively recently
in the overall span of human existence.*

*People are influenced by values, ideals, and societal institutions, as well as
by their environment.*

*A country's history influences the culture, traditions, beliefs, attitudes, and
ways of living of its people.*

Change is a constant in human society.

*The historian's view of the past is influenced by available evidence, his per-
sonal biases, his research questions, and the societal context in which he lives.*

Historical Methods of Inquiry

While most historians agree that history differs from the other social sciences,
they also contend that their methods of inquiry have much in common with
the procedures used by other social scientists. Historians such as Henry Steele
Commager and Mark Krug have described the historical method as to some
degree scientific, but also highly personal; the historian is both artist and
scientist.

Krug (1967) identifies three steps in the historian's method:

1. The collection of potentially relevant facts
2. The organization of selected facts and their pattern
3. The interpretation of selected facts and their pattern

Collecting facts requires using primary source materials. If someone
were to write a history of your life, the primary source would be you. Other
useful primary sources would be other people who know you and can add to
your story. These people can be used as witnesses. If there are no people
available, the historian can use physical remains. In the case of your history,
books that you used, your diaries, letters you wrote, magazines you read,
newspapers in your home, and your photo album would be primary source
materials. Family records might be another. In order to place your life in a
time context, the historian might visit libraries and go through newspaper
accounts and other archives. The important thing to remember is that primary sources are firsthand accounts or statements, or original documents
from a particular era.

After gathering data from primary sources, the historian turns to the
secondary sources, the writings of other historians or individuals with relevant expertise. In the case of your history, secondary sources will allow the
historian to put your life into the broader context of a particular time. What

have others written about the time when you were living in a certain place? What major events were happening and what significance did persons give to these events? In using secondary sources, the historian is able to fill in the gaps he found when collecting information from primary sources. Perhaps you noted in your diary: "Today was a most important event in our community. I played a major role." Since you did not expect anyone to read your diary, you did not identify the event. Noting the date of entry, the historian goes to the library to see the local newspaper for that day. He may also read what someone has written in a book dealing with local history.

When dealing with primary and secondary sources, the historian realizes that much of the raw material of history is perceived by the fallible human eye. He must therefore consider points of view, bias, and the authenticity of accounts and documents. The farther we retreat in time, the more fragmented the evidence becomes; part of the historian's work is to infer from limited information what might really have taken place. Inferring from scant data is part of the personal equation of history. As historians look at

Grandparents can give firsthand accounts of what life was like in another era. Here a child learns about an old-time technique for making cider.

times past, they ask: what was going on, why it was happening, and what were the results?

The answers to these questions will vary because historians interpret facts and patterns differently. Some historical scholars argue that the cause of the American Civil War was slavery, while others identify sectional differences and rivalry as the important contributing factors. Historical viewpoints fluctuate from one time to another as new concepts and generalizations from other disciplines and new perspectives provide novel ways of interpreting facts. This personal processing of data leads most, if not all, historians to realize the effects of personal bias on their research. Carl Becker has pointed out that bias permeates historical inquiry: "There is bias in the choice of subject, bias in the selection of material, bias in its organization, and presentation, and inevitably, bias in its interpretation. Consciously or unconsciously, all historians are biased; they are creatures of their time, their race, their faith, their class, their country—creatures, and even prisoners" (Snyder, 1958, p. 59).

Activity 3:1

Assessing Historical Attitude

To encourage students to think of history as more than just names and dates, we must possess the "historical attitude." This attitude is primarily a questioning one: we wish to know the antecedents to current happenings and to interpret past events intelligently. Such an attitude enriches our lives by expanding our horizons to other times and places.

Think about some particular event. Determine the level of your interests in the event as high, medium, or low, and jot down down the reasons for your interest. What questions come to mind when you consider this event? How has your knowledge of the event enriched your life? What procedures did you employ in investigating this event?

Once the data are in hand, the historian must organize the facts and denote patterns. Organization is influenced by the question, "What is going on?" After the information has been organized, the final step, *interpretation*, takes place. Recognizing the chance for personal bias, the historian attempts to reduce it at least to a level where his conclusions will have some value. These conclusions are based on fact or certainty, probability or possibility, and uncertainty. For the professional researcher, fact means that, as far as can be determined, something is true. Going back to your history, a fact would be your name. It is the truth, and can be checked out by asking people who know you what your name is or by looking at your birth certificate.

Conclusions based on probability are those that appear defensible according to the evidence. However, the historian cannot be altogether certain about the conclusion. In writing your history, the historian may have concluded from your one-year diary that you enjoy going to museums, but he cannot be absolutely certain. Perhaps you went to many museums that year because your parents insisted, or to get extra points in school. Sometimes historians find that one primary source mentions an event, but cannot locate any others that mention the same event. The historian then goes to secondary sources to find the event discussed. Mention in a secondary source is support that the event most likely did occur, but the support is in the realm of probability. Sometimes the historian draws a conclusion based on uncertainty. This is perhaps the most difficult conclusion for students of history to accept. We all like to have support for our conclusions, but historians occasionally uncover some unresolvable conflict. Two sources may offer one reason for an event, while two others may suggest a different reason. Since even primary sources may conflict, the researcher must come to some sort of conclusion, perhaps pointing out the element of mystery; he may later alter his conclusions if additional information comes to light.

History in the Elementary Classroom

Since most schools require that history be taught in the elementary grades, we really cannot choose to neglect it. Our challenge is to decide how to teach it so that students will not be bored by it, or come to see history as merely a listing of facts. Good instruction begins by carefully analyzing student interests, abilities, and concerns, and comparing this information to the school's overall aims and goals. With this information as a base, the teacher can develop interesting ways to incorporate history into the social studies program.

The decisions we make about how to teach history and what activities to schedule will be influenced by the age of the children in our classes. For example, young children do not acquire a sense of time until they are about ten years old, which is a good argument for delaying history to about the fourth or fifth grades. Prior instruction should be about the present and about the children's immediate community. Interest in their own experiences is common among all elementary children, regardless of age. (This is true even with secondary students.) Thus, when introducing the time element in history, it is best to start with a local and somewhat immediate experience, then move on to more distant times and places. Materials covering local past and present events are often not readily available, so teacher-constructed materials may be necessary.

With very young children, teachers frequently introduce history by allowing them to examine historical objects firsthand. Children love to handle objects, and local museums sometimes have special exhibits with artifacts especially selected for handling. Items that arouse children's interest are artifacts from past wars, facsimiles of important documents such as the Declaration of Independence, or the front page of a newspaper announcing a major event, such as men landing on the moon. Children can also bring in items from home that grandparents used when they were young.

Another approach for introducing children to history is to create opportunities for them to meet older people in their community. Children can take field trips to retirement communities to interview some of the residents, or older citizens can be invited to classrooms to talk about "what it was like when I was a child." Teachers sometimes discover that some members of the community are amateur historians just waiting for a chance to share their knowledge with children. When people are the resources, the teacher should prepare the children, instructing them in how to ask different types of questions. Children learn they need to ask questions that do more than just elicit facts. They need to pursue questions that help them understand why certain events occurred and the effects those events had on yesterday and even today.

Instruction in history requires more than just having students listen to the teacher tell interesting (and perhaps not so interesting) stories. Good instruction prompts students to raise questions, formulate hypotheses, however simple, conduct investigations, weigh evidence, and arrive at conclusions. History must mean more to the student than recalling what was read or said by the teacher. Teachers who accept this goal use a variety of activities and materials to get their pupils actively involved. Teachers often find these activities productive:

1. Preparing bulletin boards and other exhibits illustrating some past event
2. Tracing the history of a local industry, such as manufacturing or mining
3. Writing biographical sketches of famous people in the community, both past and present
4. Visiting museums
5. Collecting and exhibiting old photographs of the community
6. Making pictorial timelines tracing various eras in our nation's history
7. Constructing relief maps of the local area, identifying the sites of events significant to the community's development
8. Conducting a historical study of a particular community landmark
9. Having students write their own personal histories
10. Making comparisons of different accounts of the same event

Pupils find history more exciting when they can be involved in processing information. The National Council for the Social Studies Yearbook (1974), *Teaching American History: The Quest for Relevance*, presents a lesson showing how to involve upper-elementary children in investigating the story of the Jumano Indians, who vanished as a group in 1800 A.D. Students gather in groups of five or six with the objective of obtaining data to answer the question, "What happened to the Jumano Indians?" Each group is given ten cards that furnish fragments of information about the Jumano's past. An example of one of these cards illustrating a Jumano home appears in figure 3.2.

The lesson has the following specific knowledge objectives, in that students will:

1. Know that the Jumano Indian way of life ceased to exist by 1800 A.D.
2. Know that although incomplete, a variety of historical evidence is available about the Jumano Indians of the Southwest.

3. Know that any written history is interpretation.
4. Know that the history of any people or person must be classified as incomplete.
5. Know that although incomplete, the history of any group or individual can nevertheless tell us much about them.

In using these cards, pupils act like historians—gathering and organizing data and making interpretations. How might you use these materials to get pupils involved in the study of history?

Figure 3.2
Information Card for
Investigative History
Lesson

CARD 10
A Jumano Home—Archeological Finds

As you now know, the Jumanos settled in the area between present-day El Paso and the Big Bend on the Rio Grande River. There they built pueblo-type homes. We are able to know this because of the diggings done by archeologists, scholars seeking to learn more about early people by studying the articles (artifacts) or housing they left behind. The archeologist usually selects a spot where he believes early people once lived and then digs for their remains or searches the ground and caves in that area.

By digging in and around some old Jumano pueblo homes, archeologists were able to learn many other things about Jumano Indian life. An archeologist's reconstruction of pueblo homes of the 1500's follows. It is a reconstruction much like the one of the modern-day artist used for the drawing on Card 9.

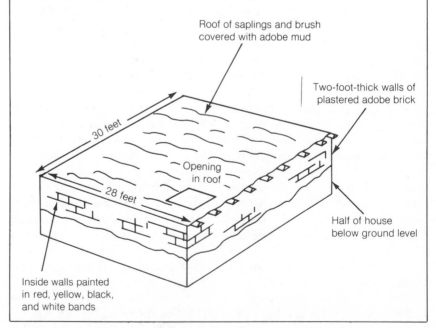

Roof of saplings and brush covered with adobe mud

Two-foot-thick walls of plastered adobe brick

30 feet

Opening in roof

28 feet

Half of house below ground level

Inside walls painted in red, yellow, black, and white bands

From Allan Kownslar, ed., *Teaching American History: The Quest for Relevancy.* Based on Newcomb, *The Indians of Texas,* p. 242. Reprinted by permission.

Geography

Geography is an integral part of the elementary social studies curriculum. But because it is a broad and integrative discipline, there is some question as to whether it belongs in the social science family. It may help to realize that all the various fields of learning, such as the physical sciences, the biological sciences, the social sciences, and the humanities, are rough classifications. Almost any area of study will not fit neatly into one particular group. There is much overlap, especially in today's cross-disciplinary specialities such as historical geography or molecular biology. The important thing to remember is that geographers consider their area of study to be first and foremost a social science.

Defining Geography

What distinguishes geography from other disciplines is its concern with the character of place. The geographer is interested in analyzing the integrated whole of a people and their habitat and the interrelations among places. The geographer focuses on a vast variety of places: mountains, plains, river systems, deserts, cities, villages. He works at obtaining information about the climate of these places, the movement of people in and out of them, the people's uses of resources, the types of cultures, and the growth and decline of

By trying out the old wringer washer, these students are reliving a piece of experience from life in early America.

cities. But geographers strive for more than just descriptions. They also develop projections as to what will happen when certain factors, such as climatic changes or new technologies, interact. They are interested in generalizing these projections to other places or regions that show similarities. This function is rather new to geography, and has come about primarily because of the introduction of sophisticated statistical methods and computerization of data. Computers can now indicate potential results of particular interactions of geographic phenomena over time. Models have been created that allow us to forecast the impact of patterns of population growth on the earth's resources. Geographers use computers to create maps of both two and three dimensions. But despite these new directions, geography is still concerned primarily with the description and explanation of natural phenomena arranged on the earth's surface. Greco (1966) notes that geography "... is a synthetic areal science which utilizes the ecological aspects of all the systematic sciences—physical, biotic, or societal. . . . Explaining area differentiation is the quest of the geographer."

Fields of Geography

Because of its scope, geography is frequently divided into different fields or specialities. Most people are familiar with *physical* geography, which is considered closely related to earth science, one of the natural sciences. This division reflects what Pattison (1964) notes as the "earth science tradition." The focus in physical geography is on the features of the physical terrain. Although much of this subject has been taken over by geology or earth science, one cannot completely ignore physical geography in the elementary school curriculum.

Figure 3.3
Fields and Traditions
of Geography

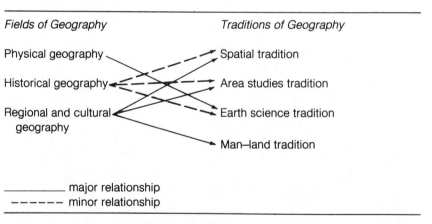

Another field is *historical* geography, which relates closely to the work and method of historians and in many ways borders on the humanities. Historical geographers analyze space in times past—they are interested in studying the relationships of patterns of movement across space. They investigate the movement of goods, ideas, and people between and among groupings of human settlements. A third field is *regional and cultural* geography, which draws on three traditions identified by Pattison: the spatial, the area studies, and the man–land tradition. The *area studies tradition,* which is frequently found in the elementary school curriculum, centers on a particular region. Geographers of this orientation may specialize in analyzing New England or the Southwest. The *man–land tradition* focuses on the cultural aspect of geography, the human race and its interaction with the physical and cultural aspects of space (Pattison, 1964). The divisions of geography and their relationships to the traditions are represented in Figure 3.3.

Structure of Geography

Figure 3.4 shows the diagram created by Crabtree (1967) that gives us a global picture of the discipline.

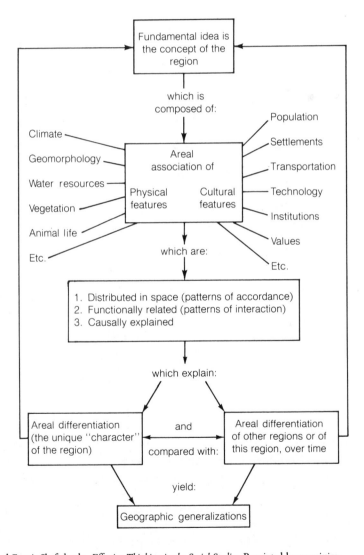

Figure 3.4
Crabtree's Model of the Structure of Geography

From Jean Fair and Fannie Shaftel, eds., *Effective Thinking in the Social Studies.* Reprinted by permission.

Geographic Methods of Inquiry

All the social sciences share some common methodology, but each discipline also has its unique approach to processing data. The major method of data processing in geography is the regional approach, which sometimes uses cartographic techniques in investigating both regions on a broad scale and topics within those regions. At one time, geographers argued that there were two major methods, regional and topical; however, most geographers now agree that the duality of the regional and topical approaches to areal phenomena has been superseded by the realization that both approaches are really different emphases of the regional method. Broek (1965) makes this point clear when he states:

> In a *regional study* one starts with the hypothesis that the area is a region and then examines its components and connections. In light of the knowledge gained, one confirms or revises the initial boundaries and interprets the "personality" of the region. Throughout the procedure, the guiding idea is to provide a synthesis of the region as a complex association of features. The *topical approach* starts with a question, such as "where are the flour mills in the United States, and why are they there?" The regional patterns of the flour mills and of all other features that seem relevant to the problem are then examined and compared. (pp. 59–60)

Geographers use the regional method to describe places in detail, to analyze events to determine relationships, and to formulate generalizations and theories that explain the relationships among places, people, and events. Recently, geographers have begun using computers and other sophisticated methods to engage in statistical prediction and model building.

Cartographic techniques are a subspeciality of geography concerned with map making and map interpretation for the purpose of discovering relationships among areal phenomena. In the early days of physical geography, maps showed the location of bodies of water, land, people, and other phenomena. Now maps have a greater variety of uses, such as the analysis of news coverage or the distribution of ideas or political views across a nation. The proportionate size of a place on a map can indicate its size relationship to other places, or the size might indicate its population density, its energy consumption, or its degree of industrialization.

Geographic Concepts

Disciplines are identified as areas of knowledge that have specialized concepts or concepts used in particular ways. Chapter 6 will explain what concepts are; for now we need to be aware only that concepts are tools with which we view and organize reality. They are mental constructs with which to organize our experiences and to symbolize vast amounts of information. Taba (1965) defined concepts as "high level generalizations" expressed in words such as interdependence, region, or change, that encompass large amounts of specifics. Concepts can be classified as lower-order abstractions, such as lake, river, or gully, or as higher-order abstractions, such as dependency, interaction, or resource.

While some may argue that geography does not have concepts unique to its field, geography does use particular concepts in its study of phenomena arranged on the earth's surface: region, ecosystem, habitat, culture region, areal differentiation, location, and spatial interaction. *Region* refers to an area of the earth in which (1) many features are homogeneous within the boundary, and (2) contrasts between the region and its surrounding area are maximized. Regions can be based on *ecosystems,* area associations that result from physical and biotic process. Regions might be *habitats,* which represent ecosystems that have been changed by human action, or *culture regions,* which are ecosystems divided according to human ways of living.

By studying the interaction of the physical and cultural features of the earth, the geographer can offer several perspectives. For example, study of an area's uniqueness results in data denoting area differentiation. Studying regions over time reveals how geographic features have changed, and studying regions on a comparative basis results in geographical generalizations and theories.

Location refers to the distance, direction, and distribution of things, natural and human-made, as they occur on the earth's surface. When studying distributions, the geographer examines patterns, density, and areal extent. In investigating a city, he might analyze its relationship to nearby cities and towns, its population density, and the distribution and area of various features of city life.

Spatial interaction refers to the links and bonds that exist among places. During the 1920s, Burgess (Bacon, 1970) developed the theory of concentric zones of urban structure. He described Chicago as a series of zones. This model has now become obsolete, with the growth of freeways, larger cities, and the megalopolis, a multicentered urban conglomerate such as the Washington, D.C.–New York–Boston combination.

Environmental perception is one concern of a new group of social geographers. This new field of study seeks to better understand the differences in the ways people view the world around them. Work is progressing in many interesting areas; for example, Clifford Russell (Bacon, 1970) has studied human perception of risk, specifically the phenomenon of people's returning to flood plains to rebuild damaged homes. He suggests that we may need to modify our idea of mastery over nature, and admit the inevitable occurrence of some losses. Instead of building better dams and bigger levies, Russell notes that we might save more lives by limiting housing development in such an area. Out of the study of environmental perception have come new mapping techniques. Geographers have revealed media reporting biases by mapping the number of times a local area is mentioned in the press as compared to the number of times other regions are mentioned.

Cultural diffusion is a concept geographers have borrowed from anthropology. It refers to the distribution of some cultural trait, such as language, education, religion, ethnic origin, or technological development, found within and throughout some particular area. Geographers are interested in locating such traits and noting their dispersion and density. They are also interested in identifying those features of the earth's surface that seem to relate to the diffusion of particular traits.

Geographic Generalizations

Concepts in geography and in other social sciences serve as building blocks to greater understanding. Geographers do not end their processing of information with the formation of concepts; rather, they organize concepts into generalizations that denote a particular relationship among the concepts. Skillful teachers of geographic content organize the learning experience so that students comprehend the relevant generalizations.

Generalizations such as the following are those most likely to appear in social studies units that deal with geography:

The sequence of a peoples' activities and cultural patterns is related to their geographic location and accessibility, and to the particular time in which they live. People in different areas react differently to similar environments.

The extent of peoples' use of natural resources is related to their level of technology and their cultural view of the resources.

Geographic factors influence where and how people live; humans shape, adapt, utilize, and exploit the earth to their own ends.

The global location of a nation or region greatly influences its roles in international affairs.

Geography in the Elementary Classroom

Geography can provide children with opportunities to deal with relationships, to fit parts into wholes, and to arrange objects and events on the surface of the earth in order to understand concepts and generalizations relating to the earth. Students led by a dynamic teacher can learn to ask questions the way a geographer does, and master the use of map language.

Elementary teachers usually find it easy to introduce geography into the social studies curriculum, for children, especially primary-age children, come to school with great curiosity about their world and seemingly endless questions about places and people. There are many activities available to stimulate and satisfy this curiosity. The teacher of primary-age children can take them on field trips in the community to observe firsthand its geographic features—slopes, hills, islands, lakes, and rivers. Children can observe the differences among various neighborhoods and the center of their town or city. They can record the distribution of various types of plants and trees, noting which are distributed naturally and which have been planted.

Field trips and class discussions during which the teacher raises thought-provoking questions will encourage children to formulate some conclusions about what is meant by environment, how people have changed the spaces in which they live, how some places can be used for multiple purposes, and why people move from place to place.

A geography lesson at the primary level might begin by having children look at the school site as a geographer would. Where is the building located? Where is the playground located? Why is the playground situated where it is? What manufactured equipment is on the playground? Why are certain types of playground equipment placed where they are? How do people get to various places in the school building?

The following lesson plan will help students analyze the school site from a geographic perspective. It involves pupils in actively processing phe-

---

Lesson Plan

Lesson Focus: Our School and Its Location

Grade Level: Primary

Objective: Pupils will understand that each place (school site) on earth has a distinctiveness that sets it apart from all other places.

Introductory Activities:
Have photographs of the school taken from various angles on the bulletin board. Tell the children they are going to pretend to describe their school to someone from another school in another town.

Have the pupils think of questions they can ask. (The teacher will have to provide some guidance as to the types of possible questions.)

Developmental Activity:
Take the children on a field trip around the school, visiting classrooms, grounds, and other areas. Have them note the locations of distinctive features and the uses of different areas of the school. Have children write a word or phrase that answers one of their questions about the school and its location. The children may be encouraged to take Polaroid pictures to record data, if they are allowed to use such a camera.

Have children engage in class discussion after their field trip. Have them decide whether or not they have answered their questions.

Have children share descriptions of the school and its location.

Note: After children feel comfortable with this type of fieldwork, have them begin applying the same questions to their own and other children's neighborhoods. How are these neighborhoods alike and different? What are some of the special features of these neighborhoods?

Concluding Activity:
Some of the children can make a bulletin board with the photographs they took and also with one-word answers to the major questions asked in the lesson.

Children may also draw pictures of their school and its location, focusing on some special feature of the school site. These pictures can be displayed.

Booklets can be developed to give to other children interested in learning about the school and its location.

Materials:
Cameras, and writing and painting supplies.

---

nomena from a geographic perspective. This involvement can be much more extensive with children in the middle and upper grades, when they can conduct intensive investigations and deal with complex questions.

For example, a teacher in the intermediate grades might plan to have students investigate the geographic generalization that successive or continuing occupancy by groups of people, as well as natural processes and forces, results in changing and changed landscapes. The lesson on page 63 has this focus.

Activity 3:2

Classroom Survey—Geography

If you are observing in a classroom or student teaching, jot down the number of social studies lessons emphasizing geography that occur in a week. Identify the focus of each lesson. What is the quality of each lesson and what is the basis for your judgment? Use a format such as this one:

Geography Lesson   *Focus*   *Quality of Lesson*   *Judgment Basis*

Lesson Title

_____   _____   _____   _____

_____   _____   _____   _____

If a geography lesson is not observed, ask the classroom teacher to share the year's general plan or the curriculum guide to identify three lessons that focus on geography.

Economics

Defining Economics

Economics is a social science that focuses on how people in a society use resources to satisfy their needs and wants. Its central concept is scarcity—that is, that there are insufficient human and nonhuman resources to satisfy people's needs and wants. The imbalance creates a need for a system in which choices are made in answer to four basic economic questions:

- What should be produced?
- How shall we produce it?
- How much should we produce and consume?
- For whom should we produce goods and services?

A dynamic interaction occurs between any society's wants and its available resources and know-how. An economic system is not static; it con-

Lesson Plan

Lesson Focus: Changing or changed landscapes

Grade Level: Intermediate

Objective: Through investigations of various places, students will conclude that, over time, human occupation of an area and natural processes and forces cause permanent environmental changes in the features of the area.

Introductory Activities:

Concepts emphasized: change, landscape, natural processes

Ask children to think of all the ways their neighborhood has changed over the last year or two. Have them decide which changes were caused by nature and which by people. This information can be recorded on a data chart.

Data Collection:

Next, have children visit their neighborhoods and/or their town and list events that are occurring or have occurred and that are changing or have changed the way the neighborhood or town looks (e.g., building new houses, widening a road, building a shopping center).

Data Chart (for recording information):

Neighborhood/town	Human made	Natural process
Changes Building new houses	*	
Widening the road	*	
Trees blown down in storm		*
Painting houses	*	
Making a waterfront park	*	

Generalizing:

Have pupils look at the information they have recorded on their data chart. Ask questions to encourage pupils to formulate conclusions as to how the people of the community have changed the area in which they live and work. Raise questions regarding which changes will have the most long-lasting impact on the community.

Evaluating conclusions:

Encourage children to decide which of the group's conclusions seem to be the most accurate. (Students will have to be aware of evaluation questions.)

Have children make judgments about whether or not the changes people are making actually improve the features of the areas. Children might also generalize as to why people engage in activities that modify the features of their environment.

Materials:

Books about the community; maps, charts, and photographs. (Most of the materials can be gathered by the students.)

tinually adjusts to such changing forces as technology, social goals, political circumstances, and knowledge and use of the planet's resources.

The flow of economic activity is pictured in figure 3.5, which shows the interactions among individuals, households, and markets and businesses. To be complete, the diagram should include government in the flow of economic activity. Government can be added to the individuals and households dimension.

Goals such as individual freedom, justice, and economic growth and stability are embodied in legislation and regulations that have a strong impact on the economy. For example, federal and state minimum wage laws set the

Figure 3.5
The Flow of Economic
Activity

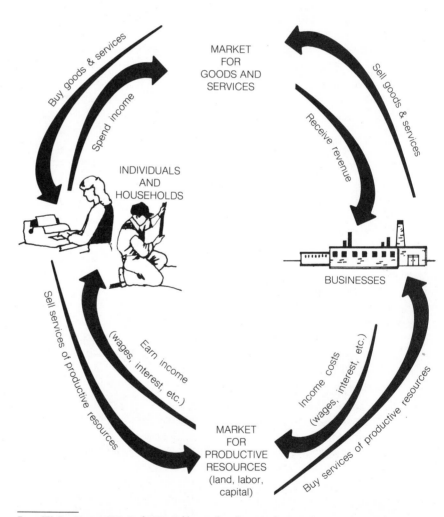

From W. Lee Hansen, B.L. Bach, J.D. Calderwood, and P. Saunders, *Master Curriculum Guide in Economics for the Nation's Schools; Part I, A Framework for Teaching Economics: Basic Concepts.* Reprinted by permission.

lower limits on wages, thus restricting employers' freedom while protecting employees. Regulatory agencies, such as the Occupational Health and Safety Administration (OSHA), set regulations for the workplace with the goals of protecting human health and life. The type and extent of the role government should play in the economy is a controversial subject in many countries, including the United States.

Economists identify four basic types of economic systems: (1) *tradition*, in which decisions are made on the basis of established customs; (2) *command*, in which decisions are made by a centralized authority; (3) *market*, in which decision making is decentralized and influenced by the activities of buyers and sellers; and (4) *mixed economics*, in which all of the three other factors operate to varying degrees. The United States exemplifies a mixed economy in which both private and public sectors are involved in economic decision making and activities. Besides studying these economic systems, some economists investigate global economic processes such as international trade, markets, specialization, international investment, and technology transfers. Figure 3.6 (pp. 66–67) presents a schematic framework of economic activity.

Economics Concepts

Economists generally agree as to the key concepts of their field and their definitions. They use precise definitions in the important investigation of production and consumption. Understanding these concepts may seem like an exercise in rote memorization, but they are important tools in acquiring a mental picture of the overall economic system.

The primary concepts in economics are scarcity, economic wants, productive resources, goods and services, consumption, division of labor, interdependence, and exchange. *Scarcity*, as noted previously, is the central concept of economics, and all economic principles and theories relate to it. The essence of scarcity is that people have unlimited wants, but the amount of resources to satisfy these wants is limited. There is, therefore, always a shortage of goods and services in light of what people want. Thus, they have to decide what goods and services will be produced with the resources available. It may seem that as more efficient methods bring increases in production, people's wants would be satisfied. But in fact, as products and services increase, so also do people's wants.

Economic wants include such diverse things as (a) the basic needs of food, shelter, clothing, and medical care; (b) modern conveniences, recreation, and entertainment; and (c) public wants, such as education, safety, parks, and highways.

Productive resources are those things used to satisfy people's wants. These may include natural resources, human resources, and capital goods. For instance, in order to meet a want for a chocolate milkshake, we would need such productive resources as a farm for producing milk, cocoa beans, and sugar, processing plants to make ice cream and chocolate, human labor, and a machine to mix the ingredients. When natural resources, people, and capital are used, the results are goods and services.

Goods are products that meet consumer wants and needs. A service refers to work aimed at satisfying consumer wants and needs. Automobiles, food, clothing, toys, and television sets are examples of goods. Benefits of services might include eating in a restaurant, having the lawn mowed, having a school to go to, or traffic control. All children have experiences with goods and services, and should therefore have little difficulty in coming to understand these concepts.

Consumption refers to the use of material goods and services. We are all consumers. When you eat your breakfast, you are a consumer of a breakfast cereal. When children go to school, they are consumers of the teachers' services. When people buy any product, they are consumers. Again, children have direct experiences with consumption.

Division of labor refers to the specialization of workers so that each worker performs a limited task in conjunction with others to increase efficiency. Production increases because each person becomes a specialist in his task, thus doing it more easily. Factories commonly employ division of labor, so each factory worker becomes skilled at a particular task. Many people together then assemble the manufactured product, whether it be an automobile or a washing machine. Even in professions such as law or medicine, division of labor exists. Some doctors specialize in treating ailments of the eyes and ears, or of the foot. The doctor's specialized knowledge about a small area of the body allows especially skilled treatment of any ailment or disease of this area. Children can begin to understand this concept by assuming specialized tasks in the classroom. Small children can be responsible for watering

Figure 3.6
Schematic Framework
of Economic Activity

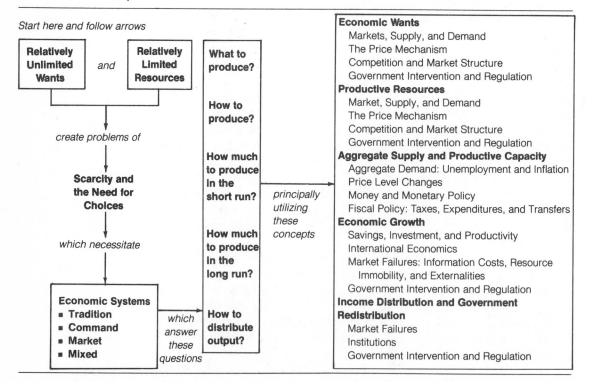

the plants, others for feeding the fish, others for keeping the library books organized, and so forth. After a while, these children will become the "class experts" in these tasks.

Specialization leads to *interdependence,* the reliance on others to produce necessary goods and provide essential services. Since most people are not specialists in medicine, they are dependent upon the expertise of a doctor. In turn, a teacher can provide the doctor with the expertise necessary to educate his children. While specialization makes a society highly efficient, it also heightens the degree of interdependence. Children can see this clearly by listing all the things they use and need that are produced by other people. We depend upon the services of others to grow our food, to bring it to the stores, to sell it to us. The people who sell food depend upon those who drive the trucks, fly the planes, and guide the trains. Specialization has produced benefits to our society, but it has also made us very vulnerable.

Economics requires that people interact with others in providing goods and services in return for other goods, services, or money. In the majority of economies, money is used to facilitate *exchange.* In a market-based economy, the interaction of buyers and sellers causes the prices of goods and services to fluctuate according to supply and demand.

Generalizations in Economics

Frequently, the goal in social studies lessons that deal with economics is to form or test generalizations. As noted previously, generalizations depict the

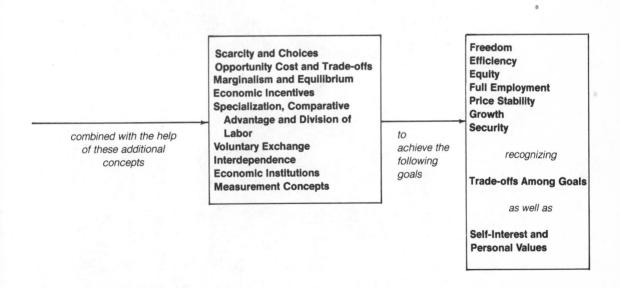

combined with the help of these additional concepts →

Scarcity and Choices
Opportunity Cost and Trade-offs
Marginalism and Equilibrium
Economic Incentives
Specialization, Comparative
    Advantage and Division of
    Labor
Voluntary Exchange
Interdependence
Economic Institutions
Measurement Concepts

→ to achieve the following goals →

Freedom
Efficiency
Equity
Full Employment
Price Stability
Growth
Security

recognizing

Trade-offs Among Goals

as well as

Self-Interest and
Personal Values

From W. Lee Hansen, B. L. Bach, J. D. Calderwood, and P. Saunders, *Master Curriculum Guide in Economics for the Nation's Schools; Part I, A Framework for Teaching Economics: Basic Concepts.* Reprinted by permission.

relationships among two or more concepts, and serve to organize vast amounts of information. These generalizations are likely to be part of an economics social studies unit:

> *The economy of a country or region is related to available resources, investment capital, and the education of its people.*

> *Peoples' wants are unlimited, whereas the resources people need to fulfill their wants are scarce. Thus, societies and individuals have to decide which needs are to be met and which ignored.*

The sexual division of labor common in many cultures illustrates both economic and sociological concepts. Here an Eskimo man teaches his son about hunting seals. An Eskimo woman, attended by her daughter, scrapes the skins from caught seals.

The interdependence of peoples in the modern world makes exchange and trade necessary.

Methods of Economic Inquiry

Many of the problems economists study involve quantification of data, statistical analysis, interpretation, and model building. The goals of economic analysis are to develop generalizations, theories, and laws that explain and predict economic behavior. For example, the law of supply and demand states that price is dependent on the factor of supply and the incidence of demand. The higher the price, the less demand. The lower the price, the more demand. When the price of a good or service rises, the supply tends to increase, because more producers are interested in selling the product. A decrease in price tends to reduce the quantity.

Economists cannot really use laboratory experiments because there is no way to get an entire society to behave in a certain way to test out an idea. Therefore, the economist usually conducts an intellectual experiment (Reynolds, 1966). Using this approach, he tests hypotheses by assuming that all of the variables are constant or equal except the one being analyzed. Suppose an economist is interested in determining why blue jeans are so popular in the United States. He first identifies the variables of cost, style, material, advertising, and peer pressure. Then he determines that cost, material, and advertising are not the main factors in making jeans so popular. The hypothesis is that peer pressure resulting from advertising is the reason for the popularity of blue jeans. The economist can then identify the various types of jeans on the market, and gather data as to which ones were advertised the most in magazines and on television programs that cater to teenage markets. If he finds that those jeans with the greatest amount of advertising exposure and with ads showing groups of teenagers wearing the jeans were also the ones with the greatest sales, our investigator has information that tends to support the hypothesis. Of course, in the real world, it would be more difficult to attempt to investigate this hypothesis. In reality, many factors influence sales and many of these are not known; of those known, many do not remain constant over time. Because of the complexity of the overall society, the economist engages in much research based on tenuous assumptions that result in conclusions that have to be accepted without reservation. This is one reason that different economists often suggest opposite solutions to the same problems.

Another approach to economic inquiry is *policy economics,* which is used for investigating social problems such as "What is the best way to control inflation?" Policy analysis represents an applied field of study in which the goal is not primarily to generate knowledge about economic processes, but rather to use existing knowledge to solve social problems. An economist concerned with social policy usually asks the following questions:

- What is the problem?
- What are the desired social goals we wish to achieve that are pertinent to this problem?

- What are the possible alternative ways of achieving these goals?
- What are the consequences of each alternative?
- What is the best alternative?

Economic analysis involves specialized decision making. With such analysis, the economist can help policy makers set a course of action. The difficulties arise when there is disagreement as to the best course of action. The disagreement may result from different values, or from different opinions as to the possible consequences of the alternatives. Much depends upon how tentative are the assumptions brought to bear on the problem.

Economics in the Elementary Classroom

The economic segment of the social studies program can be organized around the major concepts of the discipline. Ideally, children will have had experiences in which they have considered these concepts and their relationships to various generalizations or conclusions. Economics content can be readily integrated into units on the community or the nation.

Some will argue that the content of economics is too difficult for primary-grade children. Skillful teachers find, however, that by adjusting the difficulty of the content and drawing on the children's own experiences, it is easy to include key economic concepts. Barr, Barth, and Shermis (1978) suggest that second graders will learn the concept of division of labor with a simple activity. One group of children gathers around a large round table on which are piled items for a first aid box. A second group gathers round a rectangular table on which there are stacks of identical items arranged so that there is one pile in front of each student. Students are given fifteen minutes to place the gauze, bandages, Mercurochrome, cotton swabs, tape, and tongue depressors in each box.

The group by the rectangular table is instructed in assembly line procedure, with each child responsible for putting the item from his pile into a box and passing it to the next person. In the other group, each child works individually to collect the necessary items from the piles in the center of the table and create as many first aid boxes as possible.

At the end of fifteen minutes, the teacher asks the students to stop working and count the number of completed first aid boxes at each table. Usually, the greater efficiency of the group that practiced division of labor is obvious. This concept can be extended to other situations, such as a discussion of the development of Henry Ford's assembly line process.

Kourilsky (1978) has developed the Mini-Society Program for students in grades three to six. In this program, students create their own classroom economic system in which they buy and sell such goods as pencils, erasers, felt-tip pens, and posters, using printed "money." They also offer services such as banking, insurance, hair styling, and piano lessons. Class members who come up with good money-making ideas find that others soon are offering a similar product or service at a lower price. Pupils thus learn firsthand about competition. Teachers or students can also create inflation, by printing twice as much paper money as existed before. Children can compare the prices of goods before and after this event. With this kind of analysis, they will begin to understand that an increase in the money supply without a corresponding increase in prices may lead to inflation.

Another way to involve students in studying economics is through the island game, in which they deal with four basic economic questions. The teacher begins the lesson by asking the students to imagine that they are shipwrecked on an island that has nothing but sand, rocks, ocean fish, seaweed, and palm trees. The challenge is for the pupils to figure out how to survive. What food can they produce? What types of shelters can they build? How can they construct shelters from the materials available? How much of each thing will they want? How should goods and services be distributed? From playing this game and discussing their conclusions, the pupils can go on to examine different communities or societies to see how their people have answered the same or similar questions.

There are many other ways to have pupils study economics. The following suggestions will help teachers compose useful learning activities:

1. Read newspapers to compare the prices of various goods and services.
2. Visit local businesses and identify the types of goods and services offered.
3. Analyze the ways in which one's family obtains goods and services and where it gets such goods and services.
4. Analyze different types of advertising (both print and television) to determine how needs and wants are influenced.
5. Play simulations, such as the island game or creating the first aid box.
6. Compare the economic activities of people today with those of the past. (This may not work well with primary-age children who do not have a good grasp of time.)
7. Have children make a budget showing how they will spend their allowances.

Many other activities are appropriate, and children themselves are often most inventive when given the chance to suggest approaches to learning.

There are many materials and learning resources available for economic education. The Joint Council for Economic Education, 2 West 46th Street, New York City, 10036, is a good source of materials and resources. This agency publishes sample units, scope and sequence charts, and materials useful for background information.

Useful materials can also be obtained from business and industry. However, you should recognize that these materials may be biased regarding some social questions. Some commercially prepared materials have been criticized for presenting only one side of an issue; in some cases, the material has been inaccurate. A study by the Center of Study on Responsive Law revealed that some free materials were intended for selling a product or for selling a particular view of economics (Harty, 1979). As with any materials, the experienced teacher reviews the material carefully in order to make an intelligent choice.

71

Activity 3:3

Creating an Economics Lesson

Select a basic concept in economics and think of ways to introduce and develop it in a classroom. Have a friend react to your ideas. What are his reactions? Write down your ideas and the friend's reactions in a format something like this one, and try to use the notes to create a potential lesson plan for economics.

Economic concept:
Ways to introduce concept in classroom:
Reactions to introduction:
   Friend's:
   My reaction:
Ways to develop this concept:
Reactions to development of this concept:
   Friend's:
   My reaction:

Sociology

Just as economics has been jokingly referred to as the "dismal science," sociology has been characterized as "the painful elaboration of the obvious." This wry exchange obscures what these two social sciences have in common.

> Economists think, as do sociologists, in terms of systems and subsystems; they stress the relations between parts, especially patterns of dependence, dominance, exchange, and the like. (Inkeles, 1965, p. 20)

Defining Sociology

Sociology is more inclusive than economics because it focuses on all aspects of the effort to explain human behavior in groups. Sociologists are interested in patterns of human activity in both small groups and in larger structures such as communities and societies. These social scientists analyze why certain groups, such as the family, the tribe, or the nation, persist over time, even when they undergo experiences as drastic as war. Sociologists inquire into why groups change and in some cases fall apart. Not only are they fascinated by behaviors within groups, but they are also interested in group behavior among groups (Rose, 1965).

72

In seeking to acquire knowledge about human interaction, sociologists may well seem to describe the obvious. Some aspects of everyday living are well known to most of us, but much of our knowledge of family, workplace, and community is fragmentary and uncritical. From sociology, we can obtain a perspective extending beyond our own experience. C. Wright Mills (1959) calls this perspective the "sociological imagination."

> The sociological imagination enables its possessor to understand the larger historical scene in terms of its meaning for the inner life and the external career of a variety of individuals. (p. 5)

We all exist in a society, and our society exists within some historical sequence. Mills would like sociologists to investigate the interaction of an individual's life, society's institutions, and history, in the tradition of such familiar social theorists as Auguste Comte, Emile Durkheim, Karl Marx, and Max Weber.

Alex Inkeles defines sociology somewhat differently, as "the study of systems of social action and of their institutions." These systems of action vary in size and complexity, and include single social acts, social relationships, organizations, institutions, communities, and societies.

The major purpose of a sociologist's inquiry is to observe, measure, quantify, and interpret human behavior. What characterizes the social life of human beings? Sociologists address questions such as:

- What rules do people follow in ordering their group interactions?
- What are the important roles and institutions in society?
- How are these roles learned by the young?
- Why do group members stay together? Why do some groups fall apart?

Sociology is divided into two major theoretical fields: social organization and social psychology. People who specialize in social organization investigate the types of groups people form and to which they belong: institutions, small voluntary groups, and stratified groups such as social class. They study the human relationships within and among these groups as well as how group members interact with their environments. Most of the sociology content in the elementary social studies program draws from this theoretical field.

Social psychology is concerned with the individual in a social situation. Social psychologists investigate how the individual and the group are related. They deal with such questions as "What makes human beings human?" In search of answers, they study ways in which individuals are socialized—how they learn to function as an individual in an environment composed of various types of groups. They analyze the individual's development of self-concepts, the effects of the group on individual behavior, the development of a person's attitudes and values, and how individuals develop leadership skills (Rose, 1965).

Sociological Concepts

A discipline's major concepts and generalizations are considered its *substantive structure.*

Figure 3.7
Major Concepts of
Sociology

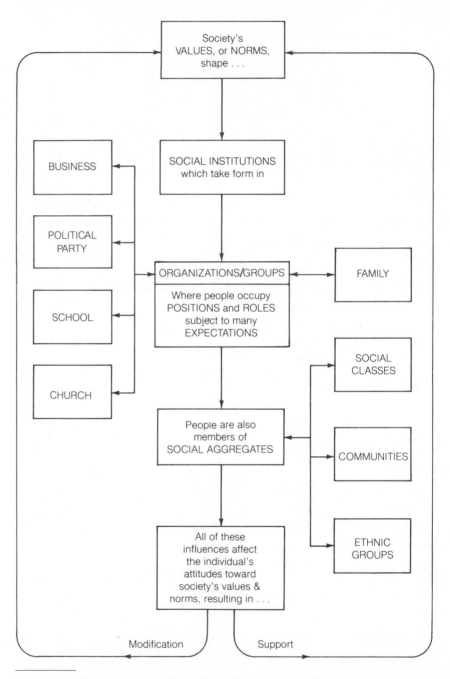

From *Concepts and Structure* in THE NEW SOCIAL SCIENCE CURRICULA, edited by Irving Morris-sett. Copyright © 1967 by Holt, Rinehart and Winston, Inc. Reprinted by permission of Holt, Rinehart and Winston.

Figure 3.7 highlights the major concepts of sociology and their relationships with each other. *Cultural values* are the widely held beliefs that certain activities, relationships and goals are important. Some values are embodied in statements about what "ought to be." *Norms* are standards or codes that guide conduct, such as classroom behavior, appropriate office attire, or the accepted form of address used by a younger person to an older person.

Values are those aspects of a culture that individuals consider worthy of high regard. They are really concepts, because they exist in people's minds rather than in reality. They represent the worth of a thing or behavior, such as standards of conduct, beauty, or efficiency. People endorse these standards and attempt to live up to them.

Values and norms comprise institutions. Institutions can be recurring, such as Thanksgiving, or they can be organized systems in which social activity has a distinct character, such as the family, the schools, or a market economy. A set of institutions make up a *social system*. People assume various *roles*, or customary patterns of behaviors, within these social systems. These roles must be learned by the members of the group through *socialization*. An eleven-year-old boy may have already learned several roles: son, friend, student, shortstop, and part-time lawn mower. Individuals learn appropriate roles in their social groups by being aware of *sanctions*—the rewards and punishments employed by groups to ensure that the group's norms and role expectations are fulfilled.

Generalizations in Sociology:

Here again, concepts are organized into statements called generalizations. As with the previously discussed disciplines, sociology has generalizations that students need to understand. These statements organize vast amounts of information that deal with humans and their social groups. It is important for students to realize that many sociological generalizations often lack empirical support, and must therefore be considered tentative, or open to additional investigation. This is, of course, a good approach to any generalization. To view generalizations as statements needing possible additional supportive data encourages one to maintain a questioning posture, which is the hallmark of the true student.

In units dealing with sociology, one is likely to find generalizations such as the following:

In most cultures, the family is the basic social unit, and provides some of a culture's most fundamental and necessary learning.

Social classes have always existed in every society, although the bases of class distinctions and boundaries have varied.

Every society creates a system of roles, norms, values, and sanctions to guide the behavior of the society's individuals and groups.

75

Sociological Methods of Research

To study social interaction, sociologists work with concepts, generalizations, and theories, using numerous methods to gather data. Often, the sociologist gathers data from people who have their own perspectives, which may or may not be an accurate picture of what is really occurring. The sociologist frequently studies a culture with which he is already familiar and about which he may have strong opinions. To counter this bias in research, sociologists learn procedures to heighten their objectivity.

The sociologist can avail himself of many methods. Field studies are undertaken on site by a sociologist or team of sociologists. In the case of *Boys in White* (Becker, Gerr, Hughes, & Strauss, 1961) the researchers spent two years on the campus of a medical school, attending classes and talking with students in the hospitals and dorms. They recorded their observations and interview data in field notes, which were subsequently analyzed according to the insights and hypotheses of the research team. In *Street Corner Society,* W. F. Whyte (1943) moved into a neighborhood so that he could study members of two rival street gangs. Whyte used this case study to make a more general statement about the importance of primary group support on personal adjustment. Both of these studies utilized the method of *participant observation,* in which the researcher becomes a part of the life of a group.

Questionnaires and surveys are important instruments in sociological research. Questionnaires offer respondents a limited number of choices so the answers can be compared, quantified, and submitted to statistical analysis. Large-scale surveys employ sampling techniques that allow the researcher to obtain representative samples of a total population. For example, rather than surveying all working mothers between the ages of 25 and 35 to ascertain their views on child rearing, *sampling* enables a sociologist to study a representative number of these women, and then make general statements to apply to the total population.

Another sociological project was that undertaken by Robert Bellah, a specialist in the sociology of religion at the University of California. Along with four other scholars, Bellah began in 1980 a three-year study of moral

---

Activity 3:4

Views of a Sociologist

Arrange for a meeting with a sociologist at your college or university. Prepare an interview, centering your questions on the value of sociology for elementary school pupils. What content is essential for these pupils? What are some ways to present content? What are some major issues in teaching sociology in the elementary school? Add other questions you consider important. Discuss the results of your interview with a fellow student and/or with your social studies methods professor. What conclusions can you draw?

commitment in American society. The researchers employed intensive interviews, personal biographies, and field studies of civic organizations such as the Kiwanis Club and Tom Hayden's Campaign for Economic Democracy. The purpose of the study was to assess "the strengths and weaknesses in the pattern of daily life of middle-class Americans that make them able to deal with the problems of late 20th Century America or make it difficult to do so." This study is an example of the use of historical analysis of a contemporary period.

Sociology in the Elementary Classroom

Most elementary social studies programs draw a wide variety of subject matter from sociology. When studying the family, pupils examine its function, the different roles played by family members, and their methods of decision making and conflict management. Children frequently read about families in other parts of the nation or world.

In the social science series *Our Working World*, Lawrence Senesh (1973) uses social science concepts throughout the six levels of the textbooks. The textbook *Families* explores with children the following major ideas through the use of stories, art and music, creative dramatics, field trips, and photographs:

1. Every member of the family occupies many important positions inside and outside the family.
2. The way a family member occupies a position is his or her role.
3. The multiple roles any one family member plays may be in conflict with one another.
4. The goals of the family may be in conflict with the goals of other institutions.

Similar major ideas are developed in many other current social studies series.

The neighborhood or community is often the next unit of study for the elementary student. Through pictures and stories about the community, children learn about the different people in their community, the work they do, and the groups they form. In an urban school, the teacher might bring to class a map of the community's bus system. Students can locate their school, their homes, and the various places they have been in their neighborhood or city. They might trace the routes members of their family travel to work, to school, to stores, or to recreation areas. A comparison of the means of transportation in rural and urban areas or during different historical periods can illustrate the impact of technology on human lives and the groups they form.

Another way to bring sociological study into the classroom is to have students use the research methods of sociologists. Such a technique has been extensively developed at the high school level in the series *Sociological Resources for the Social Sciences*, but there are also ways to introduce these processes to elementary students.

Allan Hoffman suggests having sixth-grade children use the survey method for gathering data. The unit of study might center on the changing role of women throughout history. At the beginning of the study, the teacher asks questions that will indicate the children's attitudes toward sex-role differences. Opinions are gathered anonymously. During the major portion of the lesson or unit, the teacher will use the anonymous student opinions to provoke discussions as to their validity and their popularity.

Figure 3.8
Surveying Sex Role
Differences

Questionnaire (Sample)

Person responding, please answer the following completely. Incomplete questionnaires cannot be used in our data analysis. Thank you!

Circle one:
sex—male   female
age—10–20   21–30   31–40   41–50   51–60   61–70   71–above

In your opinion, do men or women perform each of these activities better? Check your answer.

Activity	Men	Women	No Difference
Cooking			
Teaching			
Making Decisions			
Cutting Hair			
Politicians			
Managerial Position			
Driver (bus, car, taxi)			
Medical Work			

Do you feel that one sex is more likely to show any of the following traits?

Trait	Men	Women	No Difference
Practical			
Intelligent			
Open-minded			
Patient			
Nagging			
Independent			
Polite			
Nosey			

From Alan J. Hoffman, "A Case Study for Using Survey Techniques with Children (With Some Reservations)," in William W. Joyce and Frank L. Ryan, eds., *Social Studies and the Elementary Teacher: Promises and Practices.* Reprinted by permission.

To find out how students view sex role differences, the teacher introduces survey techniques. The children and the teacher jointly formulate hypotheses about the possible attitudes they will test in their survey. Hoffman suggests the following as realistic hypotheses:

1. Older males and females will feel that males and females are basically different when it comes to performing certain jobs. Young people won't be so sure.
2. All people will feel that women are the worst naggers and the nosiest.
3. All people will feel that men are stronger and better in sports.

A portion of a questionnaire that can be used in this activity is shown in Figure 3.8. Hoffman suggests that each student administer the questionnaire to four people: parents, friends, or relatives. He urges that students interview "safe" people, rather than strangers. A cover letter explaining the student project accompanies the questionnaire, along with a return envelope.

After tallying the survey results, the students review their hypotheses and modify them if necessary. If students are advanced enough in mathematics, they can apply the concepts of mean, mode, and medium to their findings. The teacher should encourage the children to analyze the questionnaire for any weak spots that might need modification. Some students may be interested in compiling a revised questionnaire to use at another time. Teachers can use the questionnaire method to have children gather sociological data for a variety of topics and issues that will arise in the social studies classroom.

Activity 3:5

Method Analysis

Select two of the disciplines mentioned in this chapter and determine the major procedures used by scholars in these fields. Compare the methods for similarities and differences and jot down ideas as to how children can be taught these methods of investigation.

Discussion

This chapter describes four of the areas from which we draw social studies content—history, geography, economics, and sociology.

History combines elements of both the social sciences and the humanities; even historians disagree as to whether its content is unique. While history records dates and facts, it is subject to interpretation, and interpretations change as the times change, so that earlier events appear in different lights. History also calls for research and inquiry, which often uncover new evidence to change previous interpretations. One's approach to research and inquiry is also subject to one's bent as either a scientific or literary historian. In addition, historical content can be organized for presentation and study in many different ways. No matter what the historian's bias, however, the historical method of inquiry breaks down into collecting facts, organizing the facts into possible patterns, and interpreting the facts and patterns. The facts appear in both primary and secondary sources. Elementary students need opportunities to work with historical research methods and to investigate facts and sources; they should not be limited to memorizing dates and events.

While history concentrates on people and ideas, geography concerns the character of place. But as many areas of study overlap, geography concerns people, too, particularly in the ways places affect people and the ways people act on their physical environment. Geographers work in several different areas of the discipline: physical geography, historical geography, and regional and cultural geography. Regional and cultural geography is further divided into the spatial tradition, the area studies tradition, and the man–land tradition. Geographic inquiry is primarily that of the regional method; cartography is the aspect of geography that people most readily associate with the discipline. Geography for the elementary student may well begin with the concept of location, perhaps with a study of the site of their own school building.

Although economics has often been considered too sophisticated for elementary students, a creative teacher can convey many of the discipline's concepts, and help children discover those concepts by themselves. The central concept of economics is scarcity, which forces each society to decide what goods it will produce, how it will produce them, how much it will produce and consume, and for whom. The four basic economic systems are those of tradition, command, market, and mixed economics. Along with scarcity, other economic concepts are those of wants, resources, goods, consumption, division of labor, interdependence, and exchange. The economist attempts to explain and predict economic behavior and, through policy economics, to help solve social problems. Elementary children can cope with many economic concepts by drawing on their own experiences, and by using classroom simulations and experiments.

Whereas economics focuses on economic behavior, sociology concerns the study of human behavior in groups. Sociologists observe, measure, quantify, and interpret behavior to find out what rules people use in group interaction, what roles and institutions a society deems important, how children learn their roles, and why some groups stay together and other disintegrate. The two fields of sociology are social organization, which concentrates on what kinds of groups people form and join, and social psychology, which studies relationships between the individual and the group.

Concepts that come under study are values, norms, roles, and socialization. To obtain data, the sociologist uses field studies, questionnaires and survey instruments, and interviews. Elementary students are capable of exploring their own and others' behaviors and feelings, and can learn to use surveys and interviews to explore values and attitudes.

References

Bacon, Philip, ed. *Focus on Geography: Key Concepts and Teaching Strategies.* Washington, D.C.: National Council for the Social Studies, 1970.

Barr, Robert; Barth, J. L.; and Shermis, S. S. *The Nature of the Social Studies.* Palm Springs, Calif.: ETC Publications, 1978.

Becker, Howard S.; Gerr, B.; Hughes, E. C.; and Strauss, A. *Boys in White.* Chicago: University of Chicago Press, 1961.

Brinton, Crane. *The Anatomy of a Revolution.* New York: Vintage Books, 1962.

Broek, Jan O. M. *Geography: Its Scope and Spirit.* Columbus, Oh.: Charles E. Merrill Publishing Co., 1965.

Burckhardt, Jacob. *Judgments on History and Historians.* London: S. J. Reginald Saunders & Co., 1958.

Collingwood, R. G. "The Idea of History." In *The Social Studies: Structures, Models, and Strategies,* edited by Martin Feldman and Eli Seifman. Englewood Cliffs, N.J.: Prentice-Hall, 1969.

Fair, Jean, and Shaftel, Fannie, eds. *Effective Thinking in the Social Studies.* Washington, D.C.: National Council for the Social Studies, 1967.

Fenton, Edwin. "A Structure of History." In *Concepts and Structures in the New Social Studies Curricula,* edited by Irving Morrissett. New York: Holt, Rinehart and Winston, 1967.

Greco, Peter. *Geography.* Boulder, Colo.: Social Science Education Consortium, 1966.

Hansen, W. Lee; Bach, B. L.; Calderwood, J. D.; and Saunders, P. *Master Curriculum Guide in Economics for the Nation's Schools; Part I, A Framework for Teaching Economics: Basic Concepts.* New York: Joint Council on Economic Education, 1977.

Harty, Sheila. *Hucksters in the Classroom.* Washington, D.C.: Center for the Study of Responsive Law, 1979.

Hoffman, Alan J., "A Case Study for Using Survey Techniques with Children (With Some Reservations)." In *Social Studies and the Elementary Teacher: Promises and Practices,* edited by William W. Joyce and Frank L. Ryan. Washington, D.C.: National Council for the Social Studies, 1977.

Inkeles, Alex. *What is Sociology? An Introduction to the Discipline and the Profession.* Englewood Cliffs, N.J.: Prentice-Hall, 1965.

Kourilsky, Marilyn. *Strategies for Teaching Economics, Intermediate Level Grades 4–6.* New York: Joint Council on Economic Education, 1978.

Kownslar, Allan. *Teaching American History: The Quest for Relevancy.* Washington, D.C.: National Council for the Social Studies, 1974.

Krug, Mark. *History and the Social Sciences.* Waltham, Mass.: Blaisdell Publishing Co., 1967.

Mehlinger, Howard, and Tucker, Jan, eds. *Social Studies in Other Nations.* Washington, D.C.: National Council for the Social Studies, 1979.

Mills, C. Wright. *The Sociological Imagination.* New York: Oxford University Press, 1959.

Morrissett, Irving, ed. *Concepts and Structure in the New Social Science Curricula.* New York: Holt, Rinehart and Winston, Inc., 1967.

Pattison, William D. "The Four Traditions of Geography." *Journal of Geography* (May 1964): 211–216.

Reynolds, Lloyd G. *Economics: A General Introduction.* Homewood, Ill.: Richard D. Irwin, 1966.

Rose, Caroline B. *Sociology, The Study of Man in Society.* Columbus, Oh.: Charles E. Merrill Publishing Co., 1965.

Senesh, Lawrence. *Our Working World.* Chicago: SRA, 1973.

Snyder, Phil L., ed. *Detachment and the Writing of History: Essays and Letters of Carl L. Becker.* Ithaca, N.Y.: Cornell University Press, 1958.

Taba, Hilda, and Hills, James. *Teacher Handbook.* San Francisco: San Francisco State College, 1965.

Whyte, W. F. *Street Corner Society: The Social Structure of an Italian Slum.* Chicago: University of Chicago Press, 1943, 1955.

Other Foundations for the Social Studies

4

The remaining traditional foundations of the social studies which we did not discuss are political science, anthropology, and psychology. Philosophy is also newly gaining acceptance as a foundation in the social studies curriculum. In this chapter, we will consider each of these disciplines from the viewpoint of their application to elementary social studies.

Political Science

If we accept political science as content organized to produce good citizens, then political science has been part of the social studies program for most of this century. However, if we look at political science as content which allows individuals to investigate the dynamic aspects of the uses of power and authority in the home, school, and other situations, as well as in government, then it is a rather recent addition to the elementary curriculum (Michaelis, 1972).

Defining Political Science

In reviewing this field, we discover argument among scholars as to its definition; the following quotations exemplify this conflict:

> Political science is an intellectual discipline primarily concerned with the question of how man governs himself.
>
> **(Sourauf, 1965, p. 25)**
>
> The study of politics is concerned with understanding how authoritative decisions are made and executed for a society.
>
> **(Easton, 1953)**

Part of the difficulty in defining political science is the fact that there are many different types of political scientists. Each type brings his or her own perspective to the investigation; each asks very different kinds of questions; each employs particular research methods; and each utilizes different concepts. Some political scientists are interested in the evolution of governments over periods of time, and rely heavily on the methods of the historian. They may investigate governments of the past, or political change in one country or area as it has occurred over time.

Other political scientists have a legal orientation—they analyze a society's laws, constitutions, and other documents in an attempt to comprehend its political system. Closely related to this orientation is the institutional approach, which gives attention to the functions of governmental bodies and officials and investigates the roles of judges and members of Congress. This approach to political science is the most common in the schools. As Jarolimek (1977) points out, political science in the schools is largely the study of government, political processes, and political decision making.

Although important, the legal–institutional view of political science tends to ignore the role of the individual in the political system. Scholars who address this deficiency follow the behavioral orientation. Rather than describe legal or political institutions, or speculate about ideal political systems, these scholars scientifically study the observable behavior of individuals in political situations, in order to create a science of politics and a body of tested generalizations and theories. As Alan Isaak (1969) puts it:

> The behaviorist argues that, although an important aspect of politics, the institution as a thing in itself is not the real stuff of politics. It is the activity within and the behavior around the political institution which should be the main concern of the political scientist. (p. 27)

While many political scientists are analyzing individual behavior within political systems, others are asking: What is the best form of government? What are the qualities of the good citizen? Such questions exemplify the normative approach, where the primary interest is in value questions rather than empirical questions. In fact, these scholars see themselves as philosophers, and attempt to use their knowledge of ideal systems and behaviors to influence political leaders and public policy. Their approach is sometimes called political philosophy or political theory.

Finally, one may view this discipline as a study of a system or series of interrelated systems that exist in a society. Political scientists of this bent have an empirical orientation, but it is broader than that of the behaviorists. Systems people focus on behavior to discover how people behave in groups and how organized pressure groups influence public policy; for example, how does the political system process incoming demands and supports in order to transform them into outgoing policy decisions?

David Easton (1957), one of the nation's leading political systems theorists, has developed a model, depicted in Figure 4.1, showing the elements of a political system. Easton identifies the research tasks of the systems theorist as the need to

> . . . identify the inputs and the forces that shape and change them, to trace the processes through which they are transformed into outputs, to describe

the general conditions under which such processes can be maintained, and to establish the relationship between outputs and suceeding inputs of the system. (Feldman & Seifman, 1969, p. 140)

Concepts in Political Science

Because of the many possible approaches to political science, no one set of concepts can sufficiently organize the subject matter. Skillful teachers must select key concepts from among the various approaches to convey to their students a global understanding of this field.

An important concept to any unit dealing with political science is that of *power*, the ability of an individual or group to influence the behavior of others. Some political scientists consider power the central concept, since struggles for power often result in *conflict* and the need for peaceful procedures to manage it. Another concept essential to elementary social studies is that of the political system, individuals, interest groups, and institutions that formulate *public policy*, the binding decisions that affect society as a whole. Focusing on this concept enables children to understand how all political elements interrelate.

People exist within *political cultures*, or their patterns of psychological orientation, attitudes, beliefs, and perceptions about political action (Patterson, 1965). Children should be introduced to this concept, with attention to the political cultures in various nations.

How people acquire their understandings, attitudes, and beliefs about the political system is called *political socialization*. As Roger Brown points out, "to learn socially relevant behavior in no sense means that all members of society must learn the same behaviors or that each generation is the simple replication of the past" (Adler & Harrington, 1970). A person is born into an

Figure 4.1
An Approach to the
Analysis of Political
Systems

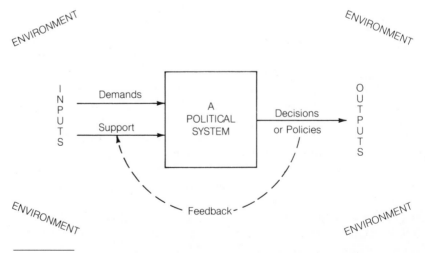

From David Easton, "An Approach to the Analysis of Political Systems," *World Politics,* Vol. 9, No. 3 (April 1957). Copyright © 1957 by Princeton University Press, illustration p. 384. Reprinted by permission.

ordered way of life in which norms, standards of judgment, and institutions are already established. What one learns depends upon societal changes as well as one's own abilities and background. The political scientists who investigate political socialization focus on (1) who provides the political messages, (2) how the child relates to the political messages in light of her own experience, and (3) the relationship between learning and behaving.

The aspect of *social control,* or how human behavior is regulated by outside social forces and maintained by laws and rules of the society, should also be included in the elementary curriculum. All institutions develop ways to manage member behavior in order to attain goals and to meet the needs and wants of their memberships consistently. These methods are usually recorded in documents, such as constitutions and legal codes, that reflect the society's norms and values. Children will have little difficulty understanding this concept, for they learn in classrooms where control is manifested by classroom rules and school policies, and live in homes where their parents set rules for them. A discussion of these rules offers a good starting place for introducing the concept of social control.

Four other concepts essential in any elementary social studies units dealing with political science are those of state, government, authority, and interest groups. There are numerous definitions of state, one of which is "an institution that has ultimate responsibility for maintaining social order." Usually, the state has control over a geographically and legally defined territory: a nation, such as the United States of America; a state, such as Massachusetts; or a province, such as Ontario. Again, children will have already had some direct contact with this concept as citizens of both their state and nation.

Frequently treated along with the concept of state, *government* refers to the agency created to manage the state. It is comprised of several institutions responsible for making legally binding decisions. A government has legitimacy when individuals accept its authority to devise the rules and regulations that order their lives. *Authority* refers to the power of the political leaders to make legally binding decisions and laws. Groups or individuals attain authority in several ways: by election to public office, by appointment, or by force, as through a revolution.

Political systems are collections or series of interconnected systems of institutions and people. People who share common concerns and goals frequently organize into *interest groups* to increase the probability of attaining their shared aims. The National Education Association is an interest group, as is the Moral Majority. These groups become active in politics when issues arise that have potential for affecting their interests.

Generalizations in Political Science

Children study political science to learn how people manage themselves as groups. The concepts mentioned above should be presented in ways that will allow children to generalize about them. These are appropriate political science generalizations for the elementary social studies curriculum:

87

In all societies, some kind of authority structure exists that can be called government. This government possesses powers to manage and direct the behavior of people under its jurisdiction.

In every society, regulations and laws emerge to manage behavior. People who break these laws receive some form of punishment.

Numerous types of political systems exist in various societies to determine public policy and to regulate behavior.

To maintain a political system, its people must support the decision-making processes aimed at settling disputes.

A society's values influence its choice of a political system and the nature of its political behavior.

Policy decisions (the output of the political process) are binding on all members of the society.

Throughout history, societies have experimented with many different forms of government.

Methods of Inquiry in Political Science

What methods a political scientist uses depend upon her approach to the discipline. As we have mentioned, some political scientists employ methods similar to those of a historian. They might use a traditional tool, the library, to analyze primary and secondary source materials. They also analyze records of public hearings, legislatures' role call votes, and public officials' private papers and speeches. Sorauf (1965) points out that probably few scholars find the indexed issues of the *New York Times* as useful as does the political scientist.

Political scientists who study the behavior of political personages often use the field study methods of the anthropologist and sociologist. For example, if a political scientist wants to investigate a political action committee formed by a corporation's employees, she could observe their meetings and conduct interviews with committee members. Political parties have been studied similarly. Another important research tool is the survey, which is often used in studies of voting behavior. Statistical techniques play important roles in analyzing interview and survey data.

Some political scientists use psychologists' methods to develop generalizations and theories about human behavior in the political context. These researchers formulate hypotheses, then design observation studies or experiments to test their theories. Political scientists frequently coordinate a variety of methods from several of the discipline's major approaches.

Political Science in the Elementary Classroom

While the aim of most elementary social studies programs has been "good citizenship," any formal treatment of political studies has been either ignored or, at best, superficial. Political science has, until recently, been reserved primarily for high school government, civics, and contemporary problems classes. Teachers are now realizing, however, that schools need to begin sooner to help children develop political understandings.

Teaching about the many forms of government, political processes, and approaches to political decision making involves high-level concepts, but there are ways to present this subject at the elementary level. It can be introduced by selecting concepts with immediate applicability to children's everyday lives. As we have mentioned, all children are aware of rules; they meet them at home and in the classroom. Children can discuss why rules are necessary and what would happen if there were none. They can discover how adults are also governed by rules. Some rules are stated formally and recorded in official documents as laws. Children can make data charts listing the rules they have to follow and the reasons for these rules. Figure 4.2 represents such a chart.

After using the charts to organize their data and analyzing the recorded information, children can formulate rules for other situations: rules for going to the movies, for going to the beach, for visiting grandparents, and for riding a bike.

Children can learn about government in many ways. The *People in Communities* (1975) series offers this example: when studying the Pilgrims' trip from England to America, the children can be asked to respond to the question, "What would happen if the Pilgrims did just what they wanted when they landed in America?" They can discuss the hardships of survival in the New World as a situation that demanded cooperation. (This is also a

Rules I have to follow:	Reasons for rules:
Rules at Home	*Home*
Rules at school	*School*
Rules in other places	*Other places*

Figure 4.2
Data Chart of Rules and Reasons

good place to discuss the need for rules.) The Pilgrim government offers contrast to the government of the Massachusetts Bay Colony, where a larger group of settlers led to formation of a representative government rather than the direct democracy of the Pilgrims.

These historical situations raise an important values question: Who should have the right to go to meetings and vote on decisions and for representatives? Colonial America offers examples of many groups who were excluded from the franchise—women, people without land, and people without church membership.

The issues of fairness or justice can be discussed in the context of the political system. Much of the curriculum in law-related education focuses on questions of fairness. In the Pro Se Court simulation (Gallagher & Hartstein, 1973), students role play situations that require a judge's decision about what is fair in a given case. In the simulation's simplest form, the teacher divides the class into groups of three. In each group, one student plays the plaintiff, another the defendant, and the third the judge. A case such as the following is presented to each group:

> FACTS: Plaintiff is assistant to the newspaper person.
>   Defendant is the newspaper delivery person.
> The defendant became sick and asked his helper, the Plaintiff, to deliver fifty papers. Plaintiff agreed to deliver the papers for $2.00. Plaintiff delivered the papers but did not place them in mail boxes or inside halls. 25 newspapers were ruined in the rain and Defendant refused to pay the $2.00 to the Plaintiff. Plaintiff sues. (pp. 28–29)

As the children role play the case, the plaintiff, the person who has not been paid by the defendant, speaks first, then the defendant has her turn. The judge is free to ask questions before reaching a decision. Each judge must explain her decision to the whole class. The students can then present a new case, switching roles and following the same procedure.

The Pro Se Court, as a special small claims court that eliminates the complicated rules and procedures of a full trial, provides an effective way to introduce students to the conflict management function of the legal system. When students become knowledgeable about this aspect of the legal system, they can move on to more complex mock trial procedures.

Another way to help students comprehend political decisions is through the "decision tree." Working through a series of activities that require decisions, pupils can learn that (1) political decisions are collectively binding on a group; (2) political decisions allocate things the group values, such as wealth, food, health, and power; and (3) members of various groups both influence political decisions and are affected by them.

The teacher might use the decision tree to have students learn about the politics of building a new city hall in their community. The key question would be, "Should our community replace its old city hall with a new one?" Children can divide into two groups, those who favor a new facility and those who oppose it. There may also be a third group, made up of those who wish to postpone the decision. The teacher tells the children they are going to make a "tree" that will allow them to decide their course of action. She explains that a "decision tree" consists of a network or chart that shows decision points and the possible consequences of each decision. Figure 4.3 shows a decision tree relating to the city hall question.

The completed decision tree can be put on the class bulletin board, so the children have in front of them available decision options and the consequences of each. Then they organize into groups based on their response to the basic question—essentially, they form interest groups. As the children work in groups to make their viewpoints known, they come to realize that as members of these groups, they both influence and are affected by political decisions.

The teacher can have another group of children act as members of the city council, to listen to the arguments of the three groups and decide

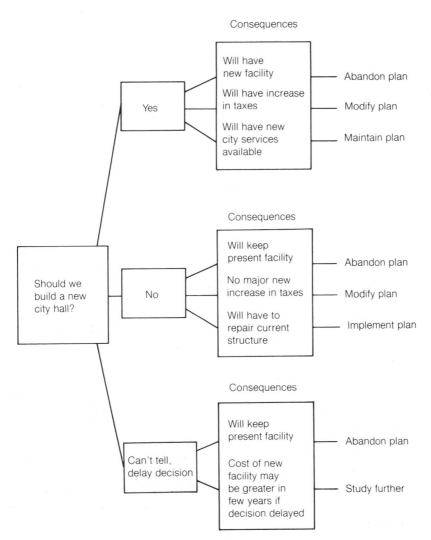

Figure 4.3
Decision Tree for
Political Science Study

whether or not to build the city hall. The council will have a difficult decision indeed if the major groups (yes, no, can't tell) each decide to press their views. Then the city council will be confronted with either abandoning the plan, modifying it, or implementing it. The teacher can require the city council members to write down the rationale for their decision. This activity can be played at varying levels of detail, depending upon the age of the children in the social studies class.

Activity 4:1

Small Claims Court Simulation

If you are observing or student teaching in a classroom, ask to do the Pro Se Court simulation. You can use either the case described in this section or others that can be found in *Law and American Society*, vol. 2, no. 2 (May 1973): pp. 26-30.

If possible, record the simulation on video- or audiotape. Play it back to yourself. How did the simulation work? What reasons might explain how children reacted to the simulation?

Anthropology

Defining Anthropology

Anthropology is a broadly based discipline concerned with the study of human physical and cultural traits. It deals with the development of language, social institutions, arts and crafts, religion, physical and mental traits, and the comparison of cultures. It is a field rich in descriptions of human life as it has existed and does exist throughout the world.

Because of its scope, anthropology has been divided into several closely related fields; the two main divisions are physical and cultural. *Physical anthropology* focuses on the evolution of humans and their relationships with other animals. Physical anthropologists investigate the unique biological traits of humans that are essential to the development of culture. Physical anthropologists frequently investigate fossil evidence of human evolution.

Cultural anthropology is the study of entire cultures; it deals with cultural change, acculturation, and diffusion. Cultural anthropology has three subdivisions: archaeology, linguistics, and ethnology. Archaeology reconstructs the prehistory of peoples and their culture. By carefully digging up ancient dwellings, monuments, objects of art, weapons, tools, and other remains left by humans, the archaeologist uncovers information about past cultures.

For descriptive and comparative purposes, *linguistics* investigates human languages. Attention is on how humans have created elaborate systems of communication and the relationships among these systems. Anthropologists who specialize in linguistics often work closely with psychologists and philosophers in pursuing such topics as psycholinguistics, semantics, and communication theory.

Ethnology compares and explains similarities and differences in culture systems. The purpose of such investigation is to allow people to understand human cultural history, the cultural patterns of a society. In the elementary school program, it is easy to stress ethnology in the study of world cultures. Anthropologists sometimes focus primarily on the social systems or structures within a culture. This emphasis is called *social anthropology.* There are many other divisions subsumed in ethnology; primitive art and ethnomusicology are but two examples.

Concepts in Anthropology

The central concept in anthropology is *culture,* which encompasses the social, learned patterns of behavior, rules, and artifacts of a people. It can refer to everything learned or produced by those people. Spradley and McCurdy (1972) define culture as "the knowledge people use to generate and interpret social behavior."

> Culture, according to the definition we shall use is *not* the behavior which occurs when someone is writing. It is *not* the product of that behavior such as letters, notes, and newspaper headlines. It *is* what one must know in order to read and write. (p. 8)

Cultural knowledge must be learned by children in every society. Social scientists call this learning process *socialization,* while anthropologists use the more general term *acculturation,* in referring to the lifelong process of assimilating culture. Acculturation is a universal process, necessary for all human groups. It allows individuals to organize group life and to anticipate the actions of others. Figure 4.4 shows several ways that nonliterate peoples educate their children about their culture. Only some societies use *schooling,* education carried on by specialists, as part of the acculturation process.

Child learns by . . .   direct moral instruction

emulating older children

observing adults at ceremonies and at daily tasks

receiving praise, admonition, punishment

direct training by adults

Figure 4.4
Acculturation in
Nonliterature Societies

Adapted from Melville J. Herskovits. *Man and His Works.*

All the members of an Amish Community turn out to raise a new farmhouse. A trip to an Amish settlement can give students a chance to examine another culture and lifestyle up close.

To study a culture, one concentrates on culture elements or traits. A culture element is the smallest unit of culture, which may be behavior patterns or artifacts. Most cultures possess a tremendous number of such traits. A typewriter, for example, is a culture trait, as is the custom of shaking hands when people meet. When combined, culture traits are identified as a *culture complex*. In the United States, children's schooling can be considered a culture complex; students proceed through various stages and complete formal education with a graduation ceremony.

Groups of people form cultural units and occupy space on the earth's surface. Anthropologists call the geographical region where a number of culture traits and complexes are evident a *culture area*. Western Europe and New England are two such examples.

Throughout history, when groups of people have come in contact with each other, they have been likely to share ideas and approaches to life. When the contact extended over time, the exchange often left one culture in a dominant position. This is another meaning of *acculturation*. The invasion by the Normans of what is now England vastly changed the life of the Angles, Saxons, and Jutes who were living there. Over the centuries, cultural exchanges resulted in present-day English culture. But acculturation is a reciprocal exchange. In their interactions with the Angles, Saxons, and Jutes, the Normans gradually changed their own language. Children will be able to grasp this concept of acculturation through a discussion of their favorite foods—pizza, tacos, spaghetti—and see how their taste in foods has been influenced by the many immigrant groups who have come to this country. While the immigrants took on "American" ways, Americans also took on some foreign ways.

Anthropologists frequently use the concepts of race and ethnic group. *Race* refers to a group of people who share several biological traits, such as skin color, hair type, and facial features (eye, nose, and lip shapes). *Ethnic group* refers to individuals who share a common culture orientation, values, behavior patterns, and religious beliefs. The population of the United States is made up of more than a hundred ethnic groups. Prominent among them are those of English, Irish, Italian, African, Asian, and Hispanic backgrounds.

Irving Morrissett (1967) has organized the fundamental ideas and concepts of anthropology as shown in Figure 4.5.

Socialization proceeds as children accompany, observe, and imitate adults.

Human needs are satisfied with the social structure of the group. The long-term practices and beliefs of a culture comprise its tradition. But culture is not static; it changes as people seek to satisfy their wants or when a new

Figure 4.5
Fundamental Ideas of
Anthropology

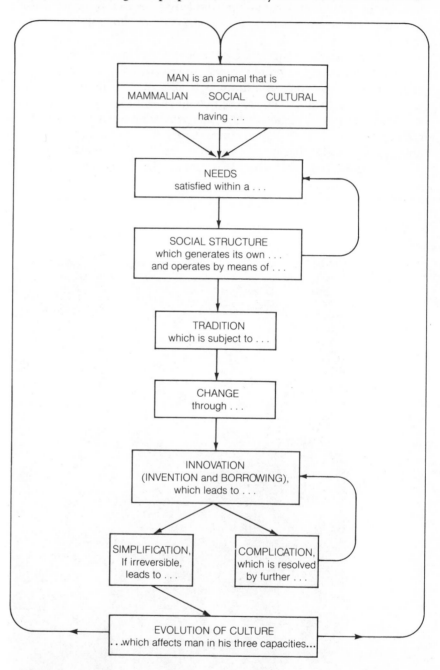

From *Concepts and Structure* in THE NEW SOCIAL SCIENCE CURRICULA, edited by Irving Morrissett. Copyright © 1967 by Holt, Rinehart and Winston, Inc. Reprinted by permission of Holt, Rinehart and Winston.

invention is introduced. Another important cause of change is contact with people of different cultures. The spread of ideas and practices from one culture to another is called *cultural diffusion*. The introduction of new ideas and practices often causes complications that lead to innovation or simplification. One example of simplification is the use of fire to satisfy needs for warmth, food, and safety. This major discovery led to the evolution of a culture.

Generalizations in Anthropology

Generalizations give direction and purpose to lessons, and social studies teachers often draw on these generalizations from anthropology:

Every society has its own artifacts, beliefs, and behavior patterns, the total of which comprise its culture.

Culture is socially learned and serves as a guide to its members regarding appropriate behaviors.

Societies must continuously evaluate and modify their cultures to adjust to changing conditions.

As a society becomes more specialized, its cultural inventions increase.

The culture in which one is reared has major impact on one's attitudes and behaviors.

Nearly all individuals can contribute to their culture groups.

The Japanese have taken on many American ways. Is acculturation always beneficial? Is it ever detrimental?

97

Methods of Inquiry in Anthropology

Because physical anthropology addresses the evolution of *Homo sapiens* (humankind) and other primates, some people have jokingly classed its methodology as that of digging up old skeletons. But many physical anthropologists carry out field research on existing human communities. They gather evidence that leads to conclusions about the predominance of certain skin and eye colors, head shapes, blood types, and resistance to disease.

The cultural anthropologists who study humanmade culture focus on its history, language, religion, law, and social structure. They employ a variety of methods, some identical to those used by physical anthropologists. For instance, archaeologists do much of their research in the field, in projects called "digs." Dr. L.S.B. Leakey has conducted some famous "digs" to gather evidence of early human life in Africa. Certain techniques are critical in carrying out a successful dig:

> Meticulous care must be taken so that excavated materials are not damaged in the digging process.

> The position and context of every object excavated is recorded by a combination of drawings, notes, and photographs.

> All significant associated items are collected and recorded: soil samples, remains of animal and vegetable materials, tools, weapons, jewels, artwork, and so on. (Pelto, 1980, p. 32)

After completing his field work, the archaeologist must then analyze and date all the materials he has gathered, through such methods as radiological dating, pollen analysis, tree-ring dating, and stratigraphy. *Radiological dating* depends upon the fact that all living things contain a fixed amount of a radioactive isotope called Carbon 14. This isotope deteriorates after the death of a plant or animal at a constant rate until all the Carbon 14 has turned chemically into Carbon 12. Archaeologists isolate the radiocarbon in the material to measure the amount of Carbon 14 remaining. They use such information to estimate the age of the particular specimen.

Pollen analysis allows the anthropologist to identify the types of plants that grew in an area where other materials were unearthed. *Tree-ring dating,* or *dendrochronology,* is supported by the fact that trees grow in an outwardly radiating pattern of rings, one ring appearing for each year of growth. The spacing *between* the rings depends upon the amount of moisture in a particular year or growing season. The number of rings determines the age of the tree at the time it stopped growing. *Stratigraphic evidence* comes from the way in which the earth or other materials are laid down in particular strata—the materials closer to the surface are newer or younger than those found deep in the ground. This method can be employed only where the investigation site has been relatively undisturbed by either humans or nature (Pelto, 1965, pp. 35–36).

As noted before, not all anthropologists deal with the past—some investigate today's cultures. To do their field studies, these anthropologists may live with a people for several months or years. In studying Tiv, a Bantu tribe in northern Nigeria, Bohannan (1957) spent 26 months in the field between 1949 and 1953. He learned the Bantu language and described and analyzed their system of justice. The report of such a field study is called an *ethnography*. Anthropologists follow many of the sociologist's research techniques in their field investigations—observations, interviews, and participation in the life of the group. When studying an unknown culture, anthropologists often employ *informants*, individuals from that group with whom they build a close relationship. An informant furnishes insights into the culture.

Anthropology in the Elementary Classroom

A vital characteristic of anthropological inquiry is an attitude of acceptance, or what Harvey (1967) calls "a willingness to take other people on their own terms, to respect them as dignified and worthy." There are many places in the elementary social studies curriculum where children can nurture this attitude. When children investigate human needs, they have a context for com-

Building a shelter typical of another culture, such as a tepee or igloo, can be an interesting social studies project.

prehending the many differences among human groups. From observing the role of the family and the activities of family members in many cultures, they come to recognize the diversity, the commonality, and creativity of the people of those cultures.

Children should of course be discouraged from concluding that other peoples are strange, or their ways less valid than those of their own culture. Looking at social studies from anthropological perspectives allows young people to understand others and their cultures, and to acquire a fuller comprehension of their own culture and way of life.

Activities in music, arts, and crafts help children consider others from an anthropological perspective. Picture books should be available in the classroom; Steichen's collection of photographs in *The Family of Man* provides students with a visual record of human differences and similarities. Creating a primitive tool, such as a spear with a stone point, arouses an appreciation of the skills that were necessary for living in the type of culture from which the tool came. Frances Emmons and Jacqueline Corbia (1971) tell of a "technical disaster" that turned out to be educationally beneficial:

> One day we attempted to make an Arunta house, not a small model but a large one that the children could enter. We went out to a nearby wooded area and collected a large supply of limbs and small branches. After we managed to get it up, it fell down on the children. We thought at first that this activity was a failure, but then we heard the children saying that the Arunta must be smart to build their own houses. (pp. 165)

Teachers today can choose from several social studies curriculum projects that emphasize anthropology: the Anthropology Curriculum Project at the University of Georgia, Man a Course of Study (MACOS) and Windows on Our World. Jerome Bruner (1966) was the primary developer of MACOS. Its curriculum continues to be controversial, because it includes customs and practices very different from American culture, and parents and educators argued as to whether major value differences should be presented to children.

The MACOS curriculum includes materials on animal and human behavior so students can determine which traits are strictly human and

---

Activity 4:2

MACOS—Yes or No?

Read the October 1975 issue of *Social Education* to understand more of the pros and cons of the MACOS curriculum. Try to locate a copy ot these materials from a local school or curriculum library and evaluate them yourself.

   If you were a member of a social studies curriculum committee for your school district, would you recommend that MACOS materials be adopted? Write a report explaining your opinion.

which link humans to animals. The first unit centers on the life cycle of the salmon. The concepts of adaptation, natural selection, and life cycle receive major emphasis. This unit is followed by one on herring gulls and baboons. The previous concepts are repeated and new ones added: territoriality, aggression, parenting, and social organization. After completing the animal studies, pupils spend the second half of the course studying a human microculture, the Netsilik Eskimos.

Bruner designed these materials to capitalize on forces he feels motivate children to learn: "curiousity, a desire for competence, aspiration to emulate a model, and a deep-seated commitment to the web of social reciprocity (1967, p. 127). By *social reciprocity,* Bruner means the interdependence that comes from a joint effort to achieve a group objective, thus ensuring the survival of the group. Children are led to feel this in relation to their own lives as well as to see it in the lives of the Eskimos.

Anthropological content can be introduced early in the elementary social studies curriculum. The following lesson might be useful in the primary grades.

Lesson Plan

Lesson Generalization: Culture is socially learned. It helps people understand the appropriate behaviors and beliefs in that society.

Grade Level: Primary

Objective: Pupils will be able to list key behaviors and major beliefs appropriate in their culture. They will be able to state the lesson generalization in sentences.

Warm-up Activity: Ask children to take a few minutes to write down briefly what they did yesterday. Then ask them to think about why they did what they did. A support might be a bulletin board showing pictures of children engaged in various activities.

Developmental Activities: Make a chart on butcher paper with the following design.

Activities I Did	Why I Did Them

Discuss the types of activities with the children. Did many do the same things? If so, how many reasons were given for these same activities? How many different types of activities were done? How might we group these activities?

The discussion can conclude with the teacher writing down one or two general statements about the things children do and why they do them. Get children to begin to think about the generalization. Their wording of the generalization may be different from the one in the lesson plan. This is all right.

The teacher can write down the conclusion and place it on the bulletin board. The statement and the bulletin board can be used to get children to continue thinking about the generalization.

At the intermediate grade levels, children can have more freedom to use some of the methods of anthropologists. The following is an example of a lesson for intermediate-grade pupils.

Lesson Plan

Lesson Generalization: Cultural adaptations result in many ways of living.

Grade Level: Intermediate

Objective: Children will use variations of the cultural anthropologist's methods to investigate several cultures and reach the conclusion that cultural adaptations result in cultural diversity. Pupils can demonstrate their understanding of this generalization either through written or verbal reports, as well as through their questions and responses to questions.

Materials Needed: Films, books, magazines, guide sheets

Warm-up Activity: Begin the lesson with several brief films showing life in two developed and two developing countries. No particular point of view is presented. After seeing the films, children work in groups to list their questions and to record and organize their perceptions. Inform the children that the questions will serve as guides to gaining an understanding of the general statement, "People's cultural adaptations result in many ways of living." They will be responsible for gathering data either to support, reject, or modify this generalization.

Developmental Activities: In teams of two, the children should answer the questions generated by the films. Furnish them with a guide sheet outlining ways to conduct observations based on the films.

Guide Sheet:
The first step in conducting an observation is to ask questions about what you see. Next, determine what information seems to be important in terms of the focus of your observation. Group and classify the information you consider important. Next, ask yourself what conclusion or conclusions you can make from the information you have classified. Note: This guide sheet can be handed out either before or after the film viewing.

After processing the information from the films, students can continue to work in the same teams to analyze commercial materials and to observe community groups, to observe people's many interests and their varied activities. (This observation can continue for several days, or for especially interested students, several weeks.)

Wrap-up Activity:
Have children role play anthropologists who are attending a convention examining Cultural Diversity. At this convention, they will have sessions for reporting their findings and for responding to questions from class members (other convention goers).

At the conclusion of this "convention," direct the children's attention to the lesson's generalization to see if their data support it.

These two lessons exemplify ways to teach anthropology in elementary social studies. Teachers have used many others with great success:

- Listing ideas that have influenced the world and tracing their history
- Recording on data charts the uses of resources and technology by particular societies
- Using simulations and role playing to get an "emotional" understanding of different groups of people
- Conducting "field investigations" in their schools and communities—playing anthropologist, in other words
- Visiting museums to view artifacts of the past and present

Psychology

Defining Psychology

Psychology does not usually appear as a separate subject or unit in most elementary social studies programs. Throughout social studies, however, there is an emphasis on children's understanding the human family and themselves as individuals. Such perception cannot be attained without some attention to psychology.

Psychology concerns the study of human mental processes and of both human and animal behavior. Psychologists investigate an astonishing variety of problems. What causes a child to be hyperactive, withdrawn, or aggressive? How can the control panel for a nuclear power plant be designed for most efficient operation? What is the impact of TV violence on young children? What is the best treatment for obesity? For phobias?

The fundamental question in human psychology is "Why do people behave as they do?" The responses to this question depend upon the psychologist's point of view and investigative approach. Psychologists who use the physiological or neurobiological approach study the function of the brain and nervous system. You may have seen pictures of experiments in which humans and animals have had minielectrodes implanted in their brains to study the reactions elicited by slight electric currents. With such tactics, psychologists have succeeded in identifying which areas of the brain produce feelings of pleasure and pain, and which handle auditory and visual sensations.

Concepts in Psychology

As with the other social sciences, key concepts in psychology are associated with the different approaches to its study. Most of us are familiar with the concept of stimulus: that which can stimulate a learner's sense or senses. The smell of fresh pizza, for example, may stimulate some change in your behavior. The action that results from stimulation and the subsequent nervous activity is called a *response*. The response can take the form of physical move-

103

ment, glandular secretion, or a mental image. Psychologists often describe responses in terms of their effects rather than their apperances. When they are so classified, they are known as *performances* (Gagne, 1970). Psychologists who work from a behavior vantage point use these concepts.

Other psychologists work from the phenomenological or humanistic stance. These psychologists emphasize the concepts of perception, self-actualization, cognitive processes, and developmental stages. *Perception* refers to the organization of stimuli by an individual based on mental set and prior experiences. *Self-actualization* refers to people's efforts to reach their maximum potentials. *Cognitive processes* apply to those mental processes that occur during perception, learning, and thinking. *Developmental stages* are periods, often chronological, that represent significant qualitative changes in perception, ability, and behavior.

Yet a third approach to psychology is that of the psychoanalytic school. The concepts that organize the "reality" of these psychologists are unconscious motives, id, ego, superego, and phobia. An individual is unaware of *unconscious motives,* or, if aware, perceives them in a distorted form. *Id* refers to that part of one's personality that seeks gratification of instinctual drives. *Ego* is the aspect of the personality that includes conscious thought processes and adaptation to reality. The *superego* represents learned moral attitudes and behavior standards. *Phobia* describes someone's persistent, irrational fears that are excessive to the actual situation.

Generalizations in Psychology

The teacher may use generalizations from psychology as guidelines for structuring learning. These generalizations will provide a focus for children's investigations into their own and others' behaviors. Some generalizations from this discipline are:

> *All individuals are capable of learning as a result of interaction between the individual and the environment.*

> *The purposes for learning serve to organize and relate the activities in which individuals are involved.*

> *Learning is multidimensional, not a one-thing-at-a-time process.*

> *The quality of children's early perceptual and verbal experiences determines to a great extent their achievements and behavior in later years.*

Methods of Inquiry in Psychology

As with the other fundamental disciplines, the methods psychologists use depend upon their approach to their field of study. Behaviorists observe and measure individuals' behavior, ignoring their internal states of mind. In the early 1900's, John Watson developed the approach that is now commonly known as the behaviorist, or S–R (stimulus–response), school of psychology. Proponents of this school examine environmental conditions; when stimuli or reinforcement in an individual's environment are altered, behaviorists expect a change in the subject's behavior. Perhaps the most famous contemporary behaviorist is B. F. Skinner, the Harvard psychologist who has greatly influenced experimental psychology as well as the applied fields of clinical, educational, and industrial psychology.

In terms of number of adherents, the second major division in psychology is the psychoanalytic school, which evolved from the work of Sigmund Freud. Freud concentrated on emotional and physical disorders, and explained human behavior largely in terms of the workings of the unconscious dimensions of people's minds. Freudians believe that humans beings are driven by powerful instincts that account for much of their behavior. This viewpoint contrasts sharply with that of the behaviorist, who considers environmental conditions the primary influences on people's learning.

The third approach to psychological methodology comes from the humanistic or phenomenological school, which focuses on how individuals organize their perceptions. Humanistic scholars reject stimulus–response psychology as too simplistic, ignoring as it does the important internal processes by which people interpret their environments. They also reject the psychoanalytic notion that indivuduals are controlled by unconscious mental processes. Humanistic psychologists see human beings as far more active in their own development than the environmental determinism of behaviorism or the instinctual drives of Freudian psychology would allow. Humanists believe that people can direct and control their lives through the exercise of free will and reason rather than controlled by irrational internal forces or environmental conditioning. Three major proponents of this school are Jean Piaget, Carl Rogers, and Abraham Maslow.

The diversity of psychological approaches has given rise to a variety of research methods. The experimental method acknowledges conditions that may vary or change among individuals, such as age, income, and learning ability. The researcher manipulates certain variables to determine which factors might cause or change certain behaviors.

Case histories are biographies or reconstructions based on the significant events and memories of people's lives. They are frequently used by clinical psychologists or psychiatrists treating patients with psychological problems. They analyze these case histories in an attempt to determine behavior patterns and causes for patient's problems. Psychologists also use observation, particularly in social psychology, where the focus is on the study of human behavior in groups.

Psychology in the Elementary Classroom

Psychology brings to pupils in the social studies classroom an understanding of themselves and of others. In effect, the concepts and main ideas of psychology are imbedded throughout all social studies content. When students study history, psychology will help them not only record what people did, but arrive at conclusions to explain those actions. Units dealing with the family, drawn from sociology and anthropology, can be even more interesting with an emphaisis on psychological concepts. Since social studies is concerned with investigating humankind, psychology directs student attention to the importance of attitudes, interests, values, and motives as key factors in human behavior.

Activity 4:3

Affective Analysis

Review several filmstrips that explore self-concept, social interaction, or character education. Discuss their strengths and weaknesses and how you feel about using them in a classroom. (Possible sources: QED Productions, *Learning About Me*, sound filmstrip series; Scholastic's Kindle Series, *Who Am I? How Do I Learn? Getting Along*; Bowmar's *Project Me: A Beginning Affective Program*; Guidance Associates, *First Things*, Elementary Sound Filmstrips.)

One way to incorporate psychology into social studies is to have students actually use the methods of psychologists. To emphasize human diversity and individual differences, they might survey members of their class to discover differences in variables such as height, number in family, birth order, mothers who work outside the home, favorite sports, etc. Fifth and sixth graders may be able to use the experimental method to investigate a topic that interests them. Ellis and Johnson (1977) offer an example of an experiment using control and experimental groups conducted by fifth-grade students. The students had learned a game that was intended to make them more careful observers. They tested the impact of this game on a group of second graders. The students tabulated all the scores for the experimental and control groups. The average score (mean) for the experimental group was 15.3; the control group had a lower mean of 10.8. Students might examine psychological research experiments to determine other ways of testing hypotheses and arriving at generalizations.

Philosophy

Defining Philosophy

In a society that considers science perhaps the most direct path to knowledge, the field of philosophy may seem irrelevant, speculative, and remote from present concerns. Philosophy, which means "the love of wisdom," might better be classified as a humanity than as a social science, yet it is still an important foundation of the social studies. Philosophy can help individuals understand the powerful ideas that have affected human history; it can satisfy the need for continuity, and serve as a bridge to other disciplines that interconnect the many areas of human knowledge. To establish continuity, the teacher can create learning situations that cater to children's natural curiosity, their natural inclination to persist until they obtain answers. Children respond best when learning is unified and complete. Philosophy augments that unity because it is characteristically a question-raising discipline; it generates questions that explore how certain aspects of reality relate to other aspects. Philosophical inquiry embodies the willingness to explore ideas, to continually engage in inquiry, and to examine ourselves and our world.

Thus, philosophy is a discipline of questioning. The questions it raises can be grouped into three types. The first is, "What is real?" Although this sounds simplistic it is actually quite profound. It allows individuals to arrive at some understanding of the reality of their world. Such a question comprises the branch of philosophy called *ontology*. Ontology has a companion label, that of *metaphysics*—the study of existence or being. An obvious reservation is whether or not elementary children would raise such questions. Put simply—children do! They ask, "What are things? What is time? What do you mean by meaning? Did all things have a beginning? What is a value?"

The social studies program *Man a Course of Study* has as one of its major objectives to encourage children to explore the nature of humanity and the related question of how we became human. Such questions have a metaphysical dimension. If social studies is the study of humankind, then we are bound to have children ask the question, "What is human?" If one answers by noting that humans are a special type of animal, children might ask, "What type of special animal?" The response might describe "an animal capable of thinking and using symbols and tools." Such dialogue is in the realm of philosophy (Lipman, Sharp, & Oscanyan, 1977, p. 20).

The second major area of philosophy is *epistemology*. This branch is concerned with the central question, "What is true?" It is directly related to the first branch in that once people have determined what is real, they want to see how true they can make their statements about reality. Is the knowledge they possess about the world accurate? When children explore this branch of philosophy, they would be guided and ecouraged to ask logic questions, which have to do with reasoning, and making judgments.

The final branch of philosophy is *axiology*. In this area, individuals ask the question, "What is good?" Such a question can be classified as ethical or aesthetic. *Ethics* centers on "What is right or proper conduct?" *Aesthetics* asks, "What is beautiful?" There are many classroom situations in which children raise such questions. They often want to know what is fair, good, or right. There will be many instances in social studies when children can discuss what is the right thing for people to do. Or, in dealing with people's rights, they can focus on what is fair for all peoples. Children want to know what things or behaviors matter and what do not. Class discussion on standards can frequently be grouped under *axiology*.

Figure 4.6
Questions in
Philosophy

Branch of Philosophy	Central Questions
Ontology—the study of being, existence	What is reality?
Epistemology—the study of knowlege	How do you know that?
Axiology—the study of what is good, right	What should we do?

Concepts and Generalizations in Philosophy

Since philosophy cuts across the disciplines of knowledge, its concepts derive from several disciplines. Concepts that come from other areas of study are those of right, freedom, equality, human dignity, the common good, responsibility, and concern for others. More purely philosophical concepts are those of knowledge, truth, values, the syllogism, and standardization.

Most teachers have a fairly good understanding of these concepts; however, the syllogistic and standardization concepts may be new to some. The syllogism refers to use of the rules of syllogistic logic. Essentially, this type of logic separates sentences into subject and predicate noun phrases preceeded by all, some, or no, and joined by a form of the verb "to be." For example, the sentence "all school buildings are red" fits this rule. One might also state that "some school buildings are red." One could note that "no school buildings are red." Sentences that do not fit this rule can be rewritten to conform. To use our first example, the sentence could have been "School buildings are red." It is easy to rewrite it to read "Some, no, or all school buildings are red." When a sentence is rewritten to fit the rules of the logic system, *standardization* has taken place. Standardization distinguishes the difference between critical and philosophical thinking. Armed with the rules of syllogistic logic, one can recognize sentences that do not apply, thus showing the limits to using such rules (Lipman et al., 1977, p. 119). Introducing children to such logic enables them to understand the mental procedures employed in processing knowledge.

Philosophy in the social studies classroom will allow students to better understand related disciplines, and also, of course, encourage comprehension of generalizations specific to philosophy. Here are some of those generalizations:

Dealing with philosophical questions allows one to deal with questions of reality, knowledge, and values.

A basic characteristic of human beings is their ability to employ formal and informal logic.

Criteria are linked to value bases, then applied to determine what is good and true.

Individuals have a need to examine ideas and proposals critically before coming to conclusions.

Philosophy in the Elementary Classroom

Philosophy in the social studies program will enable students to:

- Discover alternatives
- Discover consistency
- Support their conclusions with defensible reasons
- Heighten their creativity
- Discover part–whole relationships
- Discover situations that need investigation (Lipman et al. 1977, p. 00)

Teachers skilled in handling philosophy in the social studies class recognize and follow very closely what children are thinking. They help them develop procedures and questioning skills that facilitate reflection. Teachers find they can set the stage for philosophical inquiry if they have shown through their actions a respect for student opinions. An easy way to do this is to provide opportunities for the children to express their opinions and to challenge information reported by the teacher or fellow students.

Allowing time for discussion in social studies also facilitates the raising of philosophical questions. When studying a particular culture, pupils should be led to ask questions such as "Why do those people do those things? Why do those people believe those ideas?" How a teacher reacts to these questions determines to a great extent the quality of her pupils' learnings. A one-word response or a brief sentence will not usually elicit maximum benefit from the question. When studying anthropology units that deal with homelife throughout the world students should be shown how many of the questions they raise relate to ontology and epistemology. Teachers can encourage children to keep a list of key questions to which they can seek answers about particular social studies topics.

While philosophy fits readily into social studies, there is ongoing effort to bring philosophy as an identifiable subject into the elementary curriculum. Foremost in this movement is the work of the Institute for the Advancement of Philosophy for Children, directed by Mathew Lipman. Lipman is presently creating a philosophy program for grades K–12; two books of the series currently on the market are *Harry Stottlemeier's Discovery* and *Lisa*.

Harry Stottlemeier, the key character in the first book, is interested in logic, in right and wrong, and in language. One day he discovers that all cucumbers are vegetables but that not all vegetables are cucumbers. Excited about this new thought, he shares it with his friend Lisa. "When you turn sentences around, they're no longer true!" says Harry. Lisa hands Harry a sentence to consider. "No lions are eagles." Harry is perplexed because he realizes that the reverse is also true, "No eagles are lions." This incident leads Harry and his classmates (and the readers) to discover some principles of logic and the problems addressed by the fields of epistemology, ethics, and metaphysics. *Lisa* is a novel that deals with the relationship between logic and ethical inquiry. The characters (and the reader) consider such questions as: What are standards? What are rules? What is love? What is sex discrimination?

The Institute has also produced a sound filmstrip series entitled *Thinking About Thinking* (1978), whose cast of six characters have adventures that parallel those of Harry. Research on this attempt to teach philosophy to young children is in the early stages, but evidence suggests that teachers would need training in philosophical inquiry before materials could make a measurable impact on children.

Activity 4:4

Opportunities for Philosophy

Skim a social studies textbook or a curriculum guide for the grade you think you might teach and indicate where you could engage children in considering philosophy. Note the procedures and activities you could employ in teaching this new subject matter.

Activity 4:5

Your Philosophy

Consider your own philosophical views in relation to the human family. Jot down ways in which you could organize social studies content to be consistent with your philosophical views.

Discussion

Besides history, geography, eonomics, and sociology, the social studies foundations include the disciplines of political science, anthropology, and psychology. Some social studies programs are also beginning to draw on the field of philosophy.

Political scientists approach their discipline from one of several orientations—the historical, the legal–institutional, the political philosophy, or the systems orientation. The first approach concentrates on the evolution of governments and political change; the second, most common in the schools, concerns the study of government, political processes, and political decision making; the third is most interested in value rather than empirical questions; and the systems approach concerns group behavior—pressure groups and the processing of incoming demands into policy decisions. Political scientists study the concepts of power, conflict, political culture and socialization, social control, government, authority, and interest groups. Although political science has been taught at the high school level, teachers are now trying at earlier educational levels to develop children's awareness of political processes.

Anthropology is a broad discipline, divided into the fields of physical anthropology and cultural anthropology. Physical anthroplogists study human evolution and the relationships between humans and other animals; cultural anthropologists study cultural change, acculturation, and diffusion by means of archaeology, linguistics, and ethnology. All of these areas share a concern for culture, which is a society's behavior patterns, rules, and artifacts. Physical anthropologists conduct digs and other kinds of field work, while cultural anthropologists study culture by means of a society's history, language, religion, laws, and social structures. Elementary social studies lessons based on anthropological concepts lend themselves well to field trips and investigative study.

Because social studies emphasizes children's understanding of themselves and of the human family, the field of psychology underlies much of the curriculum, with its concentration on trying to discover why people behave as they do. Psychologists also work in various schools of thought, and may approach the discipline from a behavioral standpoint, a humanistic standpoint, or a psychoanalytic standpoint. Behaviorists work mainly with the stimulus–response theory and external environments; psychoanalysts explain behavior as responses to subconscious instincts; and humanistic psychologists believe that human beings control and direct their lives through the exercise of free will and reason. In the elementary classroom, psychology helps students understand attitudes, interests, values, and motives.

While closer to the humanities than to the social sciences, philosophy provides yet another foundation for the social studies because it is a discipline of questioning. It addresses three major questions: "What is real?" arises in the branch of philosophy known as ontology; "What is true?" comes from the branch of epistemology; and "What is good?" is dealt with in the branch of axiology. Axilogy further treats questions of ethics ("What is right or proper conduct?") and of aesthetics ("What is beautiful?"). Children often raise questions such as these, and can begin to deal with them at the elementary level.

References

Adler, Norman, and Harrington, Charles. *The Learning of Political Behavior.* Glenview, Ill.: Scott, Foresman, 1970.

Bohannan, Paul. *Justice and Judgment Among the Tiv*. London: Oxford University Press, 1957.

Bruner, Jerome. *Toward a Theory of Instruction*. Cambridge, Mass.: Harvard University Press, Belknap Press, 1966.

Easton, David. "An Approach to the Analysis of Political Systems." *World Politics* 9 (1957): 384.

Easton, David. "An Approach to the Analysis of Systems." In *The Social Studies: Structure, Models, and Strategies,* edited by Martin Feldman and Eli Seifman. Englewood Cliffs, N. J.: Prentice-Hall, 1969.

Easton, David. *The Political System: An Inquiry into the State of Political Science*. New York: Alfred A. Knopf, 1953.

Ellis, Arthur K., and Johnson, David W. "The Utilization of Experimental Research Methods by Teachers and Students." In *Social Studies and the Elementary Teacher: Promises and Practices,* edited by William W. Joyce and Frank L. Ryan. Washington, D. C.: National Council for the Social Studies, 1977.

Emmons, Frances, and Corbia, Jacqueline. "Introducing Anthropological Concepts in the Primary Grades." In *An Anthology of Readings in Elementary Social Studies,* edited by H.W. Walsh. Washington, D. C.: National Council for the Social Studies, 1971.

Erikson, Erik. *Childhood and Society*. New York: W. W. Norton & Co., 1963.

Gagné, Robert M. *The Conditions of Learning*. 2nd ed. New York: Holt, Rinehart and Winston, 1970.

Gallagher, Arlene, and Hartstein, Elliott. "Pre Se Court: A Simulation Game." *Law in American Society* 2 (1973): 26–30.

Harvey, Robert. "Anthropology in the High Schools: The Representation of a Discipline." In *Concepts and Structure in the New Social Science Curricula,* edited by Irving Morrisett. New York: Holt, Rinehart and Winston, 1967.

Herskovits, Melville J. *Man and His Works*. New York: Alfred Knopf, 1948.

Hilgard, Ernest R., Atkinson, Richard C., and Atkinson, Rita. *Introduction to Psychology*. 7th ed. New York: Harcourt, Brace, Jovanovich, 1975.

Isaak, Alan C. *Scope and Method of Political Science: An Introduction to the Methodology of Political Inquiry*. Homewood, Ill.: Dorsey, 1969.

Jarolimek, John. *Social Studies in Elementary Education*. 5th ed. New York: Macmillan Co., 1977.

Katen, Thomas. *Doing Philosophy*. Englewood Cliffs, N. J.: Prentice-Hall, 1973.

Lipman, Matthew; Sharp, Ann Margaret; and Oscanyan, Frederick S. *Philosophy in the Classroom*. Upper Montclair, N. J.: Institute for the Advancement of Philosophy for Children, Montclair State College, 1977.

Michaelis, John U. *Social Studies for Children in a Democracy*. 5th ed. Englewood Cliffs, N. J.: Prentice-Hall, 1972.

Morrisett, Irving, ed. *Concepts and Structure in the New Social Science Curricula*. New York: Holt, Rinehart and Winston, 1967.

Patterson, Franklin K. *Man and Politics: Occasional Paper No. 4*. Cambridge, Mass.: Education Development Center, 1965.

Pelto, Pertti. *The Study and Teaching of Anthropology*. Columbus, Oh.: Charles E. Merrill Publishing Co., 1980.

People in Communities. Social Science Concepts and Values Series. New York: Harcourt, Brace, Jovanovich, 1975.

Sorauf, Francis J. *Political Science: An Informal Overview*. Columbus, Oh.: Charles E. Merrill Publishing Co. 1965.

Spradley, James P., and McCurdy, David W. *The Cultural Experience: Ethnography in Complex Society*. Chicago: SRA, 1972.

Thinking About Thinking. Los Angeles: Ergo Films, 1978.

New Sources of Social Studies Content

5

In addition to the core disciplines that contribute to the social studies curriculum, other subjects add new dimensions to the study of humankind. International, national, and local current events offer appropriate material. Broad social concerns—hunger, inflation, housing shortages, droughts, and racism—can be incorporated into social studies units. Discussions about new scientific developments that may enhance or threaten the quality of life fit readily into social studies.

Environmental Studies

Most people realize that society must face environmental concerns—those of both the sociocultural and the biophysical environments. Our own and future societies may very well be threatened by today's uses and misuses of the earth's resources.

Many groups have helped to heighten awareness of environmental issues. Natural scientists, social scientists, health scientists, and scholars in the humanities have introduced problems that must be considered and solved. Attention has been directed to population and resources, environmental degradation, and environment and society (Murdoch, 1971). Humans must use the earth's mineral, energy, land, and water resources more wisely. A particular problem is pollution. Industrialized nations must limit, and try to eliminate, the pollution of air, soil, and water. They must find ways to stop the mismanagement of forests, lakes, and rivers, take steps to preserve wildlife, and halt the decay of cities.

To initiate a unit on environmental studies, the teacher might direct his students to think about the following questions:

- What are the major types of pollution?
- How long will pollution be a problem?
- What might be some consequences of ignoring pollution?
- How much will it cost to control and eliminate pollution?

In integrating environmental studies into social studies, the teacher should first consider the basic goals of the subject as they relate to knowledge, inquiry, skills, attitudes, and values. The aim is to have pupils understand the meaning of environment, to see humans as part of the ecological system, to grasp the reasons for environmental problems, and to arrive at possible solutions to problems. Students will have to process information from their environmental studies, cope with controversy, engage in forecasting, and try to arrive at workable solutions to some of our environmental problems. We also want them to develop the attitudes, feelings, and values necessary for appreciating the environment and for committing themselves to the wise use of nature's resources.

Organizing the Curriculum

Environmental content can be organized around concept clusters—those of environment, ecology, resources, food chain, land use, conservation, pollution, and erosion. Environmental studies can focus on both rural and urban environments, on human and natural resources, and on weather and climate. One cannot consider the human environment without including attention to population, numbers and distribution, density, growth, and migration.

Environmental units or topics can focus on resources: mineral, energy, soil, water, plant, and animal. The study of natural resources will lead students to investigate land use, which can then lead to considering the characteristics of rural and urban areas. Ideally, students will focus on the interaction between humans and the environment, which is a facet of ecological analysis.

Pollution is one of the negative hallmarks of an industrialized society. The teacher will want students to confront the different types of pollution: air, soil, food, water, sound, and visual.

One aim of environmental studies is for students to become conservation minded—to develop the attitudes necessary for the intelligent use of resources. Conservation should focus on human, resource, and wildlife conservation. Although conservation refers to wise use, not nonuse, of resources, wise use occasionally translates into restricted or aesthetic use, as exemplified in the creation of national parks.

After becoming acquainted with such concepts, pupils will be able to reach generalizations such as:

The earth is a self-contained system that subsumes numerous ecosystems. These are dependent upon solar energy and work in ways that support life.

The cultural and technological levels of human development will influence how people perceive and use their environment.

Current environmental problems are not localized. Air pollution generated in one part of the world affects people in other parts of the world.

115

Environmental problems require both immediate and long-term action.

Population growth is putting immense pressures on the earth's various ecological systems.

Solving the problems of pollution poses an immediate challenge to modern humanity—so that we will not poison ourselves, our plants, and the animals upon whom we depend. We hear almost daily that certain products in our environment cause serious health problems, such as emphysema and cancer. Children will have to confront these problems, and a lesson similar to the one on page 117 will help them develop an awareness of them.

Energy use is often considered in environmental studies units. Nuclear power is an especially current topic. The following case study shows how one teacher involved his students in investigating this topic.

The fifth graders burst into the classroom on Tuesday morning with paper bags full of supplies for an art project. Before the class begins, one group of students gathers in the corner. Their discussion draws the interest of others in the class, including the teacher, Mr. Alonso.

Jack: My dad says that nuclear plants are a lot safer now, and we have nothing to worry about.

Lou: Oh yea? How would you like to have radiation leaking into the river, the air, and everywhere?

George: I think if the big cities along the coast need more power, they should have the plant in their own backyards, not in our town.

Jacki: They don't want to build near the coast 'cuz of earthquakes and all the people and stuff.

Lou: Oh, that's really great! So they stick the plant out there in the desert so just a few thousand of us die when it explodes.

(Note: It's time for these students to continue the study of the Civil War period in American history. If you were the teacher of this class, would you end the discussion or allow it to continue?)

Mr. Alonso decides to conclude the discussion, but he wants the students to explore this important change in their town. Before beginning the history lesson, he suggests that the students gather as much information as possible about the proposed nuclear power plant. He informs the class that on Friday, instead of the usual current events lesson, the class members will share what they have discovered. "If there's enough interest, we might study the power plant as a combined Social Studies/Science project," Mr. Alonso adds.

On Friday, the students' desks are full of newspaper clippings, and their conversations reflect personal opinions and rumors. Mr. Alonso begins the discussion of the nuclear plant by asking about its size, location, and the amount of time needed for construction. Then he asks which community groups favor and which oppose building the plant near their town. A list of reasons favoring or opposing the plant is written on the chalkboard. The students' own reasons are added to the list.

Lesson Plan

Lesson Focus: Fresh water pollution

Objectives: Students will explain why we need unpolluted fresh water. Students will be able to identify the causes of fresh water pollution and will be able to suggest feasible ways of elimi-
nating such pollution.

Warm-up Activity: Start the lesson by having pupils list all the ways they have used water during the
last week. Have students conclude that fresh water is essential to human, animal,
and plant life. Introduce, via pictures and/or a film, the notion that many of our
fresh water sources are being ruined by pollution. The purpose of this lesson is to
show the ways in which water is polluted and how to reduce the incidence of such
pollution.

Developmental Activities: Have students list questions for guiding their investigation of this topic.
Some students may wish to group the causes of and solutions for pollu-
tion. A data chart such as the following might result:

Data Chart: Pollution Sources		
Source	Consequence/s	Solution/s
Run off from cities	Ruined streams, lakes	Surface planting
Sewage	"	Treatment
Rains washing polluted air	Ruined crops, reduced plant growth	Cutting down air pollution

Some pupils may wish to investigate agricultural drainage, erosion, radioactive isotopes, toxic
wastes, or thermal pollution.

Students can map out their questions and the strategies they plan to use in conducting their
investigations. Students who study agricultural drainage and its effects on water pollution might take
field trips to local farms to see different types of ground cover and how farmers dispose of waste
water. The children can also analyze what happens when farmers use chemical fertilizers. In
advanced classes, children might take water samples from streams that border the farms to see what
chemicals are present.

Pupils who investigate erosion might travel around the community to take pictures of erosion.
They can classify erosion as to type, cause, and solution. Students may also visit the local or state
agencies responsible for managing erosion. Many of these agencies will furnish students with information packets. Pupils who work on these topics can prepare reports for class distribution. Some
students might even prepare film reports for class presentation. (The depth of investigation can be
adjusted according to the children's abilities.)

Concluding Activities: One way to conclude this lesson is with a Pollution Seminar, at which students
can discuss their findings and their feelings. Parents and community members
might be invited to participate in the seminar.

During the discussion, the class identifies several important issues. Is a nuclear power plant safe? Does the state really need more power? Are there sources of energy other than nuclear? Will all of the people moving here and all of the new jobs help or hurt our town?

Students form groups to study these questions. Mr. Alonso requests that each group prepare a chart, and uses the safety question as an example of how to organize the charts:

Research Question: Are nuclear power plants safe?	
Yes	No
Facts supporting nuclear safety 1. 2. 3.	Facts showing nuclear plants unsafe 1. 2. 3.

The Friday lesson triggers a more extended treatment of the topic. The students discover that finding information about this important com-

The construction of nuclear power plants could serve as the focus for a unit on environmental studies.

munity issue is not difficult. Special programs are being aired on television, and the newspapers furnish diagrams of the proposed plants, explanations of nuclear power, and many articles about the impact of the proposed plant on the community. Community members are invited to the class to discuss the issue and to answer student questions, including a member of the Sierra Club (opposed), a member of the city council (in favor), a representative of the power company (in favor), and a lawyer who leads an opposition group. In this particular case, the nuclear power plant was never built in this little desert community. The power company failed to prove the need for the plant and to obtain a license from the state. Mr. Alonso and his fifth graders were well informed about the issues and felt themselves participants in an important local event.

Activity 5:1

Materials Analysis

Review two or three social studies series and determine where and how the content of environmental studies is considered. Is the treatment balanced, that is, does it deal with both the ways in which humans have improved the environment as well as ways in which they have threatened it?

Humanizing the Classroom

Recent attention to human interaction and personal growth offers another source for enriching the social studies curriculum. Spurred by the studies of psychologists such as Abraham Maslow and Carl Rogers, many educators have turned their attention to the educational implications of self-actualization and group dynamics.

Education cannot be restricted to teaching the basics, to individualizing instruction, to administering cognitive tests and measures. Formal instruction occurs in groups, thus creating an important dimension to learning that cannot be ignored. Many argue that by paying attention to classroom interaction and helping students develop skills in working with and for others, teachers can improve the learning of math, history, and language. Aspy (1974) found that certain dimensions identified by Carl Rogers as facilitating integration, when present in the classroom, related significantly and positively to student achievement.

119

The concept of the humane person as one who exhibits qualities of empathy, brotherly love, and trust is a part of many religious traditions and the subject of philosophers of many ages. With an increasing world population, shortages of essential resources, and new technological developments that give humans the power to make this planet uninhabitable, the world can appear to be a frightening place. The need for humane individuals, capable of relating effectively to others and to the environment, has never been more evident.

Reflecting this interest in humanizing education, many current classroom materials contain suggestions and activities that emphasize small-group work, role playing, simulation, and classroom discussion. Educators are coming to accept that the *process* of learning may be as important as, or more important than, learning actual content. Consider the probable difference in atmosphere between the classroom in which facts and values are presented to students by authority figures—teachers and textbooks—and the classroom in which inquiry, open-ended discussions, and team projects are encouraged.

There are several ways to observe and analyze classroom interaction. For example, Figure 5.1 shows how Ned Flanders (1965) developed an interaction analysis instrument that compares the amount and type of "teacher talk" with student talk. Metfessel, Michael, and Kirsner (1969) modified Bloom's Taxonomy of Educational Objectives so that it is now possible to determine the type of interaction between teacher and student as well as the type of cognitive activity that is taking place.

The ability to work with and for others is an important dimension of learning.

TEACHER TALK	INDIRECT INFLUENCE	1. Accepts Feeling: accepts and clarifies the feeling tone of the students in a nonthreatening manner. Feelings may be positive or negative. Predicting or recalling feelings are included. 2. Praises or Encourages: praises or encourages student action or behavior. Jokes that release tension, not at the expense of another individual, nodding head or saying "um hm?" or "go on" are included. 3. Accepts or Uses Ideas of Student: clarifying, building, or developing ideas suggested by a student. As teacher brings more of his own ideas into play, shift to category five. 4. Asks Questions: asking a question about content or procedure with the intent that a student answer.
	DIRECT INFLUENCE	5. Lecturing: giving facts or opinions about content or procedure; expressing his own ideas, asking rhetorical questions. 6. Giving Directions: directions, commands, or orders with which a student is expected to comply. 7. Criticizing or Justifying Authority: statements intended to change student behavior from nonacceptable to acceptable pattern; bawling someone out; stating why the teacher is doing what he is doing; extreme self-reference.
STUDENT TALK		8. Student Talk—Response: talk by students in response to teacher. Teacher initiates the contact or solicits student statement. 9. Student Talk—Initiation: talk by students which they initiate. If "calling on" student is only to indicate who may talk next, observer must decide whether student wanted to talk. If he did, use this category.
		10. Silence or Confusion: pauses, short periods of silence and periods of confusion in which communication cannot be understood by the observer.

Figure 5.1
Flanders's Interaction
Analysis

From *Interaction Analysis in the Classroom—A Manual for Observers* by Ned A. Flanders, copyright © 1965 by the University of Michigan Press. Reprinted by permission.

Carl Rogers (1961, 1969) has theorized that certain core conditions—empathy, positive regard, congruence, and concreteness—determine whether or not an interaction is facilitating. Empathy is the ability to place oneself in another's situation. Positive regard is the respect accorded an individual just because he or she is a person; it is independent of that person's actions. Congruence involves the quality of being genuine in a relationship, rather than deceptive, withholding, or dependent on a facade. Concreteness of expression has less research to support it as a core condition; there is some evidence, however, that communication can be facilitated by saying things in a specific, concrete way, using a vocabulary suitable to the person who is listening.

Using the ideas of many psychologists, especially those of Carl Rogers, Thomas Gordon has developed training programs to help people learn ways of interacting effectively, based on his books *Parent Effectiveness Training* and *Teacher Effectiveness Training*. Figure 5.2 shows how Gordon classifies twelve categories of "the language of non-acceptance, roadblocks to communication." The first five teacher responses try to solve the problem for the student, and in doing so, slow down or stop communication with a troubled student. The next three categories (6, 7, and 8) Gordon calls "judgment, evaluation, and put-downs." Nine and 10 are "attempts by teachers to make a student feel better, to make the problem go away, or to deny that he even has a problem."

Figure 5.2
Gordon's Roadblocks
to Communication

---

1. Ordering, commanding, directing

2. Warning, threatening

3. Moralizing, preaching, giving "shoulds" and "oughts"

4. Advising, offering solutions or suggestions

5. Teaching, lecturing, giving logical arguments

6. Judging, criticizing, disagreeing, blaming

7. Name calling, stereotyping, labeling

8. Interpreting, analyzing, diagnosing

9. Praising, agreeing, giving positive evaluations

10. Reassuring, sympathizing, consoling, supporting

11. Questioning, probing, interrogating, cross-examining

12. Withdrawing, distracting, being sarcastic, humoring, diverting

---

Reprinted with permission from the book *Parent Effectiveness Training* by Thomas Gordon, copyright 1970. Published by David McKay Co., Inc.

Gordon's interaction training is designed for students who have problems and for teachers wishing to help them. As an alternative to judging, preaching, ignoring, and questioning the student, Gordon recommends passive listening—saying nothing at all, but indicating through verbal and nonverbal cues that one is paying attention to the other. Active listening is a process in which the teacher tries to "decode" a student's comment by stating what the teacher thinks the student means.

Strategies for improving interpersonal communication attempt to help both teachers and students with the complexities of human interaction and group dynamics. The assumption underlying approaches such as Gordon's is that this skill can be learned and practiced, thus resulting in improved relationships. The insights students will gain from viewing themselves as humane people will also heighten the quality of their social studies learnings.

Activity 5:2

Library Visit

Check in the materials section of your campus library to determine how many social studies curriculum guides specifically treat the human dimension of people. That is, do the materials stress human qualities and how to make children sensitive to others?

Activity 5:3

Improving Interpersonal Communication

Roadblocks to communication have been presented. List ways in which you can improve interpersonal communication. Tie your suggestions to specific topics that you might teach in the grade level of your choice.

The teacher can indicate through verbal and nonverbal cues that she is paying attention to the student.

Group Dynamics as Social Studies Content

Regardless of the emphasis on individualizing and personalizing instruction, most classroom social studies experiences involve pupils in groups. Thus, an understanding of group dynamics facilitates effective group membership. Additionally, an understanding of groups is basic to the content of the social sciences.

Group dynamics concerns the discovery and use of knowledge about group process. It is a subarea of psychology that rarely (if ever) appears as a unit or theme in elementary social studies. We believe it should be included.

Characteristics of Groups

People comprise a group when they exhibit one or more of the following characteristics:

1. Definable membership—a collection of two or more people identifiable by name or type.
2. Group consciousness—the members think of themselves as a group, have a collective perception of unity, a conscious identification with each other.
3. A sense of shared purposes.
4. Interdependence in satisfaction of needs—the members need the help of one another to accomplish the purposes for which they joined the group.
5. Interaction—the members communicate with, influence, and react to one another.
6. Ability to act in a unitary manner—the group can behave as a single organism. (pp. 40–41)

From *Introduction to Group Dynamics* by Malcolm and Hulda Knowles. Copyright © 1972, National Board of Young Men's Christian Associations. Used by permission of Association Press/Follett Publishing Company.

Groups have common properties. All groups have a *background* or lack of background which influences their behavior. If children have worked together before, that joint work becomes part of their background. If not, this lack of prior contact will influence their interaction. People, including children, always approach group involvement with some kind of expectation. They may look forward to the experience, believing other people will contribute greatly to their investigation, or they may be unsure of how the group will work because they have little or no data on the members of the group.

In addition to background, all groups develop a *participation pattern* that exists over time and can be described at any particular moment. In a group of three children, for example, a pattern might emerge in which one child dominates the discussion with the other children listening attentively; in another group of three, there may be an equal exchange of views by each child.

All groups have the property of *communication,* which refers to how well members understand each other and how well they express their feelings, attitudes, and information. Children with very different cultural and/or experiential backgrounds may have difficulty making themselves understood by others in the group.

All groups exhibit *cohesion*, the bonds uniting the individual parts. Team spirit and group morale are outward signs of group cohesion.

Groups have the tendency to create *standards*, or rules of conduct necessary for remaining in the group. In social studies classes, the teacher may establish the standards and responsibilities for the group members. For example, he may appoint a group leader to keep notes that can be shared with the rest of the class. It is essential that everyone who participates in a group understand its standards, the expectations others have for each person's performance.

People in groups of three or more are often assigned particular roles that define the relationships among members. In these cases, the group has a particular *structure and organization*. Sometimes the teacher assures a formal structure by assigning roles, and at other times allows the structure to remain informal, with roles and tasks shifting during different lessons. Sometimes the children's backgrounds and varying abilities determine group structure. Some social studies teachers organize groups so that children of varying abilities but shared interests are together.

All groups have *procedures* and *goals*. Goals refer to the end points toward which the group strives. Procedures are the means group members use to attain the goals. Most goals in elementary social studies groups will be short or midrange. Procedures will vary according to the complexity of the task or topic, the age of the pupils, their ability levels, and the time available for carrying out the group tasks. The procedures can be formal or informal, again depending upon the nature of the topic (Knowles & Knowles, 1972).

Students work together in groups more effectively if they know the rules, procedures, and roles they can play.

Purposes of Stressing Group Dynamics

We recommend group dynamics in the social studies curriculum for two reasons: (1) to provide pupils with a way to understand and improve their actions in groups, and (2) to use the information of group dynamics to analyze groups as they encounter them in social sciences content.

Lesson plans often include the directive, "Have pupils work in groups to discuss the questions of the unit," but lack specific information as to how to get pupils to work effectively in those groups. While teachers need more specific directives, pupils also need to know the rules, the procedures, and the roles they can play.

A widely accepted classification of membership and leadership functions (Knowles & Knowles, 1972), useful for social studies teachers who want to guide pupils toward becoming effective group members, creates two classifications: (1) group-building and maintenance roles and (2) group task roles. The group-building and maintenance roles contribute to cresting relationships and group cohesiveness; group task roles are those that assist the group in performing its assigned work. The group-building roles are those of:

The encourager: the person who provides praise, is responsive to ideas, accepts contributions of others.

The mediator: the person who moderates conflicts among group members, is responsible for making compromises.

The gate keeper: the person who tries to make it possible for another member to make a contribution to the group. Makes statements like "let's hear from Susan."

Standard setter: the person who makes known the standards for the group to employ in addressing a topic, in conducting group activity.

Follower: the person who goes along with the group, playing a somewhat passive role.

Tension Reliever: the person responsible for diverting attention from unpleasant to pleasant matters. Interjecting some humor into group discussion.

From *Introduction to Group Dynamics* by Malcolm and Hulda Knowles. Copyright © 1972, National Board of Young Men's Christian Associations. Used by permission of Association Press/Follett Publishing Company.

The task functions are those of:

Initiating: suggesting new ideas or another way of viewing a group problem or goal.

Information seeking: asking for information needed to conduct the group investigation.

Information giving: providing information related to the group's activities.

Opinion giving: stating a pertinent belief of opinion having relevance to the group's investigation. Clarifying, elaborating, proving for meaning, or asking that additional information and examples be furnished. Giving examples is part of elaboration.

Co-ordinating: showing the relationship among various ideas, attempting to tie ideas together.

Orienting: defining the focus of the discussion.
Testing: checking with the group to determine if the members are willing and able to make a statement or take some action.
Summarizing: reviewing the content of past discussions.

From *Introduction to Group Dynamics* by Malcolm and Hulda Knowles. Copyright © 1972, National Board of Young Men's Christian Associations. Used by permission of Association Press/Follett Publishing Company.

These functions and tasks need not be presented in formal lessons; teachers can acquaint pupils with them via handout sheets written in language geared to the children's ages and grades. They might also place such lists on the bulletin board. The information will not only facilitate group functioning, but will also enable students to apply it in critiquing and understanding other groups in various social studies units. It may help them comprehend how individuals working together arrive at particular conclusions or solutions. Children can focus on determining whether groups are authoritarian, democratic, or laissez-faire. They can use their new-found information to analyze their social studies group and the roles their classmates perform. Information about group dynamics can be integrated throughout the social studies curriculum. Its effectiveness as a new foundation for social studies depends upon both the teacher's commitment to the field and his creativity in introducing the information to his pupils.

Activity 5:4

Group Analysis

If group dynamics is to be considered as social studies content, then you as a teacher will have to understand this content field. Drawing on the information presented in this chapter, classify three groups to which you belong and explain their common properties, the roles people play in these groups, and the tasks these people play.

Group 1 (Student Group)

Properties:

Roles people play: Person playing role:

Tasks assumed by people: Person assuming task:

Group 2 (The class in which you are practice teaching)

Do the same analysis.

Group 3 (You select this group, consider the same information.)

The Arts as Social Studies Content

Visual Arts

The arts offer yet another rich source for social studies content. Through the arts, children encounter the many ways humankind celebrates life—its beauty, surprises, spirit, and purposes. From the earliest of times, artisans have interpreted life through media such as painting, sculpture, and weaving. The genius of artists and artisans have contributed to the quality of our dwellings and our clothing, and have made utensils not only functional but pleasing to the eye (Michaelis, 1972).

In the reality of the social studies classroom, it is difficult to avoid integrating the arts into almost all curriculum units. Units dealing with various cultures should have students studying the way art influences and

Studying the art of another civilization is one way to step into the world view of another culture.

enhances the cultures. Drawing content from art gives pupils insights into and appreciations of how people perceive what is creative and beautiful. Today's art has a major impact on homes, buildings, furnishings, and even schools. Children gain new understandings of history by considering the works of art of people who lived during those times and artistically recorded their observations.

The study of art in social studies should naturally be multicultural. Children should have opportunities to experience the art of European, Asian, African, and different Native American cultures. For example, viewing sculptures of India (or replicas of them) allows children to be touched affectively by the culture. The beauty of the Taj Mahal and the genius of the people who built it are even more marvelous when children realize this structure was built during the same time the Pilgrims came to the New World.

Examples of the beautiful calligraphy of Arab cultures gives children an appreciation for these peoples' artistic dimensions. Pictures of Japanese paintings will suggest how culture affects the "eye" of the artist. Looking at pictures of Egyptian sculpture, and perhaps comparing it to that of Greece and Rome, encourages children not only to reflect on beauty and creative genius, but also to make comparisons among cultures, to see how art forms have evolved over the years. Children's emotions, feelings, appreciations, values, and creative abilities are stimulated through art.

Teachers can involve children in art through both creative and appreciative activities. Most encounters are aimed at appreciation and understanding, but there will be times when children can actually produce art forms. Whether such activities are part of social studies or art classes depends upon what the teacher has the children do with their art. If the art is intended not

The visual arts in social studies can be emphasized through both creative and appreciative activites.

only as a means to express an emotion but also as a vehicle for getting to
know oneself and others, then the activity would be appropriate for social
studies. Art production activities suitable for integration in social studies are:

Free painting	Making models
Drawing illustrations	Wood carving
Block printing	Making batik designs
Painting murals	Weaving
Ink sketching	Constructing furniture
Clay modeling	Making mobiles
Making mosaics	

Many museums make special arrangements for students to visit and learn
about the paintings, sculpture, and artifacts on display. Docents frequently
conduct special programs and exhibits for furthering children's understanding
of the museum's artwork.

Many communities display art works in their public and private
buildings and parks. A tour of the community will show children that art is
ever-present, that it continues to express our desire for the beautiful, the
pleasing, and the functional.

Most communities claim at least one local artist, either a painter,
sculptor, or designer. Architects can also be considered part of the art community. These people are usually quite willing to discuss their areas of expertise in the schools, and will often bring examples of their work.

Dramatic and Performing Arts

In every society, some individuals express their creativity through acting or
dancing. Social studies teachers have always been taught how to involve their
pupils in dramatic activities, but little attention has been given to how to
draw content from the performing arts. Just as paintings and sculpture offer
insight into a culture, so also do theater and dance furnish students with
opportunities for insight as well as enjoyment.

More and more communities accept the importance of the dramatic
and performing arts, and support special theaters and dance groups for children. Some theater groups perform at the schools. The Seattle Repertory
Theater, for example, toured the state of Washington to take drama to the
students. These encounters provide pupils with opportunities to experience
good theater, and thus to understand humankind more deeply.

Children can also participate in dramatizations of social studies topics.
This kind of activity is structured, and requires a script, some type of staging,
and rehearsals. Children can sometimes read plays orally, then discuss them.
From such dialogue, children arrive at a more complete view of some event
in time or the reasons for someone's actions.

Some communities have children's theater, in which all roles are taken
by children. The groups put on plays that present information in dramatic
form, and the children in the audience have a chance to see their peers in a
different light.

The dramatic and performing arts offer many teaching opportunities; some of the forms and their educational type are:

1. Dramatization—quite structured
2. Dramatic play—an informal and creative portrayal of experiences
3. Pageants—used to portray a sequence of events, usually related to some topic in a social studies unit
4. Pantomimes—somewhat spontaneous occurrences in classrooms, to give students a better understanding of a particular happening
5. Marionettes and puppets—used either for dramatization or dramatic play
6. Role playing—children assume particular roles to help them understand others' problems, feelings, or ideas

Auditory Arts and Music

Through music, children can extend their communication to other peoples, other cultures, even other times. Music can be integrated into all social studies

Through dramatic presentations students can learn about the language, dress, customs, and values of another time period.

units. In history, children can learn and discuss songs from the past. In anthropology, children can learn to play musical instruments unique to the groups under study. When studying the pupils' native country, a teacher can use the power of music and song to impart the love of country that inspires so much of its music.

The usual activities for integrating music into the curriculum are singing, rhythmic encounters, listening, and producing. Singing is probably the most common activity. Many songs help children identify more closely with certain peoples and times. Awareness and appreciation of particular jobs can come from folk song. Folk songs also frequently deal with social problems, which invite student analysis. Analysis of lyrics might flow naturally into a brief survey of a culture's literature. Teachers are turning to the use of song in the classroom in response to the increasing attention to the affective dimensions of learning.

Rhythmic activities allow children to sense the pulse of life, to express their emotions in unique and common ways. Especially in the primary grades, children enjoy bodily expression and performing folk dances. Not only do they get enjoyment, but grace and poise are also cultivated along with a higher affective and cognitive orientation to the study of humankind. The teacher can incorporate rhythmic activities with activities that address the dramatic and performing arts, especially dance.

Through songs from the past students can become aware of the meaning of events to the people living at the time.

Listening is a greatly neglected skill throughout the elementary school curriculum. While a part of the language arts curriculum, listening needs to be cultivated in all elements of the curriculum. Listening to music makes the pupil a critical consumer of this art form. Listening does not just mean being quiet; rather, it means creating a purpose for listening and raising questions as one listens. Becoming a critical listener enables a person to be intellectually aware of music at the same time it enhances one's level of enjoyment. It allows the person to move much closer to the human spirit, to human needs and interests.

In anthropology units, children can listen to native music and make comparisons with music from their own culture. What kinds of sounds are pleasing to a people? How is music used in their culture? What types of instruments do they use?

Music is all around children. They carry it with them on their portable radios and listen to it on home stereos. Usually, however, listening to music is random. In social studies, it can become a planned activity for stimulating a more complete knowledge of the human family.

Music listening is easy to schedule, and materials are widely available. Teachers have access to records and audiotapes. They can take children to symphonies to hear contemporary and period music, and local community groups are often willing to visit schools with musical performances.

Pupils are often interested in *producing* music to express their feelings, either individually or as a class activity. When pupils are planning a special class report, they may enjoy creating background music for the report. A class

---

Activity 5:5

Incorporating the Arts

Note the various arts that can be utilized in social studies lessons and indicate how you might develop lessons or activities integrating the arts.

Activity 5:6

Making an Art Resource List

Considering your local community, make a file on various persons who can serve as resource people for the different arts. Note specifically what these individuals might do to make the arts a vital part of children's social studies learning.

---

that is working on a film about some social problem can create a sound track to set and carry the film's mood. Children who are gifted in music find such a project exciting.

Class members might create music to accompany dramatic play. Producing may not involve actually writing music or lyrics, but perhaps simply arranging music already composed. Many educators shy away from such activities because they don't feel qualified to lead pupils in music production, although it is easier than it might seem at first. For those who feel this is beyond their competence, there are usually others on the school staff who are glad to assist. Most elementary school staffs have several members who have studied music and who play instruments, and the school's music director is always a good source of guidance. Producing can also refer to making rhythm instruments for class use. Drums, blocks, and rattles are easy to create, and other rhythm instruments, such as bells, triangles, cymbals, gongs, and tambourines, can be purchased.

Discussion

In chapters 3 and 4, we discussed in detail the disciplines from which social studies content traditionally draws. In this chapter, we have explored areas other than the traditional that also offer materials and methods for inclusion in elementary social studies. Current events, important social concerns, and new scientific discoveries are legitimate foundations for lessons and units.

Environmental studies are particularly timely for elementary students, who can investigate their environment through concept clusters such as ecology, resources, conservation, and pollution. A lesson plan offered one approach to the study of fresh water pollution, and a case study showed how one teacher helped his fifth graders investigate the construction of a nuclear power plant.

A psychological perspective on human interaction and personal growth also deserves a place in the social studies classroom, with the goal of bringing students to a sense of self-understanding and a familiarity with principles of group dynamics. Educators have begun to accept that the process of learning is perhaps as important as the content learned, and that learning occurs best in a classroom that encourages humane behavior, empathy, and respect for the individual.

Because so many social studies activities involve group work, learning about group dynamics can help children become more effective group members. All groups are influenced by background, and develop participation patterns and methods of communication. They exhibit cohesion, create standards, and define relationships among members by establishing a structure or organization, and they develop procedures with which to accomplish goals. Studying group dynamics helps elementary students understand and improve their own group participation, and helps them analyze groups when they encounter them in social studies content.

Social studies teachers may also draw from the arts when creating lessons. The visual arts provide an infinite source of supplementary material for cultural studies and offer endless opportunities for "hands-on" learning. The dramatic and performing arts offer insight and enjoyment, and can appear in the classroom as full-scale dramatizations or as brief role-playing activities. Music, singing, and rhythmic and listening activities also have an important place in today's elementary social studies.

References

Aspy, David. *Toward A Technology for Humanizing Education.* Champaign, Ill.: Research Press Co., 1974.

Flanders, Ned A. *Interaction Analysis in the Classroom—A Manual for Observers.* Ann Arbor: University of Michigan Press, 1965.

Gordon, Thomas. *Teacher Effectiveness Training.* New York: David McKay Co., 1974.

Knowles, Malcolm, and Knowles, Hulda. *Introduction to Group Dynamics.* New York: Association Press, 1972.

Metfessel, N. S.; Michael, W. B.; and Kirsner, D. A. "Instrumentation of Bloom's and Krathwohl's Taxonomies for Writing Educational Objectives." *Psychology in the Schools* 7 (1969): 227–231.

Michaelis, John U. *Social Studies for Children in a Democracy.* 5th ed. Englewood Cliffs, N. J.: Prentice-Hall, Inc., 1972.

Murdoch, William W., ed. *Environment, Resources, Pollution and Society.* Stamford, Conn.: Sinauer Associates, Inc., Publishers, 1971.

Rogers, Carl. *Freedom to Learn.* Columbus, Oh.: Charles E. Merrill, 1969.

Rogers, Carl. *On Becoming a Person.* Boston: Houghton Mifflin, 1961.

Social Studies Content

Types of Social Studies Content

In order to create meaningful curriculum units, it is important to understand not only the major concepts and generalizations but also the ways in which knowledge is organized. Thus armed, one can select the types of social studies content that will meet the objectives and guide children in realizing the nature of knowledge itself.

This chapter concerns the several ways in which content is organized: facts, concepts, generalizations, and theories. We will also discuss the major curriculum designs available to the social studies teacher.

Facts

Facts represent things that actually exist or that really occurred in the past. They also denote the locations of places, dimensions of objects, the activities of individuals, and the dates of events. Their proof rests upon the presence of empirical evidence. These are examples of facts one might find in social studies units:

- George Washington was the first president of the United States.
- Boston is the capital of Massachusetts.
- France is a West European country.
- The Treaty of Paris was signed in 1783.

Notice that each of these statements refers to a particular individual, place, event, or situation. Each can be verified by data. Because facts are restricted to a particular time, event, or person, they tend to have little transfer value. Knowing that Boston is the capital of Massachusetts does not help one to know the capital of Idaho.

Teachers frequently use too many facts, organizing the social studies program around, perhaps, the major events and key figures in American history. Facts are essential, but they should not be the goal in social studies learning. They are important only as they relate to and support concepts, generalizations, and theories.

138

Which facts should students learn? To answer this question, one must consider the context in which the facts will be learned and used. A person in Kansas might need to know facts about different soil types; such information may have little meaning to a person living in Boston. To a person who lives in a community that has subways, knowing the dates of subway openings may contribute to her awareness of mass transportation; however, a native of Montana may find such information completely irrelevant. There are, of course, some facts that should be part of all students' information base; all pupils should know facts about the organization of the American government, for example, and the facts relating to our economic system.

A specialized type of fact is a rule. Teachers decide which rules are necessary for successful functioning in particular situations. Students who drive cars need to know the rules and facts of the road; children in elementary schools need to know the rules of behavior for group activities.

Concepts

Unlike facts, concepts do not depend upon evidence; they are definitions, and they exist because they have been explained in a certain way. They are "givens" in knowledge that serve as building blocks to create more general knowledge, primarily at the level of generalizations. For example, the concept of "mountain" is not proven true by gathering evidence from reality. A mountain is a mountain because geographers and geologists have agreed to define a particular topographical feature as a mountain. A topographical formation that has a particular shape and a certain minimum altitude can be called a mountain. In this case, the attribute of altitude may be more crucial than that of shape; a land form with the same shape as a mountain but with an altitude of only 1500 feet above sea level would, in all likelihood, be called a hill.

As noted previously, facts refer to single objects, events, or individuals. In contrast, concepts refer to classes or clusters of objects, events, or individuals that share something in common. For instance, *school* functions as a concept because there are several organizations, numerous behaviors, and various groups that can all be included under this organizer. There are primary schools, elementary schools, colleges, universities, technical institutions, and community colleges. All these institutions share common attributes (they focus on learning and have a formal curriculum) that the people who study schools say are the essential characteristics of schools.

Concepts represent our attempts to organize our world—to make sense out of the diversity of reality, to make reality intelligible. John Wilson (1967) explains:

> We observe that certain features of our experience keep cropping up, that certain experiences are recurrent. If the same experience recurs often enough to make it worth our while, we invent a word or sign to use on any occasion when we wish to communicate the experience. We see that pillboxes, poppies, and stop-lights are similar in one respect; and so we use the word "red"

to express this similarity. We perceive that certain things are similar in many respects; say, they are all small, circular and hard; and we invent a noun for the occasion when we wish to speak of any of these things, the noun "penny". We observe the penny doing something on various occasions, which we afterwards call "rolling." (pp. 20–21)

Concepts are mental constructs created by individuals to describe characteristics common to a number of experiences. Concepts allow people to relate a great amount of individual and separate "bits" of information and to categorize such "bits." In so doing, we can communicate vast amounts of specific information via a particular concept. Mention the concept "social group," and a great number of specifics about groups are suggested (Bruner, 1956).

How has the concept of the school changed since the days of the one-room schoolhouse?

Kinds of Concepts

Concepts can be organized according to level or degree of abstraction and concreteness. A concrete concept is one that can be learned through the senses and perceived in reality, such as girl, mountain, or house. Abstract concepts, on the other hand, are not directly observed, but are inferred from analyzing reality or ideas, such as revolution, interdependence, power, or freedom. Abstract concepts are often learned as definitions, to be applied whenever appropriate for comprehending a particular situation (Hunkins, 1980).

Concepts can also be thought of as classifications. Bruner and others identify two kinds of classification concepts: conjunctive and disjunctive. The conjunctive concept is defined by the presence of two or more attributes that contribute to its meaning. Fraenkel (1973) gives the concept of "tourist" as an example. This conjunctive concept includes the characteristics of "travel for pleasure" and "permanent home elsewhere." The concept of "professional athlete" includes the characteristics of "plays for money" and "plays on a regular schedule."

A disjunctive concept is one for which there must be one or more defining attributes present before it has meaning. These attributes are not additive, but each contributes equally to the concept's meaning. Two examples are "creative genius" and "political activist." Any number of attributes can describe these concepts; no set number of properties must be present. Fraenkel uses the example of "extra point" in football. An extra point can be earned (after a touchdown has been scored) either by kicking the ball through the goal posts, by running the ball over the goal line, or by completing a pass over the goal line. Any one of the three qualifies for the extra point.

Fraenkel discusses a third type of concept, the connotative. The connotative concept is usually highly complex; its meaning is defined not by observing reality, but rather by referring to other concepts. For example, the concepts of empathy, honor, and bravery are connotative in that their attributes are essentially other concepts.

A final type of concept is the *relational*, which is defined by a specifiable relationship between attributes. The concept "speed" is an example. It points out the relation of a distance covered in units of time. The relational concept of "mental age" notes an association between a level of intellectual functioning and chronological age.

Even though people create concepts to make reality clearer, some concepts can be comprehended only at the common-sense level. One such concept in social studies is "fully functioning individual." This concept is difficult to define precisely, yet people usually nod in agreement when asked if they understand what is meant by this type of individual. One reason for the difficulty in attaining precise understanding is that people define such concepts with other concepts that, in themselves, lack clear definitions of commonly accepted attributes.

Social studies frequently deals with such complex concepts as democracy, socialization, acculturation, privilege, empathy, and culture. Social studies teachers who understand the nature of these difficult concepts will be more successful in teaching them than the educator with only superficial knowledge.

Concept Attributes

According to Kagan (1971), all concepts have four important qualities: degree of abstraction, complexity, differentiation, and centrality of dimensions. *Degree of abstraction* relates to the nature of the concept's characteristics. In labeling concepts as concrete or abstract, we are considering degree of abstraction. Concrete concepts can be pointed to or experienced directly by the senses: for example, house, garden, lamb, or automobile. Concepts that are abstract cannot be pointed to nor experienced directly, and are frequently defined by referring to other concepts; examples are nations, revolution, freedom, or integrity.

The next quality, *complexity*, relates to the number of attributes required for defining a concept. The more attributes necessary, the more complex the concept. The concept of "cow" is easily grasped. There are only a few attributes to evaluate—four-legged, hairy, warm-blooded, it moos—before visualizing the concept of cow.

A concept such as integrity is much more difficult, because it is defined by drawing on other concepts, such as concern for others, honesty, consistency of action, and conscious action. Each of these concepts has attributes of its own. The teacher must consider the complexity of concepts when planning social studies units, since the more complex the concept, the more difficult it will be for students to learn. All concepts, however, are learned through experience. When dealing with concrete concepts, students should have experiences that involve the senses. In teaching the concept "noise pollution," the teacher might plan a field trip or a simulation in which students can actually hear noise pollution. The concept of "texture" can be learned only by touching objects that have smooth or rough or slippery surfaces. Abstract concepts can be experienced when students have opportunities to discuss the concepts, demonstrating their understanding by employing symbols such as words and occasions.

Kagan's third quality of concepts is *differentiation*. As he notes, concepts vary in the degree to which their basic characteristics can assume differing, yet related, forms. For example, the concept of "hammer" is not finely differentiated. To most people (excluding, perhaps, carpenters) it takes one form, with no other words appropriate to describing different kinds of hammers. The concept of vegetable, however, is highly differentiated—we can speak of potatoes, onions, corn, radishes, beans, and beets. Kagan points out that highly differentiated concepts are usually central to the culture. In the United States, the concept of "marketplace" is expressed in shopping center, central business district, grocery store, banking center, and port. In the Eskimo culture, there are numerous words or concepts for various types of snow. For most Americans, snow is just snow. We have only one word.

The final quality shared by all concepts is *centrality of dimensions*. The meaning of some concepts derives from one or two key attributes. The meaning of the concept "professional athlete" rests with the attributes "plays for money" and "plays on a regular schedule." "Plays for enjoyment" is not critical, although it might be clustered among the attributes (Kagan, 1971).

Concepts are crucial to students' comprehension of social studies. Concepts help people identify and comprehend the multitude of objects in the world, and classify vast amounts of information. Learning concepts eliminates the necessity of relearning all social studies information continuously. Once an individual has learned the concept "mountain," she does not need to constantly reconsider specific attributes such as shape, altitude, and location. Because concepts allow people to organize information, they are then able to solve problems.

Activity 6:1

Concept Classification

Go to the school or university curriculum center and select two or three elementary social studies textbooks. Choose one unit in each and make a list of the concepts mentioned or emphasized. Classify the concepts as to their type—either abstract or concrete.

Note how the concepts are treated. Are they presented much like facts, or are there questions that encourage pupils to consider the concepts? Are pupils given examples of the concepts?

From your analysis of the textbook units, what general statements can you make regarding the treatment of concepts?

Generalizations

Facts support concepts, and concepts underpin generalizations—statements of relationships among two or more concepts. Generalizations, like facts, can be supported or refuted by observable evidence. For example, the concepts "individual" and "family" bring several questions to mind. What can one say about their relationships? First, individuals belong to family groups. Most students would have little difficulty comprehending this, and they can validate the statement through their own experiences.

Generalizations must consist of an "if–then" relationship (if this occurs, then this happens). Using the previous example of individuals and family, we could state, "If individuals belong to the same blood group, then they are members of a family." Another generalization is "The economy of a country or region is related to available resources, investment capital, and the educational development of its people." This can be adjusted to read, "*If* a country has adequate resources, sufficient investment capital, and sufficiently educated and skilled people, *then* it can engage in productive economic activity." Generalizations are usually not worded in the "if–then" format, but this format can be used to check the accuracy of the generalization and its level of general applicability.

Banks (1977) ranked generalizations according to their level of generalizability. High-order generalizations are those with universal scope. The previous generalization about the economy of a country is a high-order generalization. It applies to almost all countries. The scope of intermediate-order generalizations is more limited, but they still apply to wide areas or times or peoples. One might generalize about the interaction of the American economy, noting relationships applicable only to the United States, yet the entire nation is considered in the generalization. Low-order generalizations are situation- and often time-specific. The soil conditions and climate of the eastern part of Washington make ideal conditions for growing grapes. This generalization, while true for a region of Washington state, is not useful in studying eastern Idaho. These low-order generalizations are often called "descriptive" generalizations rather than "if–then" generalizations.

Using generalizations, tremendous amounts of information can be organized into concise statements. But generalizations, since they are propositional, are true only to the degree that evidence can be gathered to support them. Both teachers and learners may have to modify generalizations from time to time as new evidence raises questions about the validity of a statement. At one time, the generalization that the geographic area of a culture determined its nature was widely accepted. This was called *geographic determinism.* Using this generalization, one concluded that several peoples who lived in the extreme northern climate zone would have the same, or very

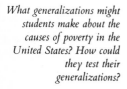

What generalizations might students make about the causes of poverty in the United States? How could they test their generalizations?

similar, cultures. But evidence disputed this generalization. Investigators found that the Laplanders in northern Scandinavia did not have the same culture as the Eskimos of North America. Neither did the Indians of Alaska have the same culture as the Eskimos, even though they frequently live in the same region. Thus the evidence called for modification of the accepted generalization.

The testability of the generalization is important. Armstrong (1980) notes that generalizations are "terse consolidations of 'truths' whose veracity is supported by the best information available at present." Students should learn that generalizations can be modified as new evidence appears. Also, students need to realize that these propositional statements can frequently be adjusted to address data about specific situations. The generalization from geography that a nation's resources and resource use are related to its level of cultural and technological development must be adjusted to describe the concepts as they relate to specific countries.

Using Generalizations to Plan Social Studies

Generalizations are aids to thinking and understanding. Whereas facts refer only to unique events, individuals, or situations, generalizations depict relationships referring to numerous examples. Generalizations thus represent ideas of varying power. High-order generalizations are more powerful than low-order generalizations. In planning which generalizations to include in a lesson, one must apply certain criteria to distinguish the more powerful ideas from the less powerful.

Fraenkel suggests some questions to use in determining the power of ideas:

1. To how many varied areas, events, people, ideas, and objectives does the generalization apply? (applicability)
2. How likely is it that the relationship the generalization suggests does indeed exist in actuality? (accuracy)
3. To what degree does the generalization as stated lead one to other insights? (depth)
4. To what extent does (do) the relationship(s) the generalization suggests describe important aspects of human behavior and explain segments of today's world? (significance)
5. How much information does it encompass? (breadth)
6. How many powerful (complex) concepts does it include? (conceptual strength) (p. 105)

From Jack R. Fraenkel, *Helping Students Think and Value: Strategies for Teaching the Social Studies*, © 1973, p. 105. Reprinted by permission of Prentice-Hall, Inc., Englewood Cliffs, N.J.

Applying these criteria to the generalization, "The culture in which one is raised affects the individual's attitude and beliefs," one can see that it is more powerful than the generalization, "In the United States, there are many supermarkets."

145

The planning of social studies curricula should start with identifying powerful generalizations, proceeding then to major concepts and then to supporting facts. Figure 6.1 indicates the relationships among levels of knowledge, the direction of curriculum planning, the directions of both inductive and deductive learning.

Figure 6.1
Levels of Knowledge,
Directions of
Curriculum Planning,
and Directions of
Learning

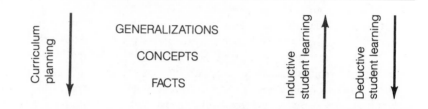

As suggested previously, effective social studies curricula are organized around generalizations or major concepts. The advantage of beginning planning with a generalization is that it will point to a specific, broadly applicable, learning outcome. For example, learning about the impact of culture on individual behavior can be transferred to the analysis of other cultures.

Selecting Generalizations

Where can we find good generalizations for planning social studies? One source is the Social Science Education Consortium, in Boulder, Colorado, which has monographs that contain many generalizations. Lists of generalizations can be found at the back of many social studies methods books. Of course, the teacher can create generalizations of her own; for example, observing and classifying the phenomena of Americans' social activities can lead to a propositional statement that notes the relationships among two or more concepts.

Figure 6.2 shows David Armstrong's matrix for selecting generalizations for social studies units.

Activity 6:2

Sample Planning

The diagram in fig. 6.1 shows how the teacher proceeds from generalizations to facts in planning social studies content.

Select two generalizations you think would be appropriate for students at the grade/age level at which you intend to teach. List the generalizations, then note two or three concepts you would include in teaching such generalizations. Select some supporting facts you think students would need to consider. Write them down under the headings Generalization; Concepts to Emphasize; and Supporting Facts.

Figure 6.2
Generalizations
Decision Matrix
(with sample data
checked)

Possible Generalizations that might be selected to guide instruction related to a given topic	Characteristics of Alternative Generalizations									
	Interest of Students		Concept Difficulty		Teacher's Background in Area		Availability of Learning Resources			
	Hi	Lo	Hi	Lo	Substantial	Minimal	Textbook Only	Textbook Library	Audio Visual Media	Other
Generalization 1	X		X		X				X	X
Generalization 2	X			X		X	X			
Generalization 3		X	X			X	X			
Generalization 4		X	X		X		X			
Generalization 5	X			X	X			X		X
Generalization 6	X		X		X			X	X	
Generalization 7	X			X	X			X	X	X
Generalization 8	X			X		X		X	X	
Generalization 9		X	X			X	X			
Generalization 10		X		X	X			X	X	X
Generalization 11	X		X		X			X	X	X
Generalization 12		X		X	X			X	X	

Reprinted with permission of Macmillan Publishing Co., Inc. from *Social Studies in Secondary School*, by David G. Armstrong. Copyright © 1980 by David G. Armstrong.

Activity 6:3

Material Orientation

Selecting from two social studies series either in the curriculum materials library or in use in a local school district, examine a primary and an intermediate textbook and identify the number of concepts introduced per chapter. What generalizations are developed or taught drawing on these concepts? What is your opinion regarding the conceptual load of these materials? What other generalizations might also be introduced using the concepts stressed in these materials?

Theory

Theory is the main goal of scholarly inquiry. In the social sciences, theory is used to describe, explain, and predict human behavior. It also guides human behavior and directs further inquiry. Most scholars describe theory as a set of interrelated, law-like propositions or high-level, testable generalizations. These propositions must (1) show clearly the relationship between variables or concepts; (2) constitute a deductive system that is logically consistent; and (3) trigger additional testable hypotheses. The following two descriptions of theory are useful.

> In its simplest form, a theory is a symbolic construction designed to bring generalizable facts (or laws) into systematic connection. It consists of (a) a set of units (facts, concepts, variables) and (b) a system of relationships among the units.
> **(Snow, 1973)**

> A theory may be defined as an integrated body of definitions, assumptions, and general propositions covering a given subject matter from which a comprehensive and consistent set of specific and testable hypotheses can be deduced logically.
> **(Rose, 1953)**

Fraenkel (1973) furnishes criteria for ranking the power of theory:

1. How many propositions are interrelated? (breadth)
2. How complex are the propositions that are interrelated? (complexity)
3. To how many varied areas, events, people, ideas, or objectives does the theory apply? (applicability)
4. To what extent do the relationships suggested by the interrelated propositions contained within the theory describe and explain important elements of human behavior and explain important segments of today's world? (explanatory power)
5. To what extent does the theory lead to other insights? (depth)
6. How many powerful (i.e., complex) concepts as opposed to facts does the theory include? (conceptual strength)
7. How testable are the hypotheses that can be derived from the propositions interrelated within the theory? (testability)

From Jack R. Fraenkel, *Helping Students Think and Value: Strategies for the Social Studies*, © 1973, p. 106. Reprinted by permission of Prentice-Hall, Inc., Englewood Cliffs, N.J.

Organizational Designs for Social Studies Content

In addition to understanding the content of social studies, teachers must also be aware of the numerous ways to design or organize social studies curricula. Curriculum design deals with the elements of the curriculum (objectives, content, experiences, environments, resource materials, and personnel) and the manner in which these variables are organized for student learning. Figure 6.3 shows that curriculum designs have two basic structures—horizontal and vertical. Horizontal organization involves the concepts of scope and integration; vertical organization is concerned with sequence and continuity. (Hunkins, 1980).

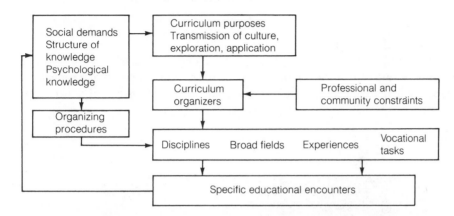

Figure 6.3
Conception of
Curriculum Design

From Francis P. Hunkins, *Curriculum Development: Program Improvement,* p. 224. Reprinted by permission.

Subject-Centered Designs

Separate Subject
This is the oldest curriculum design available to a teacher of social studies. When school subjects follow this design, their content is arranged so that it represents a specialized and common area. Subjects are chronologically organized, with (1) prerequisite learnings carefully noted; (2) stress on whole-to-part mastery; and (3) deductive learning. With this design, the teacher is the major classroom performer and students take a passive role, memorizing information and demonstrating mastery through tests or through immediate application.

Elementary social studies teachers frequently opt for this design, arguing that it allows children to learn essential cultural elements. They are also comfortable with this design because adequate materials, primarily textbooks, are readily available.

Teachers who select this format should realize the danger of presenting information in a nonintegrated manner. Learning tends to be compartmentalized, with excessive emphasis on mnemonic skills. Additionally, subjects tend to be detached from the students' real world.

Discipline Design
The discipline design is an extension of the separate-subject design, but it involves students in processing information. Students are taught the methods unique to each discipline. Teachers who use this design draw on the basic structures of each social science discipline.

149

This curriculum design still presents the risk that, if poorly organized or taught, the students' conceptualization will be fragmented. Teachers can avoid this fragmentation, however, if they relate the disciplined knowledge to other realms of knowledge and student experiences. Many teachers find this curriculum design easy to use since, as with the separate-subject design, commercial materials frequently reflect this organization.

Correlation Design

With the correlation or multidisciplinary design, similar content topics or subjects are scheduled for simultaneous study while their separate identities are still maintained. Students might study both the history of a particular

Knowing how to design and organize a social studies curriculum is as important as understanding social studies content.

country and its literature, but the identity and integrity of each discipline remains separate. A specialist may teach each discipline. Such cooperative teaching might occur when a teacher wishes to correlate art with a unit on anthropology. In this case, the social studies teacher presents the anthropology section and the art teacher the art lesson.

Because separate subjects or disciplines are being taught, there is still the chance of fragmentation, but an awareness of this possibility can help the teacher prevent it.

Broad Fields Design

The broad fields or fused interdisciplinary design goes a step beyond the correlated design. Logically related subjects are clustered together, often around some shared organizer. This organization overcomes the compartmentalization of subjects and gives students a sense of unity. The content (generalization, concepts, and supporting facts) draws from more than one discipline, with the result that the identity of the discipline becomes secondary to the topic organizer itself.

By its very nature, social studies *is* a broad fields design, since it includes history, geography, sociology, economics, anthropology, and political science, as well as other content areas related to the study of humanity. Figure 6.4 illustrates this structure.

MULTIDISCIPLINARY DESIGN

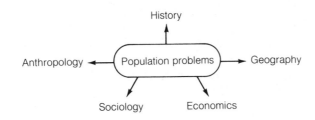

Figure 6.4
Broad Fields Design

INTERDISCIPLINARY DESIGN

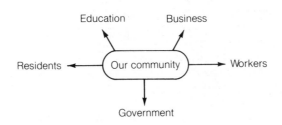

151

Grouping subjects into a single field points up the interrelationship of content and enables students to relate school subjects to their daily world. The broad fields design has the advantage of presenting the essentials of a culture in an orderly and systematic manner, and allows integrating related content into meaningful clusters so that students will perceive knowledge as a meaningful unity.

When organizing social studies content, most teachers will have some units that are discipline oriented, some that are multidisciplinary, and some that are interdisciplinary. The value of knowing the various subject matter designs is that you can take advantage of options and match designs to the topic at hand, taking into account student needs and interests, and the demands and expectations of the local community.

Learner-Centered Design

As you might assume, the learner-centered design emphasizes the learner. With this design, the teacher gives primary attention to the individual's development, needs, interests, and reasons for attending to the particular subject. Taba (1962) furnishes a well-stated rationale for this design:

> People learn what they experience. Only learning which is related to active purpose and is rooted in experience translates itself into behavior changes. Children learn best those things that are attached to solving actual problems, that help them in meeting real needs that connect with some active interest. Learning in its true sense is an active transaction. (p. 404)

Since this design is relevant to the students' worlds, it permits them to be active learners. All curriculum designs have deficiencies, however, and for the learner-centered design, there is the possibility that students' interests and

---

Activity 6:4

Design Identification

If you are student teaching, obtain a copy of the social studies curriculum guide used in your school and identify the type of curriculum design suggested. Refer to the discussion on designs in this textbook to help you in your identification. If no curriculum guide exists, ask to see the lesson plans of the supervising teacher. You may also ask your supervising teacher to tell you which design is used.

Whether you have studied the curriculum guide or discussed the design with your supervising teacher, determine the rationale for the design in use.

If you are not student teaching, analyze a curriculum guide in some educational material or curriculum in your college or university library.

expressed needs may not be valid or lasting. Student interests may not reflect the knowledge they will need to function successfully in the general society. Also, students from particular environments may be inadequately prepared to discern their own needs and interests. Educators should realize that part of their responsibility is to create needs as well as to respond to them. A more practical limitation of the design is that few commercial materials are produced with this focus. Furthermore, if individuals *are* totally idiosyncratic, then no curriculum can be created or a design selected before students arrive. Upon their appearance, the teacher will have to plan and supply unique curricular experiences for each individual.

In the reality of the elementary school, teachers will use aspects of each curriculum design in attempting to make social studies interesting for their students. Readers of this text are encouraged to be creative in selecting and organizing various design options.

Understanding the dimensions of knowledge and the major types of curriculum design furnishes essential information for planning social studies. The effective social studies teacher also brings to the decision-making task an understanding of supplemental disciplines and of the relationships among the various types of information.

This foundation furnishes information for the decision making we will discuss in the next chapter.

Discussion

Content can be arranged according to facts, concepts, generalizations, or theories. Facts represent verifiable data; they are restricted to a time, person, or event, and have little transfer value. Their importance is in relationship to and support of concepts, generalizations, and theories.

Concepts do not rely on evidence; they are definitions to be used as building blocks to create more knowledge, usually at the level of generalizations. Concepts refer to classes or clusters of objects, events, or individuals that share something in common. Concepts are attempts to organize experience, and can be categorized according to their degree of abstractness or concreteness. They can also be classified as either conjunctive or disjunctive; Fraenkel identifies a third classification, that of the connotative, by which concepts are defined by reference to other concepts. Still another classification for concepts is that of the relational. All concepts share the qualities of (1) degree of abstraction, (2) complexity, (3) differentiation, and (4) centrality of dimensions. Concepts help classify information, which contributes to the ability to solve problems.

Generalizations state the relationships among two or more concepts, and express an "if–then" relationship. They may be regarded as high-order, with universal application, intermediate-order, with broad application, or low-order, with only specific application. Low-order generalizations are often of the "descriptive" rather than the "if–then" type. Since generalizations represent propositions, they are true only to the degree of their supporting evidence, and must often be modified as new evidence appears.

Because generalizations express relationships among many examples, they contribute to organizing thought, and are basic to the planning of social studies curricula. The social studies planner would begin by identifying high-order generalizations, break those down into their major concepts, and then break the concepts down into their supporting facts. Beginning with generalizations and moving to facts provides a basis for deductive learning. The opposite is true for inductive learning.

Theory is the goal of inquiry; the social sciences use theory to describe, explain, and predict human behavior. Theories are considered to be sets of interrelated and testable generalizations.

These four vehicles for organizing knowledge—facts, concepts, generalizations, and theories—are important for the teacher to understand when she designs a social studies curriculum. Curriculum design follows either a horizontal (scope and integration) or vertical (sequence and continuity) structure, and includes the elements of objectives, content, experiences, environments, resource materials, and personnel. Curriculum designs are either subject-centered or learner-centered. Subject-centered designs are the separate subject design, the discipline design, the correlation or multidisciplinary design, and the broad fields or interdisciplinary design. The learner-centered design relies heavily on the student's expressed interests and identified needs, and on intensive individualization. The creative social studies teacher will ultimately use elements of all the curriculum designs.

References

Armstrong, David G. *Social Studies in Secondary School.* New York: Macmillan Publishing Co., 1980.

Banks, James A. *Teaching Strategies for the Social Studies.* Reading, Mass.: Addison-Wesley, 1977.

Bruner, Jerome S. *A Study of Thinking.* New York: John Wiley & Sons, 1956.

Fraenkel, Jack R. *Helping Students Think and Value: Strategies for Teaching Social Studies.* Englewood Cliffs, N. J.: Prentice-Hall, Inc., 1973.

Hunkins, Francis P. *Curriculum Development: Program Improvement.* Columbus, Oh.: Charles E. Merrill, 1980.

Kagan, Jerome. *Understanding Children: Behavior, Motives, and Thought.* New York: Harcourt Brace Jovanovich, 1971.

Rose, Arnold M. "Generalizations in the Social Sciences." *American Journal of Sociology* 59 (1953).

Snow, Richard E. "Theory Construction for Research on Teaching." In *Second Handbook of Research on Teaching,* edited by Robert M. W. Travers. Chicago: Rand McNally, 1973.

Taba, Hilda. *Curriculum Development, Theory and Practice.* New York: Harcourt, Brace & World, 1962.

Wilson, John. *Language and the Pursuit of Truth.* Cambridge: Cambridge University Press, 1967.

Decision Making
in Planning
Social Studies

7

Planning As Decision Making

Teaching involves both decision making and action that will stimulate student learning. When certain decisions and actions occur prior to the actual class period, planning is taking place. When decisions and actions occur while students are present, instruction is taking place. Actions and decisions that follow student involvement are classified as evaluation. This chapter focuses on the decision making and actions necessary for planning social studies. We will discuss the decision making and actions required in instruction in chapter 8, and chapter 14 will deal with evaluation.

Shavelson and Borko (1979) show, in figure 7.1, the factors that affect decisions in planning. The model suggests questions that need to be asked

Figure 7.1
Factors in Planning
Decisions

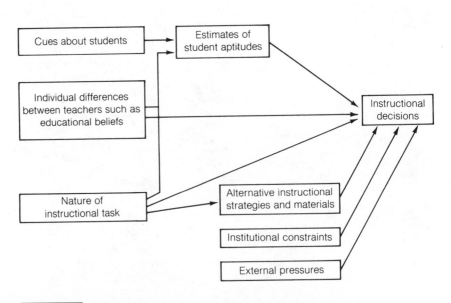

From Richard J. Shavelson and H. Borko, "Research on Teachers' Decisions in Planning Instruction," *Educational Horizons* 57 (1979): 183–189. Reprinted by permission.

during this planning process: What information is available for making decisions? What instructional strategies and materials might be appropriate? How do institutional constraints, external pressures, and individual differences affect these decisions?

In studying the model, one can see that cues about students gained from standardized tests, reports from past teachers, observations, and knowledge of individual learning styles affect instructional decisions. Individual differences among teachers and the nature of instructional tasks and content also affect planning. Finally, decisions may be influenced by outside factors such as the school's and school district's policies, the materials available, and the demands of society.

This model shows clearly that planning is a complicated process. To do it all alone would be overwhelming. But few teachers have to work independently in making decisions about their social studies programs. Most of the time, teachers can get assistance from numerous agencies and organizations at the national, state, and local levels. They frequently work in teams. Whether working alone or with others, however, teachers must realize the central position they occupy in curriculum decisions making. It is they who ultimately decide what aspects of the curriculum will be implemented in their social studies classes.

Planning Instruction

Planning includes more than arbitrary decisions about "what I'm going to teach today." And while thorough planning will not by itself ensure successful student learning, it does increase the likelihood of success. The teacher must consider three levels of planning: first, the resource unit—an overall plan for extended periods of time and for a general group of pupils; second, the teaching unit—a more detailed plan for a shorter period of time, usually one or two weeks, created for a specific group of students; and, third, the lesson plan—a plan for a brief period of time, usually two to five days, developed for a particular class. Each level has the same major components: objectives, suggested content, materials, and instructional methods. The teacher may sometimes plan for arranging the classroom environment as well.

Essentially, the resource unit is created for a hypothetical group of students. The teacher selects objectives and content appropriate for a general group of pupils. This part of the plan contains more instructional possibilities than can possibly be used with any particular class.

Then, drawing ideas from the resource unit, the teacher creates a teaching unit, in which he lists objectives, content, materials, and instructional methods appropriate for the specific class. From this teaching unit, the teacher selects objectives and content for a specific lesson. Figure 7.2 shows the relationship among the three types of plans.

157

CHAPTER 7
Decision Making in
Planning Social
Studies
Figure 7.2
Relationships in
Planning

Resource Unit (General, long-range for potential pupils)

Teaching Unit (Specific, mid-range for specific pupils)

Lesson Plan (Specific, immediate time, for particular class)

Developing the Teaching Unit

A well-developed teaching unit* contains:

1. A rationale
2. Major generalizations
3. Goals
4. Objectives
5. Content to be taught
6. Instructional strategies
7. Educational activities
8. Suggestions for suitable learning environments
9. Support materials and personnel required
10. Means of evaluation

Teaching units are usually influenced by three factors: (1) the overall curriculum prepared by the state department of education; (2) the curriculum resource unit; and (3) the series of adopted textbooks (Hunkins, 1980).

Developing any type of unit requires several major steps: conceptualizing, diagnosing, selecting and organizing content, and selecting and organizing experiences. These steps are followed by implementing (teaching) the unit, evaluating its effectiveness, and developing the means to continue its use over time.

Step 1: Conceptualization

Conceptualizing involves identifying the reasons why studying the subject is important to students. During this stage, the teacher notes his view of social studies, their importance in the curriculum, and the student audience for

---

*What is said regarding the teaching unit also applies to the resource unit. The units and their preparation differ in degree, not in kind.

which the unit is intended. While teachers usually have little choice about who will be in their classes, the effective instructor will learn as much as possible about those class members so that the instruction he selects will be as meaningful as possible. Insight comes from knowing students' levels of physical development, their achievement levels, their emotional and social development, their intellectual and creative potentials, and their individual differences. Information about community and home and family life is also useful. To obtain such information, educators may do a "needs analysis" focusing on the students' levels of knowledge, skills, and attitudes. This stage need not be time-consuming; a few simple diagnostic procedures can provide enough information to create profiles of pupils' competencies, interests, and backgrounds. Additional data can come from teacher-made diagnostic tests, anecdotal records, interest inventories, checklists of students behaviors, and teacher–student conferences.

Step 2: Diagnosis

Social studies instruction concerns the attainment of multiple objectives. The objectives address facts, concepts, generalizations, principles, and theories derived from the foundations of the social sciences and from incidental knowledge. Objectives also relate to the skills and attitudes we wish students to acquire. Our decisions about objectives are probably the most important we make, for they furnish the bases for systematically and purposefully choosing content, learning activities, instructional strategies, and instructional materials, as well as identifying standards of performance.

As we saw in chapter 1, social studies emphasize several types of objectives: cognitive, affective, and process.

Considering Open and Closed Objectives
There has been much debate over the appropriateness of objectives. Some educators argue that objectives, when stated precisely, are more appropriate for training activities than for educational activities. Nonetheless, there are certain objectives we wish all students to attain at certain levels. These guiding statements are closed and prescriptive. Two examples of these objectives are:

> *Given a wall map of the United States, pupils will, in a five-minute period, locate the state capitals with 90% accuracy.*

> *Given a globe of the earth, pupils will accurately, in a five-minute period, compute air mileage between Atlanta, Georgia, and London, England.*

In contrast, open objectives are descriptive, divergent, and can vary as to content, experiences, behaviors, and the criteria applied. They are suitable

159

to the social studies because they allow us to individualize or personalize the experience. Open objectives provide structure but are not limiting. Two examples of open objectives are:

Students will state at least two reasons why they believe concern should be shown for all cultural groups.

Students will explain why they believe a campaign against litter should be started at their school.

We need both open and closed objectives in the social studies.

Considering Elements of Objectives

All objectives, whether open or closed, or general or specific, include the same components:

"Given a wall map of the United States, students will, in a five-minute period, locate the state capitals with 90% accuracy."

1. The behavior the student will demonstrate (stated or implied).
2. The conditions under which the student behavior is to occur (stated or implied).
3. The type of behavior that will be accepted by the teacher (stated or implied).

The behavior frequently is stated in the form of an action verb, which many educators consider the objective's crucial dimension. Examples of action verbs that occur in stating objectives are: predict, write, outline, name, define, identify, label, list, state, specify, describe, group, classify, match, arrange, distinguish, discriminate among, summarize, draw, make, formulate, and diagram. How specific to make these action words depends upon the teacher's general purpose. The following paradigm may prove useful.

General Purpose of Unit	Objective Suggested	Degree of Specificity Needed	Objective Statement
Questions relating to what you want to do.	Ideas for objectives. Directions to go with the lesson.	Question(s) as to whether objective needs to be open or closed.	The final polished statement of the objective.

The second component, the statement of the conditions under which the student will perform the behavior, notes environmental factors or constraints that exist in the classroom. These are some sample statements that address this condition:

With the aid of an encyclopedia . . .
When given the names of the states . . .
Using a map . . .
From memory . . .
With the aid of an atlas . . .

The third element common to all objectives is the definition of acceptable performance. Examples are:

. . . identify five out of eight . . .
. . . within five minutes, with no more than two errors . . .
. . . with 90 percent accuracy . . .

Activity 7:1

Creating Objectives

Select a social studies unit topic for a particular grade and state two or three open and closed objectives for the unit.

The teacher can easily manipulate the level of detail and specificity of these components. An open objective might call for a pupil to make hypotheses relating to population distribution and imply that a standard for meeting the objective will be supplied. Conditions may also be implied.

The final decision to make about objectives is to determine their appropriateness. Can students learn them? Can you meet the objectives with your teaching skills? Do you have sufficient time to deal with them? Are the necessary support materials available, or can they be obtained? Are the objectives worthwhile in light of the unit's rationale?

These sample objectives are from a unit dealing with the forest products industry:

Students will identify selected trees from leaves, cones, branches, and wood supplies.

Students will explain the processes involved in logging in the Pacific Northwest before 1900.

Students will contrast modern logging methods with those used in the nineteenth century.

Students will summarize the contributions lumbering makes to the Puget Sound economy.

Students will explain the reason(s) for tree farming (Pasco Public Schools, 1975).

The feasibility of an objective depends, in part, on available resources and materials

Note the action words of the objectives. Since these are general, open-ended objectives, the exact conditions under which they will be accomplished and the standard of acceptable performance have been left open. These details will be specified when the teacher incorporates the unit objectives into a lesson plan. How would you make these objectives more specific?

As we noted earlier, objectives can address both the cognitive and affective domains, and can focus on content, processes, skills, and attitudes. Consider these illustrations of each kind of objective.

Content Objective: The student will specify *(behavior)* at least three characteristics *(level of performance)* of a mountain by analyzing photographs and topographic maps showing mountainous regions *(conditions)*.

Process Objective: The student will summarize *(behavior)* the information on energy resources and furnish three generalizations *(level of performance)* that are warranted. (The conditions are implied to be from processing classroom materials.)

Skills Objective: Using materials found in the library *(conditions)*, the student will draw *(behavior)* a graph showing the cost of various sources of energy. (In this objective, the level of performance is left open.)

Affective Objective: The student will describe *(behavior)* his feelings after listening to a speech by a conservation advocate *(condition)*. (Here the level of performance has been left open.)

Step 3: Selecting and Organizing Content

As we saw in chapter 6, content refers to the facts, concepts, generalizations, and theories included in the social studies curriculum. It also refers to the processes employed to generate content. You recall that a number of social sciences contribute subject matter to the elementary social studies program. The humanities and interdisciplinary fields such as environmental, law-related, and human relations education also furnish content.

Many current social studies programs are organized around "big ideas" drawn from the various social sciences and related disciplines. These big ideas, or generalizations and concepts, provide the program's foci. Teachers get these "organizers" from master lists of generalizations frequently found in resource units or in books that deal with the social sciences.

Knowing what criteria to use in selecting content will facilitate this specialized decision making. The following list will prove useful:

■ *Significance:* The importance of the content to be learned is the first criterion. Content is significant only to the degree to which it contributes to basic ideas, concepts, principles, generalizations, etc. Significance also pertains to how the content contributes to development of particular learning

163

abilities, skills, processes, and attitudes. Finally, it relates to the degree to which content will last over time. Significant content will have not only contemporary relevance but will also be of value and interest to students in the future.

- *Validity:* This refers to the authenticity of the content. We apply it when we are selecting content, and we must also question it at regular intervals throughout the program. Validity also pertains to whether the content we select is sound in relation to a unit's objectives. If an objective states that students will learn the relationships between one's cultural approaches to life and the potential in one's environment, then the teacher has to be sure the content will enable pupils to perceive this relationship.

- *Interest:* Social studies should not only address students' interests, it should also create interest. When dealing with this criterion, the teacher can address these questions: Is the content potentially interesting to students? Are students' current interests of long-lasting educational value? Will this content expand the range of students' concerns? In attending to this criterion, we need to allow for students' maturity, their level of schooling, their prior experiences, and the educational and social value of their interests.

- *Utility:* This refers to content usefulness. Pupils frequently want to know why they should learn certain information. They are impatient to use the information, skills, or processes learned in class. In some cases, content can be applied immediately in reading, in map interpretation, in cooperative games, or in group investigations. Other content is useful in furnishing pupils with foundations for later learnings; this kind of content is usually difficult for students to appreciate.

- *Learnability:* The content we select should be learnable. Although this may seem to state the obvious, educators are coming to realize that students have various learning styles that make some content and its organization more difficult to learn than others. Some students are "field dependent," and approach learning somewhat holistically—that is, they find content that stresses isolated parts and the analysis and recombination of such parts difficult to learn. Also, they experience difficulty in isolating key concepts for analysis. When we consider learnability, we are asking ourselves if the unit material is appropriate for our intended student audience.

- *Feasibility:* This criterion asks: "Can the selected content be taught in the time allowed, with the resources available, with the expertise of the current staff, with the political climate present in the community, with the current legislation, and with the amount of monies allocated for the program?" (Hunkins, 1980)

Steps in Selecting Content

Armed with the previous criteria, we can select content for our units by proceeding through the following decision-making steps:

1. Consider the available content.
2. Select which content and topics to cover.
3. Determine the scope and sequence of the content.

Activity 7:2

Utilizing Content Selection Criteria

Obtain a teaching unit for a particular elementary grade and, applying the content selection criteria presented in this chapter, critique the content included. If the content in the unit does not meet a particular criterion, indicate what you would do to correct the content deficiency.

In step one, we acquaint ourselves with the content available on the topic we plan to teach. We become familiar with the key ideas, we read the various lists of generalizations, and we formulate ideas by reading state curriculum guides for social studies.

In step two, we choose from the available content the major generalizations applicable to our objectives, keeping our student audience in mind. The generalizations suggest both explicitly and implicitly the key concepts and topics we will cover.

Once we have specified our topics, we ask ourselves, in step three, how much detail will we give to each (scope) and when will we teach each one (sequence).

Following these steps, we might create a data sheet similar to this one about Egypt.

Egypt: Ancient Land in Modern Times

Central Generalizations from the Disciplines

Human societies have undergone and are undergoing continual though perhaps gradual changes in responses to various forces. *(history)*

Guidelines for understanding thought and action in contemporary affairs can be derived from the society's historical backgrounds. *(history)*

Places on the earth have distinctions about them that differentiate them from all other places. *(geography)*

The art, music, architecture, food, clothing, sports, and customs of a people help to produce a national identity. *(anthropology)*

Specific Ideas for Unit Attention

Since ancient times, agriculture has been a main activity in Egypt.

The Nile River has influenced the culture of Egypt since ancient times.

The Egyptians presently are trying to bring more industrialization to their country.

165

Concepts Upon Which to Focus

Society, change, contemporary affairs, place, region, customs, culture

Scope and Sequence of Content

Topic 1:   Egypt, its location

Topic 2:   The Nile, Past and Present

Topic 3:   Agriculture in Egypt
Past agriculture
Present agriculture

This data sheet shows the major content to include in a teaching unit. Skilled teachers use such a list to guide their final selection and organization of content. From these specific ideas and topics, related facts and concepts are detailed. For instance, the statement that Egyptians are presently trying to industrialize their country can trigger the following related statements, directed primarily at topic 3, Egypt's present-day agriculture:

The Egyptians are working cooperatively to modernize agriculture.

Modern technological machinery, such as electric and diesel pumps, is helping to irrigate fields more effectively.

New types of fertilizer and seeds are being used in current Egyptian agriculture.

Egyptians are cooperating to form a more modern society. Other nations are assisting Egypt in modernizing its agricultural effort.

Step 4: Selecting and Organizing Experiences

Answering the question "What content shall I teach?" leads to the next: "How shall I teach what I have chosen?" Often only the latter question arises, since content is provided in the resource guide, teaching unit, or textbook supplied for the class.

Whether we ask the question of "how" after or during content selection, we cannot ignore this step in planning. Our response will depend on our view of social studies. If we believe social studies to be primarily the transmission of knowledge to rather passive learners, then we will specify experiences that emphasize student listening, memorizing, and writing. If we consider social studies as an opportunity for students to think as social scientists and to become increasingly aware of their world, then we will designate experiences that foster active participation. Teachers who emphasize active student learning create situations that allow pupils to gain skills in information-processing procedures. Some teachers who accept this goal fall short in attaining it. They may have students read geography books, but supply few opportunities to compile data as a geographer would. They may have pupils study occupations without the associated sights and sounds of real jobs. Students frequently study history without using primary source materials. To facilitate student involvement, the lessons must give students both direct and vicarious experiences: for example, they must learn to use reference tools, gather and interpret data, conduct interviews, compare different points of view, make surveys, role play, work on community projects, participate in field trips, take part in games and simulations, brainstorm, and conduct case studies.

Social studies experiences include both teaching methods and educational activities. Teaching methods refer to specific teacher actions (often verbal) that are aimed at causing students to learn. Examples of teaching methods are lecture, exposition, demonstration, discussion, and inquiry. There are various ways to approach each of these methods, which we will discuss in chapter 8. Educational activities are happenings in which students interact with people and materials. The teacher may not need to be present or, if present, need not specifically direct the students. Examples of educational activities common in social studies are taking field trips, listening to audio tapes, reading books, doing independent investigations, watching films, and making maps.

Because so many variables characterize any given social studies classroom, decisions as to methods and activities are quite complex. Every teacher has unique personal strengths, abilities, and experiences to rely on; on the other hand, each pupil brings different likes, interests, values, abilities, experiences, and needs to the classroom. These differences will provide an equal number of varying responses to you and your lesson. It is thus essential to consider student variables carefully when making decisions about teaching methods and educational activities.

Unit plan experiences and methods can be determined only by reviewing your previous decisions regarding the student audience, the goals of the program, the major objectives, and the specific content. You will want to consider the following guidelines in choosing activities and methods; are they:

1. Valid?
2. Feasible from the standpoint of staff expertise, time, and resources?
3. Such that they will foster development of students' cognitive, affective, and psychomotor domains?
4. Such that students will encounter various types of instructional materials?
5. Such that they contribute to multiple learnings?
6. Stimulating, so that students' interests will be broadened?
7. Relevant?
8. Meaningful?

Many of these questions are similar to those you must ask when selecting content. Asking whether the activity or method is valid relates to whether or not it will allow students to achieve the stated objective; the other guidelines are self explanatory.

After deciding on methods and activities, the teacher must select appropriate materials. Chapter 12 deals with materials and support technology in greater detail, but a few comments are appropriate here. Certainly, teachers need to use more than books in their lessons. Pupils should have opportunities to use primary source materials, such as documents and newspaper articles. Teachers should select films, videotapes, filmstrips, maps, charts, photographs, records, and bulletin boards. The surrounding community can even be considered course material.

Teachers are usually thinking of materials while selecting content and experiences. In fact, many instructional strategies depend on the availability of appropriate materials. In planning, skillful teachers note which specific materials will or can be employed in the unit. Merely to indicate in a unit on agriculture that newspaper clippings will be used is too general. If particular clippings have not been gathered, the lesson will have to stop until they are obtained. This breaks the flow of learning.

Reading and browsing in a variety of books on a certain topic is a good warm-up activity when beginning a new study unit.

Teachers should seek variety in materials. As we have noted, students vary greatly in their capacity to profit from individual materials: not all read at the same level of accomplishment; some learn more effectively from listening; others are more visually oriented. The materials should allow for these differences, thus providing opportunities for every student to experience some success (Armstrong, 1980).

Arranging Our Plans

Decisions about objectives, generalizations, key ideas, topics, teaching methods, and educational activities result in a teaching unit. Most teachers begin to organize the unit plan on paper as they proceed through these stages. By then, the instructor is really polishing the organization, or layout, of the unit.

A variety of formats are appropriate for unit plans, but most share three common elements: some type of overview, a statement of objectives, and an activities section. (You will find sample pages of unit plans later in this chapter.) The body of the unit is usually divided into warm-up, developmental, and concluding activities.

Warm-up activities should trigger student interest and set the stage for the teaching unit. At the same time they arouse curiosity, they can also relate the topic to what students already know and to the outside world. The teacher can also use warm-up activities to assess children's knowledge of a topic.

Creative teachers look continuously for motivating ways to introduce units so that pupils become acquainted with the unit's general scope and major emphasis. The following warm-up activities have been used with good results in many classrooms:

- Showing a film, filmstrip, pictures, maps, or objects, followed by a discussion.
- Posing a question or problem for the group to solve.
- Asking children to react to the topic.
- Asking children what they would do if they found themselves in a particular situation.
- Arranging a bulletin board with maps, charts, graphs, or pictures that relate to the topic.
- Having children spend time in the library acquiring general background information on the topic.
- Having children start a display table of relevant artifacts.
- Doing a dramatic presentation, perhaps inviting students from other classes to participate.
- Having a general "rap" session on the topic.
- Having children read the introductory section of their textbooks, noting questions or reactions.

The major portion of a unit consists of *developmental activities* geared to its various topics. Working through these activities may take a few days or several weeks. As general guideline, a teaching unit at the primary level should not last more than three weeks; at the intermediate level, not more than six weeks; and at the middle-school level, not more than ten weeks.

During this developmental stage, students encounter the content, think about it, ask questions, formulate procedures for investigation, process information, experiment, and use materials pertinent to the unit's objectives. Teaching methods and management techniques should be geared to the activities being carried out.

Developmental activities can be divided in several ways. *Research activities* require students to read, write, conduct interviews, take notes, code data, use references, write reports, and conduct experiments. *Presentation activities* involve class members in announcing, describing, reporting, demonstrating, pantomiming, or relating events. *Production experiences* find pupils drawing, sketching, modeling, illustrating, painting, constructing, writing, dramatizing, and role playing. Not only are the end products important, but the experiences through which the products are created are of vital interest.

Activities can also be clustered under such categories as appreciating, observing, listening, experimenting, organizing, and evaluating. Each of these groupings subsumes other supporting actions, such as questioning, assisting others, recording data, collecting, planning, outlining, summarizing, and conducting meetings. These are some time-tested developmental activities:

- Asking questions to assist students in solving problems.
- Collecting books, pictures and other materials necessary for particular investigations.
- Planning a field trip to a place under study.
- Formulating rules and procedures for working in groups.
- Building card files on topics to be investigated.
- Reading textbooks, reference books, and other written materials.
- Listening to reports and stories by the teacher or other students.
- Viewing films, slides, and filmstrips.
- Observing demonstrations, experiments, and people at work.
- Having a resource person visit the class.
- Studying maps, globe, and charts.
- Conducting interviews with resource persons in the community.
- Classifying information discovered in investigations.
- Conducting panel discussions.
- Engaging in simulations.
- Constructing models of settlements or of objects being investigated.
- Drawing or painting pictures.
- Arranging bulletin boards.

Add some of your own activities to this list, then categorize them by type, as to research, presentation, or production activity.

Culminating or wrap-up activities conclude the unit. Their purpose is to help students synthesize and summarize the values, attitudes, and understandings they have acquired during the unit study. They allow students to share experiences and information, to summarize content, and to relate what they have learned to topics studied in other units. Skillful teachers often use these activities as transitions into other units, or as stimuli for getting pupils to raise additional questions for investigation.

These wrap-up activities can also be used to evaluate children's levels of understanding skills, but they must consist of more than taking teacher-made tests or completing worksheets. Carefully planned culminating activities are closely related to, and flow out of, the developmental activities; for example:

- Making a document highlighting the aspects of the unit that pupils consider important (the document can be a newspaper, a movie, or slide-tape presentation).
- Taking students on a field trip to check out tentative conclusions reached earlier in the unit.
- Inviting a guest speaker to summarize major points of the unit and to suggest new directions for inquiry.
- Having students make a scrapbook.
- Having pupils work in the community. (For unit on community pride, students might work on a community park.)
- Engaging students in a group discussion to summarize the points of the unit study.
- Having pupils complete unfinished stories.
- Having a happening: a play, a party, an art show, a debate, a round-table discussion, a mock town meeting. Perhaps invite another class to participate.
- Having pupils formulate major generalizations to discuss and include in a student notebook.
- Having pupils take a teacher-made or pupil-made test.

Never shortchange the wrap-up activities. How a teacher concludes a unit is truly important, for it can leave students with a strong impression. If the end of a unit finds them merely filling in facts on a worksheet, their final impression may be that the unit was only "a bunch of things to remember for a test." The time spent planning the wrap-up is as important an investment as that put into the introduction and development of the unit. Michaelis (1972) presents a list of useful questions to ask when planning culminating activities:

- Will the culminating activity help to clarify relationships among main ideas or problems?
- Will it contribute to children's ability to organize and share information around basic concepts and generalizations?
- Will it provide for a review of fundamental learnings and contribute to evaluation of objectives set for the unit?
- Will it provide additional learning opportunities for each child? (p. 102)

From John U. Michaelis, SOCIAL STUDIES FOR CHILDREN IN A DEMOCRACY: Recent Trends and Developments, 5th ed., © 1972, p. 102. Reprinted by permission of Prentice-Hall, Inc., Englewood Cliffs, N.J.

Activity 7:3

Analyzing Unit Activities

Obtain another teaching unit or the same one used in activity 7:2 on page 165 and classify the types of activities incorporated. Critique these activities using criteria presented in this chapter or your own criteria. What general impression do you get regarding the activities in the particular unit critiqued?

Unit Back Matter

Some teachers include in their unit plans appendices of useful background information, such as lists of materials to use with various topics, bibliographies of teacher and student materials, lists of films, slides, exhibits, and records appropriate for the unit. They may also include a complete list of generalizations and skills appropriate to the unit. Whether a teacher puts such information at the back of or in the body of the unit depends greatly on preference and the amount of material available. If there are twenty available books on the topic, the best place to list them is most likely in the appendix, rather than to take up space needed for teaching methods and activities.

Format 1:

UNIT TITLE: _____   TOPIC: _____
THEME/S: _____
_____
INSTRUCTOR: _____

LEARNING INTENT	TOPICS	ACTIVITIES	MATERIALS
(Objectives, major ideas, concepts and generalizations)	(Content to be covered)	(Initiating)	(Text references)
		(Developmental	(Supplementary references)
		(Culminating)	
(Skills, attitudes)			(Media support)
			(Community resources)

Unit Formats

Although most units have the same components (objectives, generalizations, content topics, activities, teaching methods, and materials), the teacher is of course free to arrange these components however she wishes. The primary criterion for unit arrangement is that it be clear and easy to follow. A real test of clarity is whether or not a substitute teacher can successfully teach the unit in the way its compiler intended. Two formats for the body of a teaching unit are shown on pages 172

Format 2:

UNIT TITLE: _____

Topic to be Developed	Key skills	Attitudes and values to receive attention
Generalizations, concepts for emphasis		
Key questions to stimulate thinking		
Research Activities	Presentation Activities	Production Activities

Activities to tie the unit to other curricular areas (math, art, music, science)

Materials

Textbook references:

Supplementary references:

Support materials:

Community resources:

Activity 7:4

Creating a Unit

Drawing on the guidelines presented in this chapter, create an initial draft of a curriculum unit for a social studies topic. As you read other chapters in this textbook, make additions to the unit as you deem appropriate. Share your unit ideas with a fellow student.

The following unit is appropriate for second or third grade.

Unit Plan

UNIT ONE: OUR EXPANDING COMMUNITY*

THEME: PEOPLE EXIST IN A TIME SEQUENCE

Rationale: Children seven, eight, and nine years old are experiencing an exciting phase of their lives, extending their interests beyond their families and immediate neighborhoods. In an increasingly mobile society, children need to begin to grasp the basic concepts dealing with the community and the interrelationships between and among people. Such early beginnings can enable children to obtain a firm understanding of themselves and others. Children need to commence to grasp the concepts of "Spaceship Earth."

This unit is developed around topics and activities that will provide opportunities for children to confront various expanding communities. Children will have opportunities to raise questions and to answer questions about people. It is hoped the teacher will utilize this unit to enable pupils to develop an inquiring awareness of their world—both immediate and distant.

Generalizations: Geographic factors influence where and how people live and what they do; man adapts, shapes, utilizes, and exploits the earth to his own needs.

Human societies have undergone and are undergoing continual, though perhaps gradual, changes in response to various forces.

The affairs of human societies have historical antecedents and consequences; events of the past influence those of the present.

In order to meet individual and group needs, societies organize themselves into subgroups, which in time become institutionalized; individuals are members of several such subgroups or institutions.

General Objectives: Pupils will gain an understanding of the concept "change" as it relates to their own community both past and present.

*From Auburn Public Schools, Auburn, Washington, *Social Studies Resource Guide, K–3*. Reprinted by permission.

Pupils will understand the various causes creating change within a community and will be able to develop a hypothesis regarding the reason for community changes in the past, present, and future.

Pupils will understand the growth of their own community and will be able to describe the significance of changes that have occurred in the last century.

Pupils will understand the effects of community changes upon the individuals within the community.

Outline:　1. Outside our neighborhood—the community

        A. Our community—past time

           1. Land use of the grounds before the school was built
           2. Historical development of the school

        B. Our community—present time

           1. The school and its adjacent community at present
           2. Auburn as it is now

Topic I:　Outside our neighborhood—the community
      A. Our community—past time
         1. Land use of the grounds before the school was built

Learning Intent	*Activities*
Disciplines Stressed	Introductory Activities
History, geography	1. Show a picture of an area which might include woods, a lake or stream, hills, and wild animals. By group inquiry, with the teacher acting as the resource person, the pupils could discuss when the picture might have been taken, where it was, what might be in this place, and what people would be able to do if they went there. Would it be a place you would like to visit or live in? How might people change it if they did go there? (Note—refer to Taba strategy.) Post the picture on the bulletin board. Ask pupils to draw pictures of what might happen if people moved to the area. Follow up with another discussion on what might happen. How would you feel about that? (Note—refer to Rath's Values and Teaching.)
Generalizations Geographic factors influence where and how people live and what they do; man adapts, shapes, utilizes, and exploits the earth to his own ends.	
Human societies have undergone and are undergoing continual, though perhaps gradual, changes in response to various forces.	2. Later show another picture of the same area after buildings have been constructed. Lead the discussion to why men changed the area. What is different? What is the same? How do you explain the differences? Try to get the pupils to make a general statement.
Concepts	

Area, past, present, future, resources, change, chronology	Materials:　Two pictures of the same area, but different times in the history of the area
	    1.　The area in the natural state before man came.
	    2.　The same area after man had changed it by building on it.

Processes	
Discussing, interpreting, inferring	Resource:　Historical Society

Learning Intent

Activities

A bulletin board for posting these pictures in a corner or another place in the room where pupils could observe and discuss the pictures in small groups. The pictures should be posted at eye level of all pupils and, if possible, should be left for a week or a month.

Developmental Activities

Objectives

The pupils infer what happens to a wilderness area when people move in.

The pupils explain concept "change" in their own words.

The pupils point out how selected examples of change affect people's lives.

The pupils differentiate among examples taken from different points in time and explain changes which have taken place.

Processes

Listening, interpreting, inferring, discussing, comparing, contrasting

1. Read aloud *The Little House* and stop frequently for pupils to discuss with each other the progression of seasons in the early part of the story. Divide pupils in groups. Give each group five minutes to come up with as many ideas as they can as to why the area is changing. Bring class together. Share ideas. Ask pupils to explain their reasons for selecting the ideas they developed in the groups. Lead the pupils to tell what changes are evident and then give them time and encouragement to tell how they think this might change the lives of the people in the house. Let them express their feelings. (Note—refer to Rath's Values and Teaching.)

2. *The Sneetches and Other Stories.* The story "Mr. Zaks" in this book is designed to teach the concept of change. Use "Mr. Zaks" for the class story time. Ask pupils to give examples of change from the story. How did people feel about those changes? What can you say about how people feel about change in general? How did you feel about those changes? (Note—refer to Rath's Values and Teaching.)

3. Have pupils ask parents and grandparents about what subjects they studied in elementary school when they were children. Divide blackboard into three parts—label one "parents," one "grandparents," and one "us." Ask pupils to tell you what they found out from their conversations with parents and grandparents. Write information under appropriate category. Under "us" write in subjects studied by your class. Ask pupils to look at the three lists and group and label. Follow this up with a discussion comparing and contrasting educations at the three points in time. Why are there differences? How do you explain those differences? What has happened? (Note—refer to Taba strategy.)

Materials: *The Little House*, Virginia Lee Burton, IMC, School libraries; *The Sneetches and Other Stories*, Dr. Seuss, School libraries

Objectives

The pupils generate defensible hypotheses supported by logical argument.

4. Divide pupils into groups of five or six. Tell each group to pretend that something has happened to eliminate all electricity in the world. Give each group ten minutes to think of as many ways as possible that their lives would be changed. Bring groups together and discuss. Lead toward generalizations about how inventions change our lives. What would happen? Why do you think so? How do you feel about that? Why?

Learning Intent

The pupils infer that technological innovations cause change.

The pupils create a future model indicating changes necessary to bring it into existence.

The pupils differentiate between historical and contemporary school environment.

The pupils explain reasons why historical and contemporary schools are characterized by different physical facilities.

Activities

5. Referring to the story, *The Little House,* you might have pupils write a story or draw a picture of the way they think new houses will look 100 years in the future. Share pupils' work. Ask each to explain changes that have taken place. How do those changes reveal themselves in houses of the 21st century? Would you like to live in that kind of house? Why?

6. From old school records in your district, if available, if not elsewhere in the state, construct a diagram showing physical lay-out of a school around 1900 (date is optional). Have pupils, in conjunction with their art class, draw a diagram showing the present physical lay-out of the school. Discuss. What things do you see in the 1900 diagram (list, group, label)? Use these labels and list data for today's school that pupils see in their diagram. What are similarities? Differences? What has happened? Can you make a general statement about today's school and the one in 1900? Note—refer to Taba strategy.

Culminating Strategy

1. Write and illustrate stories about what they think it was like long ago when children went to school such as the one in 1900 described in activity 6. Pupils could write and illustrate stories of what it is like now in our schools. Make a bulletin board. Have pupils bring in pictures from magazines illustrating things in today's schools that the 1900 school lacked. A discussion can follow.

Materials: Half-ruled newsprint, school classrooms

"Our Expanding Community" comes from a resource unit, but a teaching unit would have the same features, differing only in the number and specificity of suggestions and, perhaps, objectives. Think of ways you would develop a teaching unit. What would you include in a unit on a topic of your own choosing?

Activity 7:5

Available Units

Check in the curriculum materials section of your library for social studies units. Compare at least three units, concentrating on their organization, usefulness, and appropriateness of topic. Write three descriptive statements and use these statements to trigger discussion with a classmate about teaching units.

Activity 7:6

Viewing Classroom Reality

Visit a classroom where a unit that interests you is being taught. React to the unit as written down and observe how it is translated into actual classroom experiences. Think how you would teach the same unit. Is there a great deal of difference between the unit as planned and the unit as implemented? Jot down the reasons for the agreement or lack of agreement. Chat with the teacher to discover why he changed the implementation of the unit or kept it just as planned.

From Units to Lesson Plans

Earlier in this chapter, we stated that levels of planning move from the very general (a resource unit) to the specific (a teaching unit) to the very specific (a lesson plan). The aim of decision making is to create lesson plans that can be used at a particular time and place with a specific group of students. The ideas for such plans are derived from teaching units. A specific lesson plan may be written to cover a day or a week.

All lesson plans can be divided into five components: (1) goals and objectives; (2) content topics; (3) procedures; (4) materials and equipment; and (5) evaluation suggestions. The objectives can be open or closed, but they are usually quite specific as to the type of pupil behavior expected. The content can be divided into generalizations, concepts, skills, attitudes, and facts. The procedures denote the specific teaching method or educational activities. Some teachers indicate in their lesson plans a particular warm-up experience to stimulate student interest and to build readiness. Some also note one or more developmental activities that will comprise the greater part of the lesson. Most mention one or more culminating activities, often under a "summary". Materials and equipment are usually listed alongside a particular activity, although some teachers prefer to list materials separately. Evaluation plans can be noted either at the end of the lesson plan or wherever they would more naturally fall during the lesson.

Essentially, we plan lessons by proceeding through the same stages of decision making we use for developing a teaching unit. We ask ourselves about our particular students, we determine important objectives, we identify potential content that addresses the objectives and our pupils' interests, we determine the methods and activities appropriate for the class, and finally, we decide on suitable materials. While raising these questions, we most likely are jotting down ideas. Using these procedures, we might arrive at lesson plans similar to the following examples.

These two examples show the varying degrees of detail in lesson plans. The more knowledgeable the teacher is about a topic, the less detail she may need to spell out. This is not a license, however, to be satisfied with a lesson plan that notes only that social studies will be from 9:15 to 10:00 each morning.

Lesson Plan

Topic: Varying Uses of Land in My Community.

Content: Geography, economics, history

Grade: Three

Objective: Pupils will identify five ways land is used in their community. They will state orally or in writing the reasons for the variety of land use.

Activities	Materials
Introductory-Developmental Activity	
If students have had little prior experience with map study, use map kit for background in map reading.	Map reading kit
Begin this lesson by having pupils list all the ways that land is used in their community. Pupils could be asked to group and label the uses of land identified.	Maps. Pictures of the community showing land uses.
Ask the pupils to share their ideas.	
Concluding Activity:	
Have the children make a data chart that shows the types of land use. Inform children that these data will be used in the next lesson focusing on reasons for various uses of land.	Data chart, paper

---

Lesson Plan

Topic: The American City in the Nineteenth Century*

Intended Student Audience: Upper elementary level

Suggested Time for Classroom Use of Materials: Five to seven class periods.

Materials for Classroom Use: 8 pictures, each of which depicts political, economic, social, and cultural aspects of city life. 5 data charts.

---

*From Francis P. Hunkins, "What to Ask and When," in Alan O. Kownslar, ed., *Teaching American History: The Quest for Relevancy.* Reprinted by permission.

179

Major Objectives for Lesson:

Within cognitive domain: Upon completion of this lesson, students will:

Knowledge

    a. Know the reasons for the growth of cities in America during the last century.

Skill development

    a. Identify the stages in technological growth affecting the American city during the 19th century.

    b. List the major inventions that affected the growth of cities and explain why these inventions affected the city as they did.

    c. Summarize the working conditions in factories.

Within Affective Domain: Upon completion of this lesson, students will:

Appreciation

    a. Be able to express verbally that they appreciate the contributions of various groups of individuals to the growth of American cities.

    b. Value the functions of questioning as a way of learning new data.

Teaching Suggestions

Lesson overview:

Today, many cities are confronted with many problems, but these problems cannot be understood without analyzing their historical foundations. This lesson focuses on the following topics: factories and workers, eras affecting the growth of cities, inventions assisting the growth of cities, the influence of transportation on the city, and migration and immigration as they affected the urban growth.

Introducing the lesson:

Before the students begin the lesson, select eight magazine pictures, two of each, that illustrate political, economic, social, and cultural dimensions of city life. Display these pictures on the class bulletin board labeling each pair with the phrases "Political Parts of a City" (for pictures A-B), "Economic Parts of a City" (for pictures C-D), "Social Parts of a City" (for pictures E-F), and "Cultural Parts of a City" (for pictures G-H). Have students observe the pictures and the appropriate phrases accompanying each and then record their reactions. Allow ten minutes for this brainstorming, and then ask students to share their reactions with classmates. How many reactions are statements and how many are questions?

Record in two columns the major statements and the major questions about the city. Have students explain their reactions, and during the discussion direct their attention to the questions raised. Allow sufficient time for discussion.

Implementing the lesson:

In group discussion have pupils generate needs for considering the topic of cities in the last century. These needs can be recorded by each student on a chart. On the chart, the pupils can record the need, the information required to satisfy the need, and a specific example. In analyzing the data chart, the students can generate topics they wish to investigate and formulate key questions to trigger their investigations.

Team pupils who wish to work with a classmate.

Allow pupils time to obtain information in response to the questions raised.

Concluding the lesson:	After several days, have pupils share the results of their investigations. This sharing can take several variations: you can have pupils role play being historians at a conference on the American city to report their research findings. Other "historians" at the conference can challenge the conclusions of their "colleagues." Several groups of pupils can meet in separate sessions to consider the conclusions in light of the growth of cities.
References:	Urban Study Filmloops, Hubbard Scientific, Inc., Modern American Cities, Quadrangle Press

Discussion

Planning must occur before instruction can take place, and for the social studies teacher, planning is a decision-making process. Major factors to consider in planning are: (1) the students—what one knows about them from standardized test scores, previous teachers, observation, and their learning styles; (2) the teacher—his individuality and instructional style; (3) the content—its nature and that of the requisite learning activities; and (4) outside factors—school and district policies, available materials, and society's demands.

The teacher must conduct instructional planning at three levels. He must first plan the resource unit, an overall, long-term plan intended for a general group of students. Second, the teacher must create a unit plan, more detailed than the resource unit, covering a specific time period and directed at a particular group of students. Third, the teacher develops a lesson plan for a specific class, ranging over one or two to about five days. For each planning level, the teacher must make decisions about objectives, content, materials, and methods. The more thorough the planning, the greater the likelihood of successful student learning.

The resource unit will be quite broad, and should include more possible objectives and content than the teacher could expect to use with one group of students. From the resource unit, the teacher will draw specific objectives, content, materials, and methods to formulate a unit plan to use with a specific class. He will then draw his individual lesson plans from the unit plan.

The major steps in developing any type of unit are (1) conceptualizing, (2) diagnosing, (3) selecting and organizing content, and (4) selecting and organizing experiences. After developing the unit, the teacher must implement it, evaluate its effectiveness, and provide for the unit's continued use in the future.

In making planning decisions, the teacher will address both cognitive and affective objectives; both areas include closed and open objectives. Closed objectives are prescriptive; they define a particular behavior we wish to see a student demonstrate at a particular level. Open objectives are descriptive and

181

divergent, and the conditions for meeting them can vary. All objectives have three components, each of which can be either stated or implied: (1) the expected behavior; (2) the conditions under which the behavior is to occur; and (3) acceptable performance.

When the teacher plans content, he must base his decisions on the criteria of significance, validity, interest, utility, learnability, and feasibility. He considers available content, selects the particular content and topics to cover, and determines the scope and sequence of content with these criteria in mind. It is hoped that the teacher will choose those methods and activities for conveying content that promote active learning; the choice of teaching methods and learning activities will determine what materials the teacher decides to use.

The several common formats for arranging teaching units usually provide an overview, a statement of objectives, and an activities section. The activities section includes warm-up, developmental, and concluding activities. Finally, the teacher will wish to write lesson plans that specify: (1) goals and objectives; (2) content topics; (3) procedures; (4) materials and equipment; and (5) evaluation suggestions. The unit and lesson plans in this chapter illustrate the decision making involved in instructional planning.

References

Armstrong, David G. *Social Studies in Secondary Education.* New York: Macmillan Co., 1980.

Hunkins, Francis P. *Curriculum Development: Program Improvement.* Columbus, Oh.: Charles E. Merrill Publishing Co., 1980.

Hunkins, Francis P. "What to Ask and When." In *Teaching American History: The Quest for Relevancy,* edited by Allan O. Kownslar. Washington, D. C.: National Council for the Social Studies, 1974.

Michaelis, John U. *Social Studies for Children in a Democracy.* 5th ed. Englewood Cliffs, N. J.: Prentice-Hall, 1972.

"Our Expanding Community." Social Studies Resource Guide, K–3. Auburn, Washington: Auburn Public Schools, 1973.

"People Produce to Live." Social Studies Resource Guide, 7–9. Pasco, Washington: Pasco Public Schools, 1975.

Shavelson, Richard J., and Borko, H. "Research on Teachers' Decisions in Planning Instruction." *Educational Horizons* 57 (1979): 183–189.

Effective Instruction in the Social Studies

8

Teaching Methods and Educational Activities

Teaching methods in social studies can range from lecture to discussion to inquiry. Rather than spending time searching for the "best" method, teachers should identify which methods work best for which students according to which content. Methods will vary according to the variety of content, the time needed to process information, the degree to which the information is new to the student, and the degree of flexibility of space necessary. Further, certain methods are more effective than others with individual students. Ascher (1966) divides common methods into telling, showing, and doing, as follows:

Telling	*Showing*	*Doing*
lecture	demonstration	role playing
discussion	modeling	practice
exposition	pictures	exercise
debates	written words	inquiry procedures
panel discussion		simulation

Some of these are not teaching methods, but are more appropriately referred to as educational activities, or experiences that involve students with the subject matter. The most appropriate type of activity depends on the nature of the subject, the objectives the teacher and students want to attain, and the pupils' abilities and experiences. In some cases, the most suitable activities will call for students to interview, describe, explain, hypothesize, or summarize. In other cases, the most effective activities might require hands-on creation of maps, charts, models, reports, murals, or essays. Other activities may find students listening to a record, watching a demonstration, going on a field trip, or playing a game (Fraenkel, 1977).

According to Fraenkel, different types of educational activities serve different functions. For example, reading, listening to records, viewing films, and interviewing provide for intake of information. Students must perform these activities to acquire necessary information; they need information before they can solve problems or think critically. A second type of educational involvement helps students organize information. Outlining, graphing,

Figure 8.1   Functions of Learning Activities

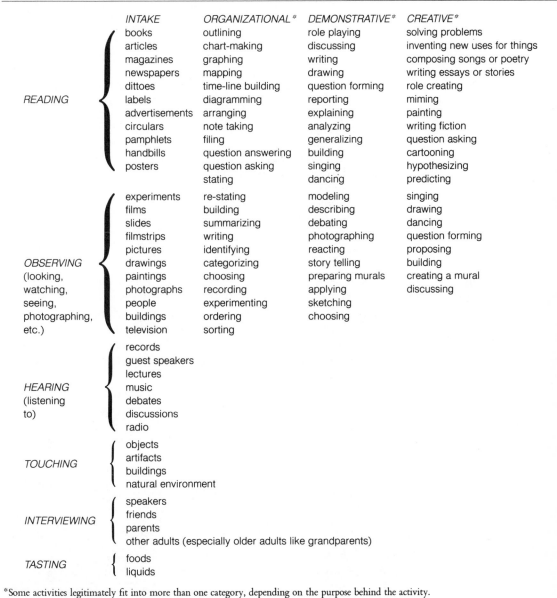

	INTAKE	ORGANIZATIONAL*	DEMONSTRATIVE*	CREATIVE*
	books	outlining	role playing	solving problems
	articles	chart-making	discussing	inventing new uses for things
	magazines	graphing	writing	composing songs or poetry
	newspapers	mapping	drawing	writing essays or stories
	dittoes	time-line building	question forming	role creating
READING	labels	diagramming	reporting	miming
	advertisements	arranging	explaining	painting
	circulars	note taking	analyzing	writing fiction
	pamphlets	filing	generalizing	question asking
	handbills	question answering	building	cartooning
	posters	question asking	singing	hypothesizing
		stating	dancing	predicting
	experiments	re-stating	modeling	singing
	films	building	describing	drawing
	slides	summarizing	debating	dancing
	filmstrips	writing	photographing	question forming
	pictures	identifying	reacting	proposing
OBSERVING	drawings	categorizing	story telling	building
(looking,	paintings	choosing	preparing murals	creating a mural
watching,	photographs	recording	applying	discussing
seeing,	people	experimenting	sketching	
photographing,	buildings	ordering	choosing	
etc.)	television	sorting		
	records			
	guest speakers			
	lectures			
HEARING	music			
(listening	debates			
to)	discussions			
	radio			
	objects			
TOUCHING	artifacts			
	buildings			
	natural environment			
	speakers			
INTERVIEWING	friends			
	parents			
	other adults (especially older adults like grandparents)			
TASTING	foods			
	liquids			

*Some activities legitimately fit into more than one category, depending on the purpose behind the activity.

From Jack R. Fraenkel, in *Social Studies and the Elementary Teacher: Promises and Practices*, edited by William Joyce and F. Ryan. Reprinted by permission.

note taking, summarizing, map making, building time lines, and charting help students make sense out of the information they take in. Discussions, sociodramas, role playing, preparing murals, and writing comprise yet a third type of activity, one that enables students to demonstrate what they have learned. Such experiences allow students to use their skills and demonstrate their thinking capabilities. A fourth type of activity encourages students to apply what they know to creating a new and different product. Examples include composing a poem, building an original model, and solving problems. (Figure 8.1 shows more examples of activities in each category.)

> A realization of the idea that different kinds of learning activities serve different functions should help us design learning activities that will assist students to learn in a variety of ways. In too many classrooms, students are engaged for the most part in the same kinds of activities every day—they listen to teachers talk; they read; they write. The kinds of activities are obviously very important. But different students learn in different ways. And many students do not learn very well at all via talk and the printed word. They need to be more directly or actively involved. . . . It is important, therefore, that we take steps to insure that students have open to them as many ways to learn as possible. But all four types of activities—intake, organizational, demonstrative, and creative—are essential if learning is to take place. (Fraenkel, 1977)

If there is one thing educators know about how students learn, it is that they learn differently. Some students learn easily through reading; others need to see, to hear about, and to touch objects with which they are working. Some students work effectively by themselves; others work best with a group. Social studies teachers are sometimes not as careful as they should be about selecting appropriate teaching methods and educational activities. Consequently, many social studies classes become just another formal reading class. To avoid this, methods and activities must be geared to the individual needs of a diverse group of students. The diversity becomes increasingly complex as we address the needs of the gifted and the learning disabled.

The drawing of a mural is both a demonstrative and creative learning activity.

Individualizing Instruction

The term "individualizing instruction" has several meanings. Sometimes it means that all students are exposed to the same materials, teaching methods, and educational activities, but are allowed to progress at their own rates. It may mean that students pursue objectives unique to their personal interests and abilities. It may also mean that students proceed through the same curriculum at their own pace, but are allowed to choose among different activities and demonstrate mastery in different ways.

Individualized (or "personalized") instruction does *not* mean that the teacher always works with individual students or that students work alone. Broadly, individualizing refers to the adaptation of teaching methods and activities to students' individual needs. Pupils are provided with learning experiences that are personally relevant.

Most instruction involves both small groups and large groups. The teacher should not place students in permanent groups, however; she should move them from one group to another in ways that will help each one learn in her own best way. As Jeter (1980) reminds us, "Perhaps the best approach is to think of individualization of instruction as the attempt to accommodate the needs of individuals within a particular group through a balance of instructional activity (independent study, one-to-one, small-group instruction, large-group instruction) that is appropriate for the members of that particular group and the goals the teacher wants to attain. It is also important to remember that because each student is a unique individual, assistance and instruction should be personalized to fit emotional as well as intellectual needs.

Individualizing instruction requires knowing each student's background, achievements, interests, and abilities. The teacher must also determine under what circumstances each individual learns best. One child may be able to meet objectives while working alone because she is highly motivated. Another may also work effectively alone, but because of an introverted personality. Other students may function more effectively in groups of various sizes.

Some students learn by listening to the teacher and to others, or by watching a film or filmstrip. Others acquire understanding by manipulating objects. It is important for teachers to gather data constantly on pupils' learning styles and to use this information in instructional decision making. Cumulative records offer one source of information, but actual classroom activities are equally important. For example, when students prepare reports, make murals, or interpret maps and graphs, teachers can detect their interest and identify which pupils need special help and which have achieved the desired skills and understandings.

In making diagnoses, instructors should be wary of the self-fulfilling prophecy. Students are often classified as slow learners strictly on the basis of achievement and intelligence tests, and instruction is shaped to fit the classification rather than the individual. Expectations are often set too low, and pupils are not challenged to move to higher levels of achievement.

Educators have their own particular styles and preferences and develop their own ways to individualize social studies, but they also find it necessary to blend various methods and procedures as they address individual students' unique learning needs.

Activity 8:1

Visit an Elementary Classroom

Visit an elementary social studies class and observe the following:
1. Student differences in use of language, work habits, etc.
2. Strategies the teacher uses and activities she provides to meet individual differences.
3. Use of learning centers in the classroom.

Grouping

Classroom grouping in social studies usually falls into four categories: independent, one-to-one, small group, and large group.

Some students work best in groups while others work effectively alone.

The independent mode allows students to work alone to meet objectives that they and the teacher mutually decide can best be met by this method. Individual research projects that involve reading, writing, note taking, collecting data by interviewing, or reporting lend themselves easily to independent study. Effective learning will not result, though, if students constantly work by themselves without the opportunity to interact with others. One-to-one, small-group, and large-group activities must be included so students can share ideas and plan activities cooperatively.

The one-to-one mode permits a variety of combinations of individuals. The purpose of the activity should determine the pairing. For instance, two students might be paired, or a student and a teacher or other adult might collaborate. The teacher may be needed to supply assistance or to clarify a difficult concept. Or, two students might work together in an educational game. One-to-one is useful for students who need a great deal of individual attention, as it allows them to talk intimately with someone.

The small-group mode affords many alternatives. Nussel, Inglis, and Wiersma (1976) list five types of small groups, identified by the activities that take place in each: (1) task groups, (2) didactic groups, (3) discussion groups, (4) brainstorming groups, and (5) inquiry groups. The task group is actually a working committee organized to complete a particular assignment. For example, if a class is studying early colonial settlement, the students might present an original play depicting one of the early settlements. One small group might be assigned the task of planning, designing, and making scenery for the play. Another small group might write the script.

In the didactic group, the teacher performs the traditional instructional role. She might, for example, talk to the students to help them understand the economic concept of supply and demand.

In the discussion group, Nussel, Inglis, and Wiersma recommend that the instructor be a somewhat inactive participant so as not to inhibit the free flow of discussion. The teacher should remain quiet most of the time, except perhaps to interject a comment when students stray from the subject.

In a brainstorming session, students spontaneously offer ideas on a specific subject. Every idea is accepted and listed. At the close of the session, students can review all the ideas and eliminate those that could not be carried out. A possible topic for brainstorming is: "What do we need to prepare a model of a Southern plantation in the 1800s?" Students present ideas, then eliminate those that cannot be used. Brainstorming can be helpful for clarifying ideas, for obtaining a wide sampling of opinion, and even for getting students to participate who might not do so in a more structured situation. Brainstorming can easily get out of hand and become noisy and confusing, so the teacher usually needs to stay firmly in control.

The inquiry group resembles the brainstorming session in some ways; the difference is that students are given an opportunity to solve problems under teacher direction. The instructor does not talk *at* the students, but instead creates an environment that encourages them to identify issues and to state and test hypotheses. (Inquiry strategies are discussed in more detail later in this chapter.)

The panel discussion is an excellent example of a small-group technique frequently used in social studies. It is more formal than many small-group discussions. It generally begins with a short presentation by each panel member, followed by general discussion. Panel discussions are usually conducted before an audience, and each panelist is considered an "expert."

This is how one sixth grade in Louisiana conducted a successful panel discussion. The topic before the panel was a community problem involving conversion of the Atchafalayan Basin (a very large swamp area controlled by the U.S. Corps of Engineers that serves as a flood control area and home of wildlife for southern Louisiana) into a privately developed industrial area. The teacher asked class members to volunteer to represent each of the following: (1) an engineer from the Corps of Engineers; (2) a citizen who makes his living fishing in the basin; (3) a Sierra Club member; (4) an oil company executive who plans to drill for oil there; (5) a state senator; and (6) the panel moderator. The students were given ample time to research their topic and prepare for the discussion, which was conducted in front of the rest of the class.

Large-group instruction is used when all the students can benefit from the same activity. Introducing a unit of study, showing a film, conducting a demonstration, hearing a guest speaker, and summarizing a unit are common large-group activities.

Most social studies groups should be temporary. They are sometimes formed on the basis of a common interest, such as when a group of students works together on a display or mural. Other groups might be formed on the basis of common need. For example, the teacher might work with a small

In a small inquiry group, students ask questions and solve problems under teacher direction.

group to clarify a difficult concept or develop a map skill while the other pupils work independently. The teacher should particularly avoid fixed groups that separate young people into low, medium, and high achievers.

By making groups temporary, the teacher can prevent cliques from forming in the classroom. Also, students can experience a greater mix of personality types as well as learn to work with children of varying intellectual strengths. But not all grouping needs to be teacher initiated. In some investigations, children should be allowed to select other members who share the same interests. This gives children a chance for some degree of control over their learning experiences and personal encounters.

Varying Learning Activities

A variety of activities should be provided to meet individual differences, such as: (1) self-directed activities, (2) teacher-guided activities, and (3) teacher-directed activities.

Self-directed activities are facilitated by providing an attractive learning center in a corner of the classroom. A learning center is not a collection of interesting games and toys to keep students occupied. Instead, it offers varied learning activities based on specific objectives and materials organized around a topic, theme, concept, or skill. A well-designed center does not require the teacher's continuous direction. It presents activities at varying levels of difficulty and provides some degree of choice for the students. It also includes a method of record-keeping and a means of student assessment. According to Johnston et al., (1978), learning centers should:

1. Contain a varied and extensive collection of materials related to fundamental concepts or skills;
2. Provide for the needs, interests, and learning styles of the students;
3. Be designed to provide specific learning experiences, carefully sequenced within practical time limits;
4. Seek to stimulate interest and encourage active learning;
5. Be related to and build on past experiences or provide readiness for new learning experiences;
6. Seek to develop problem solving, creative thinking and valuing;
7. Provide an opportunity for exploration, discovery, and student interaction; and
8. Accommodate a wide range of abilities.

A learning center is an effective organizing mechanism in traditional, individualized, and open classrooms. Regardless of the type of classroom, learning centers help motivate students to become more independent learners.

In summary, probably nothing is more important in meeting individual differences than the teacher's attitude toward her pupils. Educators who value differences and recognize each student's uniqueness are the ones who plan most effectively to address individual differences. They care about their students. Without this sincere concern, a teacher may not be motivated to spend the extra time and effort required to individualize instruction.

Activity 8:2

Learning Center

Sketch a social studies learning center. Show what you would include in it, and make lists of the various individual and group activities that could take place in your learning center.

Dealing with Exceptionality

All teachers realize that students in regular classrooms represent a wide range of diversity in interests and abilities. The range of pupils encompasses both the learning disabled and the gifted and talented.

The Learning Disabled

Historically, children with handicapping conditions were placed in isolated classrooms. In the mid-1970s, educators and members of the public began to realize that many of these students did not need to be isolated from their peers in regular classrooms. Changes in values and attitudes, from nonawareness to acceptance to a demand that these children be given their full rights, resulted in legislation in 1975 that some have called the Bill of Rights for the Handicapped. This law, P.L. 94-142, mentioned in chapter 1, serves as the basis for bringing many special children into the regular classroom, in the process called mainstreaming.

Almost all teachers are affected by this legislation. Students with handicapping conditions are not automatically placed in regular classrooms, since some cannot function in such an environment. Many children, however, have handicaps that do not prevent their participating in the regular classroom. Children with hearing difficulties and visual problems can be rather easily accommodated in regular classrooms. Children with special learning difficulties may need only adjustments in material, teaching methods, and activities.

192

Instructional Approaches for the Learning Disabled

Many of the suggested methods for individualizing instruction are applicable to learning disabled children. Grouping is a primary means of addressing these children's unique needs. Lowenbraun and Affleck (1976) note that social studies teachers can create "skill-specific" groups in which they direct the student's attention to one specific fact. For instance, several of these pupils could make a mural of their community. Some could gather pictures; others might interpret simple maps of the community; others might put up the mural. Children without learning handicaps can assist their classmates in the special groups with the final stages of the group tasks.

Homogeneous grouping is often effective. The instructor can have children with the same reading difficulty work together to understand a booklet about some particular topic, perhaps "Our Community." (The teacher may have to rewrite the booklet to these special pupils' correct reading level.)

Instructors with mainstreamed children may have them work with a nonhandicapped peer. For example, a learning disabled child who is just acquiring a particular skill can be grouped with a peer who has demonstrated proficiency in the skill. A child skilled in reading maps can collaborate with a child who is just meeting maps for the first time. Of course, the teacher may need to instruct peer tutors in ways of working with their fellow classmates.

Creating new social studies units is another approach for helping special children. Pupils who are only mildly handicapped may not need extensively rewritten materials, but some adjustment in the wording or in introduction of topics not in the "regular" units may be needed. Turnbull and Schulz (1979) present questions to keep in mind when determining social studies topics appropriate for mainstreamed children:

1. Will these topics help the student become more independent in the community, at home, or in employment?
2. What is the danger if the student does not know this information or is unable to master this skill?
3. Will the student be receiving this information from other sources? (p. 260)

Using these questions as guidelines, teachers can create social studies units that will address the needs and interests of the special students.

Teachers need not always develop new courses for mainstreamed students. It is frequently only necessary to make adjustments in the available textbooks and workbooks. Necessary modifications might include adjusting the prose to fit the reading levels of the special students. Some portions of the regular materials might need to be completely rewritten, other sections could be adapted slightly, and others deleted. Such modifications of the materials do not alter the major thrust of the social studies units designed for the regular class members. Sometimes the alterations need be nothing more than recording the books on audiotape so that children who are severely disabled readers, or blind, can "hear" the books. Sometimes just writing the words in

193

a larger print size is sufficient. Along with modifications, the teacher may need to consider new instructional strategies. She may have to present information in very small segments and frequently ask low-level questions. As more special children are included in the regular classroom, publishers will probably create specially-adjusted materials.

Worksheets or study packets can help children who have learning difficulties and handicaps keep up with the rest of class.

Lowenbraun and Affleck (1976) furnish several useful guidelines for designing worksheets and study guides.

1. Make sure that the directions are simple and clearly written. Ask questions that make the students restate the instruction in their own words. (This allows the teacher to get an assessment of just where the pupil is in his or her understanding or skill level.)
2. Have the worksheet page or assignment focus on only one specific task.
3. Keep to a common format for worksheets so that students can easily recognize the assignment. (This repetition of format allows pupils to become familiar with the tasks to do and lessens the chance for confusion.)
4. Make sure that the pupil understands what he or she is to do and also what indicates completion of the task.
5. Use visual and verbal prompts in the materials to insure pupil success in the tasks. (p. 63)

Learning Activity Packets (LAPS) are a special type of worksheet that can be employed with all class members, but are especially useful with children who have learning handicaps. These packets list objectives, and usually contain a type of pretest, activities with carefully delineated directions, and optional activities.

In reviewing the previous suggestions, a common thread becomes evident—*individualize*. It can be argued that all good instruction—materials, activities, content—needs to be individualized to some degree. Experts in special education consider individualizing instruction even more essential when dealing with children with learning handicaps. The basic structure of individualizing is the Individual Educational Plan (IEP). These plans, ideally, are used for each mainstreamed student in social studies. Each plan is a result of the teacher's working with other special teachers, counselors, and parents in analyzing diagnostic data to determine objectives, topics, instructional approaches and materials, and evaluation techniques. The proper approach to creating an IEP is identical to the planning steps outlined in chapter 7, except that the specific decisions are unique to the children's particular needs. Each IEP indicates the special materials to be used, the instructional approaches to consider with the child, and the appropriate types of group and individual activities. Figures 8–2 and 8–3 (pages 196–197 and 198) are samples of long-term and short-term IEPs.

Working with exceptional children in the regular classroom requires the regular class teacher to work closely with a special education teacher or resource specialist. The regular teacher may also need to establish cooperative relationships with tutors, coordinators of special education, and sometimes with the parents of these special children. Cooperation frequently evolves when creating IEPs. Sometimes, addressing an exceptional child's special need requires an immediate meeting. One benefit of the legislation for the education of exceptional children is that teachers in regular classrooms are becoming members of educational decision teams. All parties involved should benefit from such encounters.

The Gifted and Talented

Teachers in the regular classroom have always had gifted and talented children to motivate, but the current attention to these children's needs in new. As with learning disabled students, educators focus on the gifted and talented in four important ways:

1. Particular attention is now called to these pupils.
2. Individualized educational plans are required for them.
3. There are specialized staff plus particularized instructional procedures to buttress the regular class teacher's work.
4. Parental involvement is increased. (Reynolds & Birch, 1977, p. 236)

Some schools have established special programs for these children, but in the spirit of mainstreaming, many argue that gifted and talented children should have the benefit of working with children of more average abilities. They feel this is a more realistic approach to educating students of above average abilities.

At one time, the term "gifted" was narrowly defined to mean intellectually gifted. It has now been redefined to include not only intellectual capacity but artistic, creative, and kinesthetic talents (Reynolds & Birch, 1977).

The intellectually/academically gifted have little or no difficulty with the regular curriculum. They usually learn the essential content and skills easily and quickly. In fact, they exhibit their exceptionality by moving far beyond the regular program offerings. They delve into topics to a much greater depth than do other children. Thus, social studies teachers are challenged to provide content and experiences that extend the range for these students. The regular classroom serves as an arena where such students can engage in extensive research, using sophisticated inquiry procedures, regardless of grade level.

In the past, many educators thought that, although giving specific attention to these children would be ideal, they could succeed rather nicely by themselves; they did not really require special attention from the teacher. But teachers have learned that these students do need guidance, and that they benefit from specialized educational plans and structured learning experiences.

The challenge to teachers of exceptional children is to individualize the curriculum so these youth can reach their potential in minimum time.

Figure 8.2 A Long-term IEP

Yorktown Central School District
1982–83 Data

Originating
Teacher: _____

School: _____
Check:
Res. Room ☐ Spec. Class ☐ Itin. ☐

IEP Year
Teacher: _____

1982–83 Data

Student's Name: _____
                Last _____ First

Home District: _____
Name of Parent
or Guardian: _____
Home Address: _____ Zip _____

Date of Birth _____
Home Phone: _____

MEETING DATA

Spring Meeting, 1982:
Date: _____
Location: _____
Attending: _____   *Title or Relation*
_____
_____

Early Fall Meeting, 1982:
Date: _____
Location: _____
Attending: _____   *Title or Relation*
_____
_____

Spring (Final) Meeting, 1983:
Date: _____
Location: _____
Attending: _____   *Title or Relation*
_____
_____

Recommended Placement for the Fall: _____

SPECIAL STRENGTHS
(NOTE: Include comments for both)

WEAKNESSES
Academic and Personal/Social Areas)

Other student information: _____

Describe extent to which student will be participating in regular school programs: _____

Relevant medical information: _____

(Student's File Copy)

EDUCATIONAL TESTING DATA

	Test Name	*Score*	*Date Given*
Reading Scores:			
Incoming			
Math Scores:			
Incoming			

Instructional Level of Materials Used
Incoming (Spring) READING _____
Incoming (Spring) MATH _____

I.Q. Test Data: _____ Test Name _____
Verbal _____ Performance _____ Full-Scale _____
I.Q. _____ I.Q. _____ I.Q. _____
Given By: _____ Date: _____
Retest Data: _____ Test Name _____
Verbal _____ Performance _____ Full-Scale _____
I.Q. _____ I.Q. _____ I.Q. _____
Given By: _____ Date: _____
Other _____
Test Data: _____

	Test Name	*Score*	*Date Given*
Math Scores: End of Year			
Reading Scores: End of Year			

Instructional Level of Materials Used
End of year READING _____
End of year MATH _____

IEP—Page 1

Figure 8.2
A Long-term IEP
(continued)

Yorktown Central School District _____

Last　　(Student Name)　　First

Goal Number	Date Goal Devel.	Listing of Academic and Personal-Social Goals Established for this School Year	Summary of Progress Toward Each Goal To be completed for or at the Spring, 1983 final meeting	
			Goal Mastered State "yes" or "no"	Comment
			(Use letters of A, B, etc. . . . . if more than one goal sheet is used.)	

IEP—Page 2

Yorktown Central School District _____

Last　　(Student Name)　　First

Instructional Area _____

Goal Number (see Pg. 2)	Date Obj. Devel.	Conditions- Methods, Materials or Services To Be Used	Short-term Instructional Objectives	Standard or Criteria by Which Mastery of This Objective Will Be Evaluated	Status Report — Show prog. towards each obj. by evaluating continuously & by writing dates in approp. column			
					Init.	Prog.	Mast.	N/App
				(Use letters of A, B, etc. . . . if more than one obj.-eval. sheet is used.)				

(Student's File Copy)　　　　　　　IEP—Page 3

John G. Herlihy and Myra T. Herlihy, ed. "The IEP–Individualization of Instruction," in John G. Herlihy and Myra T. Herlihy, ed. *Mainstreaming in the Social Studies.* NCSS bulletin 62. Washington, D.C.: National Council for the Social Studies, 1980. pp. 28–29

Reynolds and Birch provide us with four useful principles to guide curriculum individualization. First, the teacher should assure that all gifted and talented students acquire the basic skills and content of the standard curriculum. Teachers should use preassessment activities to determine what information and skills these children possess before involving them in enriching activities.

Figure 8.3
A Short-term IEP

Child _____ Identification # _____

Short Term Goal(s):

Instructional Objective(s)	Current Functioning	Methods or Materials	Dates Beg.	End	Evaluation Procedure and Comments
					Objectives Met
					Yes / No / Still Progressing
					☐ ☐ ☐
					☐ ☐ ☐
					☐ ☐ ☐
					☐ ☐ ☐

John G. Herlihy and Myra T. Herlihy, ed. "The IEP–Individualization of Instruction," in John G. Herlihy and Myra T. Herlihy, ed. *Mainstreaming in the Social Studies*. NCSS bulletin 62. Washington, D.C.: National Council for the Social Studies, 1980. pp. 28–29

Second, these children should be encouraged to proceed through the standard curriculum as quickly as their abilities and interests allow. Advanced books and materials should be available to support their expanded investigations.

Third, the scope of the regular curriculum should be expanded to cater to these pupils' interests and capabilities. Activities usually reserved for junior and senior high pupils may be appropriate. For example, some students may wish to try detailed cartography, while others may want to investigate topics usually covered much later in the school sequence. When pupils want to investigate topics that occur later in the curriculum, the teacher should discuss this plan with the instructors who normally teach those topics or courses, so the students can avoid difficulty in meeting requirements later.

Last, the teacher should help each student follow any personal inclinations to expand her investigations outside the regular curriculum. Many of these children benefit greatly from informal independent study or from more formal advanced placement. In social studies units dealing with cultures, for example, some children can take on advanced topics such as ethnic and morality studies. When considering this option, however, teachers need to be in close contact with parents and have their full support for such a move.

Methods of Teaching the Gifted and Talented

There are no teaching methods specifically designed for gifted and talented students; the available instructional strategies simply require some modifications. In the next section of this chapter we will discuss generic strategies applicable to social studies. These strategies work well with children of high intellectual ability as well as with those of average ability. In using these strategies, however, keep in mind that the teaching pace most likely will need to be accelerated with the gifted. The instruction should usually introduce and emphasize more abstract ideas and concepts. Also, the activities to accompany the various teaching methods provide ample opportunities for independent study in diverse areas. Students will have time to invent knowledge classifications, synthesize conclusions, and apply their new learnings to still other areas and new situations.

The regular social studies materials often need to be supplemented. Many students can read college-level materials, and these should be made available. Gifted students may be directed to community libraries, museums, and art galleries to obtain material for independent investigations. Many of the teacher's own books might be placed in a special learning center for these children's use. It's important to evaluate these materials before encouraging children to use them, since not all adult or advanced materials are of good quality. Arrangements often can be made with school libraries for students to use the materials. It is helpful for teachers to meet with the librarians or the directors of educational communication centers to obtain lists of materials potentially useful for these students' investigations.

Many school districts do have special programs for the gifted. In many of these programs, children leave the regular classroom for several periods two or three times a week. The work they do in these special class sessions is planned to complement and expand the regular program. The gifted education specialists frequently assist the regular teacher in creating special sections of social studies units to challenge gifted pupils. These specialists should cooperate in the preassessment necessary for determining particular materials and activities.

Teaching Strategies for the Social Studies

The full range of teaching strategies, from exposition to inquiry to value analysis, may be found in the social studies. In fact, most teachers employ a combination of strategies. The teaching strategy utilized must be consistent with the objectives. If the objective is to convey information or to teach a certain skill, expository teaching or demonstration may be the most effective technique. On the other hand, if the objective is to foster thinking and problem-solving skills, an inquiry strategy may be more appropriate.

Strategies such as exposition, discussion, or demonstration are usually teacher-dominated, while other strategies, such as inquiry, are student-dominated.

Expository Teaching

When teachers present information, explanations, or generalizations to the class, or when they give reading assignments that offer such information, they are using expository teaching. When it is done well, expository teaching can be highly effective.

In this mode, teachers introduce fresh data to their class, drawing upon material to which students lack access—for example, comparative figures on the speed of different forms of travel in a transportation unit. At other times, they might introduce material by means of maps, charts, globes, or pictures. In fact, variety in presentation strengthens learning and helps hold interest.

To achieve success with *any* teaching method, the students' attention must be directed toward the important elements and key relationships among the facts. This can be difficult in expository teaching, because there is less teacher-student interaction than in other approaches. Consequently, the instructor cannot be certain that all students are attending to the discussion. However, if the exposition is organized to build toward a conclusion or series of conclusions, most students will probably pay attention. Highly interesting topics will grab and hold their attention. The teacher can usually determine whether or not students are actively listening by their facial expressions as well as by their responses to occasional questions interspersed throughout the explanation.

Successful exposition often begins with a question for focusing the students' listening. For instance, in a class lesson about cultural variety, the introductory question might be "What are some major reasons for the great variety in the cultures of the world? We will attempt to answer this question." An expository lesson that starts this way is more likely to heighten interest than if the same topic is introduced with, "In our world we find that most cultures exhibit a lot of variety." Raising a question encourages students to think about additional questions—to listen to the exposition with a questioning attitude.

Conducting a Discussion

One of the most widely used and most valuable strategies in social studies teaching is discussion. It is a thinking-together process, in which students should talk freely. But a fruitful discussion requires careful planning, so that it doesn't degenerate into a free-for-all talkfest. While skill in leading a discussion comes primarily through practice, there are some requirements and guidelines to be kept in mind.

One requirement for a successful discussion is that it have a definite purpose. Examples of some different purposes are:

- To plan a class activity;
- To arouse interest at the beginning of new unit;

- To summarize or evaluate a group activity;
- To review a difficult concept, generalization, or process;
- To discuss a controversial issue or explore values;
- To explore new ideas or ways to solve problems, that is, to develop problem-solving skills; and
- To provide opportunities for learning to accept and value people from other ethnic and/or cultural backgrounds.

The success of social studies discussions also depends upon the questions used. Discussion questions must be open-ended. They should not be answerable with a "yes" or "no," or with a recitation of facts, such as the following questions would elicit:

1. In what year was the city of New Orleans founded?
2. Who was the city's founder?
3. What countries have controlled that city?

As these questions are worded, there is really nothing to discuss, but framed differently, they might effectively stimulate discussion. Consider the reworded questions:

1. New Orleans was founded in the year 1713. How do you think the area looked at that time?
2. How do you think Iberville felt when he discovered what is now New Orleans?
3. Both the French and the Spanish controlled New Orleans for long periods of time. What French and Spanish influences do we see today in the city?

(Refer to chapter 10 for detailed information on using questions in the social studies.)

Effective discussions occur in a classroom atmosphere where both teacher and students accept and support behavior. Accepting questions might be used when a student strays from the topic: "That's very interesting, Jane. Can we come back to your comment later?" Supporting questions can be used when a student makes a mistake, such as, "Who can help Joe out on this?"

A potential difficulty in class discussion is the likelihood that a few children will monopolize it. Equal participation can be accomplished through several tactics. For example, discuss with the class the need to have many take part, or encourage shy students by calling on them when you know they are interested in or knowledgeable about the topic.

If the purpose of the discussion is to facilitate student talk, then teacher talk should be limited to what is needed to keep the discussion moving. In fact, the nature of teacher involvement has much to do with the extent to which pupils participate in discussions. There are several good guidelines for teacher participation: (1) use nonverbal cues, such as an encouraging glance or smile, as well as verbal encouragement; (2) allow students time to think about what they are going to say; (3) limit your actions to proving or clarifying comments and to acknowledging contributions; and (4) when the discussion strays from the topic, refocus the group's thinking with a comment such as, "Let's get back to the main point. . . ." Whatever you do, avoid turning the discussion into a lecture!

Activity 8:3

Observe a Class Discussion

Visit a classroom and observe the teacher's role in guiding discussion. Note the use of open-ended, clarifying, accepting, and supporting questions.

The student participants must also follow guidelines and possess certain skills and attitudes. These skills can be taught directly; for example, students participating in a discussion should:

1. Listen while others speak;
2. Consider conflicts with open minds;
3. Stick to the topic;
4. Speak clearly so everyone can hear and understand;
5. Contribute ideas at appropriate times, not dominate the discussion;
6. Be considerate of other students' feelings; and
7. Ask for clarification when something is not understood.

There are appropriate times and places for both large- and small-group discussions. The same principles and procedures apply to both types, but the advantage of small groups is that they permit greater participation by everyone. (For more specific examples of small-group discussion, refer to the section on grouping in this chapter.)

Activity 8:4

Group Discussion

Prepare a chart to use with students to illustrate points to keep in mind when participating in class discussions. Illustrate your chart in a way that will appeal to students.

Demonstrations in Social Studies

Sometimes a demonstration is the most effective way to help students understand certain content or learn how to perform a process. The elementary
social studies program offers limitless possibilities for the use of this generic
method. Demonstrations are popular for teaching students how to use equipment and materials and how to develop skills such as candle and map making. Students can be shown the proper ways to grow plants and flowers.
Students will frequently need demonstrations in the proper use of maps,
globes, and models. Sometimes, when teaching a unit about life on the farm,
the teacher can demonstrate ways to process flax, card wool, or grind corn
into meal. Demonstrations can be performed by the teacher, a child, or a
classroom visitor. Children can demonstrate how to use or make objects
brought from home.

Demonstrations are one form of large-group method. Instructors cannot be sure of the learning level of all class members, and much will depend
upon their willingness to follow the demonstration, and their understanding
of and skill in learning strategies. Following these guidelines will increase the
probability that most students will learn from the demonstration:

1. Gain attention by stating the purpose of the demonstration and informing
   the class of the likely results of observing it. Occasionally allow pupils to
   determine their own objective before beginning a demonstration.
2. Relate the demonstration to existing knowledge or to the unit under
   study, to help pupils see the value of attending to the demonstration.

*Demonstrations can be
performed by the teacher, a
student, or a classroom
visitor.*

3. Carry out the demonstration in a series of steps. Involve the students if their participation will clarify understanding. Think through the steps prior to the demonstration. Keep explanations clear throughout, and do not present too much information. When showing how to use a carding machine, for example, it's not necessary to discuss the role of wool in 18th-century life. While this may be important, it is not essential to the demonstration of how the machine works.

4. To demonstrate a series of steps, use visual aids such as charts, diagrams, photographs or the chalkboard. Be sure the materials are on hand before starting.

5. Ask questions. Demonstrations present information visually and verbally, and there will undoubtedly be times when students need to ask questions to clarify points. The teacher also can ask questions to determine whether students comprehend what is being shown and discussed.

6. Encourage summaries. When you are demonstrating particular skills or processes, students need opportunities to summarize the steps before they are called upon to perform.

7. Provide follow up and application. For students to understand what has been demonstrated and be able to apply that understanding, immediate follow up activities should be scheduled so they can practice. The teacher may review the focus of the demonstration and how this new material relates to the overall unit (Michaelis, Grossman, & Scott, 1975).

Demonstrations are usually incorporated into an overall instructional strategy; one would not teach an entire unit of demonstrations. They can often be used to clarify confusion pupils may exhibit as they respond to other instructional strategies. Resource persons invited to provide expertise on a particular unit of study often give demonstrations about their field.

Activity 8:5

A Processing Activity

Select a process—such as washing, carding, and spinning wool, candle making, or soap making— and after reading and other kinds of research, plan a demonstration to use with a group of students.

Values Formulation

Values education activities can be organized into general categories or approaches that reflect different goals or objectives (Superka et al., 1976).

The general approaches most frequently mentioned are values clarification, values analysis, and social/moral reasoning. Each of these distinctly different approaches can serve to demonstrate the relationship between human values and the social studies.

As Simon & Clark (1975) define it, values clarification represents ". . . a process for examining our lives and trying to find out clearly what we want and do not want." This procedure enables us to make personal choices, set personal goals, and examine personal roles. Although values clarification emphasizes alternatives and consequences, it does not emphasize an analysis of the societal context for value choices.

Values analysis frequently focuses on the values of others, of institutions, or of groups. It emphasizes systematical assessment of a value-oriented problem with particular stress on comparing, contrasting, and investigating the consequences of alternatives. Values analysis moves beyond the immediate decisions of personal choice toward a larger, more abstract decision-making activity applied to societal issues.

In using social/moral reasoning, one may examine either personal choices or societal issues that touch on ethical considerations. What is the right thing to do? Discussion revolves around the reasoning behind a personal decision, along with the rationales for recommending one action over another. Social/moral reasoning emphasizes consequences and role-taking as methods of developing empathy with others in our global community. One goal of this approach is the gradual development of a student's "world view" or "social perspective" in relation to value dilemmas.

Social studies represent an appropriate context for exploring a variety of value questions that center on personal choices, community issues, and social and moral issues.

Values Clarification

Kirschenbaum, Harmin, Howe, and Simon (1975) delineate the major hypothesis of values clarification as follows: "If a person skillfully and consistently uses the 'valuing process,' this increases the likelihood that the confusion, conflict, etc., will turn into decisions and living that are both personally satisfying and socially constructive."

Kirschenbaum (1977) further elaborates on this hypothesis by explaining that:

> "Personally satisfying" means that our living has value for us; that is, we pride and cherish more of our choices, beliefs, and activities. We experience higher self-esteem. We experience greater meaning in our lives. We are less apathetic and flighty, more purposeful and committed. It does not mean that we are always "happy," but that we are living vitally and experiencing the richness of ourselves, others, and the world around us, as we move toward self-selected meaningful goals. Being "socially constructive" means that we act in ways that promote the values of "life," "liberty" (i.e., freedom, jus-

tice, and equality), and the "pursuit of happiness" for all, as these general terms are further defined by the Bill of Rights and the United Nations Declaration on the Rights of Man. (p. 398)

Values clarification strategies rely on five dimensions basic to the valuing process: thinking, feeling, choosing, communicating, and acting. Many of the strategies can be adapted for use with value-laden topics in the social studies.

The teacher's role is to encourage students to clarify values, not to impart or instill specific values. An open atmosphere in which students' responses are accepted and honesty and diversity encouraged is necessary. Students learn to weigh the pros and cons and the consequences of various alternative actions.

A variety of activities based on Raths' model help students clarify values related to social studies topics (Raths, Harmin, & Simon, 1966). Four techniques of values clarification are values voting, rank order, values continuum, and unfinished sentences.

Values Voting

This activity for exploring values is an excellent way to introduce a discussion or topic investigation. The teacher begins by questioning, "How many of you . . .?" For example, in introducing a study of environmental issues, one might ask "How many of you think that gasoline should be rationed so that every driver can obtain only a certain amount?" Students who wish to vote in favor of the position raise their hands, those who are undecided fold their arms, and those who choose to answer negatively keep their hands down.

Rank Order

This procedure provides practice in choosing among alternatives. Students are given three or four options and asked to rank order them. Rank order questions might also be employed as a springboard or introduction to a lesson or topic, or to generate interest and stimulate discussion. For instance, in beginning a unit on environmental issues, students might rank order the following:

Which of these problems do you think is the greatest threat to our nation?

_____ Overpopulation; _____ Air and water pollution; _____ Depletion of natural resources.

Values Continuum

The values continuum points out the range of alternative positions on any given issue. Students identify where they stand by placing their names on a line between two extreme positions. For example:

What should the federal government policy be on control of energy sources?

Complete control _____ No control

How do you feel about immediately increasing the price of gasoline by 75 cents a gallon to cut down on gasoline use?

I agree—start tomorrow _____ No—Don't do it

How do you feel about banning the use of air conditioners in all buildings with windows?

I agree—start tomorrow _____ No—Don't do it

Unfinished Sentences

This activity allows the student to explore attitudes, interests, likes, dislikes, and so on. Unfinished sentence stems can be used in several ways, as shown in the following examples:

> The thing I liked best (least) in this unit . . .
> In the unit on the family I learned . . .
> I like best the kind of teacher who . . .
> If I were president of the United States, I would . . .

Values Analysis

The steps in values analysis are closely related to problem-solving models that begin with identifying a problem, require one to gather data, and move toward testing a conclusion (Metcalf, 1971). This approach to values education calls for detailed analysis of relevant data, using the following steps:

1. Define and clarify the value problem.
2. Gather the available facts.
3. Check the facts and select those that are relevant.
4. Make a tentative value decision.
5. Test the value principle implied in the decision. Does it apply in other situations?

Social/Moral Reasoning

Social/moral reasoning enables a person to examine either personal choices or societal issues that touch on ethical considerations. What is the right thing to do? The strategy described below is derived from the work of Kohlberg and Turiel (1971). Kohlberg recognizes three levels of moral development. On the *preconventional* level, a person responds to cultural labels of right and wrong, but interprets according to physical or hedonistic consequences. At the *conventional* level, maintaining the expectations of the individual's family, group, or nation is perceived as intrinsically valuable. The attitude is not only one of conformity to expectations in social order, but of loyalty to it. At the *postconventional* level, there is a clear effort to define moral values and principles as valid apart from the authority of the groups or persons who hold these principles.

207

To apply this strategy of values clarification, the teacher introduces a moral dilemma, determines the students' level of moral development, conducts discussion on that level, and attempts to advance their reasoning to the next higher level. Students analyze moral dilemmas, take a position, and verbalize reasons for their positions.

The main steps of the strategy, then, are to:

1. Present a moral dilemma.
2. Have students take a position and defend it.
3. Analyze positions and reasons.
4. Validate reasons further.

Activity 8:6

Values Clarification

Develop an appropriate values clarification exercise for a particular grade level.

Inquiry and Problem Solving

The main purpose of inquiry-oriented teaching is to help students develop the skills and attitudes necessary for independent problem solving. Inquiry processes require a great deal of interaction among student, teacher, materials, content, and environment. Both student and teacher become persistent question askers, interrogators, and ponderers. Inquiry-oriented teaching, then, requires an attitude of curiosity, the ability to analyze a problem, the capability for stating and testing hypotheses, and the skills to use data in establishing conclusions.

Certain classroom conditions and general procedures will facilitate inquiry. Inquiry and critical thinking flourish in classrooms where teachers are open and flexible and value diverse ideas. Teaching materials, too, affect inquiry and critical thinking, but unfortunately, materials for stimulating curiosity are rare.

Inquiry is not just asking questions; it is a systematic process of conducting an investigation. The process has been outlined in various ways, but the following steps are explicit or implicit in most versions:

1. State a question that can be answered with data and logic.
2. Hypothesize alternative questions.

3. Identify the kinds of evidence needed to support or reject each hypothesis.
4. Collect data relevant to each hypothesis and evaluate the reliability and validity of the data.
5. Test the adequacy of each hypothesis with the highest quality data obtainable and through logical reasoning.
6. Draw tentative conclusions regarding the accuracy of the hypothesis and the degree of confidence that can be placed in those conclusions.

Although this process appears to be linear, it does not necessarily operate that way. Identifying kinds of evidence, for example, may suggest a more productive form for the key question. Evaluating the adequacy of collected data may suggest another data source. The complexity of the inquiry determines the degree of effort necessary for each step and how much backtracking will be necessary.

Any inquiry activity will require a great deal of time to initiate and complete, so the teacher must schedule carefully. Inquiry requires time for students to analyze content in depth, and calls for greater interaction between learner and materials than in teacher-dominated strategies. There is also greater interaction between the teacher and the students.

The inquiry method actually reduces the amount of factual material covered, because more time is spent on developing thinking processes than on memorizing fact or content. When the aim is to stimulate high-order thinking skills, process must be substituted for some content.

Obviously, not all social studies teaching need be inquiry-oriented. The general rule is that the teaching strategy be consistent with objectives. If the objective is to convey information to students, exposition would probably be the most efficient and effective strategy. If the objective is to teach a skill, demonstration could be the best strategy. On the other hand, if the objective is to teach critical-thinking and problem-solving skills, an inquiry strategy would be best.

Expressive Experiences

Expressive experiences can extend and enhance learning in the social studies, and can help in individualizing instruction. They allow students to become deeply involved in learning activities and to express thoughts and feelings. Expressive experiences can be readily adapted to fit individual students' needs and characteristics.

Creative Writing

The social studies offer exciting opportunities for creative writing. After students have acquired basic understanding of a unit, they can express themselves by writing and sharing stories, poems, and plays.

In the early grades, before pupils can write with any degree of fluency, they can dictate their thoughts to the teacher. When they see their dictated accounts written, first on the chalkboard and then transferred to a chart, they learn that their ideas can be written down. They will soon want to do the writing themselves. As writing skills develop in later grades, students can express their thoughts in writing and share them with the class. The schedule can include time for pupils to read their creations to the whole class or to small groups. Teachers can occasionally help them share their work with one another by dittoing and passing out their creations. Over a period of time, student writings can be collected in individual journals, class scrapbooks, or displayed on bulletin boards.

Dramatic Presentations

Dramatic presentations offer limitless possibilities for students to identify with and to summarize social studies content. Presentations may take the form of spontaneous dramatic play, formal dramatization, puppet shows, or role playing.

Dramatic play, used frequently in the early grades, is an informal portrayal of an event or experience. The children do not have to memorize lines, and if costumes and properties are used at all, they are easy to improvise. Dramatization often becomes more formal in the intermediate grades. The students are interested in playing before an audience, particularly in costume. Students can take assigned roles and learn lines, and present the play to other classes or parents.

Children can use puppets for dramatic play and for more formal dramatization. Students enjoy making their puppets as well as writing the play. Puppets are often effective with shy students, helping them verbalize their thoughts and feelings and thereby build confidence.

Role playing is used to present a specific situation for study and discussion. It allows opportunities for students to change attitudes, clarify values, and to identify with the problems of others. A problem situation may be dramatized through role playing, followed by a carefully structured discussion. Shaftel and Shaftel (1967) suggest the following strategy for role playing:

1. The group discusses and interprets the problem.
2. Roles are discussed and participants selected.
3. The stage is set; questions are answered about space and the different roles.
4. The observers are prepared by clarifying points for which to watch.
5. The role playing is conducted.
6. The actions are evaluated; students are encouraged to actually "get inside" the other person.
7. The role playing is resumed.
8. The entire event is discussed, evaluated, and further changes are made.
9. The role playing is generalized to similar experiences in other contexts.*

---

*Fannie R. Shaftel, George Shaftel, ROLE-PLAYING FOR SOCIAL VALUES: Decision-Making in the Social Studies, © 1967, pp. 134–135. Adapted by permission of Prentice-Hall, Inc., Englewood Cliffs, N.J.

Young people need to comprehend how others feel. Students should be encouraged to identify with others and experiment with new attitudes as they play different roles. Role playing thus fosters insights into others' problems, feelings, and values.

Music

The spirit of a people is often revealed by their music. Since most cultures express customs, beliefs, and values in music, its study makes an important contribution to the social studies.

The social studies curriculum invites singing and dancing, listening, creating, or playing musical instruments. It is possible to find related songs to sing for almost any unit of study. Singing folk songs and ballads and performing folk dances give young people a feeling for other times and places and expand their appreciation of other cultures.

Simple rhythm instruments can be used as an accompaniment to a story or poem.

211

Besides learning about different cultures through singing and dancing, students can learn about the folk songs, events, composers, and holidays through listening experiences, which provide direct cultural contact with peoples everywhere. Though often considered a passive activity, listening to music is creative to the degree that students discover new dimensions of a people through this aspect of their culture.

The social studies allow ample opportunity for students to be musically creative. Stories and poems written by the children can be set to music using simple rhythm instruments. Upper-elementary grade students might even create the music for some of their dramatic presentations—plays, puppet shows, and so on.

Arts and Crafts

Arts and crafts provide avenues for expressing thoughts and feelings not found in other activities. These experiences not only provide personal and creative outlet, they can extend and strengthen learning in the social sciences. The kinds of art experiences applicable to social studies are unlimited; they can contribute to learning in every social studies unit. Among the most common are:

Drawing pictures	Weaving and sewing
Making murals	Finger painting
Making posters	Designing and making
Clay modeling	booklets or bookcovers
Soap carving	Painting scenery for plays
Making puppets	Making cartoons
Making masks	Constructing dioramas
Creating mobiles	and shadow boxes

In addition to the creative arts and crafts, students enjoy and benefit from many of the industrial or practical arts. They can use materials and tools to construct objects related to their social studies units. (Only simple tools should be handled, and proper use and safety measures must be taught.)

Some lower-elementary teachers have their pupils construct playhouses to use with units on the home. The children make curtains, crude furniture, and braided rugs. As children move into the upper-elementary grades, more complex construction projects continue to be appropriate. A unit on Pioneers in America might inspire construction of a model of a log cabin, for example.

The important thing to remember is that construction activities, as well as all classroom art activities, should contribute to reaching specific objectives. They should help pupils develop concepts and understandings, and should be practical from the standpoint of available materials and time.

Activity 8:7

Expressive Experiences

Select a unit topic for a grade in which you have a particular interest, and suggest several expressive experiences that might be used with the unit. Explain briefly toward what objective each experience would contribute.

Involving Students in Content

As a teacher, you will want to choose activities that will involve your students in the social studies content. The purpose of this involvement is to motivate students to think about and apply what they are being taught. The most appropriate activity for the content depends on the nature of the subject and the teacher's and students' objectives.

As part of the concept of inquiry learning, educators have begun to view students as researchers. Students can pose questions and collect relevant data; they can conduct social science experiments by manipulating variables, analyzing data, and drawing inferences.

Wheeler and Kelly (1977) outline interesting instructional implications of historical research for the elementary grades. Elementary students can actually function as historians, interviewing people and looking through old books, letters, and diaries to search for answers to questions. For example, in studying the family, students can generate a great deal of data and make comparisons with the past. The following activities emphasize the student as historical researcher:

1. Teachers and students construct a questionnaire about family size, gather data, analyze them, then make comparisons with the past.
2. Students bring in photographs of themselves and other members of the family and create family trees.
3. Students interview parents and grandparents about things they did when they were children.
4. Students look at old catalogs, magazines, and newspapers, and draw inferences about clothing, furniture, and household materials from times past.

Lee (1977) furnishes a good example of descriptive research procedures for students. In helping students conduct descriptive research, the teacher must provide an atmosphere where there is freedom to make mistakes, along with ample guidance to help pupils learn new methods as they acquire new subject matter. As topics applicable to descriptive research, Lee suggests: What examples of sexism do we find in our textbooks? Do all library books tell the same stories about George Washington? Topics such as these give students a chance to find answers to questions they consider important and interesting.

In the past, reading and writing activities have probably been overemphasized at the expense of doing, creating, and demonstrating. It is these latter activities, though, that allow students to comprehend what they are learning while enjoying their social studies experiences. To be sure, they need to learn from reading, but they also need to increase their knowledge from observing, discussing, interviewing—in essence, from actively *doing*.

Discussion

Although there is no "best" teaching method, some methods are more effective than others in certain situations. The most common methods fall into the categories of telling, showing, or doing. Some teaching methods might be more accurately categorized as educational activities, and among these, different types of activities serve different functions. There are those that provide for intake of information, those that help organize information, those that allow students to demonstrate what they've learned, and those that encourage application of knowledge to create a new product.

In addition to choosing from among different methods and activities, the social studies teacher must also contend with a variety of learning styles. Every student learns in a different way, and the teacher must cope with the different learning styles by attempting to individualize instruction—to adapt methods and activities to individual needs. One method for achieving individualization is that of grouping. The four grouping categories found in social studies classrooms are independent, one-to-one, small group, and large group. Groupings should be temporary—the teacher must shift children from one group to another and shift class activities from one grouping category to another as circumstances demand. Typical small-group formations are task groups, didactic groups, discussion groups, brainstorming groups, and inquiry groups.

Individualization can be facilitated by varying instruction among self-directed, teacher-guided, and teacher-directed activities. A classroom learning center for social studies promotes self-directed activities and motivates independent learning. Whatever methods or activities are chosen, however, the degree of individualization achieved in the classroom depends primarily on the teacher's attitude. The teacher who places the greatest importance on individual differences will do the most to address those differences in instruction.

In addition to individualizing instruction, the social studies teacher must also be prepared to cope with the diverse needs of learning disabled students and of the gifted and talented. Public Law 94–142 gives handicapped students the right to attend school in regular classes insofar as they are able.

The needs of these "mainstreamed" students can often be met with the techniques used for individualizing, particularly those of grouping. The teacher may also need to create or adapt instructional units, or modify textbooks and materials, or perhaps use new instructional strategies. Many teachers rely on Individualized Educational Plans (IEPs), prepared in cooperation with special education teachers, counselors, parents, and other support personnel.

The same approach is necessary in dealing with the gifted and talented. The social studies teacher may need to adjust content and activities for these students to help them go beyond the level of the regular classroom to achieve their potential. Again, the primary need is to individualize instruction to meet the student's needs—by accelerating the pace of instruction, introducing more abstract ideas and concepts, encouraging independent study, providing more advanced materials, and creating new study units.

In general, the social studies teacher's methods will cover the whole range of teaching strategies, depending upon the immediate instructional objectives. She will use expository techniques, conduct discussions, and carry out demonstrations.

The social studies teacher will be closely involved with values education. In this aspect of the social studies content, the three common teaching approaches are values clarification, values analysis, and social/moral reasoning. The teacher's role in values clarification is not to impart or instill values, but to help students clarify their values. Four techniques of values clarification are values voting, rank order, values continuum, and unfinished sentences. The values analysis approach follows the problem-solving model by calling for identification of a problem, gathering of data, and testing of conclusions. The social/moral reasoning approach calls for the teacher to present students with a moral dilemma; the students must take a position on the issue and defend their positions.

The social studies teacher will find inquiry-oriented instructional methods particularly effective. Inquiry and problem-solving approaches demand interaction among students, teacher, materials, content, and environment; their purpose is to encourage in students the necessary skills and attitudes for independent problem solving.

Expressive experiences are highly useful for social studies; they include creative writing, dramatic presentations, music, and arts and crafts. The choice of activity depends upon the topic and the educational objective, but the most effective activities are those that involve the student as an inquirer.

References

Ascher, R. S. "Methods and Techniques in Teacher Development." *Educational Technology,* November 1966.

Fraenkel, Jack R. "Learning Activities." In *Social Studies and the Elementary Teacher,* edited by William Joyce and F. Ryan. Washington, D. C.: National Council for the Social Studies, 1977.

Herlihy, John G., and Herlihy, Myra T. eds. *Mainstreaming in the Social Studies.* NCSS bulletin 62. Washington, D.C.: National Council for the Social Studies, 1980.

Jeter, Jan. "Guiding Thoughts on Individualized Education." In *Approaches to Individualized Education,* edited by Jan Jeter. Alexandria, Va.: The Association for Supervision and Curriculum Development, 1980.

Johnston, Hiram et al. *The Learning Center Idea Book.* Boston: Allyn and Bacon, 1978.

Kirschenbaum, Howard. "In Support of Values Clarification." *Social Education,* May 1977, pp. 218–21.

Kirschenbaum, Howard; Harmin, H.; Howe, L.; and Simon, S. *In Defense of Values Clarification: A Position Paper.* Saratoga Springs, N.Y.: National Humanistic Education Center, 1975.

Kohlberg, Lawrence, and Turiel, E. *Research in Moral Development.* New York: Holt, Rinehart and Winston, 1971.

Lee, John R. "Some Thoughts on Descriptive Research Procedures for Children." In *Social Studies and the Elementary Teacher: Promises and Practices,* edited by William Joyce and F. Ryan. Washington, D.C.: National Council for the Social Studies, 1977.

Lowenbraun, Sheila, and Affleck, James Q. *Teaching Mildly Handicapped Children in Regular Classes.* Columbus, Oh.: Charles E. Merrill, 1976.

Metcalf, Lawrence E., ed. *Values Education.* Washington D.C.: National Council for the Social Studies, 1971.

Michaelis, John; Grossman, R.; and Scott, L. *New Designs for Elementary Curriculum and Instruction.* New York: McGraw Hill, 1975.

Nussel, Edward J.; Inglis, Joan; and Wiersma, William. *The Teacher and Individually Guided Education.* Reading, Mass.: Addison-Wesley, 1976.

Raths, Louis; Harmin, H.; and Simon, S. *Values and Teaching.* Columbus, Oh.: Charles E. Merrill, 1966.

Reynolds, Maynard, and Birch, Jack W. *Teaching Exceptional Children in All America's Schools.* Reston, Va.: The Council for Exceptional Children, 1977.

Shaftel, Fannie R., and Shaftel, George. *Role-Playing for Social Values: Decision-Making in the Social Studies.* Englewood Cliffs, N.J.: Prentice-Hall, 1967.

Simon, Sidney, and Clark, Jay. *More Values Clarification.* San Diego: Pennant Press, 1975.

Superka, Douglas P.; Ahrens, Christine; and Hedstrom, Judith E., with Ford, Luther J., and Johnson, Patricia L. *Values Education Sourcebook.* Boulder, Colo.: Social Studies Education Consortium, 1976.

Turnbull, Ann P., and Schulz, Jane B. *Mainstreaming Handicapped Students: A Guide for the Classroom Teacher.* Boston: Allyn and Bacon, 1979.

Wheeler, Ronald, and Kelly, K. "Instructional Implications of Historical Research." In *Social Studies and the Elementary Teacher: Promises and Practices,* edited by William Joyce and F. Ryan. Washington, D.C.: National Council for the Social Studies, 1977.

Teaching Social Studies Skills

9

The systematic development of skills in elementary social studies is critical, for students learn by using the four basic types of skills: academic, research, thinking, and social skills. *Academic skills* focus on reading, viewing, writing, verbalizing, listening, interpreting, and creating (graphics, maps, charts, graphs). *Research skills* relate to identifying and defining a problem, creating hypotheses for solutions, locating and gathering data, analyzing data, evaluating hypotheses in light of the data, and finally, drawing conclusions. Study skills fall under research skills. *Thinking skills* refer to proficiency in describing, defining, classifying, hypothesizing, analyzing, and generalizing. These skills are activated in problem solving and critical and creative thinking. The last type, *social skills*, incorporates those skills essential for working with others in groups, being able to contribute to the efforts of others, and being both an effective follower and leader.

Jarolimek (1977) notes that below-standard achievement in social studies can usually be traced to poorly developed academic skills, primarily reading and work-study skills. Some students are unable to handle social studies vocabulary or to use reference materials. Other children cannot read maps, globes, and other graphic materials. The social studies program must, therefore, provide for systematic and sequential development of the necessary skills.

Skills are fundamental to learning; they allow the student to process and understand materials and to become independent learners. Because these skills are complex, however, they require careful teacher and student attention. Since skills are developmental, practice must be provided over extended periods of time. Teachers can incorporate such opportunities into a developmental sequence in which essential skills are carefully identified, systematically taught, and thoroughly practiced.

Academic Skills

Reading in the Social Studies

Reading is perhaps the paramount academic skill in all areas of the curriculum. Through reading, individuals identify their own and other cultures, they process information necessary for developing new concepts and general-izations, and they gather data essential for problem solving. Regardless of subject matter area, every teacher is responsible for teaching reading.

Most elementary teachers set aside a definite time during the day for concentrated attention on basic reading skills. During this time, students develop a basic vocabulary, learn various word-attack techniques, develop comprehension skills, and learn to read critically, evaluating what they have read.

Regardless of the quality of the basal program, reading from the basal is generally easier than reading social studies texts, for which students often need additional guidance. The vocabulary of social studies is usually more difficult; new terms are introduced at a faster pace and with less repetition; more facts are presented; and a large number of rather complex concepts are introduced with little explanation. Pupils frequently need to learn entirely new words or additional meanings for words they already know, such as belt, basin, source, mouth. Reading skills and other abilities associated with the social studies must be developed right along with other social studies instruction.

Building Social Studies Vocabulary

Social studies materials have a specialized vocabulary, and use words from the common vocabulary in particular ways. Many pupils find it difficult to read this material, so the social studies teacher must accept vocabulary develop-ment as a major responsibility. With both gifted and learning handicapped in the regular classroom, the teacher will also have to develop ways to address these pupils' unique vocabulary development needs. Some of the types of words students will encounter in social studies are:

- Abbreviations and acronyms—abbreviated expressions, such as NATO, UN, UNESCO, AFL–CIO.
- Technical words—words used in the social studies that are generally not found in other curricular areas, such as market, culture, democracy, senate, house of representatives, latitude, longitude.
- Figurative terms—terms that have a connotation different from the literal meaning, such as cold war, open door, closed shop, hawk, dove, carpetbag, guerrilla warfare.
- Multiple-meaning words—words that change meaning depending on con-text, such as chief, fork, mouth, hill.
- Quantitative terms—terms signifying amounts of time, space, etc., such as fortnight, score, decade, century, area.

One effective way to assist pupils with this new vocabulary is to anticipate word problems before asking students to read a selection, then designing strategies to prevent difficulties.

New words and terms should be presented and developed in context rather than in isolation. Students should not be required to look up long lists of words and write definitions before reading an assignment. The teacher should conduct vocabulary development in short, highly motivating sessions, and encourage students to use the new vocabulary in their discussions.

You can plan to use some of the following activities to help your students acquire a social studies vocabulary. Remember that the activities should correspond to the students' levels of achievement, capabilities, and backgrounds.

1. Select and use pictures, photographs, or slides that illustrate specific meanings. One picture can help clarify any number of terms, such as rice paddy, bayou, canal, etc.
2. Take field trips to observe activities and objects firsthand.
3. Observe and examine models, exhibits, or displays to clarify meanings.
4. Give examples, and distinguish them from nonexamples.
5. Have students work with synonyms and antonyms to link the meaning of a new term to a known term.
6. Introduce new words on the chalkboard in a meaningful context and encourage their frequent use.
7. Have students make models, objects, displays, murals, or dioramas.
8. Have students role play to extend meaning.
9. Encourage students to write creative stories using social studies vocabulary.
10. Show pupils how to use context clues in solving unknown words.

Activity 9:1

Specialized Social Studies Words

Select an elementary social studies textbook and find examples of the types of words listed on page 219. Write some basic guidelines showing how you would introduce the terms.

Facilitating Comprehension

Comprehending an author's meaning is a key objective of reading. Such understanding calls for a variety of reading skills and a grasp of specialized vocabulary, aids to reading, and a knowledge of how social studies materials are organized. When the reader comprehends what the author has intended, then he can extract essential facts and meanings, formulate a pattern, and sense the connections among facts.

According to DeBoer and Dallman (1974), comprehension occurs on three levels. The first is the literal or factual level, when an individual just "reads the lines." The second is "reading between the lines," or grasping the meaning but not actually as expressed in the author's words. The third is "reading beyond the lines." At this final level, the reader anticipates ways the material can be applied over and above those suggested by the author. Some reading experts refer to a fourth level, appreciative and creative, when the reader "creates new lines."

Reading comprehension in social studies consists of all of these levels. The literal or factual level provides the groundwork for moving to higher levels. After mastering the author's intended meaning, the reader can advance to more complex reading and thinking skills, such as drawing implications, making inferences, discovering relationships, formulating appropriate responses, and engaging in critical responses to the material.

Children who bring much to a reading situation also derive much. All children bring to the reading task their intellectual abilities, interests, attitudes, and experiences. For the most part, there is not much that social studies teachers can do to enhance children's intellectual capabilities. However, they can do much to capitalize on the other three qualities. Children with limited experienes can have their horizons broadened through field trips, films, photographs, and by having interesting people visit the classroom. These encounters can also influence their interests and attitudes.

Many of the suggestions regarding the basal reading program also apply in social studies. The recommended activities in reading programs are valuable in social studies for setting a purpose for reading, reading for the main idea, reading to select significant details, reading to summarize and organize, reading to derive generalizations, and critical reading.

Setting a Purpose for Reading

Sometimes the only purpose for reading will be to "get some impressions about these people." This general statement is still purposeful—that of exploring material and recording impressions. It is unreasonable to give students a reading assignment without some purpose; to tell them to "read pages 21–30 for tomorrow" is purposeless. Why should they read these pages? For impressions? For types of air pollution? For solutions to health problems?

Reading for a purpose is essential to comprehension. At times, the purpose will be convergent: to read for a specific fact or conclusion or issue. At other times, it is divergent: to read for as many facts or conclusions or issues as possible. A convergent purpose would be to "read this section of our book to find out what the author considers the four most important economic issues facing our country." You might assign a divergent purpose by saying, "Read these pages to discover as much as possible about the causes of pollution in our industrial society."

Reading for the Main Idea

All other comprehension skills depend upon reading to grasp the main idea. Good readers are able to distinguish the main idea from details and to restate that idea in their own words. Learning activities for developing this skill include:

1. Having students make a mural showing the main events of a reading selection.
2. Having students make up their own titles or headings for selections.
3. Having students read a paragraph or selection in the textbook, then state or write the main idea in their own words.
4. Having students select from several pictures the one that shows the main idea, or encouraging them to match a number of pictures with the paragraphs they illustrate.
5. Having the students select from a list of questions one that reflects the main idea of an entire paragraph.
6. Having students answer questions that focus on the main idea.

Reading to Select Significant Details

Details in social studies provide concrete illustrations to clarify a concept or generalization. Details supply evidence or data to support or reject hypotheses. Teachers present pupils with reading situations in which they are to note and remember significant details; these are two such activities:

1. After they have read a passage, have students.make a list of details necessary for: (a) drawing a picture about the ideas found in the passage; (b) dramatizing the passage; (c) preparing a chart or graph based on the passage; and (d) making an outline.
2. After reading a passage, have students find and state the details that support a main idea in a paragraph or selection.

Reading to Summarize and Organize

Selecting the main idea and identifying significant details are basic to summarizing and organizing. Skilled readers bring together the main idea and the supporting details in some logical order. According to some reading specialists, reading to summarize and organize is more closely related to interpreting material than to comprehending it. They argue that comprehension in the strictest sense involves only getting the facts as presented by the author. Interpretation goes beyond literally reporting an author's statements. Whenever students must make inferences, identify cause and effect, give examples of author bias, act as critic, and make projections from material read, they are interpreting. Remember, as noted earlier, that comprehension exists on several levels. It demands more than recall; it requires interpreting and processing information so that the reader really knows more than just what the author has written down.

These are ways to foster reading for summarizing and organizing information:

1. In the lower grades, after a selection has been read, have pupils arrange pictures in the order in which the events in the selection occurred.

2. After reading a selection, have pupils draw pictures to illustrate the main events.
3. Have pupils make an outline, chart, graph, or table that summarizes information from a particular selection.
4. Have pupils write a summary of a selection in their own words.

Reading to Derive Generalizations

Deriving generalizations is essentially an interpretive aspect of comprehension. Formulating generalizations from reading requires ability in selecting the main idea and identifying significant details, ability in summarizing and organizing information, and the capability of taking the extra leap in deriving generalizations. DeBoer and Dallman point out that students who lack this skill tend to generalize without adequate evidence and make generalizations that are far too broad based on the available information.

To help pupils generalize from reading, the teacher can:

1. Ask pupils questions that focus their attention on forming generalizations. Such questions are, "What general statement can you make about this selection? If someone asked you to summarize the main ideas, what might you say? What conclusions can we draw from this chapter?"
2. Have pupils create titles that indicate generalizations about reading materials.

Reading to Develop Critical Views

Critical reading falls in the category of interpretation rather than that of simple comprehension. To make critical judgments about what someone has written is one of the most essential reading skills. It allows the reader to judge the usefulness of material for a general or specific purpose, and to decide whether or not the information should be stored for future use. In social studies, pupils need to read materials with an eye for bias, prejudice, opinion, and accuracy. Critical reading is a deliberate process, and the skilled reader uses it to identify an author's purposes, to compare and contrast a variety of sources, to determine whether an author presents one view or several on controversial issues, and to distinguish fact from opinion. The competent critical reader is an effective questioner. (More will be said about questions and questioning in chapter 10.) People will not be able to read critically without the ability to raise analysis and evaluation questions. Heilman (1977) suggests several obstacles that often prevent elementary students from reading critically.

1. Pupils form the opinion that everything in print is true.
2. Children are conditioned to accept authority blindly.
3. Schools have relied on single textbooks, and the teacher stresses "what the book says."
4. Some schools avoid controversial topics and emphasize uniformity.

These are some ways you can help pupils learn to read critically:

1. Ask students to locate statements of opinion in newspapers.
2. Have students check the qualifications of a number of authors who have written on the same subject and determine who may be the most qualified.
3. Have pupils compare a newspaper editorial and a front-page account of the same event.
4. Ask pupils to examine several newspaper articles to identify words that signal opinions or judgments, such as "The greatest achievement of . . . "; "People in Mexico generally prefer . . . ."

Facilitating Effective Use of the Textbook

Although criticized throughout the years, textbooks have been and continue to be the school's most widely used teaching tool. One criticism is that some teachers expect all pupils to be able to read the text designated for their particular grade level. A second criticism is that some teachers expose their class only to material covered in the textbook. A third complaint is that textbooks quickly become outdated. It is evident, however, that the first two criticisms are really not aimed at the textbook, but rather at teachers' poor use of it. The third point is valid, but most books cover topics generally enough that this tendency is somewhat reduced. At today's rate of technological change, all materials are vulnerable to some degree.

Textbooks *are* important to the social studies curriculum. The challenge facing teachers is how to use them in ways that facilitate pupil learning. To vary the use of the social studies textbook, the teacher can:

1. Provide for individual differences. She can furnish reading material on a particular topic at various reading levels. The material from the text can be tape-recorded so that students who need to can listen to tapes. She can also vary the difficulty level of the activities that arise from the text material.
2. Supplement the textbooks with additional materials, such as reference books, globes, maps, charts, films, filmstrips, etc.
3. Use the textbook not as a tool for gathering data but rather as a resource for children to use in checking the accuracy of their investigations. This means that pupils conduct an investigation using a variety of reading materials and then read the textbook to compare their conclusions with those of the author.
4. Have pupils read the textbook in a sequence other than that suggested by the table of contents. So often teachers have pupils read the chapters in sequence, when allowing children to suggest the sequence themselves could produce a fresh, unbiased view. Each child may not need to read all chapters.
5. Use the textbook as a basis for debates rather than just as information to be remembered. Encourage children to read the textbook as a literary

critic might. This approach can help the children develop their critical reading skills and thus hone their abilities of critical thinking.

A good source of ways to use the textbook creatively is Patton's *Improving the Use of Social Studies Textbooks*. This publication of the National Council for the Social Studies shows teachers how to update the out-of-date, strengthen reading comprehension, study pictures effectively, correct ethnic and sex stereotypes, and evaluate the strengths and weaknesses of social studies textbooks.

Locating and Utilizing Reference Materials

The myriad print and nonprint materials available for social studies classrooms reflect today's phenomenal rate of knowledge production. Well-developed social studies units suggest many different types of materials for student use; confronted with this vast array, children must learn how to make wise use of materials. The teacher has the responsibility of instructing pupils in such practical applications. The teacher should formally teach skills related to locating information, classifying it under both the academic and research skills. Locational or "study" skills include learning the different parts of the book, learning to use basic references, and learning to use the library.

These activities help students develop basic locational skills:

1. Have pupils learn the parts of social studies textbooks by examining and discussing the table of contents, index, list of maps, graphs, and tables, and the glossary.
2. Assess the pupils' ability to locate information in their textbooks by the use of study questions and exercises. For example, guide them toward selecting the key words in an index that would help them research the request to "discuss the causes of the Civil War."
3. Provide assignments that require the use of encyclopedias, maps, pictures, and diagrams in order to gather data.
4. Have pupils use the card catalogue to locate information on a specific problem.
5. Guide the students in locating all the references available for gathering information on the topic in question.
6. Have pupils use dictionaries to find information other than spelling and pronunciation of terms. They can be directed to maps, foreign terms, and tables in many dictionaries.

One challenge in teaching the use of reference materials is having pupils become skilled in organizing and synthesizing information. They can develop this skill by seeking information from various sources and summarizing it on notecards. Students in the middle- and upper-elementary grades should learn note taking as a specialized study skill. In the early grades, the teacher might record information on the chalkboard as pupils report it. The

225

teacher often can encourage pupils to develop their own schemes for organizing and connecting information. Children can be encouraged to create their own notebooks, to keep as "data vaults" for use in later class discussions and investigations.

Teachers should encourage note taking throughout the elementary grades. It is a good idea to make pupils aware of the variety of questions they may want to raise as they process information from both the textbook and reference materials, since the types of questions will influence what information they record in the notes. If pupils are taught to ask only knowledge questions, their notes will most likely record specific facts for later recall, but if they are taught to raise questions about causes and effects or about the

Knowing how to use the library card catalogue is a basic research skill.

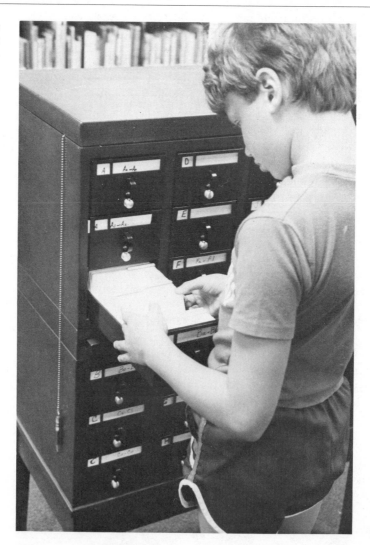

accuracy of conclusions, their notes will record relationships and ideas about which they have some doubt.

Notes need to be organized in some manner to be useful. Outlining, a subskill of academic skills, allows pupils to organize information from a variety of sources. Awareness of the organization of the original materials helps in making outlines. The table of contents or the major headings in reference materials can suggest main headings for outlines, although children should not blindly accept these organizations. They should be encouraged to decide whether the organization in the reference material is relevant to their own questions and the focus of the lesson.

The mechanics of outlining are sometimes taught in language arts. Children should ask questions about the outlines they create: Does the outline cover the major points of my investigation? Are the key subpoints listed under each major heading? Do the main points go together? Should point III

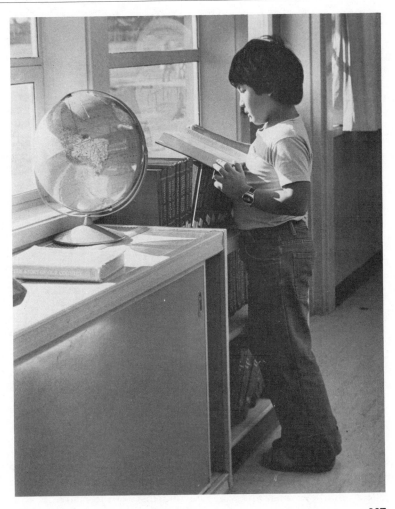

Guiding students in locating and using a variety of references is an important practical aspect of social studies teaching.

really be point IV? Can someone make sense out of my outline without my explaining it? The children's outlines can also be placed in the notebooks for later use in investigations and class dialogue.

The teacher should supply a list of current materials beyond the basic textbook. A rather standard grouping of available materials is as follows:

Reference Books	*Other Written Materials*
Encyclopedias	Newspapers
Atlases	Magazines
Dictionaries	Government reports
Almanacs	Business reports
Yearbooks	Pamphlets, booklets
Bibliographies	(published often by government
Guides to published materials	agencies, both national and
(to books in print, and to	states. Frequently published by
published articles)	various professional associations
	as well.)
	Travel folders
	Diaries and letters

Books	*Visual Materials*
Textbooks	Photographs
Picture books	Maps, charts, and graphs
Biographies	Paintings
Historical fiction	Sculptures and artifacts

A quick glance at this partial list makes it clear that pupils will need specific instruction in using these materials. All teachers must realize that reading is not taught only in the developmental reading program. Pupils need specific instruction in the reading materials geared to social studies.

Activity 9:2

Comprehending Social Studies Materials

Select a social studies textbook at a grade level in which you are interested. Outline a plan for developing the various academic skills related to reading in social studies.

Writing and Social Studies

When pupils reach conclusions, they must be able to communicate their findings to others. It is essential, then, that they be able to express themselves effectively in writing, and you will find that writing activities blend naturally into others as pupils investigate and synthesize. Avoid attempts to set aside separate times for developing writing skills. Social studies writing can assume any number of creative forms. There should be many opportunities for students to create and share stories, reports, and poems. Several short papers of one or two pages are more helpful in developing writing skills than one major long paper. Give students chances to:

1. Organize information into an outline.
2. Write paragraphs to summarize major points of an investigation.
3. Write short reports to share their individual research. (Discourage reports that essentially repeat information copied from an encyclopedia.) You can help pupils write short reports by providing counsel in choosing a topic, helping them select suitable references, showing how to take notes and outline, proofing the actual writing, and making suggestions for possible visuals (pictures, charts, diagrams, maps, graphs).
4. Write television and radio scripts. When students are studying the past, they can recreate famous broadcasts.
5. Write letters. As students investigate controversial issues such as pollution, they can write letters to editors and legislators.
6. Write poetry. Poetry writing sometimes correlates well with social studies. When studying the geography of a region, for example, hearing poems about the region will encourage children to write poems of their own that give a poetic view of the region under study.
7. Create stories as a group. With very young children, the teacher can write their stories on experience charts or on the chalkboard.

Activity 9:3

Basic Skills in the Social Studies

Many people say that young people today do not know how to read and write. Communities are demanding that schools spend more time on the basic skills. List specific tactics that can lead to integrating basic skills in the social studies.

Verbal Communication and Listening Skills

Verbal communication and listening are essential academic skills. Students often receive no assistance in thinking through ideas or in organizing the ideas they will present verbally. They need to learn to ask, "What do I want to say? Is verbal delivery the best way to present the information? How do I organize my thoughts so my audience will understand what I am trying to communicate?" Pupils often improve the organization of their verbal messages by reflecting on their written reports. Panel discussions, interviewing, oral reports, and role playing also help improve verbal communication. Even informal conversation is beneficial. The teacher who encourages verbal skills understands that verbal language skills flourish best in an environment that allows face-to-face relationships, furnishes stimulating materials, and encourages a relaxed atmosphere for sharing ideas.

Listening is also an essential skill in social studies, and is in many ways a more difficult process to master than reading or writing. Children have no control over the rate at which they listen. They cannot go back and reexamine ideas they've heard. In addition, the verbal information may not be carefully organized. Most speakers do not organize their information as tightly as when they are writing. Since children in social studies classes will spend a major portion of their time listening, listening needs to be a part of formal instruction.

Teaching listening skills is somewhat more difficult than teaching reading or writing, primarily because listening skills are not as well defined. Advocates of teaching listening skills draw heavily from selected reading skills—recall, comprehension, inference, and critical and creative listening. Indeed, there are basic parallels between listening and reading; both are receptive skills that depend heavily upon the influence of experience for quality and quantity of meaning.

Ragan and Shepherd (1977) present helpful suggestions for encouraging effective listening among pupils:

1. Make listening an integral part of the curriculum.
2. Provide a classroom environment that facilitates good listening by paying attention to temperature, seating, and noise reduction. Also, make certain that pupils are prepared to listen before material is presented orally.

Verbal communications skills can be developed through informal conversation as well as regular academic activities.

3. Develop listening readiness by relating the material to previous experience, by writing the meanings of new words likely to be heard in the oral presentation, and by writing questions that can guide the listening.
4. Give pupils a purpose for listening by having them write down the reasons for doing so. Valid reasons include: for enjoyment, for finding answers to questions, and for finding errors in statements.
5. Make sure that the material to be presented orally is suited to the maturity level, attention span, and previous experiences of the children.
6. Assist pupils in reproducing, summarizing, and explaining what they have heard.
7. Assist pupils in evaluating the programs to which they listen. Such help can instruct children in phrasing evaluation questions.

Skills for Using Maps, Globes, and Graphics

Maps and globes are essential tools in social studies; they provide an efficient way to portray a great amount of information. A good map, like an effective picture, is worth thousands of words. In the social studies, maps present selective and abstracted representations of reality. From maps and globes, children

Maps are an essential tool in social studies.

can learn to locate places in the community, the state, the nation, and the world. These places can be cities, parks, resources, ports, water bodies, historical places. Maps can even show events and populations.

Maps and globes also help pupils find direction, locate one place in relation to another, identify travel routes, determine the direction of a river's flow, and the movements of people. Maps and globes also help pupils understand distance and time between different places and areas. But they do not merely furnish facts. Children can use them to draw inferences and discover relationships among graphic data. They can analyze relationships between the distribution of resources and the location of a people, or the locations of cities in relation to topographic features. A special benefit of using maps and globes is that children develop a visual orientation to spatial relationships.

Maps and globes comprise an essential part of any social studies program. They orient children to a particular place scheduled for investigation. In planning their own investigations, children should be guided in determining when they should employ maps and globes and what types are appropriate for their inquiry. The units to be taught, the children's maturity, and their prior experiences determine what types of maps and globes to use with a class.

The following list outlines essential map and globe skills that should be developed in the elementary school.

Interpreting Maps and Globes

A. Orienting the map and noting directions
   1. Use cardinal directions in classroom and neighborhood
   2. Use intermediate directions, such as southeast, northwest
   3. Use cardinal directions and intermediate directions in working with maps
   4. Use relative terms of location and directions, such as near, far, above, below, up, down
   5. Understand that north is toward the North Pole and south is toward the South Pole on any map projection
   6. Understand the use of the compass for direction
   7. Use the north arrow on the map
   8. Orient desk, outline, textbook, and atlas maps correctly to the north
   9. Use parallels and meridians in determining direction
   10. Use different map projections to learn how the pattern of meridians and that of parallels differ
   11. Construct simple maps which are properly oriented as to direction

B. Locate places on maps and globes
   1. Recognize the home city and state on a map of the United States and on a globe
   2. Recognize land and water masses on a globe and on a variety of maps—physical-political, chalkboard, weather, etc.
   3. Identify on a globe and on a map of the world the equator, tropics, circles, continents, oceans, and large islands

4. Use a highway map for locating places by number-and-key system; plan a trip using distance, direction, and locations
5. Relate low latitudes to the equator and high latitudes to the polar areas
6. Interpret abbreviations commonly found on maps
7. Use map vocabulary and key accurately
8. Use longitude and latitude in locating places on wall maps
9. Use an atlas to locate places
10. Identify the time zones of the United States and relate them to longitude
11. Consult two or more maps to gather information about the same area
12. Recognize location of major cities of the world with respect to their physical setting
13. Trace routes of travel by different means of transportation
14. Develop a visual image of major countries, land forms, and other map pattern studies
15. Read maps of various types which show elevation
16. Understand the significance of relative location as it has affected national policies
17. Learn to sketch simple maps to show location

C. Use scale and compute distances
1. Use small objects to represent large ones, as a photograph compared to actual size
2. Make simple large-scale maps of a familiar area, such as classroom, neighborhood
3. Compare actual length of a block or a mile with that shown on a large-scale map
4. Determine distance on a map by using a scale of miles
5. Compare maps of different sizes of the same area
6. Compare maps of different areas to note that a small scale must be used to map larger areas
7. Compute distance between two points on maps of different scales
8. Estimate distances on a globe, using latitude; estimate air distances by using a tape or string to measure great circle routes
9. Understand and use map scale expressed as representative fraction, statement of scale, or bar scale
10. Develop the habit of checking the scale on all maps used

D. Interpret map symbols and visualize what they represent
1. Understand that real objects can be represented by pictures or symbols on a map
2. Learn to use legends on different kinds of maps
3. Identify the symbols used for water features to learn the source, mouth, direction of flow, depths, and ocean currents
4. Study color contour and visual relief maps and visualize the nature of the areas shown
5. Interpret the elevation of the land from the flow of rivers
6. Interpret dots, lines, colors, and other symbols used in addition to pictorial symbols

E. Compare maps and draw inferences
1. Read into a map the relationships suggested by the data shown, as the factors which determine the location of cities

233

2. Compare two maps of the same area, combine the data shown on them, and draw conclusions based on the data
3. Recognize there are many kinds of maps for many uses, and learn to choose the best map for the purpose at hand
4. Understand the differences in different map projections and recognize the distortions involved in any representation of the earth other than the globe
5. Use maps and globe to explain the geographic setting of historical and current events
6. Infer man's activities or way of living from physical detail and from latitude*

*Helen McCracken Carpenter. *Skill Development in the Social Studies.* Reprinted by permission.

The Globe

The globe, the most accurate representation of the earth's surface, is useful when pupils investigate problems concerning relative location, size, direction, distance, and the shape of land masses and bodies of water. With a globe, children can accurately plot the distances between places on the earth, obtain an accurate view of the size and shape of land masses and bodies of water, and obtain true directions. In most classrooms, maps and globes are often used together. The question for the teacher is when to use a globe and when to use a map.

Children should be introduced to the globe in the primary grades, and become acquainted with the fundamental concepts of the earth and its surface features. They can come to understand the concept of the earth's roundness, the extent of water coverage, and the shapes and sizes of the land masses. In the intermediate grades, the globe can be used to explain time zones, season changes, rotation and revolution, latitude and longitude, and hemisphere. Each classroom should have a globe, and children should have free time just to handle it and study it casually. Some formal time for discussing the globe should be scheduled as well. More time will be spent with the globe in the middle grades. The teacher must plan systematic globe instruction as a part of unit activities, as well as reinforcement of certain globe processing skills when the need arises. Many learning experiences facilitate globe use; for example:

1. Show the globe to children and point out its roundness. Perhaps the children can suggest the benefits of a round earth. What happens to our daily lives as a result of a round earth?
2. Have children become aware of the land areas and water bodies on the earth. Point out that all these features have names. In the early grades, it's not necessary to spend a great deal of time on geographic names. Many children will learn the names in their casual inspections of the globe.
3. Show children the location of the poles. Tell them that the top half of the globe is called the northern half. Children can guess what the other half is called.

4. Have children study the locations of most of the land masses. Have them suggest what effects this might have on travel.
5. Children always want to know where *they* are located on the earth. Show them their location on the globe. Have them locate places where other members of their families live. Where do the world leaders they have heard about live?
6. Allow children time to explore the globe, just taking an imaginary trip around the world, visiting places that seem interesting. Children can report their findings to other classmates.
7. Encourage children to ask questions about the globe. Schedule time for discussing these questions.

Maps and Their Language

Maps are selective and abstracted representations of reality, which show certain areas in detail. The globe is far too small to show great detail. Maps can be classified according to their content as:

- Physical—mountains, plains, rivers, oceans
- Political—boundaries, cities, states, nations
- Climate—rainfall, temperature, winds
- Population—distribution, relation to topographic features
- Economic—distribution of resources, occupations, products
- Physical-political—a combination showing political units and physical features

Students should have free time for handling and casually studying the globe.

235

A major aim in social studies is to teach children to "read" maps, to make sense out of the symbols and concepts that are unique to maps. They must first learn the concepts of *scale*. The scale of a map shows the ratio of the space used on the map as compared to actual geographic surface. For instance, how many miles of the earth's surface are represented in one inch on the map? This differs from map to map, so each map must show what scale is being used. A large-scale map shows only a small region, but gives a great amount of detail. A small-scale map covers a much larger portion of the earth's surface, but eliminates many details. The most common way to show scale is by a representative fraction. A scale of 1:62,500 or 1/62,500 means that one inch on the map stands for 62,500 units on the earth. Maps designed for elementary-age children frequently use a graphic scale, where scale is shown by a straight line on which distances have been marked off. Thus 20 miles might appear in the lower corner of the map. Children must learn to locate the scale key of each map they read. A third type of scale also common at the elementary level is in words and figures—for example, the scale might state that "one inch equals five miles."

Although they may not realize it, children are already acquainted with scale by the time they encounter maps. All children have seen photographs of themselves; the teacher can remind them of this and ask them if they are really only three inces high. Of course not! Then tell them the reason they do not look funny in the photograph is that all parts of them have been reduced proportionately. Thus, the photograph looks real. Aerial photographs offer a good way to get children to compare photographs of themselves to photographs of places on the earth shown in scale.

The second major term in map language is *symbols*. A great deal of information can be put on a map by using symbols. Mapmakers have developed a variety of symbols, some of which stand for human-made or cultural features of the landscape, such as cities, roads, and farms, while others represent natural features, such as mountains, plains, rivers, and lakes. Symbols on complicated maps may be lines, dots, circles, triangles, letters, colors, or some combination of these. Many maps produced for the elementary grades use miniature pictures of the thing being represented as symbols. The younger the age level, the more concrete the symbols. Examples of map symbols found in school maps appear in figure 9.1.

Figure 9.1
Map Symbols

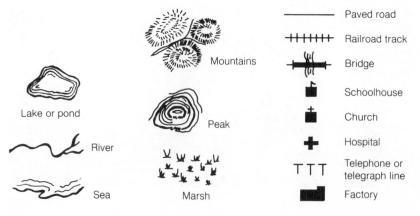

Lake or pond

River

Sea

Mountains

Peak

Marsh

Paved road

Railroad track

Bridge

Schoolhouse

Church

Hospital

Telephone or telegraph line

Factory

Most maps have a *legend* to explain the meaning of the symbols, and children must develop the habit of looking for and using this legend.

As a specialized map symbol, *color* may represent political boundaries, land elevations, population distribution and density, and rainfall patterns. To determine what a color stands for, children again need to check the legend. Children in the primary grades will understand that blue on a map usually symbolizes water, tan or green usually represents land areas, and black or red usually refers to human-made features. As children advance in the grades, more complex use of color can be treated, and children can "read" color to learn what the surface of the land is like, differences in rainfall among areas, and the relationship of rainfall patterns to wind patterns and topographic features.

Gridwork, another symbol system in the language of maps, is a network of north-south and east-west lines on the surface of a map. The reader uses the grid to establish directions and to locate places precisely. The north-south lines are called *meridians of longitude* and the east-west lines are called *parallels of latitude*. By following a grid line around the globe, children discover that all grid lines are circles or parts of circles. Meridians of longitude measure distances in degrees east and west of the prime meridian, or Greenwich meridian, an imaginary line that passes through Greenwich England. The prime meridian is labeled 0 degrees; all other meridians represent so many degrees east or west, up to 180 degrees.

The east-west parallels of latitude are lines around the globe; all points along each line measure an equal distance from a pole. The line around the middle of the globe is the *equator*. All points along this line are halfway between the North Pole and the South Pole. Mapmakers designate the equator as 0 degrees and the latitude lines as either north or south by so many degrees. The distance from the equator to a pole is 90 degrees, or one fourth of a circle.

As shown in figure 9.2, the gridwork allows one to locate places exactly. One way to teach children to use a grid is to give them a blank piece of paper with an *X* drawn on it and ask them to tell a classmate where the *X* is located precisely. They will quickly see how hard it is to be precise. Saying

Figure 9.2
Latitudes and
Longitudes

0°

Equator

that an *X* is just to the right of the center may be fine, until the paper is turned upside down. Now where is the *X*? You can then give the children a second sheet of paper of the same dimensions, but marked out with a grid noting one-degree differences between each line. Now ask the children to locate *X*. They should quickly see that with the grid, they can state exactly where *X* is regardless of the orientation of the paper.

Working with Maps

Primary grade children need to be introduced to the idea that maps are flat drawings of places on a round earth. Any such drawing that has a grid is a *projection*. (This term comes from the method of transferring the grid lines from a globe to a flat map by using a transparent globe with a light inside it. The light *projects* the lines to a sheet of paper upon which the lines are copied.)

Only a few of the many different map projections are used in elementary classrooms. Children are usually not taught the names of the projections, but teachers should be aware of the benefits and weaknesses of each. Gifted children, however, may enjoy and benefit from investigating the different types of map projections.

Tangential plane projections are made by projecting a shadow from a light source onto a flat piece of paper that touches the globe at one point. This point of projection is called the "point of tangency" or "eye point." Often this point is the North or South Pole.

Figure 9.3
Learning to Use a Grid

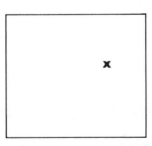

Question: Where is the X?

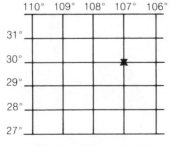

Question: Where is the X?

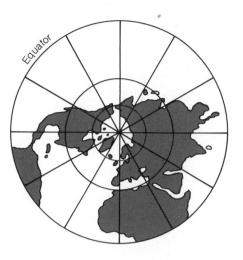

Figure 9.4
An Example of a
Stereographic
Projection

Several kinds of tangential plane projections exist. A "stereographic projection" is one in which the point of projection is on the earth's surface directly opposite the point of tangency. Figure 9.4 shows an example of this projection.

Another tangential plane projection is the "gnomonic projection," where a light source is presumed to be located at the center of the earth. These projections result in maps on which lines of longitude are projected as straight lines. Such maps are useful to pilots since they depict the shortest point-to-point distances between places lying on these lines. Figure 9.5 shows the creation of such a map.

Cylindrical projections are maps made as if the paper were a cylinder or tube that has been rolled around the globe along the equator. Figure 9.6 shows this type of projection being made. With this projection, the parallels and meridians usually emerge as straight lines at right angles to each other.

This type of map is common in many elementary classrooms; the Mercator projection is the most recognized example. One difficulty in reading this type of map is that the distances between parallels, which are the

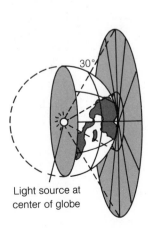
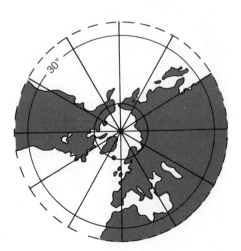

Figure 9.5
An Example of a
Gnomonic Projection

239

same on the globe, become greater and greater as one nears the poles. Thus there is a great deal of distortion in the latitudes near the poles. In a Mercator projection, for example, Greenland appears much larger than South America. Children who are being taught to read maps need to understand that all maps have distortions. One way to communicate this is to draw a face as it would appear on different maps. On a Mercator projection, the person's forehead and neck would be greatly exaggerated. This humorous presentation helps children realize how maps indeed distort. But the Mercator projection is ideal for showing sea routes and gives children an overview of the locations of the world's land masses, although it does not show their shapes or sizes in accurate proportions.

A *conical projection* map is made from projections on a cone of paper rather than on a cylinder. The cone may be designed so that only its base touches the earth, or so that it cuts through part of the earth's surface. The projection is most accurate at the points where the cone touches the earth's surface. Conical projections are frequently useful in mapping areas in the middle latitudes, such as the United States. Figure 9.7 shows how this type of projection is made.

This type of map shows true shape, and distances, directions, and areas are shown with 90 to 98 percent accuracy.

One major objective of social studies is to get children to consider their world both abstractly and spatially, to move from seeing their real community to seeing it depicted abstractly on a map. One way to encourage such perceptions with primary children is to take them on a walking tour of the school grounds and photograph the school and points of interest. After such a "field trip," they can draw their school in relation to features on the school grounds. If it is possible to have a picture of the school taken from

Figure 9.6
An Example of a
Cylindrical Projection

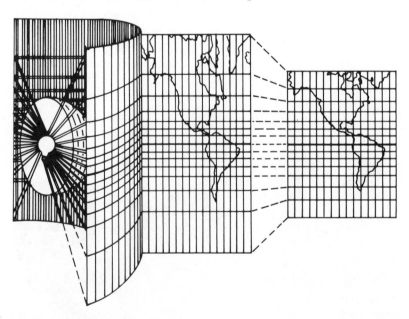

Reprinted from *Mapping* by David Greenhood by permission of The University of Chicago Press. Copyright © 1964 by The University of Chicago Press.

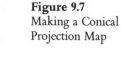

Figure 9.7
Making a Conical
Projection Map

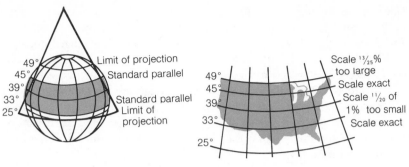

Reprinted from *Mapping* by David Greenhood by permission of The University of Chicago Press. Copyright © 1964 by The University of Chicago Press.

some elevation or even from a low-flying plane, the children will be able to see the school in relationship to playgrounds, parking lots, trees, and so on. After the field trip, young children might make a model of the area from cardboard and paper. Each child would use pictorial symbols to represent reality. Asking children questions that require them to describe the school site enables them to begin to see the relationships among human-made features (the school) and natural features (trees, grass, water).

Early experiences with maps must be kept simple. The field trip is one in which all children can participate and learn. Creating outline maps and diagrams of the neighborhood is frequently useful in introducing children to maps, and they can also map their classroom. They can record on a piece of blank paper the location of each child's desk, the teacher's desk, chalkboard, door, windows, and so on. They can perhaps make a simple grid on this to help some friend "locate" their desk in the classroom.

Teaching Direction

Direction is usually not specifically mentioned when children are first trying to make diagrams and maps, but in most cases, the concept of direction and how to locate things on a map should probably be introduced before the end of first grade. Teachers often introduce cardinal directions by putting direction signs on each wall of the classroom. They can point out the direction from which the sun appears in the morning. Once children learn where north is, they can determine the other directions. Show them how north is usually indicated on a map by an arrow pointing north. In drawings of the classroom, children can note which "side" of the map is north. Children can take field trips to the playground and note directions. If children in the Northern hemisphere stand on the playground at high noon on a sunny day, they will cast shadows that point approximately north. Young children enjoy such activities in learning directions.

Directions on wall maps are best taught in conjunction with learning about the globe. By using the globe, children learn that *north* really means "in the direction of or toward the North Pole"; *south* means "in the direction of or toward the South Pole." They can learn that west or east refers to what

241

"side" one is on in relation to a particular line, the *prime meridian*. Young children can learn this by imagining a line down the center of the room, with desks to the left or right of the line. If the room is arranged north and south, children can identify each desk's location as east or west of the classroom's center line or "prime meridian."

Map reading skills are developed throughout the elementary years, and teachers should provide many opportunities for children to note directions on maps when they use them as sources of data for class discussions. When children do map work, they can be required to point out directions as well as to read the map.

There is a vast array of maps from which to choose; these commercial materials deal with map and globe concepts:

- *Where and Why,* by Dale Brown and Philip Bacon. (A. J. Nystrom and Company, 1974.) Presents a complete map and globe program in cassette form.
- *First Book of Maps.* 12 transparencies and 14 duplicating masters that deal with all aspects of map interpretation and map making. Available through Social Studies School Service, 10000 Culver Blvd., Culver City, California 90200.
- Map and Globe Skills Kit. Deals with basic concepts and skills. (Chicago: Science Research Associates.)
- *Making Inferences from Maps.* 12 color transparencies and 14 spirit duplicating masters. (St. Louis: Milliken Publishing Company.)

The teacher's difficulty is not a shortage of map materials, but rather of choosing those most appropriate for the particular age group. You can use these guidelines to select suitable maps.

1. Is the map suitable for the maturity and background of the pupils?
2. Is the material on the map accurate, yet not overloaded with detail?
3. Can the map and related materials be used with the district social studies program? How do the map skills integrate with the general concepts and topics of the social studies program?
4. Is the map designed so that the general components of map language can be taught easily? Some maps are single-purpose, which is fine as long as such a map will be useful throughout most of the program. Political-physical maps are usually more useful than maps that represent only physical features.
5. Will the map withstand constant use by children? Can it be displayed easily?

Graphics

Children will discover large quantities of data in graphs, charts, and drawings. *Graphs* can present much statistical data efficiently. Children will need to learn that graphs carry one type of information on the vertical axis and another type on the horizontal axis. In the early elementary grades the horizontal axis and vertical axis can be called the "bottom line" and the "up-and-down line."

Early in this century, it was assumed that primary-grade children would be unable to comprehend graphs, but educators have since discovered children have no difficulty when graphs present information within their experiences. For example, primary-grade children can learn to read bar graphs by keeping a record of daily temperatures.

Circle or pie graphs can also be used with elementary pupils. In the intermediate grades, children can create a circle graph to show how much time they spend at various subjects and activities during the school day. They might also show how money is spent to run the schools. (Children will need some understanding of percentages and ratios to use pie graphs effectively.)

Line graphs accurately show changes in quantity through stated time periods or some other variable. One way to acquaint intermediate grade children with this graph is to have them record the decrease in the number of children attending schools over several years, or the price of housing over a certain time span. Figure 9.8 shows the average cost of a house in one community over a period of seven years.

You can often record more than one set of data on a line graph. A line graph might show, for example, the increased cost of education in contrast to the decreasing numbers of pupils in school.

But line graphs can be misleading. The slope of the line on the graph varies depending upon the scale of the grid. Figure 9.9 shows how the line's slope changes according to the grid.

Children become skilled graph readers by making and using graphs in their regular assignments. The teacher can require that research reports present part of the data through graphs, charts, and pictorials. Teachers should call attention to the graphs in the children's social studies textbooks, and initiate discussions about how data can be misinterpreted based on the graph design.

Teaching children to read and create graphs and charts can be both formal and informal. In formal instruction, the teacher may correlate the les-

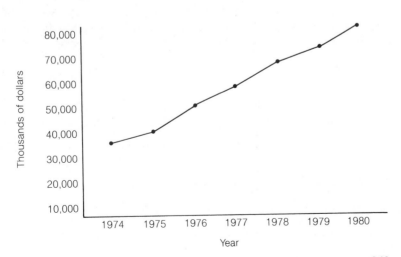

Figure 9.8
A Line Graph to
Illustrate the Rising
Cost of Houses

Figure 9.9
Grid Scales and Line
Slopes

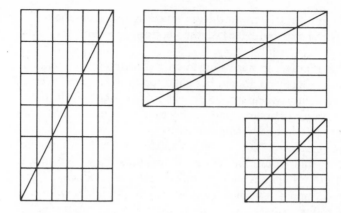

son with mathematics. She can focus on the purpose of the graph and appropriate designs for displaying information, taking into account the type of grid, the intervals between points, and the decisions necessary for determining what data points to indicate. How does one decide whether the time intervals on the horizontal axis should be one year or ten years? When children create graphs or encounter them in reading materials, the teacher may wish to schedule time for individual or class discussion on the appropriateness of the graph's design and the intervals selected. She might show examples of graphs that present data clearly and in misleading ways. Figure 9.10 shows how two graphs depict identical data with different data points (the data are fictional).

Children need guidance in formulating the types of questions to raise in interpreting graphs. They need to understand that questions other than just factual are valid and must learn to ask questions aimed at evaluating the appropriateness of the data display and questions that help determine the relationships among the data.

Children must also learn the skills associated with reading and making charts. Jarolimek (1977) identifies several types of appropriate charts: narrative, tabulation, organization, and flow charts. *Narrative charts* show the steps of a procedure or illustrate events along a time dimension. Such a chart might show how bread is made, tracing the process from growing the wheat, transporting grain to a flour mill, making the flour, to transporting the flour

Figure 9.10
Learning About
Different Data Points

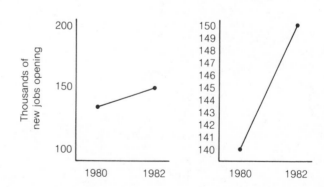

to the bakery. *Tabulation charts*, sometimes called data charts, allow the listing of data from several sources, and thus facilitate comparisons among data. When investigating different cultures, children might make a data chart that records facts about the types of housing in particular countries, as in Figure 9.11.

Types of Housing	United States	India	Japan	Egypt
Single-family dwelling	※			
Apartment	※	※	※	※
Tent				
Mud Hut		※		※
Row House	※			

Figure 9.11
A Data Chart for Comparing Housing in Different Cultures

Organization charts can exhibt the internal arrangement of organizations, such as schools, companies, or government agencies. These charts are quite common in elementary social studies textbooks. Children should be taught not only to learn the specific information presented in such charts but to raise questions as to why a company or governmental agency is organized the way it is and the relationships among the various divisions.

When children need to see how actions occur through time, *flow charts* are sometimes effective. These charts depict how one makes decisions or processes particular materials. They are similar to narrative charts in this respect, but usually present information more abstractly. These charts usually employ rectangles connected by arrows that show the direction of activity. Children can become acquainted with these charts by studying the stages one goes through in reading a chart. Figure 9.12 shows the process.

There are many opportunities for the teacher to instruct pupils in chart reading. Most textbooks and related commercial materials published by government agencies and corporations present a great deal of material by means of charts and graphs. As with graphs, the teacher will want to schedule both formal and informal lessons on chart reading.

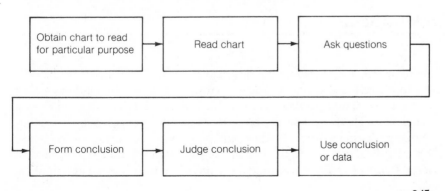

Figure 9.12
A Flow Chart

Activity 9:4

Preparing Relevant Questions

Make a list of questions that will guide students in interpreting maps. Are there some questions that are common regardless of the type of map to be considered?

Activity 9:5

Developing Map Activities

Make a list of map activities potentially useful in teaching pupils about maps and how to utilize them as information sources. Indicate when such activities would be appropriate.

Activity 9:6

Using Graphs and Charts

Create an inquiry-oriented lesson requiring the use of various charts. Try to incorporate the lesson into a social studies unit, either one selected from a school or one you have been developing.

Research and Thinking Skills

As we noted at the beginning of this chapter, research skills relate to the ability to identify and define a problem, create hypotheses for solutions, locate and gather relevant data, analyze the data, evaluate information, and draw a conclusion. Thinking skills are those that relate to proficiency in describing, defining, classifying, hypothesizing, analyzing, and generalizing. In the classroom, it is almost impossible to tightly categorize all the skills stressed in social studies. Certainly, academic skills interrelate with research and thinking skills. To carry out academic skills requires thinking, and to process information requires research skills.

In reality, the skills of thinking and research are integrated into academic skills, and the stages of research and thinking will often blend. Thus, problem formulation or definition involves the skill of describing and perhaps defining. Banks (1977) generated a model of social inquiry that begins with the stage of doubt and concern and proceeds through problem formulation, hypotheses formulation, conceptualization, data collection, data evaluation and analysis, generalization and theory derivation, and then a repeat of the process. His model is similar to the common model of problem solving: feel need, define the problem, suggest solutions, collect data, analyze the data, formulate a conclusion, then judge the worth of conclusion. One need not have consensus as to the one way of conducting research, but one should realize that it is possible for children to be systematic in conducting research: they can follow steps that involve academic skills and various types of thinking processes.

Fraenkel notes that research skills include the ability to:

1. Define a problem
2. Formulate a reasonable hypothesis as to how the problem might be resolved
3. Locate and gather data dealing with the problem
4. Analyze these data:
   a. Distinguish relevant from irrelevant data
   b. Organize the relevant data into categories
   c. Evaluate the adequacy and accuracy of the data
   d. Interpret the data as to what it means
5. Evaluate the hypothesis in light of the data that have been gathered and analyzed.
6. Draw a conclusion—accept, reject, or modify the hypothesis as appropriate.

From Jack R. Fraenkel, *Helping Students Think and Value: Strategies for Teaching the Social Studies,* © 1973, pp. 17, 18. Reprinted by permission of Prentice-Hall, Inc., Englewood Cliffs, N.J.

Fraenkel's steps are similar to those advanced by Banks. Research skills comprise what many call study skills, the abilities required for locating and gathering information. Study skills can be categorized as working with books, working with encyclopedias and other reference materials, using the dictionary, reading newspapers, magazines, and pamphlets, locating material in the library, and gathering facts from field trips and interviews. After gathering information, skills are needed to organize the information, outline, select main ideas and supporting facts, answer the questions raised, arrange events, facts, and ideas in sequence, and write summaries. The overlap of study or research skills with academic skills is obvious. A final category of research skills relates to evaluating information. Here students must distinguish fact from fiction, or fact from opinion, which promotes skills in raising evaluation questions to determine the consistency, reasonableness, and accuracy of the information or conclusions.

Throughout social studies lessons, teachers have ample opportunities to foster student skills in research. For example, when discussing the energy crisis, the teacher might give students the following hypothesis to consider: "The reason for the shortage of certain energy resources is the current political climate." The children are challenged to check the accuracy of this hypothesis. The teacher might get them started by asking: "What resources are currently believed to be in short supply? Where are these resources located? In what ways do we use these resources? What connections can we make between the location of the resources and the places where they are used? What statement might we make about the accuracy of the hypothesis? If we are not sure about what we say, how can we further check out the hypothesis?"

Teachers who stress the development of research skills guarantee their pupils numerous opportunities for posing problems, stating related hypotheses, defining terms, gathering and organizing data, evaluating such data, and formulating and evaluating conclusions.

All social studies teachers hope their pupils will become skillful thinkers, although there is some confusion as to just what thinking is. Many teachers believe that elementary school children cannot be taught to think until they have accumulated a great deal of factual information or have covered vast amounts of the material. This is reflected in teachers' attempts to "cover the book." Another invalid assumption is that only subjects such as mathematics and science enhance thinking. Another source of confusion results from the types of thinking discussed in the current literature, where teachers read about critical thinking, evaluative thinking, analytical thinking, elaborative thinking, convergent thinking, divergent thinking, and problem solving. It is safe to say that we do not really know much about thinking. Educators can perhaps agree, however, that thinking is a process that involves both psychological and psychomotor functioning, and that it also relates to the ability to process information at various levels of abstraction.

Thinking requires some degree of definition in order to create lessons that will heighten it. Thinking involves a transaction between the pupil and a particular situation; it is interactive, in that the pupil interacts with the environment, then makes some judgment, which in turn influences the environment or data. Thinking is involved in identifying problems and formulating questions to guide reflection. It is also involved in problem identification and in organizing and classifying perceived phenomena into concepts and differentiating among these concepts. It is present in developing hypotheses and assessing whether the data are appropriate for testing these hypotheses. Thinking also involves predicting possible outcomes and generalizing information. All aspects of social studies can contribute to the development of thinking skills. Most children in the regular classroom are capable of thinking, although there will be differences in quality.

The various stages of research closely parallel the stages and types of thinking. Critical thinking relates to raising questions and analyzing information and phenomena to arrive at attributes, relationships, cause and effect relationships, and overall organization of information. Critical thinking also requires evaluative judgments as to the appropriateness, accuracy, and usefulness of information. Creative thinking refers to the process of going beyond the data, elaborating from the data, making predictions, and offering alternatives. It further involves the reconstruction of knowledge, making new statements, and/or generating new problems for investigation. All thinking engages both critical and creative activity. Thinking skills are critical in the sense that pupils must analyze data, verify it, and organize knowledge to make it intelligible; they are creative in the sense that they must develop new organizations, generate new questions, formulate new relationships among data, and create new generalizations. Thinking involves both induction and deduction. These two approaches usually occur in a cycle. Pupils might process specific data inductively to formulate a conclusion, but once formulated, the conclusion is used deductively as a major assumption or premise to guide additional inquiry.

The teacher can foster thinking by providing opportunities for students to extend hypotheses to their logical conclusions. This requires not only further testing of the hypotheses, but also applying the hypotheses to other situations. Another way is to teach pupils the steps in deductive and inductive reasoning. Ennis (1962) suggests four criteria that pupils can employ in judging deductive thinking operations: evaluating the meaning of a statement; judging whether there is any ambiguity in a chain of reasoning; judging whether a conclusion follows necessarily from the premise; and judging whether a premise supports a conclusion that purports to be an application of it. Teachers who wish to foster thinking provide pupils with opportunities to classify and order data and to judge the reality of inductive inferences.

Activity 9:7

Generating Types of Thinking

Note several types of thinking you might develop in a unit and the ways in which you could foster such thinking. Compare your ideas with a student colleague.

Activity 9:8

Critiquing Questions in Textbooks

Critique a recently published textbook for the types of questions included and how these questions foster the development of various types of thinking skills.

What type of thinking is most emphasized, least emphasized? How might you alter the questions to increase the emphasis on particular types of thinking strategies?

To stimulate and improve their pupils' thinking skills, teachers need to realize that thinking is essentially a process in which an individual engages in a series of symbolic responses. For social studies to provide an avenue for developing these skills, classroom encounters must allow children to manipulate symbols into increasingly complex patterns of meanings. The classroom must emphasize pupil activity over teacher activity. Pupils must have time to confront information, to manipulate information, to relate new information to their prior experiences, and to identify patterns (Fair and Shaftel, 1967).

Social Skills

Social skills describe the ways individuals relate to and interact with others. They draw on academic skills, such as being able to speak clearly to others, but concern primarily the attitudes and feelings that pupils should exhibit.

Social skills can be categorized as those that are related to and necessary for living and working with others: respecting the rights of others, being sensitive to their feelings, and being willing and able to assist others when necessary. Another grouping of social skills relates to sharing, including participating with others in group activities. Planning with others can also be grouped under sharing.

All social studies programs consider good citizenship a major goal, and learning to act responsibly is crucial to good citizenship. The skills of self-control and self-direction are essential to responsible action. Pupils can learn to develop these skills through activities that help them estimate the consequences of planned actions or cause them to reflect on the consequences of past actions.

Social skills can be taught formally and informally. A formal lesson on group behavior can have all students reflect on the various skills they need for working effectively in groups. Theories of group dynamics can be incorporated into formal social studies lessons. Social encounters with their peers show them how they need to identify, develop, and perfect social skills. Through class discussions, children begin to develop confidence in their ability to contribute; discussions thus cultivate the skill of effective participation in groups. Here, the blending of social and academic skills is clear, since children need to be able to listen attentively, speak clearly, and to organize their thoughts for oral presentation.

Role playing and simulation activities are effective ways to nurture social skills. Role playing conflict situations helps develop the skills of communicating feelings and developing empathy for others.

In addressing social skills, the teacher provides pupils with opportunities to examine their own feelings, sensitivities, and values so they can understand themselves thoroughly and honestly. Emphasizing social skills allows pupils to gain the competencies, attitudes, and values they need to become self-actualized individuals.

Activity 9:9

Fostering Social Skill Development

Suggest activities that can be incorporated into a social studies unit to foster pupils' social skill development. Share your ideas with one of your peers.

Activity 9:10

Critiquing Social Skill Development

Arrange to observe a social studies lesson to identify the ways in which the teacher fosters children's social skill development. Discuss with the teacher the reasons for his action.

Discussion

Because learning depends upon academic, research, thinking, and social skills, the elementary social studies program must promote sequential development of those skills.

In the area of academic skills, reading is paramount, and it is incumbent on the social studies teacher, as on every other elementary teacher, to teach reading. Students may need special guidance with social studies reading, which the teacher can provide by presenting new social studies vocabulary in context and encouraging students to use the new words and terms. The teacher can promote reading comprehension by setting a purpose for reading, and by helping children learn to read for the main idea, read for significant details, read to summarize and organize, read to derive generalizations, and read to develop critical views. The teacher must also plan ways to use the social studies textbook creatively, to encourage familiarity with reference materials, and to promote writing, verbal communication, and listening skills.

Skills in using maps, globes, and graphics are essential to social studies, since so much information is presented by these means. Children should spend time learning about the globe both formally and casually; map study will include learning about scale, symbols, legends, color, gridwork, the various types of map projections, and direction. Social studies also offer chances to develop skills with graphs and charts, and the teacher should encourage students to use and make them when they do reports.

Social studies also provides many opportunities to enhance research and thinking skills. Research skills are those with which we identify and define problems, create hypotheses, gather and analyze data, evaluate information, and draw conclusions. Thinking skills are those of describing, defining, classifying, hypothesizing, analyzing, and generalizing. The research and thinking skills are intertwined with the academic skills, and the investigative nature of the social studies provides ample opportunity for developing them.

Since a major goal of all social studies curricula is to foster good citizenship, the teacher should promote social skills as well. Many social studies activities lend themselves to small- or large-group formats, and students will benefit from studying theories of group dynamics. Other useful activities for developing social skills are class discussions, role playing, and simulations.

References

Banks, James A., with Clegg, Ambrose A., Jr. *Teaching Strategies for the Social Studies: Inquiry, Valuing, and Decision-Making.* 2nd ed. Reading, Mass.: Addison-Wesley, 1977.

Carpenter, Helen McCracken. *Skill Development in the Social Studies.* Washington, D. C.: National Council for the Social Studies, 1963.

De Boer, John James, and Dallman, Martha. *The Teaching of Reading.* New York: Holt, Rinehart and Winston, 1974.

Ennis, Robert H. "A Concept of Critical Thinking: A Proposed Basis for Research in the Teaching and Evaluation of Critical Thinking Ability." *Harvard Educational Review* 32 (1962): 81–111.

Fraenkel, Jack R. *Helping Students Think and Value: Strategies for Teaching the Social Studies.* Englewood Cliffs, N. J.: Prentice-Hall, 1973.

Greenhood, David. *Mapping.* Chicago: University of Chicago Press, 1964.

Heilman, Arthur R. *Principles and Practices of Teaching Reading.* Columbus, Oh.: Charles E. Merrill, 1977.

Jarolimek, John. *Social Studies in Elementary Education.* 5th ed. New York: Macmillan, 1977.

Parsons, Theodore W., and Shaftel, Fannie R. "Thinking and Inquiry: Some Critical Issues." In *Effective Thinking in the Social Studies,* edited by Jean Fair and Fannie R. Shaftel. Washington, D. C.: National Council for the Social Studies, 1967.

Ragan, William B., and Shepherd, Gene D. *Modern Elementary Curriculum.* 5th ed. New York: Holt, Rinehart and Winston, 1977.

Questions and Questioning for Teaching and Learning

10

Of all teaching methods, none is more potentially powerful than questioning. Research shows, however, that most teachers use questions primarily for evaluation, and that their questions call primarily for the recall of information. Questions that require pupils to apply information, analyze data, synthesize, and evaluate conclusions are asked less frequently.

Teachers who effectively utilize questioning realize the power of this technique for getting students to comprehend more completely and to develop positive values and attitudes toward social studies. Teachers skilled in questioning serve as models of questioning techniques for students, and create opportunities for students to generate their own questions. Armed with skills in questioning, pupils can increase their learning autonomy and augment their understandings. The students gain not only an increased knowledge of social studies, but an effective orientation to reality as well.

Questioning in Social Studies

Many teachers believe the function of questioning is to test pupils' knowledge, often at the end of a chapter or a unit. Questions are useful for evaluating children's understandings, but while evaluation is a valid use of questions, it is not the only or primary use. Essentially, questions are tools by which pupils can process information they hear, read, or experience. They are integral components of the academic, research, and thinking skills. Questions help orient pupils to a particular lesson or unit, guide investigation, and enable one to judge the value of a research effort.

The kinds of questions teachers ask or allow pupils to raise depend upon the goals and objectives of the lesson or unit. If the primary goal is to have pupils acquire a body of facts to use in later inquiry, then the teacher's and students' questions should focus primarily on the recall of information. When the aim is analysis and evaluation, then questions should address the these levels of cognitive functioning.

Teachers who use higher level questioning in their classrooms are those who realize that questions grow out of an individual's innate curiosities, and are a means of advancing exploratory behavior. Indeed, Chaudhari

(1975) notes that student questions are "curiosity in action . . . their mind hunger." Questioning behavior flourishes best in a nonthreatening environment, where class members realize that questions are a means for dealing with errors, a way of dealing with one's level of understanding and making modifications where necessary. Questioning is an orientation for study.

Carin and Sund (1978) suggest that what separates the truly brilliant teacher from the average is the talent for posing the right question at the right time. Well-selected questions allow pupils to reach new levels of intellectual functioning and to discover creative uses for the information they uncover. Questions engage children's minds; they stimulate active learning. Effective questioning helps students realize that their role in learning is not a passive one, but one of participation. The quality of the classroom dynamics depends greatly upon the level and frequency of questions.

Classifications of questions are usually carefully described or implicitly integrated in teaching strategies. A useful scheme for classifying cognitive questions employs the Taxonomy of Objectives, Cognitive Domain developed by

---

Activity 10:1

Self-Check on Questions

Try to remember some of the questions you used this past week. Write down three or four of them, then explain how you used them. What kind of information were you seeking? What did your questions demand of those you asked?

Keep these questions and your reasons for asking them in mind, and consider your reasons as hypotheses to test as you read the rest of this chapter.

Bloom and others. This taxonomy, originally developed to note various levels of education objectives, includes several divisions: knowledge, comprehension, application, analysis, synthesis, and evaluation.

Going deeper than a classification, each level of a taxonomy subsumes those below it; analysis subsumes the levels of application, comprehension, and knowledge, and evaluation subsumes all the lower levels. The taxonomy furnishes teachers with a meaningful way of classifying questions, and provides both inductive and deductive teaching strategies. (More will be said later about placing questions in strategies.) When the objective is to have pupils work inductively, they can ask or respond to questions beginning with the knowledge level and proceeding through the higher levels. To work deductively, questioning could begin at the evaluation level, with a question to determine the validity of a statement, then move to lower-level questions. Figure 10.1 shows both approaches.

Figure 10.1
Inductive and
Deductive Strategies

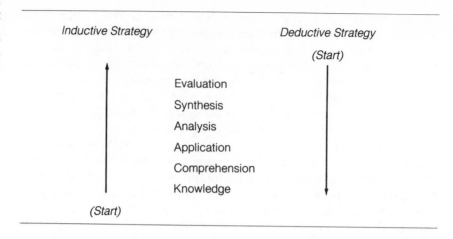

Questions in the Cognitive Domain

Knowledge Questions

A knowledge-level question asks a student to recall specific facts, methods, places, trends, concepts, generalizations, criteria, and theories. Students are not required to use the information; they merely have to recall it. Examples of knowledge-level questions are:

> *What is the oldest democracy in the world?*

> *How many years may an American President serve?*

> *How many stages does a bill go through to become a law?*

Comprehension Questions

Comprehension questions require pupils to understand the meaning of information previously presented. Comprehension questions operate at three levels. At the first level, *translation*, students translate or paraphrase information from one form to another. For example, a student might adapt information from a paragraph into line graph form. The second level, *interpretation*, asks students to derive the essential meaning of oral or written information. They may relate facts to one another, rearrange information, establish relationships by comparing or contrasting, identify essential from nonessential data, or indicate how information can be used. Questions that ask pupils to identify an author's main point are interpretation questions. The last level of comprehension, *extrapolation*, urges the individual beyond a simple recounting of information to drawing inferences. Students who have read about an energy crisis might be asked to infer the probable effects of the increasing scarcity of resources on future standards of living. Examples of comprehension questions include:

What is the meaning of the concept "cultural interpretation of resources"? (level one)

What are some of the differences between the American and Brazilian ways of life? (level two)

What can you infer from the data presented in this chart? (level three)

Application Questions

To answer an application question, the student must apply a previously learned understanding or procedure. An application question differs from a comprehension question in that the student is confronted with a novel situation that does not immediately expose what information or procedure is required. He must first study the situation, then determine which procedure or information is appropriate; essentially, he must transfer his previous learning to a new situation. These are examples of application questions:

Study the map that shows the topographic features of this region. Assume you are a demographer. Where would you expect the next major population growth to occur?

How would you resolve the conflict between pro-nuclear and the anti-nuclear forces?

Analysis Questions

Questions at this cognitive level ask students to analyze materials, situations, and environments and separate them into their component parts. There are three levels of analysis questions: analysis of elements, analysis of relationships, and analysis of organizational principles. At the first level, students focus on the basic elements in materials or the major events in some situation. They might be asked to isolate major assumptions underlying a debate. To respond to questions at the second level, students must look at the relationships between and among elements recognized in the first level of analysis. Attention can focus on determining cause and effect relationships and on identifying the parts of a discussion that support a particular line of argument. In the final level of analysis, the questions ask students to consider the interrelationships within the particular situation. They must determine the form, pattern, or organizational structure of a statement or set of ideas. Guided by the questions, pupils can detect evidence of bias in one authority's discussion on use of natural resources or of one historian's account of the French and Indian War. Armed with such questions, pupils will be able to recognize the logic or lack of logic in advertisements. As students become skilled in forming analysis questions, they also become competent in logic, at least on the common sense level. How specifically to deal with logic depends on the pupils' age and grade level. Analysis questions enable pupils to critique their own academic, research, and thinking skills. Examples of analysis questions are:

From our discussion of prejudice, what are two basic feelings we get about people? (level 1)

How does the information we have prove that waste is the main reason for shortage of resources? (level 2)

Explain the thinking of people who believe that problems of the third world are caused by the developed nations. (level 3)

Synthesis Questions

Synthesis questions ask students to take information and combine and integrate it into some new arrangement, one new at least to them. Such questions require creative thinking as well as critical thinking and problem solving. Here, emphasis is on both divergent and convergent answers. Synthesis questions operate at three levels: as the production of a unique communication, as the production of a plan, and as a derivation of a set of abstract relations.

Synthesis questions provide pupils with no clues as to how to process information, although they clearly indicate that a product is to be the result. In responding to the first level, the pupil's product will be some unique communication; in reaction to the second, the product will be a plan that could be presented for class discussion. At the third level, the result is a conclusion available for class sharing and evaluating. Examples of synthesis questions are:

What do you think about the need for alternative forms of energy? (level 1, perhaps as result of a field trip to a power plant)

Think of a plan for getting the community to become conservation-minded. (level 2)

Based on how people in your town feel, how do U.S. citizens view people from other cultures? (level 3, asking for a generalized statement new to the student)

From our study of Canadian politics, what ideas do you have that will help us gather additional information? (level 3)

Evaluation Questions

The two levels of evaluation questions ask students to judge data or conclusions. They employ either internal criteria, such as logical accuracy and consistency, or external criteria, as established by experts or community norms. Is the conclusion useful to our other investigations? Is the result good or bad, beautiful or ugly, meaningful or worthless? Such questions require complex intellectual processing that includes all the lower levels of the taxonomy. Students who encounter or raise such questions realize that one does not just accept conclusions; rather, one must first make judgments as to the worth and correctness of the conclusions. Examples of evaluation questions are:

What sorts of questions at each level could be asked of students studying the American political process?

Which of the following statements are examples of facts and which are examples of opinion? (level 1)

According to the arguments we've talked about here, what is the best thing a person could do in this case? (level 1)

After you have investigated the schools, what do you think are the best things about them? (level 2)

Activity 10:2

Creating Cognitive Level Questions

Select a social studies topic that interests you. Write a question at each cognitive level (knowledge, comprehension, application, analysis, synthesis, and evaluation) that relates to this topic. Compare your questions to the examples in the text.

Questions in the Affective Domain

One aim of social studies is for students to develop appropriate attitudes and values. Questions in the affective domain enable pupils to be more systematic in creating their attitudes and values and to be aware of their emotional and value reactions to social studies content.

Krathwohl's *Taxonomy of Educational Objectives, Affective Domain* (1964) provides a systematic guide for formulating questions geared to affect. This taxonomy contains five levels: receiving, responding, valuing, organization, and characterization.

Receiving or Attending Questions

The first level of the affective domain is *receiving* or *attending*. These questions call for students to express their awareness of a situation, phenomenon, person, or state of affairs. Receiving questions closely resemble knowledge questions, but their purpose is to determine whether the pupil has been aware of stimuli or has interest in a particular topic.

Awareness, willingness to receive, and controlled or selected attention are subcategories of receiving. *Awareness* questions probe for student awareness of a situation, person, event, or phenomena. Willingness to receive questions seek to determine a student's preference for and willingness to attend to an issue, topic, or idea. (That is, the pupil might not actively seek the information, but would attend to it as the situation demands.) Questions at the controlled or selected attention level encourage students to direct their energies toward some specific task or end point; their aim is to determine whether or not students would pay attention to a particular point in the lesson. Examples of receiving questions are:

I have some pictures here of famous government officials. Who are they? (awareness)

If you had a free afternoon, which of the following would you do? (willingness to receive)

Which of the following activities do you usually do, rarely do, never do? Read, travel, talk with people outside your class. (controlled *or* selected attention; *forced-choice inventories are effective in getting students to respond at this level*)

Responding Questions

Responding questions ask the individual to do something with the perceived stimuli, at the levels of acquiescence in responding, willingness to respond, and satisfaction in response. *Acquiescence in responding* questions seek to identify topics that individuals will tolerate if requested to do so. *Willingness to respond* questions are raised to discover if the learner is sufficiently motivated to act or react. Would she take a certain action voluntarily? Teachers often find some individuals who are totally unwilling to even consider certain questions—they guard their minds from information and situations perceived as distasteful or confusing. *Satisfaction in response* questions are structured to find out whether or not a person derives enjoyment or satisfaction from certain topics or content areas. Such questions are effective in determining student interests. Samples of responding questions are:

Consider the following situations: spending some time in the Peace Corps working in a third world nation to develop agricultural practices or *working in an office collecting funds for overseas relief. Which of the two would you most like to do?* (sublevel 1)

From this unit, select one of the five major activities as the one on which you wish to work. (sublevel 2)

Of the following events, put a "yes" beside those things that give you the most pleasure. (sublevel 3)

261

Valuing Questions

Teachers who believe that social studies should include attention to values become skilled in raising questions in three subcategories: acceptance of a value, preference for a value, and commitment.

Questions about *acceptance* of a value aim at determining if a person truly accepts a value or particular belief. *Preference* for a value questions ask the student to identify her choice through a telling statement or through the activities she chooses. *Commitment* level questions ask whether a student holds a belief or position to the extent that she would publicly defend it. The intent is to determine whether these values are accepted over some extended period. Answers to these questions are sometimes stated verbally, but at times they may emerge through an individual's behavior as observed over a few weeks or months. Examples of valuing questions are:

> *How would you classify the following events? New situations—enjoyable, not enjoyable; school—fun, boring; social studies—challenging, dull.* (sublevel 1)

> *Which of the following solutions for reducing population pressure do you feel is best?* (sublevel 2)

> *Identify the ways in which you have practiced conservation this past week.* (sublevel 3)

Organization Questions

Organization questions requiring students to begin to formulate and articulate their value systems fall into two subdivisions: conceptualization of a value and organization of a value system. At the first level, conceptualization of a value, questions center on asking pupils to relate their ethical standards and personal goals to some specific experience. Students must identify and classify concepts, especially nominative concepts, and relate them to ones already held. Questions that address the organization of a value system strive to integrate the individual's values. These questions direct students to identify and reflect on the values central to their lives. Questions at these two sublevels are:

> *Of the three social groups we have studied, which one considers major human relationships in the same way you do?* (sublevel 1)

> *Explain why you believe people must be humane when dealing with the poor of other countries.* (sublevel 2)

Characterization of a Value or Value Complex Questions

Such questions, at the zenith of the affective domain, assume that the student has identified her value system. Realistically, however, people do not reach this stage until adulthood, if then. This level of questioning also has two subcategories: generalized set and characterization. Questions at the level of generalized set seek to determine whether or not students are consistent within their system of attitudes and values. They might be asked to take a stand on energy use or to respond to a particular minority's demands. Are their views about these issues consistent with their value system? Characterization questions are asked to uncover a person's overall philosophy, her world view. Many issues in social studies require students to react holistically. Samples of these questions are:

Which of the following guidelines do you advocate we follow during the energy crisis? (sublevel 1)

Of the following goals, which would you strive to meet? (sublevel 2)

Many of the issues in today's social studies might easily involve all affective levels.

Activity 10.3

Creating Affective Questions

In reality, the affective domain cannot be separated from the cognitive domain. But, in order to increase the probability of fostering positive affect in social studies, we should be aware of and use the various types of affective questions.

    Select a social studies topic and write questions for the topic at each level of the affective domain.

Questioning Strategies

Although questions are sometimes asked in isolation, they more usually comprise part of a strategy created either by the teacher or the pupils for a definite purpose. The strategy is frequently incidental and situational rather than the result of careful planning; however, the teacher who uses questions most effectively generally plans them somewhat systematically.

Planning for Effective Questioning

Obviously, the first step in planning is to become familiar with the types of questions, their particular dimensions, the possible ways to sequence them, and their potential uses. The second step, or the first for the teacher who is already knowledgeable about the types, is to analyze the current situation. She must analyze needs on the basis of students' backgrounds, maturity levels, and intellectual abilities. An interest inventory is also appropriate at this stage. The teacher must also address other factors: Are necessary materials available? Will the schedule allow for detailed investigations? What are the community expectations? What is my level of competency as a teacher?

After analysis, the teacher considers goals and objectives. Objectives address the cognitive, affective, and psychomotor domains. Questions should enhance attainment of program objectives and specific lesson objectives.

Most social studies programs have as an objective the students' eventual ability to process content and arrive at conclusions about their nation's history. With this general objective in mind, you should plan cognitive questions at levels above mere recall of knowledge, and schedule sufficient time for processing them. Of course, there will be times when the objectives dictate mastering basic facts; for those occasions, a majority of questions might well be at the knowledge level. But when the lesson focuses on formulating concepts, appropriate questions will come from the categories of comprehension and analysis.

The next step, considering the question types, often runs concurrently with the previous steps. For example, lesson objectives and the types of appropriate questions can be planned simultaneously; question possibilities will arise during these planning steps.

The most obvious step is the actual writing or selecting of the questions. The quality of the questions the teacher selects or creates depends greatly on the depth of consideration during the planning steps. A teacher who is unfamiliar with possible question types and who only vaguely understands the objectives is unlikely to raise significant questions; this kind of teacher will probably overemphasize memory of specific facts.

During this stage, the teacher puts questions into sequence according to what is being emphasized in the class. If she is emphasizing problem solving, she might sequence the questions to parallel the steps of problem solving. The lesson plan on page 265 will give you some ideas for arranging questions.

In this example, the teacher has sketched out possible questions for herself or for students that parallel a problem-solving strategy. If another strategy were used, such as that in chapter 9 which emphasizes intellectual skills, the question sequences would be adjusted. If you were planning a deductive strategy, your questions would follow still another arrangement.

Reaction avenues provide an effective way to plan questions. They draw on the fact that teaching is a decision-making process in which you should anticipate to some extent the consequences of raising certain types of questions.

Developing a reaction avenue, as shown in figure 10.2, does not imply rigid planning. Essentially, it is a listing of questions that flow logically from

Lesson Plan

Topic: Urban Land Use

Strategy: Problem Solving

Stages	*Questions*
Problem identification	What types of land use do we find in our country? In the past year, what have been some reactions of the local community to current land use? To projected land use?
Hypothesis creation	Looking at the data we have, suggest reasons for various positions regarding land use.
Locating relevant data	Suggest possible places for obtaining information. What viewpoints have been reported in the newspapers? Indicate the distribution of several types of land use on the aerial photographs of the community. Note how some information might relate to one of your hypotheses. (Note: other questions will be suggested by pupils.)
Analyzing data	Determine why certain groups are favoring new uses for urban land in our community. What patterns can be detected among land use, people's viewpoints, and their income levels?
Evaluating hypotheses in light of data	Do the data you have gathered support the hypothesis that economic status determines how people view urban land use?
Drawing conclusions	What can we say in summary about people's views of urban land use? Do your data support this conclusion?

the first on through, and records possible responses or reactions to these questions. The reaction avenue is a suggestive device. The questions written into the avenue act as cues to directions in which the lesson can go. The questions are not to be memorized.

The sample reaction avenue shows the main directions questions might take a class when it is dealing with a basic factual question, "What types of machines were used in the early textile mills in New England?" The solid lines indicate the most likely direction of questioning; the broken lines suggest possible divergent investigations. The avenue also denotes potential pupil responses to each question and major concepts that could be addressed. Besides recording a good visual plan of the questions and their sequence, the teacher can also incorporate into the plan some notes for appropriate activi-

Figure 10.2
A Reaction Avenue

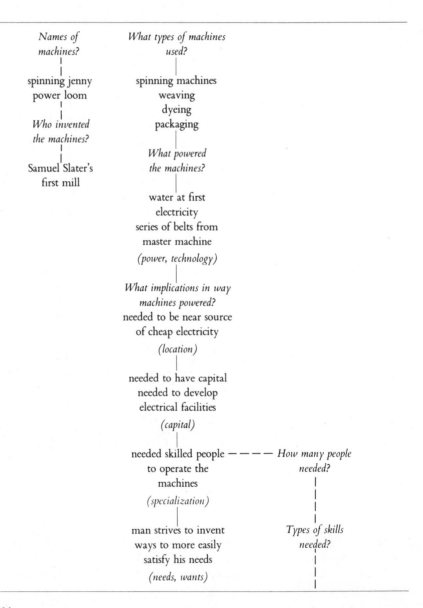

ties and support materials. Equipped with a reaction avenue, the teacher is less likely to be caught with a lesson direction for which she might not have adequate time or appropriate materials.

The reaction avenue denotes a particular questioning sequence or strategy; it is also possible to draw from specific instructional strategies and map out their stages on a reaction map. For instance, Taba (1967) developed a strategy comprised of three major stages: concept formation, interpretation of data, and application of principles. Following this strategy, one can select

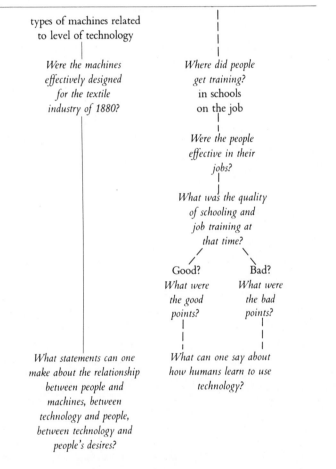

Figure 10.2
(continued)

types of machines related
to level of technology

*Were the machines
effectively designed
for the textile
industry of 1880?*

*Where did people
get training?*
in schools
on the job

*Were the people
effective in their
jobs?*

*What was the quality
of schooling and
job training at
that time?*

Good?   Bad?
*What were   What were
the good   the bad
points?*   points?*

*What statements can one
make about the relationship
between people and
machines, between
technology and people,
between technology and
people's desires?*

*What can one say about
how humans learn to use
technology?*

KEY:
_ _ _ _ _ _ _ *(possible branch investigations)*
_____ *(main stream of reaction)*

From Francis P. Hunkins, *Questioning Strategies and Techniques.* Reprinted by permission.

267

or write in a reaction avenue some questions for the first stage, then for each of the next two stages. Using this strategy to get pupils to investigate families, the teacher might plan to use questions like these:

Concept formation: How many children here have brothers and sisters?

↓

What types of things do you do with your brother or sister? (play, work)

↓

If someone visited from outer space, how would you tell them about the people you live with?

Interpretation of Data: Think about our answers to our outer space visitors about the people we live with. What are some things that were alike in our descriptions?

↓

Why do you suppose many of us do similar things in our homes with brothers and sisters? (same interests)

↓

Are people more alike or different when we consider the groups they live with?

Both the cognitive and affective domains suggest implicit strategies. Approached inductively, the cognitive domain supports questions that start at the knowledge level and proceed through evaluation. The sequence would be reversed if one wished pupils to work deductively. Questions drawing on the taxonomies can be recorded on a reaction avenue. In the sample reaction avenue about textile machines, the questions proceed inductively through the cognitive domain. "What types of machines are used?" is a knowledge-level question; the final question, "What statements can one make about the relationship between people and machines, between technology and people, between technology and people's desires?" is a synthesis question. As it relates to the problem-solving model, the last question is at the "drawing conclusions" stage.

The examples in figure 10.3 are simple representations of what would actually be a somewhat complex questioning sequence and extension of intellectual functioning. One would not always proceed linearly through the questions; there would probably be much skipping back and forth from one level to another. An actual inductive questioning pattern might look like figure 10.4.

After writing or selecting the questions for a lesson, one must judge their appropriateness before actually using them. This is the final planning step. In judging questions, we ask, "Are the questions relevant to the objec-

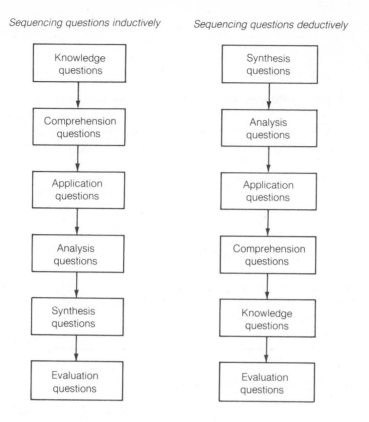

Sequencing questions inductively

Sequencing questions deductively

Figure 10.3
Inductive and
Deductive Questioning
Sequences

tives? Are the questions worded clearly and at the appropriate vocabulary level for the pupils? Will the sequence foster either convergent or divergent thinking, according to the objective of the lesson? Will there be adequate time for pupils to process the questions? Are there sufficient support materials to allow processing of the questions?" After questions have been judged appropriate for the age and grade level, for the particular objectives and goals, and for the time available, we move from planning into action.

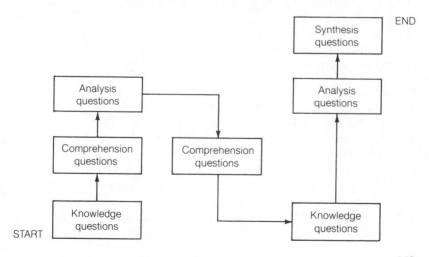

Figure 10.4
Pattern for Processing
Questions Inductively

269

Activity 10:5

Developing Reaction Avenues (Inductive Strategy)

Using the reaction avenue procedure, create an inductive questioning strategy sequence for any social studies topic. Share your plans with a peer. Arrange to use the strategy in a classroom.

Activity 10:6

Developing Reaction Avenues (Deductive Strategy)

Create a reaction avenue for a deductive questioning strategy for any grade. If possible, have a teacher critique the strategy. After the critique, try out the strategy in a classroom. Jot down your own perceptions of how it worked.

Managing Questions in the Classroom

After creating questions for possible use, the teacher can determine, at least generally, the pace at which questioning should proceed. If questions are to be integrated into materials, then the teacher should determine how much time should be alloted for dealing with them.

The pacing of questions in social studies is crucial. Mary Budd Rowe (1970) conducted research dealing with the rate at which teachers ask questions. She discovered that not only are the majority of questions in the classroom asked by the teacher, but the rate of asking these questions is extremely rapid. She noted that, on the average, the teacher waits only one second for a pupil to respond to a question. Certainly, such a time interval is inadequate to allow students to reflect or process information.

When teachers extend the amount of time they wait for a child to respond to three seconds, they achieve startling results. For example:

- The students ask more questions.
- The students' responses to questions are more varied.
- The complexity and length of student responses increase.
- Students demonstrate via their responses more incidences of speculative and creative thinking.
- Students exhibit more confidence in dealing with information.
- The teacher becomes more flexible in responding to student's responses and questions.
- The teacher actually increases the types of questions raised in the classroom.

■ Teachers begin to revise their expectations of how students should function in their learning. (Rowe, 1967)

Increasing wait time heightens the probability of effective learning. Teachers should experiment with the amount of time they allow students for processing different types of questions, and with various ways of sequencing questions in their classrooms.

When managing questions, teachers have to exert care in responding to a pupil's reactions. When a student answers a question, the teacher often verbalizes; for example, "fine, yes, all right." These statements are noncommittal; they do not denote judgment or response, but merely acknowledge that the response has been heard. Verbal acknowledgements are appropriate, but teachers often feel they must add some evaluative statement. When a teacher says to a child "yes, that is correct," however, then other children will cease to consider the question. They feel there is no need for further consideration; an answer has been offered and judged correct. Even though there may well be another "correct" answer, many children will not respond for fear of hearing "no, that is not right."

With questions that foster divergent thought at various cognitive levels, the teacher may not really know the correct or optimal answer. It is important for students to accept that they, not the teacher, must often determine the "correctness" of a response. Along with this realization, students should also be aware that just because they have studied something and answered some questions, they have not necessarily arrived at all possible conclusions. Processing questions supplies some answers and understandings, but it also generates additional queries. Inquiry is a continual activity; it requires and suggests additional questions to advance the lesson.

Increasing wait time for answers leads to more complex responses, more questions, and more creative thinking from students.

Mechanics of Questioning

As teachers practice questioning in their classrooms, they perfect ways of triggering effective student responses and additional questions. Teachers soon realize that there is more to asking questions than just phrasing them. Several techniques help to heighten the effectiveness of questioning.

Sometimes *probing* will be necessary. The instructor may see that a pupil is experiencing some difficulty responding to a question, but will be able to arrive at an answer with some helpful hints. For example, the teacher might ask a pupil some reasons for the high price of gasoline. At first, the child responds that she does not know. Instead of going on to the next class member, the teacher might say, "Well, you remember what major event happened last month?" (An OPEC meeting.) "What were some of the results of that meeting? (Pupil responds that OPEC members announced a raise in the base price of a barrel of oil.) "Fine, now what effect did the price rise have on the cost of gasoline?" (Child responds that it caused it to go up.) "All right, now we have one reason for the increase in gasoline prices. What might be some other reasons?" The teacher hopes that with these cues, the pupil will now be able to answer the question.

In probing, the teacher actually leads the pupil through a question-and-answer sequence until the pupil achieves success. Taking this time tells the child that you are interested in helping her to learn, and that you have confidence that she will be able to process the information. As a result, the child will most likely be able to keep up with the class. Other class members should be told to pay attention to such question-and-answer dialogue, for it can help them increase their own levels of knowledge. Children tend to listen only when the teacher is speaking to them personally, so they need constant reminders, at least at first, to listen carefully to the responses other students give to the teacher's questions.

Probing for details can also be used when you want a pupil to explain her response. When the child gives a correct answer to a question, probing helps her refine a response into something more specific. Children are often content, as are their teachers, with one-word responses. It is necessary to push them beyond general responses, to deal with questions in appropriate levels of detail. When probing for specificity, the teacher can ask, "What other examples can you give? How might your explanation support these other instances? Is there another explanation for this person's actions?"

A second questioning technique is *clarification-elaboration*. This is similar to probing, except that, where probing provides cues to help the child arrive at an answer, the clarification-elaboration technique offers no cues. Rather, a question to which the pupil has responded is followed by additional questions that ask the pupil to expand and improve on her response. When using this tactic, the teacher might ask "What do you mean by that answer?" or "Explain your answer; I am not quite sure what you mean. What else can you add to that statement?"

Using this technique, the teacher might ask pupils to think of ways in which an answer can apply to some other subject area. For instance, a child who is talking about the ways family members help each other could be asked to relate the concept of helping to different types of jobs in a community: "You have said that there are times in most families when individuals do certain tasks to help out. If we consider the community as a type of family, how might your answer about the family members help us understand the roles people play in the community?" In this instance, the teacher is asking the pupils to relate an answer in one area to content in another area. Teachers can sometimes use this technique to get children to make a prediction based on their answers.

These two questioning techniques, coupled with proper pacing, can enable pupils to get high "mileage" out of their reactions. It also encourages them to begin to employ these techniques themselves when they raise questions independently or work with classmates. These techniques help children evaluate their reasons for questions and responses. "Just why did you respond that way?" or "What was the intent of that question?" The intent is not to make a pupil feel uncomfortable, but to make her aware of the rationale behind a question or response.

Teachers must emphasize that one never arrives at an absolutely final answer to a question—there is always another question to consider. Probing and calling for clarification and elaboration foster the notion of the incompleteness of conclusions, and thus help to stimulate intellectual curiosity.

The Atmosphere for Good Questioning

Effective questioning strategies require an atmosphere of freedom. Pupils must feel free to raise and pursue questions that interest them, and they must have time to solve questions.

In such an atmosphere, both teacher and students are accepting of other people's interests, conclusions, and feelings. Pupils know the reasons for questions at the outset of class investigations. They realize that everyone has the right to pose questions and that everyone's questions have value. In an ideal atmosphere, students recognize textbook and teacher questions as starting places for additional inquiry, not as end points for assessing conclusions.

The ideal setting for classroom questioning is one in which (1) both teacher and pupils introduce materials that provoke questions; (2) adequate materials are available for pupil investigation; (3) students have time to plan their own questions; and (4) the questioning process itself receives formal attention. Raising questions about questions and thinking about the process of acquiring answers are valuable facets of learning.

Children need to see that the purpose of questions is to get them to think about the potential directions an inquiry might take, or to guide them in a particular investigation. To promote this awareness, the teacher can demonstrate how to plan questions, sometimes by sharing her reaction avenues with the children, or by showing how different types of questions meet varying needs.

Wilen, Dietrich and Owen (1977) have made some suggestions that summarize many of the points in this chapter. They suggest that the teacher:

1. Create a learning environment within which students feel, realize, and are encouraged to voice their ideas, opinions, and values,
2. Spend more time in preparing lessons whose objectives require students to engage in higher level thought,
3. Familiarize students with the levels of questions and thought that can be expressed in the classroom,
4. Encourage students to clarify, expand, and support initial responses to higher-level teacher questions,
5. Stimulate non-volunteering students to participate in discussions and balance the contributions of the volunteering students,
6. Use formal and informal analysis of teaching techniques as a means to assess progress toward making improvement in questioning practices.

Activity 10:7

Classroom Atmosphere

List the factors that contribute to an atmosphere conducive to good questioning by both teacher and students. Observe a social studies class over three or four lessons and write an assessment of the atmosphere the teacher has created and how the atmosphere affects the level, frequency, and use of questions by both teacher and students.

   If you feel the atmosphere does not contribute to good questioning, include the actions you would take to improve the atmosphere.

Discussion

Questioning is the most potentially powerful teaching technique. Unfortunately, it is used most often merely for evaluation and for recall of information. Although evaluation is a valid use of questioning, it is a more effective educational tool when it calls for students to process information. Questioning can help orient students to a lesson or unit, guide investigation, and help to evaluate research.

   The goals and objectives of the lesson suggest what types of questions are appropriate for teacher and students to raise, ranging from questions for simple recall to higher-level questions requiring analysis and synthesis. The teacher can use questioning to engage the students in active learning, and can structure questioning for both deductive and inductive learning.

   Questions in the cognitive domain are knowledge questions, comprehension questions (which call for translation, interpretation, or extrapolation), application questions, analysis questions, synthesis questions, and evaluation questions. Since the social studies teacher is concerned also with attitudes and values, she will find places to use questions that draw on the affective as well as the cognitive domain. Questions in the affective domain are receiving or attending questions, responding questions, valuing questions, organization questions, and value complex questions.

Effective questioning is the result of some systematic planning, although questioning strategies are often incidental and situational. To plan questioning strategies, the teacher must be familiar with the types of questions. Then she must consider goals and objectives, and choose appropriate types of questions accordingly, following with the actual writing or selection of questions. Reaction avenues are useful for planning questioning strategies, since the teacher can anticipate some possible responses and select questions to accommodate the various directions the questioning might take.

Research shows that a problem with classroom questioning has been failure to give students adequate time to respond. When students have enough time to answer a question, they begin to derive greater benefits from questioning strategies and to participate more actively. Other important aspects of good questioning strategies are acknowledging responses appropriately and encouraging the notion that questions often have no correct response or lead to other, different questions. Probing, calling for clarification or elaboration, and proper pacing enhance questioning strategies and stimulate discussion. The proper classroom atmosphere for good questioning strategies is one of freedom, where students feel comfortable raising questions and will not be embarrassed or shy about offering responses.

References

Bloom, Benjamin S., ed. *Taxonomy of Educational Objectives, The Classification of Educational Goals. Handbook I: Cognitive Domain.* New York: David McKay, 1956.

Carin, Arthur, and Sund, Robert B. *Creative Questioning and Sensitive Listening Techniques.* 2nd ed. Columbus, Oh.: Charles E. Merrill, 1978.

Chaudhari, U. S. "Questioning and Creative Thinking: A Research Perspective." *Journal of Creative Behavior* 9 (1975): 31.

Hunkins, Francis P. *Questioning Strategies and Techniques.* Boston: Allyn and Bacon, 1972.

Krathwohl, David R., ed. *Taxonomy of Educational Goals Objectives, The Classification of Educational Goals. Handbook II: Affective Domain.* New York: David McKay, 1964.

Rowe, Mary Budd. "Wait-Time and Rewards as Instructional Variables: Influence on Inquiry and Sense of Fate Control." In *New Science in the Inner City.* New York: Columbia University Press, 1970.

Taba, Hilda. *Teachers' Handbook for Elementary Social Studies.* Reading, Mass.: Addison-Wesley, 1967.

Wilen, William; Dietrich, Raymond; and Owen, David. "A Study: Guidelines for Improving Questioning Practices." *OCSS Review* 13 (1977): 16–22.

Environments for Social Studies Learning

11

According to John Holt (1974), "We would have to worry a lot less in our schools about 'motivating' children, about finding ways to make good things happen if we would just provide more spaces in which good things could happen." The quality of the educational space, or classroom environment, is crucial to meaningful educational experiences. Curtis and Smith (1974) note that when children are exposed to a creative environment, they are much more likely to realize their potentials and to have heightened excitement about learning. As Holt postulates, space creates activity; it allows students to generate places and to mold moods.

Teachers are beginning to realize that the environment of the school or the community can be as important to learning as the experiences incorporated into the master curriculum plan. Educational space and the physical phenomena that bond such space should be considered an educational tool (Hunkins, 1980).

Today's and tomorrow's teachers need to be successful designers of educational environments. This responsibility requires some knowledge of the field of environmental psychology. An environmental psychologist, concerned with understanding the complexity of the physical settings in which people live and interact, might perceive educational space much as a geographer perceives a region of the earth.

An educational environment can be any space where people react to objects and interact with people for the purpose of learning. It need not be only the classroom; it may be a community park, where students investigate how people use parks, or a local store, where students analyze the factors that influence how people decide what to buy.

The Environmental System of the Classroom

Planning an environment that fosters social studies learnings requires an understanding of environmental variables. Moos (1979) classifies four such variables: the physical setting, organizational factors, the human aggregate, and the social climate.

Physical Setting

The physical setting, the most obvious variable, consists of the architecture and the physical design of buildings and other structures. In their research of school designs, Myrick and Marx (1968) categorize designs as either cohesive or isolating. Schools with a cohesive design have one or two main classroom buildings; schools with an isolated design have several separate buildings. These researchers found that in schools with an isolated design, teachers and students spent more time traveling to and from rooms and thus had less time to interact informally before and after classes. Students in schools with a cohesive layout interacted more with their fellow students.

Besides architecture and design, the physical setting also includes furniture, hardware, and materials. The variables of student types, class size, and learning and teaching styles influence the selection of these physical elements.

Organizational Factors

Organizational factors refer to school size, room size, faculty–student ratio, classroom organization of teachers and students, and faculty organization.

Human Aggregate

All educational environments involve many people in various roles: student, teacher, resource person, evaluator, planner, manager, counselor etc. When planning social studies lessons, teachers need to consider their students' ages, ability levels, socioeconomic backgrounds, and prior educational achievements as well as any handicaps. They must also consider to some degree how the scheduling of specific content and experiences will affect people as individuals or groups.

Social Climate

The last environmental domain to consider is the *personal systems* or *social climate*. When planning the personal system, educators must weigh the individual characteristics that influence different responses to different environments. To explain differences in response, environmental psychologists study people's backgrounds in terms of age, sex, ability levels, interests, preferences for particular activities, coping styles, and drive for exploration. This kind of data allows educators to adapt the setting so as to heighten its learning potential.

There are no hard and fast rules for structuring this personal system. Current debate focuses on the advantages of open classrooms over the more traditionally structured ones. Advocates of open classrooms testify that stu-

279

dents appear to be happier and more involved in learning, resulting in a positive attitude toward learning in general. Epstein and McPartland (1976) note that positive reactions to school increase the likelihood that students will stay in school until completion, will develop a lasting commitment toward learning, and will utilize the institution to optimal advantage.

One cannot avoid the personal system, for individuals in the classroom are rarely isolated. In activating this system in social studies, teachers draw on their understanding of group dynamics, and consider ways of optimizing students' social intercourse. Social studies educators usually hope that students will develop cooperation, manage competition, accept themselves and others, and formulate role expectations for themselves. These objectives can best be achieved in a healthy social environment. Finally, teachers should also consider their own actions in this social system.

Activity 11.1

Analyzing Classroom Space

Interview some teachers to identify their reasons for organizing their classrooms as they have.
Explain how educational space in the particular school where you are observing or interning is perceived and utilized.

The Classroom as Primary Educational Space

The classroom will continue as the primary educational arena for the foreseeable future. Therefore, this facility should be organized to address the social needs of students, their feelings of security, and their feelings of belonging; it should allow pupils to develop both an inner awareness and appreciation, and an increased awareness of others. The classroom as the primary educational space should enable students to obtain the knowledge, attitudes, values, and skills essential for successful living.

The classroom should be organized so that the planned types of learnings cannot help but occur. If students are to accept the concept of responsibility, then the environment should facilitate their being responsible. Transfer of learning occurs whenever previous learning influences the learning or performance of new responses; such transfer is most likely to occur when a person confronts a new situation that he recognizes as similar to other situations for which a particular behavior or knowledge was appropriate. Castaldi (1977) notes that the greater the similarity between school experiences and the anticipated real-life experiences, the higher the level of transfer of learning.

In designing classrooms, then, teachers need to employ this concept of transfer; educational space should be similar to real space. The design should stimulate purposeful student activity and allow for depth and range of learning activities. The educational milieu must provide more than a warm environment for book learning.

The Hidden Curriculum

Not all that is learned in social studies classes is written into lesson plans. And, not all that is learned in social studies classes is positive. A "hidden curriculum" exists both inside and outside the school—those contents, attitudes, skills and values that are suggested and directly taught by the environments, the structure, the selected content and its emphasis and sequence, the manner of teaching, the types of experiences allowed, and what is taught by peer groups and significant others. For example, the goal of the teacher may be to motivate students academically, but if this goal is not valued by the majority of the student population, there will be little or no task orientation, and students who might otherwise desire high academic performance will be inhibited.

Often teachers interpret humanistic education in terms of creating a relaxed classroom environment, yet researchers show that a relaxed setting can coexist with low expectations and performance standards. An effect of this type of environment is that there is little incentive for students to strive for excellence, resulting in poor social and academic functioning.

Teachers who strive for efficient classroom management frequently instill in their pupils an overdependence on authority. Students in authoritarian classrooms may learn that in order to be successful, one does not challenge authority; individuality is stifled to achieve the rewards of the system. Students in such classrooms also develop a resistance to taking risks or asking questions that relate to learning.

Discussion in the 1970s centered around assurances that students were learning successfully, which some people interpreted to mean that students should be put in "failure free" classrooms. One result of such a classroom environment is that some children do not learn how to deal with failure or how to use it to achieve success in future learning. Good mental health requires a proper perspective of one's abilities, and when they are excluded from any failure, students do not develop a realistic self-image.

Teachers frequently create learning situations that stress competition to the neglect of cooperation. A teacher may state, "We are going to record our data about population growth on charts. Let's see who can finish first." This kind of direction turns the activity into a race, and communicates to the children that finishing first is more valued than learning how to analyze data and record it in chart form. Or, the teacher's attitude may imply that politely raising one's hand to add to class discussion is more important than the content of the discussion. Often the curricular activities one plans for the classroom tell students that the rewards will go to the first to complete the assignment or to those who "behave." Choice of activities can also implicitly

281

communicate that those individuals who do not have "learning problems" will succeed, while those with learning difficulties will fail.

Social studies teachers occasionally emphasize personal growth to the extent that some students develop anxieties. Epstein and McPartland (1976) found that in some alternative schools, excessive emphasis on responsibility and self-reliance causes many students to develop school anxiety and stress. Of course, one may also overemphasize an authoritarian classroom structure to the point that children become overly dependent on that particular structure; they "learn" they must not act before an authority has "set the stage."

Research suggests that structured classes are better for students new to the subject, while more "open" classes can be scheduled for students with some prior knowledge. The research of Nielsen and Moos (1978) supports the view that students who exhibit a need for achievement adjust better and gain more from classroom environments with limited structure, but additional research is necessary before this can become an all inclusive principle. We do know that motivated students learn best under conditions of high expectation and demand, as often exist in highly organized classrooms. In the meantime, teachers must make an effort to understand the processes at work in the classroom to learn more about the hidden curriculum.

Activity 11:2

Making the Hidden Curriculum Visible

All classrooms have a hidden curriculum. Analyze the classroom in which you are observing or student teaching, and note all those things that are being taught indirectly—through the use of space, methods of grouping, use of materials, and the way time is scheduled.

How would you classify the hidden curriculum in this classroom?

What are the consequences of the hidden curriculum on student learnings and behaviors?

Suggest things to do to heighten the positive aspects of the hidden curriculum.

Indicate how you would lessen the impact of the negative aspects of the hidden curriculum.

Planning Educational Space

The most productive learning spaces, whether in the classroom or community, result from imagination, educated guesses, good intentions, and enthusiasm for the task at hand. There is much teachers do not know about the educational environment; for the present, they must, to some degree, assume the roles of risk takers and inquirers. Instructors need to observe what happens with their students as a result of some environmental manipulation. Teachers have tended to ignore the environment because it is so familiar. Individuals walk through it, play in it, reflect in it—yet, because they are accustomed to it, it eludes their view. Teachers also know little about how the child perceives the environment. It might be productive for educators to visit their classrooms on a Saturday—to sit on the floor, play in the area designed for play, and crawl on their knees to see how the world looks from that angle. Teachers could wear earplugs, to help them develop empathy for those special students with hearing impairments.

On the days students are in class, teachers can keep a note pad handy to record pupils' reactions to and interactions with their spaces and identify factors in those spaces. Such observations should generate questions such as these: How are the children reacting to the planned spaces? Where does that shy child go most of the time when given the opportunity to select his space? Is the social conversation space such that children feel at ease talking? Do they disturb others in the classroom? Do some children feel ill-at-ease standing on the classroom platform? How do they react to the "cushion space" designed for individual reading?

It is sometimes a good idea to focus on only one observation and generate as many questions as possible as to the appropriateness of the space, the ways it could be used, its efficiency, and its "emotional" aspect. By generating such questions, instructors can make some educated guesses as to how to create effective classroom space.

Steps in Planning Educational Environments

Step 1
Assess your educational space. Then, review the four variables of educational space and record the actions necessary to accommodate each of these domains.

An example of a planned educational space: a comfortable corner for individualized reading.

Step 2

Reflect on the specific goals and general objectives for the planned social studies lesson, the types of environments that allow students to achieve these objectives, and whether the appropriate environment can be created in the classroom or requires the use of the community.

Step 3

Next, analyze the specific content to be taught. What types of environments will best enable students to learn this content? For each aspect of the selected content, the teacher can jot down possible activities with notes as to what kind of space will be best for each activity.

Assume, for example, that students are to study the agricultural methods of the American West. The question is, what type or types of environments will facilitate such study? To answer this, one needs to identify possible educational activities for the lesson. The form in figure 11.1 can be used to gradually arrange your data under the three column heading to guide yourself to a proper decision.

Step 4.

Figure 11.1 deals only with matching content and activities to the physical environment or setting. The organizational, human aggregate, and social climate variables must still be considered. If students are to view films, will they be watching them with other students who are similarly interested? Will students be allowed to share perceptions and to challenge each other about ways to address some of the problems that confront Western farmers?

The mechanics of this step can be handled by organizing questions and the resulting data as shown in figure 11.2, which would accompany figure 11.1.

Although figure 11.2 does not include all aspects of the lesson, it does indicate how to organize information in order to choose an environment for teaching about agriculture in the West.

Step 5.

Step 5 may be performed along with step 4; in this step, the teacher judges the educational space he has tentatively selected. Castaldi suggests three criteria for judgment: adequacy, efficiency, and economy.

Adequacy refers to both the number and size of spaces. Are they large enough to accommodate the number of students? Adequacy also refers to environmental controls. Is the light adequate? Are the visuals large enough for good viewing? Is the image on the screen large enough? (These two questions are especially important if there are children with visual handicaps in the class.)

Content Selected	Possible Activity	Possible Educational Space
Agriculture in the American West (geography, history, economics)	Reading materials	School classroom School library City library
	Viewing films	Classroom Film center
	Discussion groups	Classroom (Social studies interest center) Seminar room
	Experimenting	Classroom, interest center Laboratory Farm School grounds for garden experimentation
	Field trips	Local garden, truck farms Chamber of commerce Dairy farms Meat processing plants Home gardens

Figure 11.1
Relating Content and
Activities to
Educational Space

Educational Space Selected	Organizational Factors	Human Factors	Social Factors
Film Center	Students will view the film in groups of five	Match independent learners with those needing great support	
	Have separate room for viewing film, soundproof so as not to disturb other students		Allow time for students to share perceptions
			Arrange for debriefing room where students can sit around a table for discussion

Figure 11.2
Adjusting for Other
Variables

285

Suitability is a factor in the adequacy of the space; that is, the environment should suit its intended function. Is the space for projecting the film really suitable for small-group viewing followed by discussion? Modern classrooms are usually designed for demonstration and discovery as well as exposition, so it is usually a matter of selecting the right spot for each activity. And, is the classroom suitable for pupils confined to wheelchairs?

Adequacy also refers to the relationships among the spaces. How does the space designed for viewing the film relate to spaces intended for other uses? Will students have to disrupt the rest of the class in order to view and discuss this film? Is the classroom space designed for small-group film viewing also appropriate for small-group discussion? Will students be able to get from this area back to their main work areas without further disruption?

Efficiency refers to those characteristics of a space that improve its instructional effectiveness or operation. Does the environment allow the activity to be accomplished with minimum effort? Will it facilitate the greatest amount of learning? Will students and teachers find it convenient to work in the space? When viewing a film, will a small film viewing center facilitate such learning? Can students view the film in some other type of space—perhaps at a local farm bureau or at a classroom interest center—with equal or greater benefit?

The final criterion is *economy,* one aspect of which is savings of capital outlay. How much does it cost to provide this experience in one's regular classroom? In another space? What is the cost of purchasing or renting a film? Will it provide students with information and attitude development that could not be provided in some other, even better way?

Economy refers not merely to saving dollars, but also to the amounts of energy students and teachers must expend in order to teach and learn. Time is a resource, and teachers must design social studies environments that enable students to meet the lesson's or unit's objectives with the most efficient use of energy and time. Attention to economy does not mean the teacher should always select the shortest and cheapest route to social studies education, of course. There will be times when spending large amounts of time on an activity enhances learning. This might be true, for example, if students are to gain appreciation for the western farmer; they cannot do this with a fifteen-minute film or one short visit to a truck farm. Instructors do not want an educational activity to run longer than necessary, but they should strive to design environments that facilitate the greatest amount of learning in the least amount of time.

Step 6

The final step is deciding to use a particular activity or instructional method within one or more environments.

Some readers may react to these suggestions with the thought that they have only a classroom to work with, and cannot determine the nature of the educational space. But in most instances, the teacher *does* have total control over the nature of his classroom space. It is not necessary to accept the existing classroom space as unalterable. Mini-spaces for specialized activities can be created within the confines of the regular classroom. Many teachers create interest centers where exhibits and books are located. Some classrooms have reading centers arranged with bean bag chairs and separated from the main class space by a row of plants or a bookcase. The authors have observed classrooms where spaces have been defined by macramé wall hangings that reach from ceiling to floor. One teacher personalized his classroom space by building a loft in the regular classroom, where children could climb to get away from the classroom activities for reflection or quiet reading. The loft also created a cozy space underneath it.

In schools where teachers team teach and classrooms are arranged in pods connected by a learning resource center, one will find many opportunities to manage not only one's immediate classroom space but the spaces of the adjoining room and the learning resource center as well. Some classrooms of this type have a raised stage in one corner of the room which is observable to children in two classrooms when a room divider is opened.

Many teachers do not have such flexible classroom arrangements, but even in a basically square room, you can change the internal spaces by arranging desks in circles or creating mini-spaces with bookcases or even aquarium tanks. Banners can define personal spaces for children. One teacher pitched an old parachute as a "tent" for the children to crawl into for "get away time" and resting. There is no reason to assume the teacher's desk must be at the front of the room and the students' chairs arranged in rows, and that all activities must conform to such a spatial arrangement. Most teachers are not free to rebuild their classrooms, of course, but imagination and creativity can go a long way in producing an interesting and useful educational environment.

The Impacts of Classroom Settings

Does the environment in which they work really affect student behavior and learning? Investigators are finding that environments definitely influence the selection and success of people's coping styles. All participants in a social studies class can observe and determine which of several learning methods would be most productive. If students perceive that the teacher encourages inquiry, they may select a style of active investigation. If, however, the teacher has made it clear that authority will not be challenged and that attention must be given to covering the prescribed text, students may cope by merely reading the book and doing the assigned activities. Since elementary school students are not free to leave a classroom they dislike, their only option is to adjust—to cope as best they can.

Moos feels the effects of environment on student learning is greater than initially thought. He postulates that learning environments contribute to stability and predictable change more than to differential change. Classrooms tend to perpetuate known behaviors or changes within easily perceived limits rather than to encourage highly unanticipated behavior.

287

In considering the impacts of classroom settings, researchers have found that most social environments are created by people's behavior. In effect, they create spaces in which they can grow. There seems to be a mutual interaction between people and their environments; overall, students appear to be more influenced by settings than those settings are modified by students. Educational settings affect students both positively and negatively. Knowing this, instructors must consciously choose whether or not to structure a learning environment. Ideally, learning areas should foster student involvement, allow for teacher support, and enable clear identification of rules. Finally, our social studies education spaces should permit innovation.

Currently, there is much talk about individualizing or personalizing instruction; a learning space can also be personalized. Students need places to call their own—to satisfy their desires for territoriality and privacy. A sense of ownership can be heightened by allowing students to decorate the room and organize desks and chairs in particular patterns. They can design and personally control these areas according to their needs and desires. Allowing students to manipulate and personalize their environment contributes to positive self-concepts and encourages them to find the classroom a happy place.

Mapping the Classroom

We have discussed steps to take in environmental planning in terms of a chart based on a particular topic and its possible activities and potential environments. To set up a classroom for social studies instruction, one can incorporate that information into a specialized map, to show the spatial or physical arrangements of potential groups, possible activities, and even materials and equipment. In the map in figure 11.3 (showing a type of diagram developed by Castaldi), the main area of the room is reserved for large-group presentations, either teacher- or student-directed. This suggests that, for at least part of the lesson, the experience will be organized for the entire class. Other grouping arrangements and activities are noted in relation to this central area of the classroom; you can show the degree of relationship on the map by the number of lines connecting the areas.

Three lines denote a close relationship. When planning such a relationship, be sure the work areas are adjacent. In figure 11.3, the large group has a very close relationship with the research materials space as well as with the smaller discussion centers. In a regular classroom, this most likely would mean that research materials (encyclopedias, reference books, charts, pictures, etc.) would be nearby for ready reference and use. The small-group media viewing space is next to the media center, so that students can use the materials without disrupting the rest of the class.

Two lines show a strong relationship between activity areas, and these spaces should be in the same general area. In our classroom, the spaces for small discussion groups should be in the same general vicinity as the research center, and the map center within easy reach of the large-group area and the media center. The map center may be included in the media center, depending on the amount of space available.

Those areas linked by *one line* are clusters that would be nice but not essential to have in the same general area. There is no real need to have the space allotted for individual tutoring next to the small-group discussion center; in fact, such a space may be outside the classroom.

An *absence of lines* between any two groups or spaces means that no relationship exists between them, and they may be placed anywhere. For instance, one might include a space for relaxation, denoted by a circle, but it would probably not be connected to any of the other spaces since there is really no reason for such a space (a recess area) to be in close proximity to the classroom.

Figure 11.3 depicts the mapping of activities in one classroom. Similar maps can be created for the entire school and even the community. Various classrooms might be identified by one cluster each, and other clusters can show student activities centers, the library, the auditorium, the special education center, and the like. Figure 11.4 shows such a map. The map reveals a strong relationship between the classrooms and the resource center. The special education center should be near or preferably next to the resource center. The classrooms are linked by one line to the faculty work spaces—it is nice for them to be nearby, but not essential. Ideally, in a continuous-progress school with a differentiated staffing arrangement, the classrooms interact with one another. There may be primary and intermediate wing clusters, with like classrooms alongside each other. These maps usually describe a school's present arrangement, but more importantly, they can be used to show better relationships among clusters. In such instances, decision-making must take the human aggregate and social climate into consideration.

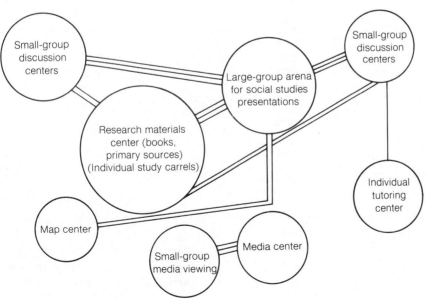

Figure 11.3
Map of a Classroom Arranged for Social Studies

Such maps help in planning various types of spaces and in generating activities to take place in them. They also provide a vehicle for analyzing created environments to determine if they are conducive to the types of intended learning. Think about how you would map your "ideal" classroom.

Figure 11.4
Cluster Map of an
Elementary School

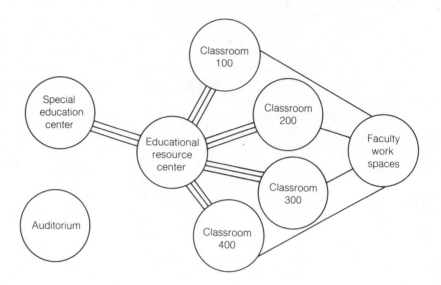

Activity 11.3

Mapping a Classroom

Using the symbols discussed in this text, create a map of the classroom where you are now observing or teaching. (If you are not currently in a school, arrange to observe in one.)
　　What relationships exist among the various classroom areas?
　　How would you reorganize the classroom? What is your rationale for your plan?

The Community as Educational Space

For most of this century, educational environment referred to the classroom, where one was concerned with methodologies, teacher–leadership styles, and an established reward system. Today, people realize that educational space requires a broader definition; it needs to include both school and non-school sites. Indeed, classrooms provide only a fraction of the total possible educational experiences. Students of the future will probably have their greatest educational experience outside the formal school classroom, and the major impact on the student will probably be made by someone other than the teacher. It is perhaps humbling to note that parents and peers are twice as influential in student learnings as are teachers (Hunkins, 1980). Current research indicates that the influence of significant others on student achievement is extremely important, and that peers and parents have about equal influence on learning.

Surrounding the school is a powerful learning environment—the community. And, there is always some intended learning that will be facilitated by taking advantage of that environment.

Armstrong (1980) notes that the community is really a laboratory for the social studies. As such, students can obtain practice in gathering information, analyzing their data, generating tentative conclusions, judging the worth of such results, and incorporating final judgments into the knowledge they have. As educational space, the community provides opportunities for students to apply their information-processing skills from the various social sciences.

It is essential to carefully plan the active use of the community, because when students actually experience this learning space, they are confronting reality. They can experience it, observe it, record people doing things, and grow in emotional experience. The community adds realism—it provides students with living examples of many of the social studies concepts. It allows them to "put the pieces together" in ways not possible through merely reading textbooks. When employing the community as a major educational space, educators allow their students to act as both observers and participants. They are not just playing investigator, they are actually gathering data from reality. The students are really engaged in generating knowledge.

By using the community as a learning environment in the early grades, pupils gain an interest in studying human society. They also develop an interest in themselves and others as they observe people, places, and things firsthand. These young investigators can visualize directly the problems of group living. They can observe the government in operation. In a visit to an open market, they can gather information about the production and distribution of goods. Visits to historical places generate excitement about their national heritage. All places have a history; every community has places to visit for emphasizing a particular person, event, or site in local history. Field trips to various parts of their cities or nearby cities bring alive to children, in ways more effective than classroom lecture, that we are indeed a diverse nation. A list of the community churches can lead to making some type of map of the numerous religious groups in the United States. Community study enables students to see instances of harmony and conflict among groups and individual citizens.

Using the Community

Teachers often do not make optimal use of the community, because their overall plans frequently lack a framework of meaningful organization. Arm-

291

strong and Savage (1976) recommend two considerations in planning community use: (1) stimulus experiences, and (2) anticipated student learnings.

In considering the community as a potential social studies resource, look for artifacts to serve as stimuli and events and other phenomena in which students can be participants or observers. These experiences can be organized into three general categories: (1) historical residues; (2) present interactional processes; and (3) likely future patterns.

According to Armstrong and Savage, historical residues are the remainders of the history of the community. These include records, documents, photographs, historical buildings, and any other physical evidence of past life in the community. Historical residues can be the focal point of a variety of social studies units. For instance, a fourth-grade class might use old photographs of a particular area as a starting point for a study of urban development. They can examine the photographs for topographical features such as buildings or parks, then visit the area to determine the ways in which it has changed. Have new buildings been built? How has the landscape been altered? What are some possible reasons for the changes they see?

Primary-grade children might enjoy a trip to an old school building simply to compare it with their new school. What are the differences between the two buildings? What is the same? What types of activities can be done easily in the new building that could not be done in the old building?

Centering on one historical residue can trigger interest in others. An interest in the photographs of an area or an old house might provoke a trip to the local museum. Historical residues can be tied into regular classroom activities as well—a visit to the site of the original central business district can introduce pupils to a unit on economic activity. After the visit and after completing related content activities, students could go on to assume the roles of economists and geographers, answering questions about the central business district and mapping out questions they wish to have answered.

Students and teachers in some communities are fortunate to have an outdoor museum close at hand. Sturbridge, Massachusetts, and Williamsburg, Virginia, are two famous examples, as are Plymouth Plantation and Jamestown. But with a little digging, teachers in other parts of the country can discover many outdoor museums for students. In Ohio, Hale Farm allows students to "get into the spirit" of a farm community of the 19th century. In Washington State, numerous forts provide data on particular time periods, and Californians can visit several of the old Spanish missions. Many cities in the process of urban renewal are rebuilding the old sections of town, recreating their original ambiance, if not their original uses.

Armstrong and Savage's second category, present interactions, refers to the "current scene." Students can visit the central business district, walk through the railroad freight yards, or see the industrial wharves in a coastal city. In planning such interactions, a teacher can map out the community to show the types of resources in the same style as the map showing classroom spaces. This map might be drawn on clear acetate and laid over a political map of the community.

The map in figure 11.5 reveals a close relationship between the industrial wharves and the factory section of the city, while there is only a marginal relationship between the wharves and the central business district. There

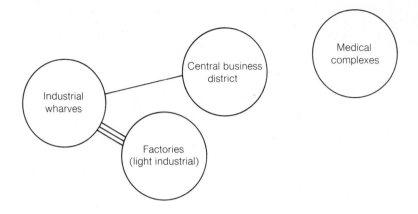

Figure 11.5
Mapping Present
Community
Interactions

is no relationship between these sections of the city and the area of medical activity. When you construct such a map, you can also identify the location of the numerous activities and interactions, and list questions to consider in light of each of these interactions. You should also anticipate possible types of student learning. With this kind of unit, students are likely to gain some understanding of the relationships among the community's industrial, factory, and central business sections. What in the central business district is connected to the factory section? Children could see that banks in the central business district would have dealings with factories. Of course, the depth of analyses will depend upon students' ages, learning capabilities, and grade levels.

One way to help pupils make the best use of their community is to have them record what they see on their visits on data retrieval charts, as in figure 11.6.

Community Activities	Where Performed	Comments, Impressions
Storing imports	South of the city	Land flat and allows this activity
Banking	In central business district	Lots of tall buildings, major banks in one or two city blocks
Selling clothes	Major stores in central business district. Specialty stores spread out	Clothing stores seem to be matched to the types of occupations found in the central business district

Figure 11.6
A Student's
Community Data
Chart

These data charts allow children to record information and compare interactions with those recorded in the "mapping" of the community. Pupils in the upper-elementary grades can make maps to show where specific activities take place. They can compare this "use map" with other maps that note population patterns, location of ethnic groups, income level, etc. Again, the students are obtaining their data from observation rather than from just listening to the teacher.

The final category Armstrong and Savage use for classifying community experiences is "likely future patterns," which draws on futuristics. In this aspect of study, pupils are encouraged to think about what a place will be like at some future time, what activities they think will occur in the community five years from now, and to estimate the population in five or ten years. One way for pupils to conceptualize likely future occurrences is to have them look at the past. Photographs of past developments in the local community can furnish ideas as to what it might be like in five or ten years. Plotting population data from the past ten or twenty years can furnish information for projecting future population. Teachers can bring in community resource people to give their ideas and projections as to what the community will be like in the future.

Up to now, we have discussed having pupils go to the community for data. Class time for discussing the data and challenging tentative conclusions must accompany such experiences. The learning environment can also be enhanced by bringing the community into the classroom, in the form of resource persons or artifacts. Historical residues can often be brought to the classroom, especially in the case of photographs or primary source materials such as documents.

There are several ways to bring the community into the school; for example, students can bring materials from home; local libraries often lend the schools artifact packets; and local museums frequently have education departments or resource persons who are happy to bring materials to the school. At the University of Washington, an on-campus museum has traveling "boxes" of artifacts that are loaned to schools to enable children to experience "hands-on" learning. The teacher must decide when to take the

Historical photographs can furnish information about what community life was like in the past.

children to the community and when to have the community come to the classroom. Some educators (Jarolimek, 1977) suggest that, as a matter of principle, it is advisable to take elementary school children into the community only for experiences that cannot be duplicated in the classroom, but we do not feel this principle should be interpreted to mean that students take only one field trip per year.

Planning to Use the Community

Using the community as educational space and bringing the community into the classroom require careful planning. Mapping major community activities and formulating potential questions must occur prior to the actual field study or to inviting classroom visitors. It is also wise for teachers to survey the community areas they might wish students to visit. If there are citizens in the community whom students might meet, it is prudent first to talk with or meet these individuals. Not all community experts in a particular field have a knowledge of children and how they learn.

When creating curriculum units or lesson plans, it is good practice to jot down those aspects of the community that have potential as learning environments. Such notes will be valuable when teaching the lesson or unit at another time. The teacher must also prepare students ahead of time for using this specialized learning environment. Pupils can list their questions and indicate where in the community they might find information to answer them. They can determine ways to gather information, and can plan to take notes and pictures.

When a resource person is to visit the classroom, children should be given time to list questions for the visitor. In fact, they might send the questions to the person before his visit. Most resource persons appreciate this, since it shows them the children's interests and helps them prepare their discussion or demonstration.

A poorly planned field trip may be worse than no trip at all. If a visit is not thoughtfully planned or if students are unsure of how to record their observations, negative learnings might be created, or the children could be endangered, or negative attitudes could arise in some areas of the community that would make it difficult for other students and teachers to arrange a similar visit.

Planning to use the community requires more than just making educational decisions. Teachers must work closely with administrators to fulfill legal requirements, especially with regard to transportation. Time must be allowed for obtaining parental permission slips. Some field trips will require children to bring money for purchasing their lunches, or replicas of artifacts, or for an admission charge. Teachers will certainly need volunteers to help manage the field trip.

The teacher must be sure all arrangements with the host institution have been worked out well in advance. Often when planning a unit, the teacher will write to a particular institution requesting information as to schedules for visits, particulars for entry, rules and regulations, and perhaps even suggested readings to prepare children for the visit.

295

In these initial plans, teachers may also create enabling tasks, so the children will get as much as possible from the trip itself. Sometimes children will be assigned special tasks to do during the visit or immediately after it. A child who is interested in photography might be assigned the role of "group field photographer."

When setting up trips into the community, the teacher must also plan ways to discuss, synthesize, and evaluate the information gained on the trip. Resource persons at the host institution can sometimes be engaged to participate in such debriefings.

Activity 11:4

Matching Community Places with Educational Activities

The following list notes places students might visit in the community. Think about what content area of social studies you could address in each of these places, as well as what you would have your students do in each place. Create a chart showing the possible content and activities for each location: mountains; flood plains; dams; business buildings; airports; zoos; parks; shopping centers; art galleries; farms; libraries; museums.

Discussion

Educational space has come to be regarded as an important instructional tool. To use space as a tool, the teacher must be familiar with aspects of environmental psychology, and must consider the variables of physical setting, organizational factors, the human aggregate, and the social climate.

The classroom continues to provide the primary educational space, and the teacher must organize it so as to encourage the transfer of learning from school to real-life situations. At the same time, the teacher must also learn to utilize space outside the classroom—in other areas of the school and in the community at large.

An important factor in learning is the "hidden" curriculum—the attitudes of peers, the importance the teacher seems to attach to cooperation vs. competition, children's perceptions of their chances for success, and teacher expectations for performance.

In planning educational space, the teacher will have to take some risks, but there are some steps to rely on in creating effective environments. First, assess the educational space according to its important variables; second, consider a lesson's goals and objectives; third, analyze specific content according to the types of space necessary. After considering space in relation to content, the teacher must, in the fourth step, give attention to the other variables—organizational, human aggregate, and social climate factors. The fifth step is to judge the selected educational spaces as to adequacy, efficiency, and economy; the sixth is to decide on one or more educational spaces for each activity or instructional method.

The classroom environment influences the choice and success of students' coping styles. Researchers have also found that there is a great deal of interaction between environments and behavior—behavior creates the social environment. The social studies environment should foster student involvement, allow for teacher support, enable clear identification of rules, and permit innovation. The teacher can map the classroom for most efficient use of the available space.

The community becomes an important educational space when the teacher plans field trips carefully, or arranges for outside speakers, activities, or exhibits to come into the classroom. As with internal classroom space, the teacher must match content and activities to the available external space.

References

Armstrong, David G. *Social Studies in Secondary Education.* New York: Macmillan, 1980.

Armstrong, David G., and Savage, Tom V., Jr. "A Framework for Utilizing the Community for Social Learning in Grades 4 to 6." *Social Education.* March 1976, pp. 164–67.

Bell, Paul A.; Fisher, Jeffrey D.; and Loomis, Ross J. *Environmental Psychology.* Philadelphia: W. B. Saunders Co., 1978.

Castaldi, Basil. *Educational Facilities, Planning, Remodeling, and Management.* Boston: Allyn and Bacon, 1977.

Curtis, Paul, and Smith, Roger. "A Child's Exploration of Space." In *Learning Environments,* edited by Thomas G. David and Benjamin D. Wright. Chicago: University of Chicago Press, 1974.

Epstein, J. L., and McPartland, J. M. *Classroom Organization and the Quality of School Life* (Report No. 215). Baltimore: Center for Social Organization of Schools, Johns Hopkins University, 1976.

Holt, John. "Children are Sensitive to Space." In *Learning Environments,* edited by Thomas G. David and Benjamin D. Wright. Chicago: University of Chicago Press, 1974.

Hunkins, Francis P. *Curriculum Development: Program Improvement.* Columbus, Oh.: Charles E. Merrill, 1980.

Jarolimek, John. *Social Studies in Elementary Education.* 5th ed. New York: Macmillan, 1977.

Moos, Rudolph H. *Evaluating Educational Environments.* San Francisco: Jossey-Bass Publishers, 1979.

Myrick, R., and Marx, B. S. *An Exploratory Study of the Relationships Between High School Building Design and Student Learning.* Washington, D.C.: U.S. Dept. of Health, Education, and Welfare, Office of Education, 1968.

Nielsen, H. D., and Moos, R. H. "Exploration and Adjustment in High School Classrooms: A Study of Person-Environment Fit." *Journal of Educational Research* 72 (1978): 52–57.

Technological and Material Supports for Social Studies Teaching

12

We hear more and more about educational technology, hardware, software, instructional design, systems analysis, programmed instruction, feedback, combination linear-branching, multimedia audiovisual technology. What does all this mean? One component of educational technology refers to new devices, such as computers, films, videotape, and cassettes. Another area refers to the human thought and design involved in arranging things in a logical order. According to Kenneth Komoski,

> By reflecting on this more fundamental view of technology we can see that *the hard work* of logically ordering the thoughts that make up a computer program and *not just the hardware* of the computer is the technology. (Lipsitz, 1971, p. 12)

Komoski further states that educational technologists see the teacher as one who consciously analyzes "instructional techniques, actions and artifacts, and effectively rearranges them into reproducible, improvable environments for effectively producing and reproducing learning." This complex task places a high priority on developing instructional objectives, a specific course of action, a systematic evaluation of the impact upon the learner, and a subsequent modification of the plan. Thus, the objectives must include a list of observable and measurable behaviors.

Some feel this view of the teacher is narrow and dehumanizing. They argue that the teacher should not be considered an "instructional agent," like a textbook, computer program, or television program. They reject the argument that programmed instruction has proven, as Charles Stack (1971) tells us, "that teaching is best defined as the arrangement of information for learning, rather than as the physical presence of a human being." On the other hand, Ralph Tyler notes: "Technological media, devices and systems can furnish constructive help to the teacher, but they cannot substitute for human communication, expectation, and concerns" (Tyler, 1980).

Printed Materials

Social Studies Textbooks

Of all the materials available to the teacher, the textbook is no doubt the most important. An excellent textbook can serve as a reference, offering up-to-date information collected by scholars and presented by educators and skillful editors. The teacher can use a textbook to introduce a unit of study by presenting a concise body of information to the class. The maps, photographs, charts, and graphs in the text can be used to enrich pupils' learning. Having the materials in one book saves the teacher the task of collecting them from various sources. Ideas, trends, and movements are highlighted in a good text, organizing factual content in a way that facilitates learning. The teacher's guides that accompany most textbook series suggest activities, additional resources, and techniques for individualizing instruction.

The textbook has not escaped criticism, however. In 1957, Handlin reported that textbooks were "dogmatic and dull, an obstacle rather than an aid to learning. There has been no basic alteration in the assumption . . . that learning consists of remembering and the function of the book is to supply the material to be remembered." Teaching by the book becomes an easy way to teach, since it relieves the teacher of planning topics and organizing content. But such an approach limits the students' social studies experience, and tends to encourage memorization of what the author says. A single grade-level text can limit the teacher's expectations of student performance, leaving little room for differences in learning style, reading ability, or intellectual ability.

Recent studies show that many teachers rely on the textbook as the primary instructional tool. Referring to math and science classes as well as to social studies classes, researchers for National Science Foundation field studies observed:

> In most classes . . . from third grade through twelfth grade, the students had few materials to manipulate, many materials to read and write on. The teachers explained some points and added a touch of personal experience, but spent most of the time directing the attention of the students to the information contained in the readings. (Stake et al., 1978)

The conclusions of three studies on the current state of social studies education by the National Science Foundation note that:

1. The dominant modes of instruction are large group, teacher-directed discussion and lecture, with primary reliance on the textbook.
2. Students are expected to learn and respect the knowledge that comes from others, "assumedly validated but by processes that are not explicated."
3. The materials from the "new social studies" national projects of the 1960s and 70s are not in general classroom use. Inquiry teaching is rare.
4. Students generally find social studies content and teaching uninteresting (Shaver, Davis, and Helburn, 1979).

Many social studies textbooks are similar in content and approach. As publishers compete for sales, they must try to avoid offending any groups and frequently emulate the best-sellers in the field. Stanford University historian Thomas Bailey (1979) affirms, "If you want to sell a maximum number of books, you have to make them so bland that you don't get into the tougher issues. But you also don't tell the truth." Steven Jantzen, a free-lance writer of social studies texts, has identified potential textbook options that might characterize the future. He predicts (figure 12.1) that the leading text in the next few years will not be a thoroughbred, but a crossbreed, "combining the particular strengths of Old Reliable, All Together Now, and Easy Rider."

Figure 12.1
Entries in the
Textbook Race, 1985

Old Reliable: Texts from the 1950s—or imitations of them—grow in popularity and general use. They stress the learning of factual content—not critical thinking, decision making, and values.

Once More With Feeling: There is a great revival of interest in progressive, student-centered education. Innovation again becomes the watchword. New texts, like those of the late 1960s, stress inquiry, values, critical thinking.

All Together Now: New texts represent a synthesis of the old social studies (1950s) and the new social studies (1960s). Emphasis of texts is distributed evenly among three areas of learning: knowledge, skills, and values.

Next Exit: Hardcover texts recede in importance as new packets of materials are developed that teach specific skills. Students spend most of their class time working with these learning packets. Completion of each packet represents mastery of a discrete skill.

Easy Rider: Taking account of declining student reading scores, new texts become more readable. Reading formulas are rigorously applied. Chapters are kept short and manageable.

Out of Nowhere: Social studies curriculum changes drastically. The nature of the change cannot yet be predicted, but whatever it may be, it leads to the creation of totally new types of text materials.

From Steven Jantzen, "What Textbooks Will Be Like in 1985." Reprinted with permission. Originally published in *Media & Methods* magazine, January 1979.

Activity 12:1.

Textbook Critique

Look at three textbooks each published a decade apart. What are the differences, if any, among the three books? Which would you use? For what reasons?

Effective Use of the Textbook

Viewing the textbook as one instructional aid rather than as the exclusive tool available will allow many teachers and even writers to overcome these drawbacks. Cronbach (1955) recommends considering the modern textbook as an "assistant teacher in print," for the teacher to use with ingenuity and care.

Once the goals, objectives, and main ideas are designed for a unit of study, the teacher can consider the selection and use of a particular textbook. The following checklist will help you plan the use of this resource tool.

1. What is the reading level of the text? Have I planned activities and individual work for the students who will find the text too easy or too difficult?
2. How difficult is the vocabulary? Have I planned appropriate and sufficient activities so that students will be able to master new words and new concepts?
3. Is there anything in the text that would be a good introduction to spark the students' interest?
4. Is there anything happening in our community that would expand the text content?
5. Are there stories, music, or poems we could use to enrich the text presentation?
6. What values questions are raised by this material? How should I discuss these values with the students?
7. What other materials (filmstrips, films, pictures, etc.) could I use in conjunction with the text to emphasize unit objectives?
8. Have I designed discussion questions that go beyond simple recall of facts?
9. Have I planned activities in which students can actively gather and evaluate information to complement the text presentation?
10. Does the text present the subject accurately and realistically? If not, what can I do to present a more balanced viewpoint?

Activity 12:2

A Hypothetical Class

You are the teacher of a fourth-grade class in which eight of your students are at the first- or second-grade reading levels. What types of small-group work could you do with these students to help them use a social studies textbook in which the reading level is too difficult?

Selecting the Textbook

School systems periodically establish committees to review current texts and preview new ones, and teachers often participate on these grade-level or subject-matter committees. These committee reviews are important, because school systems usually use textbooks from three to five years, and sometimes much longer. Publishing companies send representatives to the schools to demonstrate the components of their new social studies series. These series often include testing programs, audiovisual aids, activity cards, workbooks, transparencies, and other components.

Figure 12.2 presents Warming and Baber's checklist for selecting a textbook.

Some excellent social studies textbooks are currently available that incorporate a greater degree of social reality, highly effective visuals, advance organizers, values analysis, and a multidisciplinary base, as well as other improvements.

Activity 12:3

Textbook Selection

Use the "Touchstones" list and evaluate three current social studies textbooks. Share your assessments with your class peers.

Selecting appropriate and stimulating learning materials is a creative part of social studies teaching.

	*excellent 5	adequate 3	inadequate 1
1. Appropriate readability level	_____	_____	_____
2. Author(s) reputable in field	_____	_____	_____
3. Indicates successful field-testing of text and assessment instrumentation	_____	_____	_____
4. Published by reputable firm	_____	_____	_____
5. Table of contents exhibits logical development of subject	_____	_____	_____
6. Meets course objectives	_____	_____	_____
7. Language appropriate for intended students	_____	_____	_____
8. Presents major concepts thoroughly and accurately	_____	_____	_____
9. Defines difficult/important ideas and vocabulary in context or in a glossary	_____	_____	_____
10. Contains visual illustrations of key concepts	_____	_____	_____
11. Levels of abstraction appropriate for readers	_____	_____	_____
12. Provides chapter objectives	_____	_____	_____
13. Provides chapter summaries	_____	_____	_____
14. Format interesting and material well presented	_____	_____	_____
15. Avoids stereotypes and sexist language	_____	_____	_____
16. Provides for concrete application of abstract concepts	_____	_____	_____
17. Recommends resources and research projects	_____	_____	_____
18. Suggests alternative resources for students experiencing difficulty	_____	_____	_____
19. Provides teacher's guide or manual	_____	_____	_____
20. Provides for assessment of instructional objectives	_____	_____	_____
Subtotals	_____	_____	_____
Total score		_____	

Figure 12.2
Touchstones for Textbook Selection Inventory

Text _____

Author _____   Reviewer _____

Publisher _____

Publication date _____   *Some inventory users will wish to assign extra weight to certain "touchstones."

Date of review _____

From Eloise O. Warming & E. C. Baber, "Touchstones for Textbook Selection,"in *Phi Delta Kappan* 61 (1980): 695. Reprinted by permission.

Encyclopedias, Atlases, and Other Reference Books

Reference materials are important tools for students. Even young children can use picture encyclopedias and dictionaries, and will often voluntarily sit down and look through such books. But teachers must think of ways to motivate students to use reference materials.

George Otero, a teacher in Taos, New Mexico suggests one approach. He showed students a film about Bukashi, a national sport in Afghanistan. He ran the film without a sound track to explain the game; the children heard only music while they watched. The unknown and confusing game triggered many questions, which Mr. Otero listed on the chalkboard. Then the students speculated as to what the lives of people in Afghanistan might be like and developed hypotheses which were also recorded on the board. Each student chose the hypothesis that most interested her to research. Encyclopedias, maps, atlases, and books became important learning resources as students collected data on life in Afghanistan.

Teachers can work closely with librarians in arranging for reference materials to complement the textbook. Biographies, collections of old newspapers or magazine articles, old Sears catalogues, and many other sources offer rich supplements to textbook presentations.

Photographs, Illustrations, and Cartoons

Many materials for primary-grade students are accompanied by photographs to illustrate a point. Current textbooks contain beautiful photographs, illustrations, and political cartoons, aids that can be especially effective with students who have difficulty reading.

When drawing attention to a picture, a teacher asks students to view it differently from their first casual glance at it. Simple, low-level cognitive questions redirect pupil attention to elements in the picture they have previously missed. How many people are in this picture? Is it summer or winter? What kinds of clothing are they wearing? What tools are they using? What are they doing? What time of day is it? A careful look at the elements of the picture lays the groundwork for higher-level cognitive questions: students can be asked to differentiate among the people or activities in the picture, to predict what will happen next, or to infer what happened before the moment captured in the picture.

It can be helpful when focusing on a specific topic to employ a collage of pictures that show differences. For example, pictures of the Mohave Desert, the Rocky Mountains, the Florida Everglades, and a Wisconsin farm can trigger student examination of the variety of climates in the United States. The students might discuss where they would most like to live or how people's lives might differ because of where they live. When a textbook fails to show the ethnic diversity of the American people, pictures of various peoples can be brought in to correct the misrepresentation. Bulletin boards offer an excellent display area for pictures before and after they have been discussed.

Simulations and Games

Simulations and games suitable for the elementary level complement textbooks and other printed materials. Appendix B contains a bibliography of simulations and games that include grade levels, amount of class time, number of players, cost, and a brief description. The games are also coded according to the area of social studies with which the activity is associated: anthropology, sociology, economics, geography, history and political science. Textbooks sometimes include games in the student materials or in the teacher's guides to supplement the expository material.

The purpose of simulations is to present to students a simplified model of selected aspects of reality in an action-oriented, highly involving way. The simulation has often been used to study human behavior by creating a highly realistic, yet simplified operating model of a physical or social reality. Games often refer to a contest among adversaries operating according to given rules for the purpose of winning. Shaftel and Shaftel (1967) summarize the similarities of simulation, role play, and gaming as a concern with:

- Conflict of interest (personal, interpersonal, intergroup)
                    in which
- Players face alternatives from which to choose
- And must make individual decisions.

In social studies, the terms games, role playing, and simulation are frequently used interchangeably. Role playing always includes a dramatic ele-

The overhead projector is especially useful for displaying maps and charts.

ment in which students explore the ways they believe a person would act in a particular situation. Role play is followed by group discussion to evaluate individual and group problem solving and decision making. This evaluation, often called "debriefing," is vital for placing the group's activities in a larger context from which important concepts and ideas can be drawn out of the experience.

Simulations and games often require extended time; some games may take an hour, others as long as three weeks. Teachers must select simulations worthwhile to the learning objectives and appropriate to the time available. A highly complex simulation may be worth six class periods because of the social interaction and problem solving it elicits. The teacher must read the instructor's manual carefully to gain a clear picture of the sequence of activities and the necessary preparations. Simulation can be one of the high points of the class for both teacher and students, and provide a shared experience to talk about again and again.

Programmed Instruction

The classroom teacher's role changes dramatically when she deals with programmed instruction. The central relationship is between the writer of the program and the student; the teacher serves as a monitor, facilitator, counselor, and administrator. There is no stand-up teaching, group discussion, or lecture. Each student, using a workbook or computer terminal, works through a program at her own pace.

The information is divided into small parts, and presented in sequence, moving to increasingly complex levels of understanding. If a student makes an error, the program is designed to provide feedback by indicating the error and directing the student to related problems. When the student succeeds at the related set of problems, the original question that caused the difficulty is presented again. If the student correctly answers the question, she is directed to the next element or frame. This process is described in figure 12.3.

In the 1960s, most programmed materials were in printed form. Workbooks offered extensive lessons characterized by step-by-step tasks. Tyler (1980) summarizes the impact of these materials on students;

> When these programs were evaluated and the results compared to the learning of students who used the traditional type of textbooks and supplementary materials, it was found that only a minor fraction of the students learned more when using the programmed materials. Most of these were so-called slow learners. One can conclude that there are students who benefit by the use of programmed materials, but the need for this detailed sequencing is not universal.

Vast changes have occurred since the early workbook days of programmed instruction. With computer assisted instruction (CAI), the speed with which students can work their way through programs has increased dramatically, as has the programs' sophistication. Individualization has been heightened by providing extra examples as well as a record of student responses that determines the presentation of the next parts of the program. A computer system in widespread use today is PLATO, an instructional system of Control Data Corporation.

Computer-assisted instruction (CAI) is an expensive piece of educational technology. Each program must be developed from a clear set of objectives and tested on groups of students. It is then revised, and the feedback, branching, and prompting techniques modified. These empirically-based revisions are a costly process. James Popham (1980) recalls an experience in the 1960s in which an encyclopedia publisher who wanted to develop programmed booklets was discouraged by the slow progress. A company representative said that this "*yet unfinished,* but trice-revised programmed booklet has cost 20 times more than it would have in the old days to give an author an advance on royalties and wait for the manuscript." The expense is not only for the software, but also the hardware.

Programmed instruction is an innovation that has not expanded to the degree expected, generally because of the high cost to schools for implementation as well as to publishers for development. Another important explanation from Charles Slack relates to the terminology associated with this field:

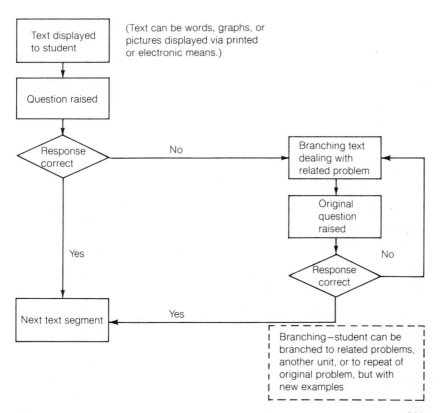

Figure 12.3
Programmed
Instruction

Writers aren't supposed to write materials anymore, they "design systems"; teachers aren't supposed to pass out materials anymore, they "apply systems"; educators don't write lovingly about the "art of teaching" anymore, they write coldly about "instructional systems"; and worst of all, the large educational corporations, in whom we all placed our hope and who ought to be moving us forward, aren't getting the point that the name of the game is publishing *self-instructional materials*. (Lipsitz, 1971, p. 42)

Teachers perceive this terminology as threatening to their jobs and as a cold, impersonal approach to education.

But the teacher can view programmed instruction, both electronic and printed, as a valuable resource rather than as a threat. Individualized instruction is difficult to accomplish with twenty-five to thirty students in five or six different subject areas. Reading, vocabulary development, learning important concepts in the U.S. Constitution, and developing map skills are all areas that can be taught through programmed instruction. Each child can move at her own pace, freeing the teacher for personal teaching, to do the things that instructional apparatus cannot do.

Activity 12:4

Materials Analysis

Arrange to visit a classroom and list the types of written materials employed in teaching social studies. Note the ways in which such materials are used. Assess the effectiveness of the materials employed.

Activity 12:5

Resources Check

Visit a school curriculum materials center and examine the types of written materials available for social studies instruction. Make a list of those you might use in your teaching, indicating your reasons for selection.

Audiovisual Materials and Other Resources

Television

Since children today already spend more hours watching television than they spend in school, it may seem unnecessary to bring television into the classroom. But television is an important resource both technologically and in terms of its content. Some school districts have a videotape and film library from which teachers can select prerecorded programs and specials. Presently, few schools have video equipment for taping students or guest speakers, but where it is available, students have an opportunity to play an active role in television production. Tapes, and now video disks, can either be saved or reused, depending on the teacher's objectives.

Activity 12:6

Assessing the Impact of Television

Using a current guide to periodicals in education, review any new research studies that show the impact of television on children. What evidence is there that skills, school performance, and behavior are affected by television viewing?

Commercial and public television have both been criticized for portraying excessive violence, using stereotypes, showing too many mindless programs, and airing too many commercials aimed at children. Early attempts to develop instructional television for use in elementary, high school, and college classrooms usually produced boring lectures that did not hold student interest. The University of Mid–American (UMA), a federal experiment in public television, discovered that students in a television accounting course performed as well on tests as students who had used only the printed text and study guides. The important difference was the much greater expense of producing the TV segments, which nonetheless yielded results no different than those obtained by traditional methods.

Television can be a powerful medium, but its strength seems to lie in its success at arousing emotions, curiosity, and awareness. It can bring the world into our homes, expanding our knowledge of the unfamiliar and remote. It can dramatize abstractions such as freedom of speech, honesty, and justice through stories and characters that absorb our attention. It loses its effectiveness, however, when it is used in the same way as the printed medium. A lecture may be a useful way for students to learn important aspects of the culture of ancient Egyptians. Worksheets and other written

311

work can reinforce and expand on those ideas. But a television program that takes students on an exploration of the mysterious pyramids can serve as the motivating device that sets the stage for later lectures and worksheets.

Using Television Effectively in the Classroom

There are several ways for teachers to use commercial and public television in social studies. Reading skills can be developed by using a short story or novel in conjunction with a television series or special. Dr. Seuss's *The Cat in the Hat* and Laura Ingalls Wilder's *The Little House on the Prairie* are examples of complementary books and programs. Combined social studies and reading projects are being developed that draw subject matter from children's favorite television stars and shows. Hamilton (1975) reported that almost half the books preteens read *by choice* are movie- or TV-related.

Some educators have been working to make television an instructional aid to help students develop critical viewing skills. For example, the organization Prime Time School Television attempts to act as a bridge between the television industry and teachers. This group publishes monthly student study guides to highlight forthcoming programs of interest to teachers. More extensive curriculum units are being prepared on a number of subjects; "Television, Police, and the Law" and "Television and Economics" are two units of particular interest to social studies teachers. These units use television as a distributor of information, and encourage students to assess the reality of the programs.

The TV Viewing Logs pictured in figures 12.4 and 12.5 help students apply concepts and consider issues by employing a checklist, chart, or sentence completion worksheet. In using the logs, Linda Kahn (1979) recommends a Monday-through-Friday format. On Monday, the teacher discusses the concepts, distributes the logs, and lists possible TV programs. The list of programs should include a variety of times and topics so that student viewing can be integrated with that of other family members and personal schedules. The logs are completed during the week, and on Friday, the students bring their logs to class and compare results.

Critical TV viewing can focus on types of programs. Rosemary Lee Potter, a teacher in Clearwater Florida, had her fourth graders use their new colored pen sets to create posters showing the ways people use TV:

> My group made a list of specific TV uses, such as listening to weather forecasts, learning about new scientific procedures, and discoveries, finding out about how other people live and discovering the availability of new products. When these colorful personal expressions were complete, we displayed them in the media center.

Police shows, worldwide news coverage, and decision making by characters as they deal with conflicts provide opportunities for students to examine television offerings critically. They can monitor their own viewing habits for a number of hours, and note what types of shows they watch and whether they watch alone or with family or friends, to become more conscious of the ways they use this influential medium.

Figure 12.4
Scarcity Guide
Questions

GENERAL:

Economists say that all resources are scarce. What resources are mentioned most frequently on the news? Why do you hear a great deal about some resources and not about others?

ENERGY:

(1) Were there any news reports about exploration for energy-producing resources?

(2) Are there reports about OPEC? What has happened to the price of oil recently?

(3) Is there enough fuel to heat homes, schools, industries?

(4) What are the alternatives to our heavy dependence on oil and natural gas?

(5) Were any reports about coal?

(6) Were any reports about nuclear energy?

SITUATION PROGRAMS:

(1) Was a character in any of the shows faced with a choice? Why did the character have to choose? Could the character have had both things? What resource was scarce? What did the character have to give up to get what he or she wanted?

(2) Was time a scarce resource in any of the situation programs? Explain.

(3) What were some of the ways the TV characters could have eased their scarcity problems?

(4) How could savings or conservation ease a shortage problem?

(5) How do shortage problems depend on what a person values?

From Prime Time School Television (Linda Kahn, Director of Curriculum Development), *Television and Economics*. Reprinted by permission.

Very young children can study commercials. Camille Faith, a teacher in Baltimore County, Maryland, supervised her kindergarten class while they experimented on the validity of TV commercials. Such firsthand experience led to an increased awareness that commercials often exaggerate the truth about a product. Older students could watch commercials with the sound turned off to study such factors such as the occupations portrayed in the commercials, sex role differences, stereotyping, physical appearance, and types of products.

Television viewing can provide the basis for analyzing programming, as skill development, as a motivation, and as a way to apply concepts and ideas to new situations. When the teacher assigns television viewing as homework, it is helpful to let parents know the reason for the assignment. A short letter describing what the child will be doing and the purpose of the assignment will eliminate confusion by parents unaccustomed to this type of homework, and may provoke family discussion about the assigned show.

313

Videodiscs

Television use in the schools has been affected by the video recorder which allows one to record television programs and to replay them later as appropriate for a particular lesson. Most of the recorders use videotape enclosed in a cassette. However, the videodisc is beginning to make some impact in education. The videodisc has the advantage of having a radial surface like a phonograph record. This makes for ease of handling and storage.

Perhaps one of the best features of the videodisc is that the user may view any of the material contained on it in any order. The only factor affecting the order is the user's need. With videotape, one usually has to view the entire taped program from beginning to end.

Kemph (1981) reports that there are four levels of use for the videodisc: level zero, level one, level two, and level three. Level zero is the most basic with the videodisc used to present material linearly. At this level, a pupil might view the disc's material from beginning to end as she might with a movie. At level one, the videodisc can present information in a mixture of still and motion sequence. The user selects what she wishes to view and controls the pace of presentation. At the second level, the viewer can interact with the disc according to some program. She can select the program's direction from alternatives provided. Here the videodisc is used as a type of

Figure 12.5
TV Viewing Log for
Factors of Production

VIEWING LOG 3: Factors of Production

Directions: Watch 3 news reports and your favorite situation programs. As you fill in the information below, remember these definitions: Land—natural resources; Labor—human resources; Capital—goods, used to produce other goods and services (factories, machines, etc.); Entrepreneurs—people who organize the other factors of production in hopes of making a profit.

Program	What factors of production were featurd in the news story or program?	What good or service is being produced?	What other factors of production, not mentioned, were involved?
EXAMPLE: NBC NEWS 6 PM 12/3/77	A business firm has developed a successful way to reclaim stripmined land for farming.	service - reclaiming land for farming	CAPITAL - equipment used in reclaiming the land. ENTREPRENEUR - company that is redeveloping the land LABOR - workers LAND - the strip-mined area
NEWS			

From Prime Time School Television (Linda Kahn, Director of Curriculum Development), *Television and Economics.* Reprinted by permission.

computer program. At the third level, a videodisc can be connected to an external microcomputer. Disc content can be arranged so that the student has information presented at several levels of comprehension. The disc is so programmed that the user can obtain an evaluation of her work immediately, and then receive an individualized program of additional content. The computer can be used to generate graphics and text information which can be coordinated with information contained on the disc.

The videodisc can furnish educators with a vehicle for effectively joining television and the computer.

Films

Films are a valuable medium for presenting material realistically. Children can "see" what they have been reading; they can visit distant places and meet the people; they can even travel back in time to meet historical figures. Films focus children's attention by singling out details of an event or situation for emphasis; the narration focuses on the most important elements. The greatest benefit of a film is that it shows motion, thus bringing a sense of realism to a topic.

Films can be used during any portion of a lesson. At the beginning of a lesson, they supply students with essential information for later investigations. During the lesson's developmental stages, films can expand on material found in books, and often provide information in ways that better suit some children's individual learning styles. Films provide a particularly effective way to summarize the lesson and reinforce key points.

The Preview

Before selecting a film, the teacher should first review a brief summary of its content. If it seems appropriate for the unit in question, the teacher should go on to consult the longer description in the film guide included with many educational films. The next step is to preview the film, or at least a segment of it. For first-year teachers, this can be a major time-consuming task, since they will probably not have seen any social studies films. Previewing reveals whether or not the film presents the content effectively and whether or not the visuals and sound are appropriate for the children who will be seeing it. The preview also provides the teacher with an opportunity to expand on the information in the film guide, noting difficult vocabulary, concepts, and any links to what the class has been studying.

Preparing the Equipment

Simple advance planning is important. First, find out the school's system for ordering films and equipment. Decide when you want to show the film and order it well ahead of time. If possible, set up the projector and thread the film before students come into the room, or while they are taking a test or

315

engaged in seat work. It is extremely annoying to have audiovisual equipment fail to operate, and having time to tinker with the machine and set up the film lessens the chance of something going wrong.

Preparing Students for Viewing

The teacher can introduce a film by explaining the reasons for watching it, connecting it with the material the class is studying. Allow students time to ask questions about the film. If the film is being used to introduce a new unit, some instructional materials or an activity to help set the stage might be appropriate. You might write the title, key words, and major questions on the chalkboard and direct the student's attention to them. You should point out any parts of the film to which students should pay special attention and explain any segments that may be difficult to comprehend. There are times, however, when it is better to let the students determine the purpose of the film. This allows them to gain skill in developing critical viewing and a sense of autonomy in investigations.

Showing the Film

Arrange for ventilation and draw the shades or blinds. Be sure all students can see the screen. Turn off the lights, turn on the projector, and adjust the focus and sound level. Watch the projector to be sure it is properly threaded to avoid damaging the film.

Reviewing the Film

There are many ways to follow up film viewing. One way is to start with several simple factual questions and move to more difficult ones. Students usually have some questions and comments, and discussion can begin with those. A role play can be initiated in which students take the parts of the film's characters. Further research activities can be introduced to expand on the ideas presented in the film. A test on student understanding may be helpful, but do not always link a test with a film since students will come to dread film viewing.

Filmstrips

There are times when realism is desired, but motion is not necessary. The filmstrip is an excellent medium for this purpose. It is as easy to use as a motion picture but costs less, and social studies teachers can find filmstrips on diverse topics. As with films, filmstrips can be used at any point in a social studies lesson or unit. One advantage of filmstrips over film is that they can easily be stopped or reversed to accommodate additional discussion. Filmstrips are particularly useful when the material has a definite sequence. A filmstrip showing how a bill goes through Congress makes the sequence very clear. Since filmstrips are easy to show, children can use them independently in interest or resource centers. Sound filmstrips are linked to audiotapes, which is especially helpful to those children who best learn visually and auditorially.

The best use for a filmstrip depends, of course, on the lesson or unit and the content of the film. Pupils can be informed of the filmstrip topics and encouraged to seek out those that may be useful in investigations.

Filmloops are short pieces of film arranged in a closed cartridge loop that can be shown over and over. They do not have any sound. They usually deal with one concept, event, or activity.

Slides

Slides are a low-cost, color visual that can be stored in a small space but provide a large visual display. Teachers can modify a slide presentation by adding or removing slides, depending on the lesson's purpose or the nature of the group. Slide programs may be accompanied by tape or record soundtracks, and have automatic or manual advance capability.

Although significantly cheaper than films or video presentations, slides share the same advantage. They allow the teacher to bring into the classroom visual illustrations of places, people, and situations far removed from the classroom.

Before a slide presentation, the teacher should organize the slides in a carousel or slide tray in the sequence in which they will be shown. Jamming is sometimes a problem, when a bent slide becomes caught and makes it impossible to advance the next slide. Try to find out in advance what procedures to use if jamming occurs.

Slides can be used effectively in combination with student reports. If the class is studying India, slides can be chosen to parallel the subjects of student reports. A student can present a report on Indian dress while the teacher shows slides of Indian clothing. Many teachers have personal slide collections from their travels; they should keep a record of ways they have used their personal slides so they can assemble them easily. Students may also be able to contribute slides to highlight a particular lesson.

Overhead Transparencies

The overhead projector is designed for use by the teacher at the front of the classroom. The classroom lights can remain on and the teacher can face the students at all times. The still images on the screen are created by transparencies laid on top of the projector surface. Drawings on paper can be converted into transparencies, and teachers can construct their own with the aid of copying machines. Some textbook companies offer transparencies to accompany written materials. Transparencies can also be ordered from publishers in sets that deal with a particular subject, such as the United States Westward Movement.

Vision is a vital ingredient in the way people learn. A lecture or reading on westward expansion in the United States can be greatly enhanced if the teacher and students discuss important events while looking at a transparency map of the United States. The transparency can present geographic areas and time periods highlighted by different colors. The entire class can look at this visual together, while the teacher or a student uses a pointer to refer to particular areas on the screen.

The teacher can create simple charts that summarize a class discussion, teach the vocabulary words of a lesson, or graphically illustrate the numerical values in written material, either in advance or while teaching the lesson. A grease pencil is used to write on clear plastic transparencies, thus allowing a creation of the moment that can then be erased. Teacher-made transparencies can be saved for use later in the unit or for next year's students.

Cassettes and Tape Recorders

The tape recorder is now a common piece of equipment, as the machine and cassette tapes have become increasingly inexpensive and easier to use. Many commercially published curriculum materials come with cassettes for students to use individually or with the entire class. Many educational organizations have listings of prerecorded tapes on subjects of interest in the social studies area. The National Education Association has a catalogue listing all their current programs. Many libraries have listings of special groups that offer tapes in such subject areas as international studies, law-related education, and consumer education. These listings change frequently, depending on each group's funding and resources.

The tape recorder can be used to tape a student discussion, then played back later so the teacher can identify areas of confusion and difficulty. A guest speaker can be recorded, with permission, and the recording saved for students who were absent, or for review after the speaker has gone. Students can use the tape recorder to practice presenting oral reports. They can tape a narrative to accompany a slide presentation. In addition, with the aid of a cassette tape player, students can learn how to be active and careful listeners.

Bulletin Boards

The bulletin board is a simple but effective instructional tool. A bulletin board with pictures of students and their families and names can be used at the beginning of the year to get classmates acquainted. Research on family backgrounds might be portrayed by a map linking students with other parts of the world where members of their families previously lived. Bulletin board displays can summarize a unit of study. Student work can be posted, charts and photographs featured, or a mural developed as the unit progresses. Small-group projects can be displayed, so groups can learn from each other. If

318

the class includes a student visiting from another country, a bulletin board display can help American children understand the people of that area, and make the visiting child feel more comfortable. Pictures of the foreign student's country showing people engaged in activities with which all children are familiar, such as working, playing games, going to school, cleaning, and taking care of children, shows how much people around the world have in common.

If it is used effectively and changed frequently, a bulletin board can involve considerable work for the teacher. The following suggestions may ease the preparation involved.

1. Include children in planning the board. They can assist in collecting pictures, making letters, or designing the board. On special holidays, ask students to draw a person or object that represents the way they celebrate that holiday. They can cut out their drawings and pin them on the board.
2. Use a variety of colors and arrangements throughout the year.
3. Letters for titles can be cut from many different materials and saved from one year to the next. Reusable plastic letters can be ordered from companies that advertise in publications such as *Instructor* and *Teacher*.
4. Use the bulletin board in teaching. Discuss the display with students, linking it to topics previously studied or scheduled for investigation in the near future.

Micro Computers

For several decades the computer has been a major part of our technological world. But recently, with the miniaturization of electronic circuitry, computers have been getting smaller and cheaper while still retaining amazing information processing capabilities.

For several years educators have used computers to assist in the management of the schools—processing payrolls and monitoring students' schedules. But micro computers are beginning to be used in the instructional realm of schooling. These computers are enabling students to obtain and utilize vast amounts of information in many fields. Having such expanded information bases is influencing the nature of pupils' investigations. Not only can students have access to more information, but the information available is much more current.

Schools using micro computers are redesigning their school libraries making computers integral parts of the information retrieval system. Presently, schools can be tied into on-line bibliographic data bases which should expand the range of student research projects. And this expansion of information sources is not only of advantage to pupils; teachers will also be able to expand their data base when planning social studies lessons. Presently, there are about 70 million bibliographic records readily available on line. While most micro computers may not be tied into such information systems, the potential exists.

With micro computers in elementary classrooms, children will be able to solve social problems not previously considered. They can feed the computer information gathered on some social issue, and using a particular program get a projection on the future development of the problem. Children can test out their suggested solutions to problems by having the computer furnish printouts of likely consequences of the solution after several years of implementation.

Micro computers can assist pupils in perfecting various skills essential in processing social studies content. Pupils can work on outlining information, making adjustments in the outline displayed on a video screen. Computers also can be used to perfect the reading and development of various types of maps and graphs. Some larger computers have the capacity to display drawings stored in their memory on a screen. Children can modify these drawings by touching the display screen with a device called a light pen.

Perhaps the biggest challenge for the social studies teacher using these computers is that with their use, children and teachers will have a much larger information base. This will mean that children will need to master information selection skills. The micro computer and the videodisc mentioned earlier may become as commonplace in the classroom as the chalkboard.

The Classroom as a Resource

The classroom should not be overlooked as an important instructional resource. Since the vast majority of elementary school children are in the Piagetian stage of concrete operations, their learning environment should include manipulative materials. With objects to rearrange, classify, and explore, children can learn problem solving and develop more advanced stages of thought. In addition, this is an important age for developing social relationships and language. The child is moving beyond an egocentric perception of the world to one that includes a plurality of viewpoints.

The classroom can be organized in many different ways, but it should provide areas for individual, small-group, and large-group work. Some teachers create learning centers for science, social studies, math, and language arts, and stock these centers with materials that children can use to explore areas of interest. Areas for artwork and other construction projects, a reading corner, and an area to display student work all contribute to making the classroom a comfortable and inviting place. Children also need a place to store their personal supplies and papers; some teachers use desk storage for this purpose, while others provide folders or drawers. (Refer to chapter 11 for detailed information on educational environments.)

Selecting Material and Technological Supports

In a recent study, 90 percent of 12,000 teachers surveyed said their instructional materials were the heart of their teaching 90 to 95 percent of the time. Given this role for instructional aids, how does an instructor choose which resource to use? The following suggestions may help you with your selections.

The school curriculum often establishes the goals of social studies instruction and the objectives for each grade level. Content samples may be selected or, in some cases, specific content required. The school curriculum may be responsive to the different trends in social studies education, such as conceptual emphasis, multidisciplinary studies, cognitive development, community participation, affective learning, mastery learning, minimum competencies, and individualized instruction. When there is no curriculum guide that teachers must use, many use the textbook as the beginning framework for a social studies plan. The text can define the goals of instruction and the criteria for selecting the content, but ideally goals and objectives have to be determined before an instructional aid can be selected.

The characteristics of the students also affect the selection of a resource. Their maturity, reading levels and abilities, learning styles, interests, motivation, and other factors play an important role in their reaction to curriculum materials.

Use a *variety* of instructional aids. The objectives desired and the resources for achieving them have great potential; try to include a broad range of resources in the lesson plan. This range will cater to student diversity and help to assure the inclusion of a variety of points. The National Council for the Social Studies has developed the following guidelines for the use of learning resources:

- A social studies program requires a great wealth of appropriate instructional resources; no one textbook can be sufficient.
- Printed materials must accommodate a wide range of reading abilities and interests, meet the requirements of learning activities, and include many sorts of materials from primary as well as secondary sources, from social science and history as well as the humanities and related fields, from current as well as basic sources.
- A variety of media should be available for learning through seeing, hearing, touching, and acting, and calling for thought and feeling.
- Social studies classrooms should draw upon the potential contributions of many kinds of resource persons and organizations representing many points of view and a variety of abilities.
- Classroom activities should use the school and community as a learning laboratory for gathering social data and for confronting knowledge and commitments in dealing with social problems.
- The social studies program should have available many kinds of work space to facilitate variation in the size of groups, the use of several kinds of media, and a diversity of tasks.

Selecting the proper resources is an exciting and creative part of teaching. Instructors should feel free to try new things. There are many ways to learn; no one instructional aid will always be appropriate.

Activity 12:7

Novel Use of Films, Filmstrips

Sometimes teachers use films and filmstrips as "fillers" for their lessons, the films having little to do with the main thrust of the lesson. In planning to use films or filmstrips, what might you do to avoid such a misuse?

Activity 12:8

Incorporating Instructional Resources

If you have been creating a teaching unit, incorporate into it ways in which instructional resources would be utilized to make social studies instruction dynamic. If you have not created a unit, still indicate specific ways in which various topics could be taught employing particular instructional resources. Share your plans with your instructor and/or class peer.

Discussion

While the field of education is being beseiged with the products of new technology, the textbook remains the social studies teacher's most important and most convenient resource. The textbook's accompanying teacher's guide usually suggests activities, resources, and individualization techniques. The teacher's objective should be to avoid teaching solely "by the book," however; she should use the textbook as a starting point for creative planning.

The social studies curriculum presents many opportunities for introducing children to the use of reference material, and the teacher should help children become acquainted with encyclopedias, atlases, and other reference books from the earliest elementary levels. The teacher should also help children learn how photographs and drawings augment the text. Other materials that fit well in social studies programs are simulations, games, and programmed instruction. The latter is particularly helpful in individualizing instruction, whether in the form of self-paced workbooks or computer assisted instruction (CAI).

The effective teacher will also take advantage of children's television viewing time, by planning lessons around various television programs and encouraging critical viewing. Social studies lessons can also center around commericals, which students can examine for topics such as sex role differences or stereotyping. Showing films in the classroom is a good way to introduce or summarize a topic. Filmstrips, slides, overhead transparencies, cassettes and tape recorders, bulletin boards, and micro computers are other examples of support media for the social studies classroom. The teacher's skillful organization of the classroom is in itself an instructional resource.

References

Cronbach, Lee J., ed. *Text Materials in Modern Education.* Urbana: University of Illinois Press, 1955.

EPIE Institute. *EPIE Report* (No. 76). New York: 1976.

Hamilton, H. "Try TV Tie-ins." *Instructor,* April 1975.

Handlin, O. "Textbooks that Don't Teach." *Atlantic Monthly* 200 (1957): 153.

Jantzen, Steven. "What Textbooks Will be Like in 1985." *Media and Methods* 16 (1979): 70–71.

Kahn, Linda. "A Practical Guide to Critical TV Viewing Skills." *Media and Methods* 16 (1979): 91.

Kemph, Jeff. "Videodisc Comes to School," *Educational Leadership* 38, No. 8 (May 1981): 646–649.

Komoski, P. Kenneth. "The Continuing Confusion about Teaching and Education." In *Technology and Education,* edited by Lawrence Lipsitz. Englewood Cliffs, N. J.: Educational Technology Publications, 1971.

National Council for the Social Studies. *Social Studies Curriculum Guidelines,* Washington, D. C., 1971.

Popham, W. James. "Two Decades of Educational Technology: Personal Observations." *Educational Technology* 22 (1980): 20.

Potter, Rosemary Lee. "What are They *Really* Saying?: Critical TV Viewing." *Instructor* 96 (1978): 29.

Prime Time School Television. *Television and Economics: From the Medium to the Marketplace.* Chicago, Ill.: Prime Time School Television, 1978.

Shaftel, Fannie R., and Shaftel, George. *Role-Playing for Social Values: Decision-Making in the Social Studies.* Englewood Cliffs, N. J.: Prentice-Hall, 1967.

Shaver, James P.; Davis, O. L.; and Helburn, Suzanne. "The Status of Social Studies Education: Impressions from Three NSF Studies." *Social Education,* February 1979, p. 151.

Slack, Charles W. "The Truth about Computerized Education." In *Technology and Education,* edited by Lawrence Lipsitz. Englewood Cliffs, N. J.: Educational Technology Publications, 1971.

Slack, Charles W. "Who is the Educational Technologist—and Where Is He?" In *Technology and Education,* edited by Lawrence Lipsitz. Englewood Cliffs, N. J.: Educational Technology Publications, 1971.

Smith, Richard W. "Educational Television is Not Educating." *Change* 10 (1978-79): 63.

Stake, Robert E. et al. *Case Studies in Science Education.* Vol. 2. National Science Foundation, January 1978. Washington, D. C., U.S. Govt. Printing Office, #038-000-00376-3.

Television and Economics: From the Medium to the Marketplace. Chicago: Prime Time School Television, 1978.

Tyler, Ralph W. "Utilization of Technological Media, Devices, and Systems in the Schools." *Educational Technology* 22 (1980): 15.

Warming, Eloise O. and Barber, E. C. "Touchstones for Textbook Selection," *Phi Delta Kappa* 61 (1980): 695.

Managing the Social Studies Program

13

Management Skills

A major role of the classroom teacher is that of manager. Management involves more than just directing pupil activities, however; it also refers to managing instructional materials and hardware. Glueck defines management as the "effective utilization of human and material resources to achieve the organization's objectives." He identifies the good business manager as one who understands individuals and groups, and has the interpersonal and managerial skills that enable one to work effectively with groups. These skills involve a complex set of competencies, as outlined in figure 13.1 ·

Figure 13.1
Managerial Skills

Managerial skills	Management of environmental relations
	Control and conflict management
	Organizing
	Decision Making
	Planning
Interpersonal skills of managers	Managerial development
	Communicating
	Influencing peers, superiors, and others
	Leadership: influencing employees
Understanding people at work	Individuals and groups
	Motivation
	Personality
	Attitudes/values
	Perception
	Learning
	Aptitudes and abilities

From MANAGEMENT ESSENTIALS by William F. Glueck, copyright © 1979 by The Dryden Press, a division of Holt, Rinehart and Winston, Publishers. Reprinted by permission of Holt, Rinehart and Winston, CBS College Publishing.

As manager of a classroom, the teacher needs many of these same understandings and skills. Indeed, Wallen and Wallen (1978) feel that a major reason teachers have difficulty achieving effective classroom management is because they lack an adequate repertoire of management procedures. Generally speaking, teachers are not taught such procedures, and receive little formal training in group dynamics.

While management specialists could assist teachers in determining their management needs, it is still the teacher who deals daily with students and must consequently diagnose their individual needs. The leadership a teacher provides greatly influences the classroom climate and the level of learning that occurs. Teachers must not only exert leadership; they must also work productively with outside groups such as the PTA, teacher inservice committees, curriculum planning committees, school boards, and parent committees.

One does not learn to be a good manager in a few months. More realistically, educators should view management as a developmental process that is acquired and improved upon over the years.

Behind the Classroom Door

What actually occurs in the classroom? What problems do teachers face as managers? What conditions constitute a "good day"? Several observational and interview studies have addressed these questions. Goodlad, Klein, (1970) visited and interviewed teachers in 150 classrooms in four southwestern states. The activity the investigators observed most frequently at all grade levels was reading (with the exception of kindergarten). The language arts—reading, phonics, spelling, writing, story telling, and grammar—dominated formal instruction to the apparent neglect of almost all other subjects. Children's major activities were responding to teacher questions or directions, or engaging in seat work. Large-group instruction was typical.

The investigators noted that the most frequently used techniques for controlling student behavior were praise, other verbal rewards, and reminders of expected behavior. Teachers used few threats, and seldom resorted to physical punishment. Classes varied in the permitted degree of work independence; kindergarten children were given the most freedom, but that freedom diminished in the later primary grades. Some teachers assigned work to be done at the children's desks, while others permitted them to move about the classrooms, occasionally encouraging independent activities chosen by the child.

Having a "Good Day"

In his book *School Teacher,* Lortie (1975) describes the results of interviews he conducted with 124 teachers. In reponse to the question, "What happened within the classroom on a good day?" two teachers gave the following description:

A good day for me . . . is a smooth day. A day when you can close the doors and do nothing but teach. When you don't have to collect picture money or find out how many want pizza for lunch or how many want baked macaroni or how many want to subscribe to a magazine. If you could have a day without those extra duties—that would be a good day.

Well, when things you planned go well. For example, you have a subject to teach that's not always an interesting subject but one of the dull factors that has to do with mechanics and suddenly you get results. You see that youngsters see what you have and get it easily and quickly and apply it and it comes back to you as you want it to come back. I think that is a satisfying day—a day when you feel you've accomplished your job as a teacher. You taught something.

It appears that a good day involves several elements, the first of which is what the teacher brings to the day. If the teacher is rested, feeling well, and encounters few problems before starting class, the day will most likely be a good one for both teacher and students. In the Lortie study, many teachers said they had a good day if they were able to motivate students to learn. If the results at the end of the day were visible and in agreement with planned outcomes, these teachers felt a strong sense of accomplishment; for them, it *had* been a good day.

In contrast, teachers identified a bad day as one plagued by interruptions, distractions, and negative moods of both teacher and students. Some teachers found that weather and holidays greatly affected student moods. One teacher gave this description of her bad day:

It's a day you're being pushed for reports, you're being pushed for this and you don't feel as though you have the time and sometimes the energy to put across the subject that you need to put across in your classrooms and so your approach is perhaps not as calm as it would have been on a good day and, as a result, you don't get results and you feel it's been a completely frustrating day.

Effective Classroom Management

Kounin (1970) conducted a videotape study of self-contained elementary school classrooms. His analysis indicated that certain teacher behavior seemed to trigger student misbehavior, while other teacher behavior seemed to facilitate students' becoming highly and productively involved in their work.

These investigators generated a list of guiding principles for managing social studies classes. The first principle is to *make smooth transitions*. Before shifting from one lesson or activity to another, give students a warning that change is to occur shortly, for example, "In a few minutes, we'll be starting our work with the new *Weekly Reader*." The teacher can facilitate smooth transitions by listing the daily schedule on the board so children know what to expect each day; for example:

8:30–9:00	Class business
9:00–10:25	Reading/language/spelling
10:25–10:45	Recess
10:45–11:35	Math
11:45–12:30	Lunch
12:30–12:50	Quiet Reading Time
12:50–1:25	Social Studies
1:25–2:00	Science
2:00–2:30	Open period, for class discussions, independent work, evaluation for the day

While a schedule can represent only an "average" day, it does enable students to plan their time in relation to the day's major events.

The second principle Kounin advances is to *reduce the number of distractions*. Once students are working quietly at their assignments, the teacher can work with individuals or small groups. There should be no general announcements about holidays, parents' night, or other special events during class time; this information should be given between classes or at the end of the day. This is sometimes difficult because many schools make announcements over the school intercom, but the teachers can keep an announcement log to remind him of what needs to be relayed to pupils at the end or beginning of the school day.

Another principle Kounin identifies is to *avoid overdwelling and fragmentation*. Overdwelling refers to excessive preaching or nagging. This kind of teacher behavior slows progress and redirects students' attention from learning tasks to minor problems. Some teachers routinely spend the majority of classtime directing students in proper classroom conduct: the right way to line up, the correct way to distribute materials, the proper way to sit, the appropriate way to enter and leave a room. Such behaviors limit the amount of time available for academic work. *Fragmentation* refers to the breakdown of a task into its distinct parts. This occurs when teachers give unnecessarily detailed instruction or require that something be done by one student at a time, thus making the entire class wait. Having each student give a brief statement of what they did over the weekend while the rest of the class waits, often not listening, is an example of this behavior.

Kounin's fourth principle is to *keep students alert and accountable*. He found that teachers who vary the way they call on students keep their attention. A teacher may select students at random to answer questions, or ask them to hold up papers for a quick scan for accuracy. Instructors sometimes create a feeling of suspense that is helpful in fostering alertness. The teacher may raise a question but inform students that they should think for a bit before responding. This allows pupils to prepare their responses and to anticipate that they may be called on for the answer. Informing pupils that a classmate's answers may provide clues to their own investigation points out the need to listen carefully to class dialogue.

Another principle that makes classrooms manageable and enjoyable is to *provide variety*. Teachers can provide diversity of content, instructional strategies, educational activities, seat work, visual aids, and grouping patterns.

329

Variety should even be considered when allocating the type and amount of student responsibilities.

As noted earlier, successful classroom management demands a wide repertoire of strategies and instructional approaches: lecture, demonstration, discussion, experimentation, role playing, debates and panel discussion, simulation and gaming, and viewing films and slides. These approaches can be used with large or small groups, and often with individual children; the activities can be teacher-directed or student-directed. In responding to these instructional procedures, students have a variety of behavior options from which to choose: listening, observing, note taking, reading, speaking, valuing, defining, questioning, decision making, planning, creating, data gathering, and writing. Such variety of responses allows all pupils to participate in ways that address their learning styles. Pupils who can approach social studies from their own vantage points, realizing what is expected of them, are most likely to be productive class members who increase the probability that both teachers and students will "have a good day."

According to Kounin, teachers skilled in classroom management exhibit "with-it-ness," a quality of knowing how students perceive their classrooms and how they react to peers and teachers. Such a "with-it" teacher notices when behavior problems are brewing and moves to control them quickly. These skilled managers can work with an individual student while simultaneously monitoring the progress of others, an ability Kounin calls "having eyes in the back of your head."

Other researchers have discovered that the effective teacher employs control techniques that reduce student frustration. Student frustration arises from innumerable causes—they may be sick, hungry, hot, tired, have problems at home, or be unable to complete a complicated task. They may deal with their frustrations in a classroom outburst or by withdrawing from class activity.

Redl and Wattenberg (1975) found *hurdle help* effective in controlling student frustrations produced by difficult academic tasks. Worksheets with clear directions and hints for students who do not understand may be helpful. A teacher might provide hurdle help by giving directions in three different ways: by explaining them to the entire class, by referring to directions written on the chalkboard and by circulating among the class members to answer questions, and by sometimes responding to a child's questions loudly enough that others who are also confused can hear.

Another useful technique in reducing student frustration is *restructuring the situation*. When a teacher picks up cues that the plan in force is not working, he then revises the plan and attempts a new approach. Sometimes *laugh therapy* lessens the intensity of a frustrating situation. By using humor, a teacher can release tension and help everyone see the situation from a different point of view. Redl and Wattenberg report that one teacher used humor to change the behavior of one of her aggressive students who blurted out the answer to a question or exclaimed, "Ooo, ooo, I know." The other pupils were becoming annoyed, so the teacher said to the class, "Oh, no! Someone in here has the ooo, ooo disease." The children, even the culprit, laughed. The point had been made and no one was angry or embarrassed.

Children, especially young children, usually like to know what they are to do. Cellar (1975) found that *establishing routines* was an important frustration-preventing technique. Pencil sharpening, lining up, collecting papers, cleaning up, and other classroom routines can be organized so that students quickly learn the appropriate behavior. Clean-up routines in social studies should include a place to put complicated assignments, time to clean desks and return materials, and a place for students to prepare or gather for the next activity.

Skilled classroom teachers exhibit *firmness, follow-through,* and *task-centeredness.* Students are more likely to work effectively when they know the teacher means what he says. Task-centered teachers link behavior problems to the task objectives. For instance, a teacher might say, "Stop talking. You won't be finished with your work in time to go to the next class." In contrast, a teacher who is teacher-centered would more likely say, "Stop talking, I don't like all that noise." The task-centered approach appears to be the more effective management technique.

The Behavior Modification Approach

Although debate rages over the appropriateness of behavior modification for managing students in regular classes, the technique is widespread. It draws on B.F. Skinner's theory that behavior that is reinforced tends to be repeated, while behavior that is ignored or punished tends to weaken or disappear. Many commercial programs for classroom management and discipline draw heavily on behavior modification. Essentially, the theory is that the consequences of a student's action are important in molding his future actions. The technique involves manipulating rewards and punishments in order to produce more socially desirable behavior.

When reward is emphasized, a student is rewarded when he behaves in a desired and defined way and ignored when he does not. With the punishment approach, the teacher ignores proper behavior and acts only when the pupil misbehaves. As a general rule, the reward techniques are most productive. Wallen and Wallen note that teachers should consider four factors when planning a reward program:

1. Create a clear definition of the desired behavior.
2. Establish a suitable reward.
3. Create a system for dispensing rewards chosen.
4. Create a schedule of periodic planning and evaluation conferences with the students.

Some educators decide to deal with behavior problems through punishment. They believe negative behavior will be modified when something unpleasant accompanies that behavior. Detention, extra assignments, losing recess, and even spanking are some of the punishments used. For the most part, punishment methods are not as effective as reward methods, but several discipline procedures incorporate some punishment component.

Regardless of whether one views behavior modification from a punishment or reward stance, the technique requires the teacher to establish a *baseline,* a measure of the level at which the student's behavior is occurring or at which a learner is functioning. Observation is very important. Let us take the case of Nancy, who is always out of her seat, wandering around the room, finishing very little of her work, and distracting other students. The teacher observes Nancy at various times during the day, records the number of times she is out of her seat, and how long she spends not working during a fifteen-minute period. This record provides the teacher with a baseline.

Now, the teacher must find some way to encourage the behavior he wants Nancy to exhibit. He has several methods from which to select. Using the reward system the teacher could praise Nancy and others when they are working quietly at the social studies learning center. The teacher might also try to discover Nancy's interests and build those into the tasks at the learning center. Or, he might permit Nancy to work on something that really interests her, contingent on her completing her work on the main social studies assignment.

If the teacher decides to use the punishment approach, he might inform Nancy that she will have no recess until she works at her seat in the learning center. As we have noted, however, punishers are often less effective than reinforcers. Nancy might just give up, and the teacher might have to spend the recess time supervising her rather than taking a break. Then Nancy might become even more restless throughout the rest of the day because of missing recess.

To encourage Nancy's on-task behavior, the teacher might try *shaping* the behavior; that is, reinforcing approximations of the desired response. Each time Nancy works for five minutes on social studies, the teacher praises her with a smile, a touch, an encouraging word. The reward of teacher attention is then given after ten minutes of work, then fifteen, and then intermittently.

In the case of Tom, who wants his peers' attention, the same action by the teacher may be perceived as punishment, because Tom's friends will make fun of him. The teacher will know which procedure to employ partly as a result of gathering baseline data on each pupil.

When children are overly disruptive, the teacher may try the *time-out* procedure, wherein the child is removed from the learning area for a short period, either to a specific place in the classroom or elsewhere in the school. Time out serves as a "cooling-off" time for both teacher and student. It is important that the child knows what behavior is unacceptable; he should not need to play a guessing game as to what he did wrong. If this happens, the teacher is perceived to be arbitrary. Teachers who say "be good and stay out of trouble" are not specific enough. Also, some children enjoy a little risk taking, and will try certain behaviors just to test the teacher. Students should realize that time out is a time for gaining self-control. This is best conveyed by a simple explanation rather than a lecture. The important point is to avoid reinforcing behavior by attention of the class and the teacher.

Schoolwide Discipline Programs

Several approaches to classroom management advocate that all teachers in the school use the same methods. A schoolwide system can be useful in establishing procedures for use by homeroom teachers, the reading specialist, the physical education teacher, and any other instructors children encounter in a school day.

The Inglewood School District in Los Angeles has implemented Canter's (1975) "Assertive Discipline" strategies. Each classroom has rules posted and each teacher determines the consequences of rule violations.

Classroom Rules:

1. Follow directions.
2. Keep your hands, feet, and objects to yourself.
3. No name calling or teasing.
4. Raise your hand and wait to be called on.
5. No gum or candy.

Consequences:

1. Name on board
2. ✔ after name = 15 minutes after school
3. ✔✔ after name = 30 minutes after school
4. ✔✔✔ after name = all of the above and note or phone call to parents
5. ✔✔✔✔ after name = all of the above and sent to the office

Severe:

1. Instigating a fight
2. Fighting in class
3. Disrespect to any teacher or teacher's aide

Consequence: Immediately sent to the office.

Although you might conclude from this list that the system is primarily a punishment approach, it involves rewards as well. At the kindergarten level, a jar of marbles is a visual symbol of good behavior. When pupils have been exceptionally good, the teacher places a marble in the jar. When the jar is full, the class is rewarded with a special event, such as a picnic, a popcorn party, or a field trip. At the upper grades, rewards more appropriate for the age group are used. Check marks may be used instead of marbles to record the incidence of appropriate behaviors. In one class, children earn "money," which is used to purchase student-contributed items at the end-of-the-year auction. A bottle of volcanic ash went for "$27,000!"

Glasser (1969) also offers a schoolwide approach to discipline, based on his "Reality Therapy". He believes that five factors produce good discipline in a school:

1. The school must be a good place from the student's point of view.
2. Students must know the school rules.
3. Students must agree with the rules, if possible. Rules should be explained so they make sense to the students and they can understand their purpose.
4. Students should participate in making rules when the classroom situation creates the need for new rules.
5. Students should know the consequences for rule-breaking.

Glasser attempts to move away from manipulation of rewards and punishments, to encompass a view of the student as a reasonable person capable of problem solving and group participation. When a student misbehaves, Glasser recommends that the teacher help the child identify the problem behavior, evaluate its consequences, and plan new behavior. The student must then make a commitment to the plan and be ready to accept the consequences should the commitment be broken. Glasser suggests task-oriented classroom meetings as one way to identify standards of behavior.

Schoolwide discipline systems have advantages as well as disadvantages. An important factor in creating a productive classroom climate is the teacher's personality. Some teachers find a behaviorist or a problem-solving approach very hard to implement. Also, given the differences in classes, it is difficult to apply one system in all situations. But elementary pupils spend increasing amounts of time with several teachers during the day, so standardization of rules and consequences may be helpful to them. It is also easy to explain a schoolwide system to parents, enabling them to assist in solving some discipline problems.

The Environment for Effective Management

The classroom environment is established early in the school year. Students soon learn about the work flow, the teacher's expectations, the tolerable noise level, the acceptable emotional level, the degree of competition, and other elements of the classroom environment. What combination of these factors facilitates the teaching and learning of social studies? The answers to this question depend upon one's beliefs about learning, students' learning styles, and teachers' personalities. Since the goal of social studies is effective citizenship, one can argue that the classroom should operate on democratic principles. Elements such as representative government, majority rule, minority rights, rule by law, and universal suffrage might all be part of the democratic classroom.

A teacher who wishes to model the classroom on democratic principles might well remember Dewey's view that democracy can be defined as a way of life, a social and moral philosophy.

But they [political forms] rest back on the idea that no man or limited set of men is wise enough or good enough to rule others without their consent; the positive meaning of this statement is that all those who are affected by social institutions must have a share in producing and managing them... The foundation of democracy is faith in the capacities of human nature; faith in human intelligence and in the power of pooled and cooperative experience.

(John Dewey, 1937)

Guidelines for Democratic Classrooms

Random behavior produces random results. The following guidelines are useful for systematic classroom management.

A primary goal of social studies is to foster awareness of our pluralistic society and a tolerance of diversity.

Establishing Rules

All people must live by rules: some are federal, state, or local; some relate to school board policy and others to school building procedures. There is often no choice about which rule to follow and no opportunity to participate in making the rules. The rule that all pupils must attend school is not for class debate; neither teacher nor children can change it. Some rules, however, can be discussed and agreed upon by teachers and students. They can discuss general rules, such as respect for others. If a group of pupils makes fun of one student's art project, the problem can be discussed with the entire class. Some classes make a list of "killer words," words and phrases that hurt people and show lack of respect. Such words or phrases might be stupid, retard, dummy, nigger, fatso, wierdo, or four-eyes. Confronting these "killer words," children come to realize that each person has the right to work without fear or ridicule. Every pupil has a right to be himself. Discussing killer words gives pupils an opportunity to understand the concept of respect and concern for others, and to incorporate these attitudes into their lives.

Providing for Individual Differences

Equality of opportunity is an important principle in American society, and should be reflected in the democratic classroom. Each pupil should be given the chance to improve, given his own abilities and interests. Thus, a pupil is not locked into one style of learning or plugged into only one level of achievement. Children should be allowed to achieve at various levels. A teacher who provides for different learning styles, interests, and abilities creates an atmosphere in which all children achieve success in learning. In this kind of unpressured atmosphere, children see that each person makes an important contribution to the group, and that differences can be accepted and tolerated, if not appreciated.

Living with Diversity

Allowing or encouraging children to function according to their individual differences creates a classroom in which pupils exhibit considerable diversity. If children are to have the freedom to possess different philosophies, interests, and ways of living, they must accept that others will frequently make choices different from their own. A social studies classroom that does not include materials and activities to foster student awareness of society's pluralism is not preparing them for life. It does not allow them to learn to guide their lives in concert with others, or to build tolerance of diversity, a basic democratic principle.

Working in Groups

Group participation is a characteristic of all societies. Children have experiences with many groups: family, friends, church, school. Democratic decisions can be achieved through committee, but the committee members must often compromise with others who have different concerns. The teacher who man-

ages a democratic classroom furnishes group experiences that will be beneficial to many future activities in the child's life. The teacher tries to give
children experiences in which they have to balance their personal goals with
group goals.

Decision Making

The well-run classroom provides numerous opportunities for decision making. Few people follow a course without facing choices along the way; decision making is a necessary tool for choosing from among alternative courses.
What is the issue, dilemma, or problem? What are the alternative courses of
action and their probable consequences? Processing such questions can be tied
closely to encouraging independent learning, wherein the student has the
opportunity to make choices and mistakes without an authority figure's providing a complete set of directions. Independent learners will have the ability
to adapt to change, to initiate action, and to make judgments without having
to rely continually on an authority figure. Teachers encourage decision-making skills by letting children make choices, and children grow in self-confi-
dence when they are provided with opportunities to make choices and to
regulate some of their own behavior.

Taking Responsibility

In the democratic classroom, children more readily accept responsibility for
their own actions because they have participated in deciding what the appro-

---

Activity 13:1

Racial Tension

Mrs. Lee was working with her sixth-grade class on a unit about Africa, in which the textbook emphasized the Ibo, a tribe in southeastern Nigeria. Her class was composed of 20 white students and 15
black students. She planned to have students do some map work and reading and writing assignments, including a special research project on Biafra. During the second week of study, Mrs. Lee
heard an argument in the hallway between black and white students. The white students were making fun of Africans, calling them "primitive," "backward," and "dumb." A couple of the white girls
were dramatically trying to carry books on their heads as they had seen Ibo women do in a photograph in the textbook. They laughed at their repeated failures. Mrs. Lee went into the hallway and
found some of the black girls walking away, looking angry and arguing among themselves. Pushing
and shoving between black and white boys was just beginning. She instructed the students to come
into the classroom.

     If you were the teacher, what would you do now? How would you modify the study of the Ibo
so that you could deal with the racial problem that arose?

priate actions are. Teachers furnish opportunities for taking responsibility by having children help with clean-up tasks, collect workbooks, take the roll, take charge of pet and plant care, assist other students, and complete individual assignments in a group project. The reward for such action is internal— the feeling of being personally responsible, which is a much more powerful reward than an extra five minutes of recess.

Activity 13:2

Problems from Home

Mr. Alexander is worried about the behavior of one of his students. Jerald, a third grader, has become increasingly withdrawn, refusing to participate in group work, class discussions, and homework. This is a remarkable change from his usually outgoing personality and above-average academic record. After calling Jerald's home and speaking with his grandmother, Mr. Alexander learns that Jerald's father has left home after a violent argument with his wife. The grandmother does not expect him to return. She knows that Jerald is worried, but assumes he will soon get over it and stop missing his father.

Mr. Alexander relays this information to the school psychologist, who will try to schedule some time to talk with Jerald. In the meantime, Mr. Alexander continues his social studies unit, "Families Around the World."

If you were a teacher, what could you do to help Jerald? Could a social studies unit such as "Families Around the World" be of any assistance to Jerald?

Managing Social Studies Groups

The effectiveness of either a political or a classroom democracy depends upon the successful functioning of a variety of groups. These are appropriately named "healthy groups" (Knowles and Knowles, 1972). Such groups have members who are able to:

1. Participate effectively in decision making.
2. Adjust differences with others in a cooperative and peaceful way.
3. Maintain an open-minded attitude.
4. Develop a capacity for trust and solidarity.
5. Be willing to accept the leadership of others, and to accept responsibility for leadership themselves.

In classrooms where teachers realize they are working with groups of children as well as with individuals, children develop feelings of belonging and status and a sense of ease in working with social studies content. They also grow in self-esteem. They have opportunities to test some behaviors against reality and to gain control over their actions.

Teachers who successfully deal with groups in their classrooms understand group dynamics. As defined in chapter 5, successful groups are those composed of a definable membership and group structure, cohesiveness and a shared sense of purpose, group standards, and defined procedures. In the majority of classrooms, teachers deal with groups of varying sizes. Even when children are working on individual projects, the teacher is likely to explain directions and structure to a group of children who are at the same level of functioning or who have the same need for guidance.

Some of the reward and punishment strategies we have already discussed can be effective in working with groups. Children often work on group projects that require group management strategies. When working with such groups, the teacher must strive for peer influence rather than teacher influence to have a major effect on pupil functioning.

Group projects offer several advantages. In groups, each student has a greater opportunity to participate in planning, discussing, and evaluating the task. Learning from one's peers is a useful experience in understanding multiple perspectives, in clarifying personal ideas, and in appreciating classmates as additional learning resources. Groups can be organized on the basis of individual differences in skills, needs, or interests. It is likely that the class as a whole will learn more about a topic if several small groups investigate different aspects of a subject and share their findings with the class.

Teachers should allow pupils to assume positions of leadership and decision making in a group. Teachers sometimes make the mistake of not delegating full responsibility for their actions to the members of the group. To use group projects as productive learning experiences as well as a classroom management tool, the participants must feel they have full responsibility for the groups' outcomes and successes (Wallen and Wallen, 1978).

Teachers often feel their students are not mature enough to assume such responsibilities; however, if pupils are ever to assume control for their actions, they must be allowed to try, to enjoy, and to suffer some of the natural consequences of their behavior. If group members argue about who is going to do what, to whom, and when, they will have to face the consequence of their project's coming in late. Some teachers want children to have a good feeling about school, so they try to protect them from failure. But if a group has not functioned efficiently, the worst the teacher can do is to make excuses and protect the members from failure. The children quickly see that if they waste time and do not attend to the task, the teacher will always make allowances—"There is no need to worry." This is a disservice to children; they never really learn to take charge of their own behavior.

Students should take turns assuming positions of group leadership. A checklist can help group leaders learn appropriate actions; for example, the checklist might ask group leaders the following questions:

1. Did I encourage each person in my group to speak?
2. Did I listen and ask others to listen when a person was talking?
3. Did I speak loudly enough for my group to hear?
4. Did I keep the group's attention on our topic or problem?
5. Was I sensitive to others' feelings and viewpoints?
6. Did we finish our work?

As they learn more about their students, teachers will be able to identify which ones require a great deal of structure when working in groups, either large or small. They might place these students together, and work with these children at the beginning of a project to assure them of getting a good start. Once they are working, the teacher can circulate throughout the class to supervise, advise, and check work with other groups.

It is important to allow time for each group to share its work with the entire class at the end of the period or at some point during the social studies unit. When particular children have worked well together, the teacher can mention this to the entire class, pointing out the kinds of cooperation that enabled them to accomplish their assignment. Problems experienced by an individual group can sometimes be discussed with the entire class. If one pupil dominates discussion and rejects others' contributions, the teacher might suggest that the group have a timekeeper, who makes sure that everyone has only three minutes to speak. This is an artificial mechanism, but it may help students realize what their group can be like when everyone has a chance to contribute.

Figure 13.2
Checklist for
Anticipating Problems
in Small Heterogeneous
Groups

1. Did you assign each group a place to work?
2. Did you choose, or suggest that the group choose, a leader?
3. If needed, did you choose, or suggest that the group choose, a recorder?
4. Did you verify that each group understands its task or purpose?
5. Do the students need materials?
6. Have you provided a means whereby the students can find materials or resources?
7. If reading is required, are there at least two members of the group who can read the needed resource material?
8. If graphs, charts, or maps are to be used, do the students have the necessary skills to perform their task?
9. If group-to-group interaction is necessary, are the students aware of the process they are to use?
10. Is there a time limit for the group work? If so, do the students know what it is?
11. How will you get the students' attention if you need to? Have you communicated the means to the children?
12. What should the students do if they need help? Have you communicated the system to them?
13. What should some groups do if they finish before other groups have concluded their tasks? Have you communicated your plan to them?

Figure 11-1 "Checklist for Anticipating Problems in Small Heterogenous Groups" (p. 52) from CLASSROOM MANAGEMENT by Johanna K. Lemlech. Copyright © 1979 by Johanna Kasin Lemlech. Reprinted by Permission of Harper & Row, Publishers, Inc.

Students will tend to work best in groups in which the activities are perceived to be intrinsically motivating. Ideally, the teacher should not have to employ extrinsic incentives such as grades or points to encourage them to participate. Wallen and Wallen note that an activity will usually be motivating if it furnishes pupils with chances to be active, to socialize, and to feel confident. A way to check on this motivation is to watch students faced with removal from a group. If a student is really interested in participating, he quiets down very quickly when he realizes that continued talking jeopardizes his chance of involvement. Of course, if the activity is of low interest to the child, a threat of removal may be taken as a benefit.

Students also manage their behavior quite well when involved in projects that have meaning to them. All teachers know that pupils learn best when they are highly motivated; on the other hand, they either procrastinate or comply only under pressure to those tasks that seem irrelevant, boring, or too difficult. All teachers confront the problem of balancing required curriculum and related activities with the needs and interests of the students.

Teachers who manage classrooms well not only make the curriculum meaningful, but also build student morale. High morale enables groups to develop increased cohesion and sense of purpose and heightens the joy of belonging. The more attractive a group is to students, the more they will be influenced by its standards. Participating in such groups is highly satisfying, and brings about positive behavior. Teachers who build class morale also build classroom atmospheres conducive to good learning.

A teacher heightens class morale by making children aware of the various attractions the class offers. He can begin by presenting them with a list of possible activities, an overview of just what types of things are possible, and the types of roles that are open. Class morale is also developed by giving praise when warranted. It is also a good idea to create ways for class members to get praise from sources outside the classroom. Children are pleased to have their good work or actions recognized by other students, teachers, the principal, and parents. Inviting outsiders to "grand summaries" at the conclusion of units allows pupils to receive praise from significant others.

Activity 13:3

Classroom Observation

Arrange to observe both a primary teacher and an intermediate teacher teaching social studies. Note the way(s) in which each instructor manages the classroom. Specify any differences in management approaches and indicate what you think is the rationale for the differences. Report how you might approach the management of the same classroom.

Managing Individual Behavior

Successful classroom managers realize that all students' behaviors, regardless of type, are purposeful, and directed toward attainment of some need or needs. These teachers realize that a pupil misbehaves for some reason, although that reason may not be known to the pupil. Students who frequently misbehave have misinformation about what is appropriate behavior and have developed socially unacceptable ways to address their needs. They often have negative self-images. Teachers need to furnish them with opportunities to develop more constructive approaches to satisfying needs. It is important to let these children know that their needs are genuine and worthwhile, and that it is only the *manner* in which they are satisfying them that is questionable.

Misbehaving students develop better ideas about themselves when the teacher wins their confidence and has them think about their behaviors and ideas. When young people realize they act up in class to gain attention, the teacher can point out that desiring recognition is fine, but that it can be gained without disrupting the class. Recognition achieved through productive behavior is likely to be longer lasting. Of course, if the teacher uses a behavior modification strategy based only on punishment, and does not praise achievements, he will fail to address these children's needs.

Teachers usually deal with children who may exhibit behavior problems but do not really have serious personality maladjustments. Most teachers are not trained counselors or psychologists. If a child does have a serious emotional problem, the teacher needs to recognize the symptoms, but also realize the situation requires assistance from other professionals. A child's

Motivation for learning and class morale are high when learning activities are interesting, relevant, and challenging.

problem may be caused by a situation outside the school; a neglected or abused child cannot be helped by the teacher alone. The assistance of a social worker and a family therapist may be required. The teacher should make sure that the people in the classroom, including himself, do not add to the problems of a maladjusted child.

Children with positive self-concepts usually do not present serious problems in the classroom. There are always some days when a child does not feel "up to par," but that is minor. For the most part, children who like and feel comfortable with themselves relate well to both teacher and other students. Teachers must realize that self-concepts are affected positively and negatively by environmental experiences. If pupils achieve success, receive praise, and have time to gain a realistic sense of their skills, they will most likely develop positive self-concepts. As more and more parents pursue careers, the school may have to become increasingly involved in providing experiences that foster this important aspect of a child's development.

Students in a classroom that reflects realism learn strategies of adjusting or coping. Toffler (1970) notes that the successful person of the future will be able to cope with change. Teachers in social studies classes should provide both formal and informal guidance for coping with stress and change.

Educators should help children develop positive means of coping. Various types of physical activity reduce stress, and some individuals cope with a difficult situation through physical activity. When a child feels frustrated by a particular learning task, he may decide to walk around the room; others may begin to push another student; still others may need only to put the book down for a moment, then be ready to return to the task. Teachers should point out that certain behaviors are productive and others are not. Pushing a neighbor will not only get a student in trouble with the teacher, it will also fail to reduce the frustration of the task.

An effective way to cope with a new situation is to talk it through with someone. Wise teachers sometimes let children chat with peers about a problem. Through discussion, pupils sometimes discover ways to solve the problem, often because of a classmate's suggestion. Besides helping to solve some school problem, chatting provides productive contact with another human being who cares. Sometimes the teacher can be the listener. This tells a child: "I recognize you as a person who has something to say or a problem that is real." Sometimes, a child just needs to hear the teacher say, "I know how you feel, that happened to me once," which gives the child a chance to put the problem in perspective—others have felt that way too. "They survived, I guess I will also." There are other ways for children to cope with stressful situations, and the successful teacher works with children in seeking the approach or approaches that are effective, whether physical activity, talking, taking time off from the task, or getting a "pat on the back" from a friend.

Of the many roles instructors play, those of counselor and friend are essential to managing the social studies classroom successfully. The teacher does not become one of the students, but he does indicate true interest in each pupil's welfare, and makes this interest known to all. He should make this attitude clear the very first day of class, when the teacher sets the stage for the year's relationship. Some instructors are inclined to be hard-nosed at first: "You can always give the students more leeway later in the year." However, this attitude suggests to pupils that they are somehow the "enemy," to be held in check until an alliance can be set up (Foshay, 1980).

Jersild (1954) believes that a communication of caring can be achieved

> . . . by being an understanding adult who lets the child know that the teacher realizes the struggle the child is undergoing. He can do this by means of a glance or by noticeably keeping his mouth shut. He can do it by a kind of understanding patience which allows the child to express his annoyances . . . or to voice his grievances.

A good friend listens and empathizes. In expressing their feelings, students identify them and begin to establish acceptable ways of dealing with them. In listening, a teacher learns what is bothering students and what they consider important. This information can be incorporated into plans for social studies lessons. Children who have a teacher who listens realize the teacher is interested in them, which enhances the development of positive self-concept.

Listening helps teachers find ways to reach children through learning experiences. Instructors can pass on alternative ways for doing things, encourage children to talk through a problem, or suggest approaches for investigating a social studies project.

Managing a social studies classroom well requires educators to deal with children as people, as fellow students, as coinquirers, as individuals who

Successful classroom managers foster in students a sense of responsibility, a respect for others, and a respect for themselves.

are worthwhile and worth knowing. Children are not an enemy to be overcome. "Showing them who's boss" will not facilitate the creation of a classroom in which children behave appropriately because of the joy of learning, a sense of responsibility, a respect for themselves, and a respect for others.

Discussion

A primary role for the social studies teacher is that of classroom manager. For the most part, however, teachers receive no formal training in management skills, even though the teacher's leadership influences the classroom atmosphere and the students' level of learning. Research shows that most teachers manage their classrooms by conducting large-group activities and assigning a great deal of seat work, and control behavior with praise and by reminding children of behavior expectations.

Most teachers seem to feel that a successful school day is one in which they have accomplished what they planned to do with minimal interruptions and distractions, and when they and their students have been in good moods. The teacher's mood or attitude has a strong influence on student behavior. Besides attitude, certain teacher behaviors can also contribute to managing the social studies classroom in a way that will cause children to become involved with their work. The teacher should plan smooth transitions, reduce distractions, avoid overdwelling and fragmentation, keep students alert and accountable, and provide variety. Skillful classroom managers also understand how students perceive their classroom and how they react to teachers and peers.

An important technique for good classroom management is knowing how to reduce student frustration. Providing "hurdle help" with difficult academic tasks, restructuring tense situations, and establishing routines tend to reduce frustration. A teacher's firmness, follow-through, and task-centeredness also contribute to the student's sense of security.

Despite controversy over the use of behavior modification techniques, they are often applied to classroom management. The teacher manipulates rewards or punishments so that students come to recognize the consequences of their behavior; the goal, of course, is to reinforce desirable behaviors and extinguish undesirable behaviors. Some researchers feel that a particular management system should be employed schoolwide; an obvious advantage to the student is that rules of behavior are standardized from one class or teacher to another.

From the viewpoint that one goal of social studies is to produce effective citizens, an excellent case can be made for the benefits of managing the classroom along democratic lines. To do so, teacher and students must establish rules, provide for individual differences, learn to live with diversity and to work in groups, make decisions, and accept responsibilities. And by the nature of both democratic and social studies activities, there will be a great deal of emphasis on groups, for which both teacher and students need to be aware of the principles of group dynamics. Students tend to function best in groups where the activities are intrinsically motivating. Another important factor in good group work is that of morale.

On the whole, the teacher will achieve good classroom management by attending to individual behavior, and by recognizing that all pupil behavior, whether desirable or not, is motivated by some purpose, to fulfill some need. The teacher must at all times convey the attitude that while a particular behavior may be unacceptable, the student's need for recognition is valid. The democratic classroom tends to foster positive self-concepts and socially acceptable coping strategies; in this kind of atmosphere, the teacher can also fill the roles of counselor and friend as well as manager.

References

Canter, Lee. *Power to the Teacher: A Guide to the Use of Assertive Discipline with Contemporary Classroom Behavior Problems.* Seal Beach, Calif.: Canter and Associates, 1975.

Cellar, Sydney. In *Maintaining Discipline in Classroom Instruction,* edited by William F. Gnagey. New York: Macmillan, 1975.

Dewey, John. "Democracy and Educational Administration." *School and Society,* April 1937.

Foshay, Arthur W. "Curriculum Talk." In *Considered Action for Curriculum Improvement.* Washington, D.C.: Association for Supervision and Curriculum Development, 1980.

Glasser, William. *Schools Without Failure.* New York: Harper and Row, 1969.

Glueck, William F. *Management Essentials.* Hinsdale, Ill.: Dryden Press, 1979.

Goodlad, John I., et al. *Behind the Classroom Door.* Worthington, Oh.: Charles A. Jones, 1970.

Jersild, A. T. *Child Psychology.* 4th ed. Englewood Cliffs, N.J.: Prentice-Hall, 1954.

Knowles, Malcolm, and Knowles, Hulda. *Introduction to Group Dynamics.* New York: Association Press, 1972.

Kounin, J. S. *Discipline and Group Management in Classrooms.* New York: Holt, Rinehart and Winston, 1970.

Lemlech, Johanne K. *Classroom Management.* New York: Harper and Row, 1979.

Lortie, Dan C. *Schoolteacher.* Chicago: University of Chicago Press, 1975.

Redl, F., and Wattenberge, W. In *Maintaining Discipline in Classroom Instruction,* edited by William F. Gnagey. New York: Macmillan, 1975.

Toffler, Alvin. *Future Shock.* New York: Random House, 1970.

Wallen, Carl J., and Wallen, LaDonna L. *Effective Classroom Management.* Boston: Allyn and Bacon, 1978.

Evaluating Social Studies Learning

14

Evaluation encompasses the processes of gathering and analyzing information to determine whether or not what was planned actually occurred. Ideally, evaluation occurs at all levels of educational activity, from selecting an overall purpose for an educational program down to the specific intent of a particular activity. When applied to curriculum, evaluation is used to discover the extent to which the curriculum as designed, developed, and implemented produces the desired results (behaviors and/or knowledge) in students.

Evaluation provides feedback to both teacher and student as to the value of the curriculum, the effectiveness of the teaching, and the level of learning. The teacher uses evaluation to judge the appropriateness and effectiveness of general and specific objectives: "How will this information or experience benefit children?" It is used to judge the value and utility of information intended for curriculum guides. It provides the teacher with profiles on children's academic achievement, on their attitude and skills development, and on their levels of interests. These profiles furnish data that enable the teacher to determine whether to continue, adjust, or discard some particular aspect of the curriculum, and how to strengthen the program. Evaluation also functions as a source of information for communicating to parents and others the success of the social studies program and, specifically, the effectiveness of its teaching. Figure 14.1 shows graphically the flow and relationships of these processes.

Evaluation Principles

The steps in conducting evaluation should be considered within the context of recognized principles. First, teachers should realize that evaluation is central to the educational process. Without it, neither child nor teacher really has any notion of how she is doing. Evaluation is part of each stage of instructional decision making, from determining general objectives to selecting specific instructional strategies and materials. This principle calls for some kind of evaluation every day, by both teacher and pupils. Evaluation occurs in three forms: as diagnostic appraisal, as formative evaluation, and as summative evaluation. *Diagnostic appraisal* refers to determining individual and group needs. It reveals the status of children's current learnings, experiences, interests, learning styles, and strengths and weaknesses. Ideally, all teachers take time to assess formally or informally "where children are" in relation to a particular unit, to guide their curriculum and instructional decisions.

Formative evaluation is the ongoing evaluation that accompanies every educational activity. It gives the teacher a picture of how daily lessons are going and how instruction should continue. *Summative evaluation* deals specifically with how well objectives have been attained; it uses data from daily assessments to determine the children's concluding understandings of a total unit. It also allows the teacher to determine the nature of the next social studies lesson or unit.

Another important principle is that evaluation is made in relation to the general and specific program objectives. As figure 14.1 shows, objectives provide necessary input into the instructional process and serve as integral components in the educational system. It is not possible to judge the output (student learnings) without reference to the program's objectives.

The more specific the objectives, the easier they are to evaluate. Global statements such as "children will appreciate the many cultures of the world," although valuable for overall curriculum guides, must be rewritten into more specific objective statements to furnish direction in evaluating pupil progress. What behaviors and actions will indicate that children appreciate these various cultures?

Third, numerous methods of evaluation should be employed. There are many instruments and techniques for determining children's ongoing learning as well as their ultimate understandings, including samples of children's work, teacher-made tests, standardized tests, case studies, anecdotal records, behavior journals, inventories, checklists, rating scales, logs, sociograms, cumulative records, and questionnaires.

Selecting Evaluation Techniques

The evaluation technique depends upon what general objective is being evaluated, the classroom context, the backgrounds and learning styles of the pupils, the time available, and the type of behavior involved. If a teacher

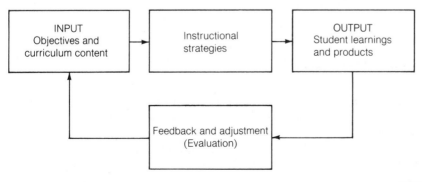

Figure 14.1
Evaluation as Part of a System

wishes to determine how well children can apply a particular approach to processing information, she might have them role play or conduct a simulation. If the intent is to determine students' factual background, a teacher-made test with multiple-choice items might be appropriate. The point is that the teacher does not use only one evaluative approach, but instead orchestrates several techniques, as necessary. The type of data needed for educational decisions determines which technique to use.

Certain criteria assist the social studies teacher in selecting appropriate evaluative instruments. The first and most essential criterion is *validity*. Does the instrument measure what it claims to measure? Is it truthful? A second crucial criterion is *reliability*; that is, does the instrument measure consistently what it purports to measure? *Objectivity* refers to the capability of the instrument to produce similar results regardless of who uses it. *Feasibility* considers whether or not the teacher can administer the instrument given her level of experience, the time factor, and the children's backgrounds. A final criterion is that of *appropriateness*: does the instrument measure what has been taught in the particular social studies program?

At one time, teachers felt they had sole responsibility for evaluation. Now, most educators urge that evaluation be cooperative, involving not only other teachers but students and parents as well. This is especially important when judging the worth of program objectives. There are often instances when students and teacher can judge together the appropriateness of certain types of materials or activities. Involving pupils in evaluation enhances their skills in assessing their own learning and the materials they use. To become independent learners, students need opportunities to practice assessing their own needs, monitoring their own progress, and judging the effectiveness of their approaches to learning. Through self-evaluation, children gain competence in critiquing the levels of their skills and understanding, and the appropriateness of their attitudes.

To help children take part in the evaluation process and engage in self-evaluation requires that teachers clearly show the nature and purpose of evaluation. Even though most children want to know "how they are doing," they are often extremely uncomfortable about evaluation, usually because they know evaluation will be used to grade and rank them and perhaps to separate children into high and low groups. But if children perceive evaluation as an essential ingredient of determining progress and adjusting behavior, they will be more comfortable with the experience.

Stages of Evaluation

While there are numerous techniques and instruments for assessing social studies learnings, the stages of evaluation do not vary greatly regardless of the instruments.

The first stage in evaluation is that of focusing on the phenomena to be evaluated and the range of evaluation activities required. Two substages include spelling out the objectives of the evaluation and noting the constraints and policies under which it is to be conducted.

The second stage is the actual collecting of the information. This involves

1. Identifying the sources of information essential for consideration and noting the levels of current information
2. Identifying the means of collecting the information (tests, interviews, observation schedules, etc.)
3. Noting the procedures available, the best methods for obtaining the information
4. Developing a schedule for carrying out these steps

Once the information has been collected, it must be organized, in the third stage, so as to be useful to the teacher and others, including students. Here the teacher considers the means by which the data will be classified, organized, recorded, and retrieved.

The fourth stage is to analyze the information. The actual analysis techniques depend on the evaluation's focus and degree of formality. The techniques can range from computing a group's mean score on a teacher-made test to sophisticated statistical computation to isolate factors influencing student learnings.

The final step is to report the information: to students, to parents, or to colleagues. The reporting process is geared to the characteristics of the audience that will receive the information; for example, ongoing evaluation can be reported in informal conversations with students and in parent conferences. At other times the reporting will need to be more detailed, especially if the information is for the use of a special education teacher to determine approaches for dealing with a learning difficulty. Other recipients can be curriculum leaders, supervisors, other instructors, or parent/community advisory committee members.

Evaluation Strategies

Observation

Observation is a basic evaluation strategy. Day-to-day observation gives the teacher a developmental picture of the pupil's learning accomplishments and capabilities. By observing each child, working alone and with peers, the teacher gains insights into the child's attitudes, feelings, and interests.

Social studies provides numerous opportunities for instructors to observe pupils. During discussions, teachers can observe who is interested, which children are always ready to contribute, and which ones never enter the discussion. During group activities, the teacher can observe children working together. Are they sure of their committee roles? Do they share ideas and materials? Do they engage in cooperative decision making? Do they defend their views?

The opportunities for observation are as numerous as learning activities created for the social studies curriculum. Besides those mentioned above other activities for observation are panel discussions, dramatic play, oral reading, questioning, and sharing of information. Observation can furnish data on children's approaches to work and play, their ability to function in groups, their management of time, their interests, their questioning abilities, their skills levels, their physical ability, their emotional adjustment, their dedication to task, and their maturity levels.

Effective observation is not a casual affair; it requires understanding of the process and of the behaviors observed. It requires focus; not all observable behaviors reveal the same motivations or mastery of learning. For example, some children are very good workers because they really enjoy the subject they are investigating, while others are equally diligent, but for an external reward promised by a parent. Some children who assume responsibility in a group activity are not exhibiting maturity, but rather are attempting to gain the teacher's praise. Only the skilled observer can detect these various moti-

Day-to-day observation allows the teacher to assess a student's capabilities and accomplishments.

vations and meanings. Thus, to focus observation, the teacher considers several factors. Just what questions are to be answered through observation? What evidence is necessary to make some assessment statement? It is not possible to observe the whole class at the same time, but certain pupils can be observed for the time necessary to obtain sufficient data. The observation may focus on a particular situation: "What does John do when he has to work with others in a group?" or "How does Marie react to situations in which the information differs from her views?"

It is the rare teacher who can commit to memory all the significant behaviors observed during a day of teaching. Therefore, she will need recording devices. A well-designed checklist is most helpful for recording information; it is easy to use and specific as to the behaviors to be observed. It often draws on the lesson's objectives, which supply a desired behavior, content to be mastered, and levels of performance to be sought. Teachers can let children create checklists and observe their own behaviors on videotaped class activities.

Checklists are often useful in social studies situations: for example, when children report investigative findings, when using visual materials, during small-group discussions, and when children work independently. Figure 14.2 shows a checklist for tallying the types of questions a child raises.

When children are working in committees, the teacher might find the checklist shown in figure 14.3 useful:

The checklists in figures 14.2 and 14.3 focus on children's behaviors. Other checklists can furnish data on children's products. For example, a teacher who wishes to assess a child's written report might employ the checklist shown in figure 14.4.

Question Checklist

Student: _____

Subject area: _____

Day: _____

Types of cognitive questions used:

Evaluation _____

Synthesis _____

Analysis _____

Application _____

Comprehension _____

Knowledge _____

Figure 14.2
Checklist of Student Questions

Figure 14.3
Checklist for
Committee Work

Name: _____	Grade: _____
Subject: _____	Group Activity: _____
Date: _____	

Initiates ideas	Helps clarify ideas
Seeks information	Challenges ideas of others
Gives information	Ignores data
Gives opinion	Disrupts the group

One can also employ rating scales to record observed actions. To gather data on a child's work habits, the rating scale in figure 14.5 might be used.

Teachers must be aware that their own feelings and prejudices may surface during observation. While it is probably impossible to eliminate personal feelings entirely, teachers who are aware of the potential bias can try to counteract this problem. They should also be alert to each child's uniqueness. Two children's similar behaviors may have entirely different causes. Teachers sometimes make the mistake of recording their reactions to behaviors instead of just describing the behaviors. Checklists and other recording devices must report what actually occurs; later, the teacher can interpret the event and perhaps even react to it. Useful observation requires obtaining sufficient data on each child. While it is not possible to observe every child in detail each week or month, it is desirable to accumulate several detailed observations on

Figure 14.4
Checklist for
Written Work

Name: _____
Subject: _____
Grade: _____

Written Report

Organization:
_____ Appropriate title
_____ Headings and subheadings
_____ Appropriate topic sentences

Accuracy of data:
_____ Data backed by authorities
_____ Uses several sources for data
_____ Shows checks for accuracy of data

Appropriateness of examples:
_____ Examples relate to topic's points
_____ Uses more than one example to make a point

Format:
_____ Title page
_____ Table of contents
_____ Footnotes
_____ References and/or bibliography

each child by the end of the year. Some teachers may have teacher aides or volunteers to help record pupil behaviors, and should discuss with the observer precisely what is to be observed and what the data will be used for.

Conferences

Teachers must take time to have one-to-one discussions with each child. These encounters provide information about the child's understandings, interests, abilities, attitudes, and needs. To heighten the usefulness of the conference, the teacher should have a definite purpose in mind—perhaps to determine if a child is enjoying a particular unit or activity. To keep the conference on target, teachers can prepare several questions ahead of time to guide the conversation. Conferences should not take place only when a child is experiencing difficulty; they should be considered opportunities for children to share their views with the teacher.

Work Habits

Name: _____

Grade: _____

1. Uses time to advantage:

_____

Always   Occasionally   Never

Remarks:

2. Gets work in on time:

_____

Always   Occasionally   Never

Remarks:

3. Uses appropriate references sources:

_____

Always   Occasionally   Never

Remarks:

4. Suggests independently topics to be investigated:

_____

Always   Occasionally   Never

Remarks:

Figure 14.5
Rating Scale for
Work Habits

A conference gives both teacher and pupil a chance to talk and listen. If the teacher does all the talking and the child all the listening, the conference won't be very sucessful. Many pupils dread such conferences as occasions for listening to the teacher "spout off." Finally, the assessment conference should not be used as a time for dispensing discipline.

A successful conference is most likely to occur when children realize its purpose and are shown how to prepare for it. They should come to a conference with their own questions and goals in mind, and feel free to express their interests and frustrations. They should also be encouraged to verbalize their understandings of particular topics, since children who have difficulty expressing themselves in writing will welcome the opportunity to "tell what they know."

Since conferences do take time, teachers cannot have meetings with all their students within a week, but the benefits of conferences should encourage teachers to schedule at least a portion of each day in five- or ten-minute conferences, perhaps during independent study or homeroom periods. Flexibility in conference schedules allows pupils with special needs to talk with the teacher at once, to prevent the damage that can occur if a child has to wait a week to discuss some personal difficulty.

Group Discussion

Although scheduling individual conferences can be difficult, most social studies teachers use the group discussion rather extensively. During these dialogues, children evaluate their work, assess their skill levels, determine the

Sometimes a teacher aide or volunteer can help observe and record student behavior.

productiveness of their research activities, and share perceptions and conclusions. They can also use these to compare their groups' performance with that of other groups.

All children should have a chance to participate in group discussion to allow the teacher to determine each child's progress. She can note the contributions of individuals and committees. Many teachers prepare questions to initiate and guide group discussion. The reaction avenues discussed in chapter 10 help sequence discussion questions.

It is ideal to schedule group discussion time at the conclusion of each lesson. At this point, pupils and teachers can assess their levels of knowledge, and generate plans for the next lesson based on what has and has not been learned. They can identify concepts that need additional study and skills that need more attention.

Not all class discussions need to be structured; children often initiate the most rewarding ones spontaneously to address their problems and questions. The class schedule should be flexible enough to allow such meetings. In group dialogue, children often reveal their attitudes toward the content, their reasoning ability levels, their content needs, and their skills in dealing with others. During these informal experiences, the teacher can observe what is happening and take notes for use in overall assessment.

Children can be guided in self-evaluation during group discussions but they must be taught what questions to ask in doing so. They must also be informed of and perhaps have participated in creating standards for determining behavior and understanding. In sharing conclusions, children should understand the standards of judging the value of content. Criteria for determining relevant content (mentioned in chapter 6) may be useful as well. Children need to determine whether the content or conclusions are valid or truthful. Is the information useful? Can it be used to form some conclusion, or to perform some task? Is the source of information reliable? Children can also learn standards of group work and assess their participation in group discussions. Did I work well with my peers? Did I attend to the task? Did I listen attentively to other committee members? Did I make wise use of my time?

Case Studies and Anecdotal Records

Case studies involve the recording of rather extensive information on a pupil over an extended period of time. A teacher usually does not make more than one or two such studies during a year. Information on the pupil's home background and prior school experience, health and psychological profiles, anecdotal records, and test data from both teacher-made and commercial tests can be included. In classrooms where children with learning disabilities have been mainstreamed, case studies are extremely useful in assessing and recording their progress.

Although she compiles case studies on only one or two children each year, the teacher creates anecdotal records on each child. These are usually begun in kindergarten or first grade and passed along at each succeeding grade level. An anecdotal record briefly describes some incident or situation in the pupil's life, and from these incidents, a profile emerges that gives the teacher an outline of unique needs and interests.

Anecdotal records provide information gained through observation and reactions to a child's work. They should include the date and time of the incident, the context in which the incident occurred, and an objective description of the incident. Teachers should also record their interpretation of the incident, separately from the description. Figure 14.6 is an example of a teacher's anecdotal record on one child.

Teachers often simplify the process of creating anecdotal records. Some teachers have a page with each child's name at hand just in case they need to record some information that day. Anecdotal records are most useful if they are systematic. Ideally, the instructor should decide in advance what to observe and relate the observational foci to particular objectives regarding a child's performance. It is best to record a specific behavior or action as soon as possible after observing it. Do not think you can reconstruct the situation at the end of the day. The anecdotal records must contain sufficient data from several observations to allow for some interpretation. Beginning teachers might wish to have a colleague also observe a child, so the recorded data and interpretations can be compared for reliability. Discussions with a colleague help one gain the skills necessary for developing useful anecdotal records.

Documentation Files

To assess a child's continuing progress, most teachers save work samples over a few weeks to discuss in conferences with both pupil and parents. A written

Figure 14.6
An Anecdotal Record

Anecdotal Record

Student: Alex Sullivan

1/22, Classroom. Alex did not start working with others on the assignment. Pushed pieces of paper around on his desk.

Interpretation: Alex doesn't seem to be interested in this topic. He is aware of our approach in that it is similar to one he did previously with success.

1/25, Classroom. Alex worked well with the other members of his group. He contributed several suggestions as to how to solve the problem.

Interpretation: Alex has found some part of the subject of interest. The conference I had with Alex trying to direct his interests seems to have paid off.

1/28, Classroom. Alex played a small part in sharing his group's conclusions to the study. He spoke clearly and used visual aids.

Interpretation: Alex demonstrated he knew the subject, and that he eventually did enjoy working with the group. He also seemed to enjoy speaking before the class.

---

report from the beginning of the year can be compared with a child's report made at midyear. Children are often pleasantly surprised to see how much better written their second report is.

Work samples are usually written, and may include special projects, daily quiz work, and teacher–made tests. Pictures of the child's projects can be kept in these folders, as well as artwork and mapwork. If the teacher wishes to get a "picture" of how well a child presents oral information, she can make tape recordings to keep in the file. Children who have physical handicaps and cannot write clearly may have their reports on tape.

The teacher might have pupils list their current activities and how successful they are with them. Daily logs or diaries can provide a running account of experiences in social studies. Information in a log allows a child to go back and determine why she arrived at a particular conclusion.

Children can be encouraged to make their own logs with some standard form, which facilitates the use of the records. A useful format appears in figure 14.7.

The log or diary is created solely by the individual pupils. It gives them an opportunity to be responsible for what they learn and to participate in their own assessment. Having them maintain these materials brings home the cooperative nature of learning and evaluation.

Sociograms

Teachers sometimes wish to get a reading on the classroom's social-psychological dynamics. To do this, they use a sociogram such as the one shown in figure 14.8. The device notes children's names and shows the interactions among them with arrows. The sociogram tells the teacher which children are the "stars" in the class and which are the "isolates." Data indicate the group's structure at a particular time. In the early elementary grades, the social

---

Log

Name: _____

Date: _____

Activity: _____

Topic: _____

Questions raised: _____

Ideas discovered, conclusions made: _____

People I worked with: _____

My feelings about this activity: _____

Figure 14.7
Student Log

dynamics change frequently. Best friends on one day may ignore each other for several days, then return to the "best friend" category.

Sociograms are probably more appropriate with intermediate-grade children because their social dynamics are most constant and longer lasting. In addition to determining the "major performers" and the "perpetual observers," sociograms allow the teacher to identify whether children are assuming leadership roles, whether their preferences for others have changed, and whether cliques have been modified over time.

Figure 14.8
A Sociogram

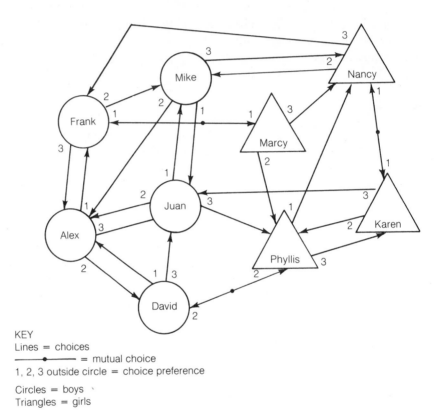

KEY
Lines = choices
——•—— = mutual choice
1, 2, 3 outside circle = choice preference

Circles = boys
Triangles = girls

Teacher-made Tests

The term "evaluation" often suggests nothing more than tests given at specific times, partly because of past overemphasis on summative evaluation and on the use of formal means to give children marks for their work. Elementary children also usually think of tests when evaluation is mentioned. They perceive tests as special events for which they have to study and for which they will receive a mark, usually unalterable. Children often anticipate tests with fear. Teachers should inform children that tests can be used for diagnosis and remediation as well as for giving a grade. In fact, the first two functions are more important than the grade, at least at the elementary level.

Teachers construct tests to measure a child's skills, background, and levels of understanding. A teacher can use the results from tests to plan later units, to determine effective groupings, and to determine the worth and effectiveness of content, strategies, and materials. Teacher-made tests should be an integral part of instruction.

Of the two basic types of teacher-made tests, essay and objective, the type to select depends partly on what you wish to evaluate and the method of instruction you have used. For instance, if you have emphasized factual information, you should construct an objective exam to allow children to show their knowledge of the particular facts.

Essay Tests

Essay tests are designed to make children solve problems, analyze and synthesize, point out their attitudes and interests, and make evaluations. In essay exams, students must plan their answers and express them in their own words. Pupils must respond actively to such questions, thinking about ways to respond and writing down their responses. A well-stated question permits a great deal of freedom in their responses.

Because essay tests require extended responses, they are best used to have pupils demonstrate an understanding of main ideas, concepts, and generalizations. Since essay tests must be written, they are not effective in the primary grades. In fact, any type of paper-and-pencil test is more appropriate at the intermediate level. As children move up through the grades, these tests increase in value.

Activity 14:1

Strategies of Evaluation

Interview a teacher in the field to learn which types of evaluation strategies she uses often (more than three times a month) and seldom (once or not at all during a month). Chart your data, and record the teacher's and your own general comments about evaluation.

Grade Level: _____

Strategy

Frequency of Use

General Comments:

Essay test questions are rather easy to write, but the teacher should nevertheless give careful thought to constructing them. Essay questions should be designed to elicit the upper levels of thinking, such as analysis and synthesis, and to give children a chance to show creativity. The questions should show clearly what is expected in the response. The question, "Discuss the reasons for the high price of gasoline," is too vague. A better one would be, "List two events that occurred in 1973 that resulted in higher gasoline prices. Indicate the reasons that these events caused the prices to rise."

Objective Tests

Questions on objective tests can usually be answered in a word, a phrase, or even by indicating a number. There are several types of objective tests: alternative response, multiple choice, completion tests, and matching. Instructors frequently make up objective tests that include items of all of these types.

Alternative Response Tests

Alternative response tests are made up of items written in several forms, including true–false, yes–no, right–wrong, correct–incorrect. The teacher can read a question to the class or have them read it. Asking the question aloud might work in the primary grades, if such a test is necessary at all. Examples of questions of this form are:

1. New York City is the capital of New York.   T   F

2. Thomas Jefferson was the fourth president of the United States.   T   F

3. Circle *yes* on your paper if the following statement is correct or *no* if the sentence is incorrect.
    Yes, no (a) Deserts are hot.
    Yes, no (b) Mountains are tree-covered.
    Yes, no (c) Rivers in the northern hemisphere flow south.
    Yes, no (d) Winds in the northern hemisphere primarily flow in a westerly direction.

4. Directions: Write an *X* beside each statement that is true.
    (a) _____ Geography is the study of places.
    (b) _____ The Mississippi River is the longest river in the world.
    (c) _____ The highest mountain in North America is Mt. McKinley.
    (d) _____ The Japanese Current keeps the weather of the West Coast of North America rather mild.

5. Put a plus (+) beside the statement or statements that correctly complete the sentence.
    Jet streams in North America
    (a) flow west to east. (   )
    (b) change their pathways depending on the seasons. (   )

(c) can reverse their directions at different times of the year. (   )
(d) interfere with radio transmissions. (   )

Teachers can use such tests or incorporate questions with this format when they want to determine understandings of concepts and generalizations, attitudes, interests, and basic understanding of facts.

Multiple Choice Tests

Multiple choice tests are popular with teachers because the questions provide a greater variety of responses than the alternative response format. The multiple-choice format consists of an incomplete statement or question (called a stem by test makers) followed by two or more responses. The stem may also be a complete sentence or brief paragraph. One response is the correct answer, while the others serve as distractors. Children are told to read the question carefully and select the correct response from among the choices given. Teachers sometimes vary the directions slightly by asking children to note the incorrect conclusion. Responses can be noted by underlining the correct option or by writing its designated letter or number.

These tests are difficult to construct because the question must be meaningful and clear. There must be only one possible answer among the responses and all the responses must be phrased so as to seem plausible. The teacher must be careful to word the options so they contain no irrelevant or superficial clues. She should also strive to have the questions measure something other than memory of factual material. The following guidelines should prove useful in creating such test items:

1. Make sure the stem is a clear statement of the question.
2. Make the choices of approximately equal length.
3. As a general rule, give four choices, and no more than five choices.
4. Make sure the grammar in the choices does not give away the answer, such as matching plurals in stem with plurals in response, or noting the correct use of "a" or "an." For instance, a sonnet is (a) an epic; (b) a poem; (c) an encyclopedia; (d) an essay.
5. Arrange items so that those with equal numbers of options are together.
6. Create plausible options.
7. Avoid using wording similar to that in the textbook.
8. Arrange responses so that the correct answer occurs in random order.

While these tests are difficult to create, they are extremely easy to correct. Pupils in the intermediate grades can correct their own by reading an answer sheet or by listening to the teacher call out answers. These are some examples of multiple-choice questions:

Directions: Underline the word that correctly completes the statement.

The central concept of geography is

space.   region.   boundary.   place.

Florida was obtained from

England.　　France.　　Spain.　　Mexico.

Directions: Select the person who could probably give you the most accurate
account of the Hungarian Revolution.
a. ____ An American newscaster who reported the story
b. ____ A Soviet soldier who participated in it
c. ____ An American soldier who was stationed in Europe at the time
d. ____ A Swedish newscaster who was in Hungary at the time

In considering the taxing problems of our community, which of the following would be the main source of tax revenue?
a. city income tax
b. city sales tax
c. city car excise tax
d. city property tax

Completion Tests

Completion tests ask students to recall a particular name, place, concept, date,
or rule. The test format is that of a series of sentences in which certain
important words or phrases have been omitted and blanks substituted for
them. A sentence may contain one or more blanks. You can arrange the
sentences in isolated fashion or within a paragraph, depending on the nature
of the question. Usually, each blank counts as one point for scoring.

These tests are somewhat more difficult to deal with than some multiple choice items in that the child must *recall* the response rather than *recognize* it. Both simple and complex recall items should be short; these are
usually more meaningful to elementary children. The teacher should also be
sure that each blank allows only one correct response. Social studies teachers
find that the completion test, as is true of the multiple-choice test, has wide
applicability as far as subject matter is concerned, but one must exert care to
measure more than rote memory.

You will find the following points useful when creating such tests.

1. Do not use statements with too many blanks. If too many key words are
left out, pupils find it impossible to determine what is needed.
2. Do not use indefinite statements. The pupil should not have to guess what
type of response is requested.
Inappropriate: John F. Kennedy was elected _____.
Appropriate: John F. Kennedy was elected president in the year
_____.
3. Omit only key words and phrases, rather than insignificant details.
4. Avoid using blanks of different lengths.
5. Avoid copying sentences directly from the textbook.
6. Be sure to check for grammatical clues to the answer.
7. Be sure there is only one correct response for each blank.

These are examples of completion items:

What do we call a place where little rain falls? _____.

What do we call the land form that is surrounded by water on three sides? _____.

The person who said, "Give me liberty or give me death" was _____.

The Japanese signed the surrender agreement to the Second World War in the year _____.

Matching Tests

The last major form of test or test item is *matching*. These items measure the student's ability to associate events and dates, events and persons, terms and definitions, principles and procedures, concepts and examples, causes and effects, and so forth. You should use these items only when the several pairs of items are quite similar, so that the child will need to think critically in order to arrive at the correct associations.

Such tests can be used in the primary grades by having children match pictures that have some relationships. The same format can be used in the intermediate grades; for example, students can match a picture of some topographic feature with a map symbol for the same feature.

The following guidelines are useful for constructing matching test items:

1. Include similar material in each matching exercise. Do not mix items in a single test, such as persons and events or dates and events.
2. Have only single words, numbers, or brief phrases in one list. Usually, the column with the shorter terms is that from which the choices are made.
3. Arrange the items in the response column in a systematic order.
4. Be clear as to the nature of the matching to be done.
5. Keep the matching items for each question all on the same page.
6. Be sure to avoid giving pupils grammatical clues.
7. Have at least five items, but not more than 15, in each matching exercise.

These are some examples of matching items:

Draw a line between the worker and the task that he does.

Secretary	listens to lawyers' arguments
Plumber	manages a business office
Engineer	works with pipes
Judge	types letters
Executive	supervises building construction

On the space before each subject, write the letter that indicates its major concern.

	Subject		*Major Concern*
1. _____	geography	A.	deals with culture
2. _____	history	B.	deals with groups
3. _____	sociology	C.	deals with land features
4. _____	anthropology	D.	deals with events in time
		E.	deals with distribution of
5. _____	political science	power	

In which of the sources would you most likely find the information listed?

1. Dictionary

2. Atlas

3. Encyclopedia

4. American history textbook

5. Daily newspaper

25. How to hyphenate the word geography (   )

26. Information about the growth of slavery (   )

27. The location of the major seaports of the world (   )

28. The latest views dealing with a political issue (   )

29. A brief account of the City of New York (   )

The teacher must follow several basic principles when creating tests, regardless of the format. First, only significant learnings should be assessed. All too frequently, teachers stress memorization of facts and give tests that merely measure memory rather than comprehension and use of information. Second, questions must be written so that their intent is entirely clear. Also, questions should be worded without giving unnecessary cues. Teachers sometimes use wording that so closely parallels the textbook that pupils have little difficulty recognizing the right answer. Third, be sure the directions are clear. If an objective test contains several types of questions, the directions for each type must precede each set.

It is always good practice to keep questions of the same type together. Do not write two multiple choice questions, then two true-false, then another multiple choice. Questions should be written at the appropriate levels of difficulty. Because teachers often take considerable time to prepare tests, they sometimes make the questions far more difficult than the level of the corresponding lessons. Children perform poorly on such tests not because they do not understand the information, but because of poor construction. It is helpful to keep in mind the cognitive levels of Bloom's taxonomy (see chapter 10) when creating objective and essay test items.

Standardized Tests

Standardized tests from commercial sources are available for evaluating specific subject-matter knowledge, and assessing concepts, generalizations, rules, theories, and facts. These tests also measure work-study skills and critical thinking. Teachers find these tests useful in providing an objective measure of progress and growth over a given period of time in outcomes that can be put to statistical measurement. Consequently, such tests are often used to gather data for judging the quality of the overall program and the effect of instructional procedures. These tests should not be used for determining grades nor for evaluating the teacher. Such judgments require a wider base of information than can be provided by standardized tests.

One type of standardized test is the *norm-referenced* test. This kind of test assesses a child's performance in comparison with the performance of a large sample (norm) of other children of the same age and grade. The test makers determine the average performance expected for the norming population.

Sometimes confused with the norm-referenced test, the *criterion-referenced* test evaluates specific objectives and measures the degree to which a pupil has mastered the particular objective. Criterion-referenced tests are often administered in programs that emphasize mastery learning, in which a child continues to study or work at some skill until she achieves mastery at the expected level of competence (criterion level). These evaluation instruments are popular with teachers who practice a high degree of individualized instruction. They are effective measures of skills in which the student attempts to demonstrate performance or understanding.

Standardized tests are important, but they comprise only a portion of the necessary evaluation. They must also be interpreted with the unique characteristics, experiences, interests, and abilities of the class members in mind. Teachers sometimes err in assuming that the grade norm noted for the test should be the standard for the grade, to use in determining whether pupils are making satisfactory progress. Children are thus felt to be doing less than optimal work if they are below grade level. This misinterpretation is sometimes encouraged when school districts publish the achievement results of children who have taken standardized tests.

The grade norm represents the average score for the norming group. For many pupils, this average represents a level far below their potential achievement. For other children, the grade norm may be too high. In most classrooms, children range in capability and achievement several grade levels above and below their grade norm. This range tends to increase in the higher grades. The standards of expectation should be based only on the capabilities of the specific class. It is interesting to know how one's class compares with a national norm, but this knowledge does not compel the teacher to attempt to bring all children up *or* down to the norm. Trying to bring all children up to the norm will cause frustration and discouragement; bringing children who are above the norm down to the norming level will make them lose interest in schooling because of the reduced challenge.

Standardized tests do provide guidelines as to what to expect for a majority of children. It sets a *range* of performance standards for children in a particular grade. When administered at the beginning of the year, standardized tests give the teacher some idea of how children compare with their national peers and indicate certain individual and group needs. Armed with such information, the teacher can modify her yearly plans. Most schools give standardized tests over several years (often at grades four, seven, and nine) for purposes of monitoring overall program effectiveness and identifying necessary modifications. By administering these tests over several years, educators obtain a developmental picture of the student population within the particular school system.

While there are numerous standardized tests on the market, the teacher usually does not select the test for her class. The instruments are selected for the entire school district by a district-wide committee composed of teachers, counselors, administrators, curriculum coordinators, and supervisors. As far as the local social studies program is concerned, certain guidelines are useful in selecting and using a standardized test. The first question to ask is whether the test relates to social studies and to the general program taught in the school system. Since these tests are created for all children across the nation, it is possible that the material one test covers is not covered at all in a particular school district. Another consideration is the difficulty of the test. Can the pupils in this school district read the test and deal with the questions? Is this the best test for assessing pupils on a particular aspect of social studies? It might be useful to know the nature of the norming population, which may be nothing like the children in the local school or classroom. Finally, does the test fit into the overall pattern of program evaluation? Will the test results effectively complement data gathered through other evaluation techniques?

Activity 14:2

Becoming Acquainted with Tests

Check through the most recent *Mental Measurements Yearbooks* and become acquainted with tests that would be appropriate for the grade level you wish to teach. If you are student teaching, read the descriptive information of the standardized tests the school uses or is scheduled to use.

If the school where you are or will be student teaching has a director of evaluation, arrange a meeting to discuss the testing program, with special attention to the instruments selected for evaluation.

We have mentioned several times in this book that the difficulty facing teachers is not a scarcity of materials but an overabundance. An excellent resource for identifying available standardized tests is *The Mental Measurements Yearbooks*, edited by Oscar K. Buros and published by the Gryphon Press in Highland Park, New Jersey. This resource lists virtually all commercial tests and explains what they test, the intended population, and other information useful in test selection.

Some of the more commonly used standardized tests are:

- Iowa Every-Pupil Test of Basic Skills, Houghton Mifflin Company, Boston, Mass.
- Standard Achievement Test, Harcourt Brace Jovanovich, Inc., New York, N.Y.
- Metropolitan Achievement Tests, Harcourt Brace Jovanovich, Inc., New York, N.Y.
- Sequential Tests of Educational Progress: Social Studies, Level 4, Grades 4–6, Educational Testing Service, Princeton, New Jersey.
- SRA Achievement Series, Science Research Associates, Chicago, Ill.

In addition to teacher-made and standardized tests, commercial materials produced by publishers are also available. Many publishers create tests and assessment exercises to accompany their main textbooks, workbooks, and visuals. These materials are usually geared to the objectives noted in the teacher's guides. The test format may be either objective or essay, although the objective format seems to be favored. The tests employ the various types of question formats discussed in this chapter, but you will want to critique the questions for suitability before actually using them. Many teachers find these assessments useful and time-saving since it is so much easier to use the questions from the publisher's test than to construct one's own. One should remember, however, that even though such tests are commercially developed, they have not necessarily been normed or statistically checked for validity and reliability.

Activity 14:3

Approaches to Evaluation

Skim through a social studies unit noting the types of evaluation approaches suggested and the manner in which their use is recommended. From what you have read about evaluation, what statement(s) can you make regarding the approach(es) to evaluation present in the unit?

Activity 14:4

Preparing Evaluation Instruments

Consider the objectives you have for the social studies unit you have been creating and indicate the means you would employ to evaluate whether children had obtained the objectives. (If you have not developed such a unit, select three or four general objectives you think relevant to social studies, and indicate how you would determine whether children had achieved these objectives.)

Activity 14:5

Dealing with Self-fulfilling Notions

Some research supports the idea that teachers' perceptions of children's abilities affect how these teachers influence their students' success rates and potential. If they see their students as capable, teachers will alter their instruction to assure pupil success. But, if they think children are unable to succeed in learning, teachers will behave in ways that tend to cause students to fail or be less successful.

Indicate how you might avoid this "self-fulfilling" prophecy in dealing with evaluation.

Activity 14:6

Student Self-Evaluation

While evaluation by the teacher is important, it is also essential that pupils realize the need for self-evaluation and become knowledgeable of ways in which to assess their own work and behavior. Make a list of ways to educate children in approaches to self-evaluation. Indicate the reason(s) why you think these methods are appropriate.

Coordinating Evaluation

It stands to reason that a social studies program with a great diversity of pupils, topics, experiences, and materials requires a corresponding variety of evaluation means. For effective evaluation, it is likely that you will need all of the techniques presented in this chapter. The success of evaluation depends upon the instructor's ability to choose the technique wisely and know when to employ it and with which pupils.

Evaluation has many functions: to provide data that will allow diagnosis of children's needs, interests, capabilities, and prior knowledge levels; to facilitate making wise decisions regarding curriculum and instruction; and to enable the teacher to say with some degree of certainty that program objectives have been achieved. A teacher who is in tune with current evaluation realizes there are numerous opportunities for evaluating children's understandings and abilities that resemble how children will actually use such understandings and skills in the real world. For instance, to determine how well children understand issues of conservation and recycling, the teacher may have them participate in some community project or monitor their home behavior regarding recycling materials. This may well be a more effective way to measure their understanding of the purpose and value of recycling than giving them a multiple-choice test.

Discussion

Social studies teachers use evaluation to find out whether or not what they have planned has actually occurred. Evaluation shows teachers and students the value of the curriculum, the effectiveness of the teaching, and the level of learning. It also furnishes teachers with profiles of student achievement, attitude and skills development, and interest levels.

Evaluation is central to the educational process, from planning through application. The teacher uses diagnostic evaluation to determine individual and group needs; formative evaluation to assess the effectiveness of ongoing instruction and activities; and summative evaluation to determine the extent to which objectives have been achieved. Evaluation must always occur in relation to general and specific program objectives, and several evaluative instruments and techniques should be employed to arrive at conclusions.

Selecting appropriate methods of evaluation depends on what is to be evaluated, the classroom context, students' backgrounds and learning styles, how much time is available, and what kind of behavior is involved. The teacher must judge each evaluation instrument according to its validity, reliability, objectivity, feasibility, and appropriateness.

Of the evaulation strategies available to the elementary teacher, observation is a basic method. The teacher needs to focus observation on a specific objective, and record what she observes. A checklist is one way to record observation data; we have looked at examples of checklists for a student's questioning behavior, group work behavior, and written reports, and a rating scale for work habits.

Conferences with students are also good evaluation tools, particularly when the child knows the purpose of the conference and how to prepare for it. Through an individual conference, the teacher will learn much about a child's understandings, interests, abilities, attitudes, and needs, and the student can use the time to verbalize questions, goals, and frustrations. For children who do not express themselves well in written work, a conference with the teacher gives them a chance to express verbally some of what they have learned in the classroom. Group discussions can also be used for some of the same purposes. Other examples of observation instruments are case studies, anecdotal records, documentation files, student logs, and sociograms.

Teacher-made and standardized tests have long been used for evaluation. Teacher-made tests consist of either essay or objective questions; objective questions take the form of alternative response, multiple choice,

371

completion, or matching items. Standardized tests are useful for obtaining statistical information about student performance on either a norm-referenced or criterion-referenced basis. In addition, the teacher can often use commercial tests published to accompany textbooks, workbooks, and visuals.

It is up to the teacher to choose the proper evaluation instruments to suit her purposes. At one time or another, a teacher will use all the common evaluation techniques; sometimes, she will have to devise a unique method to meet her evaluation goals.

References

Berg, Harry D., ed. *Evaluation in Social Studies*, 35th Yearbook. Washington, D.C.: National Council for the Social Studies, 1965.

Bloom, Benjamin S.; Englehart, M.; Furst, E.; Hill, W.; and Krathwohl, D. *Taxonomy of Educational Objectives. Handbook I: Cognitive Domain*. New York: David McKay, 1956.

Fair, Jean. "What Is National Assessment and What Does It Say to Us?" *Social Education* 38 (1974): 398–403.

Gephart, W. J. "Who Will Engage in Curriculum Evaluation?" *Eductional Leadership* 35, no. 4 (1978): 225.

Hunkins, Francis P. *Curriculum Development: Program Improvement*. Columbus, Oh.: Charles E. Merrill, 1980.

Hunt, B. "Who and What Are to be Evaluated?" *Educational Leadership* 35, no. 4 (1978): 261.

Krathwohl, David; Bloom, B.; and Masia, B. *Taxonomy of Educational Objectives. Handbook II: Affective Domain*. New York: David McKay, 1964.

Phi Delta Kappa National Study Committee on Evaluation (D. L. Stufflebeam, Chair.) *Educational Evaluation and Decision Making*. Bloomington, Ind.: Phi Delta Kappa, 1971.

Popham, W. J., ed. *Evaluation in Education*. Berkeley, Calif.: McCutchan, 1974.

The Future and Social Studies Education

15

One characteristic separating humans from lower orders of life is the ability to "time bind"—that is, to link the past with the present, to build transitions, and to create realities that are not just immediate, but that can stand when the future draws on the past (Strudler, 1974). To a great extent, human beings have always considered choices and selected alternatives—in effect, they have influenced their futures. Educators can apply this "future view" to the effective teaching of social studies.

Strudler feels that thinking about current and future actions and their likely consequences is a human behavior as simple and as natural as breathing. Although this may be true, such behavior has largely been random, not planned and systematic. No longer, however, must humans rely on tradition, or even crystal balls, for insights into the future. We have become increasingly aware of how much we can and do control future events. Today, the study of "futuristics" incorporates methods and techniques that allow us to identify possible, probable, and even preferable futures. (Lindaman and Lippitt, 1979).

More and more educators think about the future, and have become skillful at making forecasts about probable and preferred events. This kind of new knowledge and expertise will allow them to manage their educational world. Professionals will be able to answer such questions as: "How do we want our world to work? What do we want our world to look like?" And perhaps the major question for social studies teachers is, "How can we plan social studies curricula for the short- and long-term future so that students truly become functioning world citizens?"

The Need to Consider Futuristics

Social studies is a dynamic field of study, and educators need to be aware of, to anticipate, and manage its directions. The future need not be something that just happens; it need not be a surprise. Indeed, such a way of living is dangerous; it means that teachers are constantly caught off guard. If social studies educators do not anticipate social demands or needs, they put themselves in the position of having to rush some solution or program into effect to address student and community needs.

Futuristics is the systematic attempt to meld creative forecasting, planning, and action; it furnishes teachers with the means by which they can anticipate and plan for alternative futures. The major question they confront is still "What social studies content is most worthwhile?" In a time of flux and constant diversification, it is extremely difficult to answer. Realistically, the question needs to be modified to "*What* knowledge is of value to whom now and in the future?"

We will not, in this final chapter, provide the teacher with specific futuristics, but we will stress that the future can be created. When educators realize this, they will not have to wait for others to interpret reality and then create social studies programs; they will themselves be futurists and creators of productive social studies programs.

Futuristics will require at least some social studies educators to accept new roles and responsibilities. Adopting this future-oriented posture, teachers should be able to understand current major trends, to determine which trends seem most likely to persist, and to identify ways of actually managing educationally significant social trends. Rubin (1975) tells us that observations about future schooling should determine what shall be taught *about* and *in* the future, the organization of the school of the future, and the nature of

The increasing reliance on technology in modern societies will shape the world of the future. Social studies programs must address such significant social trends.

teaching in the future. Those who take some responsibility for futuristics will process such questions so as to make social studies teaching and curricula responsive to the times.

Projections in Social Studies Education

Future Directions

Our projections of the future greatly affect what it will be. Individuals must accept the notion that the future can be anticipated and managed. This does not mean believing in soothsayers; rather, one must realize that initiating certain actions increases the probability that certain events will occur and decreases the probability of others. For instance, if a teacher feels that future social studies students should have direct access to primary source materials, he can increase the likelihood that such materials will be available. He can explain to the program director that such materials are necessary, work with the budget committee to allocate funds for materials procurement, and mount strategies to get the parent–teacher group involved in pushing for the purchase of materials. These actions increase the probability that such materials will be part of the envisioned future. On the other hand, the person who feels this could never happen will not take steps to bring it about. If one does nothing, nothing is likely to occur—the self-fulfilling prophecy that one cannot manage the future.

All people are futurists at heart. If they want a vacation to be part of their future, they try to control the event by saving money, going to a travel agent, and adjusting their work schedules. By doing these things, they increase the likelihood of a vacation in their future.

To plan for and manage the future requires some "view" of it, an awareness and knowledge of which current events are likely to continue or which new events are likely to occur. Knezevich (1975) proposes that several current directions, likely to continue for the remainder of this century, have strong implications for educators: an increasing use of technology; the use of new structural (or building) developments; the use of new educational goods and services; an increase in the diversity of students; and the creation of campus and community schools.

An increasing use of technology implies an increase in the use of computers and new machines that work with laser beams. It is possible that by 1990, computer assisted instruction (CAI) will be replaced by laser assisted instruction (LAI). The increase in computer use will spill over into the home. By the end of the century, many homes will have education centers, of which the home computer will be the central component. The computer may be tied to the school computer network and perhaps even to other systems in distant places. Some pupils will probably be able to do intensive investigations without ever leaving home. Home computers will certainly be assisting students with their homework.

New equipment will communicate messages to students, and three-dimensional television and holography will accompany laser-assisted instruction. Such equipment will make analysis of certain social studies topics even more meaningful. Most elementary schools will have video communications setups wired for both telephone and television transmission, with which students will be able to obtain news broadcasts, library materials from distant sources, and printouts stored on the school's central computer. Some of this equipment is available today, but is used primarily at the higher education levels.

Technological systems will not only allow expanded use of primary materials, but will also enable students to engage in decision-making games, in which the computer will plot immediate and distant consequences of decisions. In the past, people could only infer what might result from some action; it is now possible to determine how a minor decision made in 1986 will affect a particular resource level in the year 2015. People will be able to draw on the computer's capabilities to "see" if they like the consequences of a decision before committing themselves to action. If the consequences appear negative, the decision can be modified.

Educational television has long been used in schools as an occasional instructional tool.

The second direction Knezevich notes is the use of new structural developments. For most of this century, schools have been arranged in an "egg crate" design, with separate rooms arranged along a central corridor. However, the design of some new schools gives attention to the types of curricula and educational activities to be offered. Matching school space to curricular intent should result in new designs that will foster greater student involvement in learning. The time is not too distant when schools will simulate world spaces in "school spaces" so students can learn by role playing essential skills.

Mock courtrooms where students study the workings of law may be commonplace. There may be "government chambers" where students engage in political and legal debates. There may be observation rooms where they observe the behaviors of animals or even their fellow classmates as part of psychology and sociology units. Certainly there will be specialized "viewing rooms" for processing film, videotapes or discs, or filmstrips. Possibly before the end of the century, schools will have "educational theaters" in which students can take field trips solely through the use of holography and three-dimensional films; these "theaters" will add a degree of realism not currently possible.

As Knezevich points out, increasing uses of new and existing technology and the use of new structural developments will necessitate *new educational* goods and services. The present generation of computers already demands software programs; video systems and simulation setups will require support systems. Some schools may rent rather than purchase these systems,

The socio-cultural diversity of students will be a continuing challenge to social studies teachers.

or own them cooperatively with other school systems. Besides materials to support the new technology, schools will need the services of new types of professionals—people who create new computer programs, simulation systems, and service them. There may also be individuals to assist teachers in planning the uses of the new technology and help them evaluate the effectiveness of the systems.

With increased access to material and varied experiences comes heightened diversity among students. This fourth direction is already well established; social studies educators are confronted with an ever-increasing socio-cultural and intellectual range of students. This diversity will continue, and will challenge teachers to discover ways to use social studies curricula to stimulate true understandings of human diversity *and* commonalities. Already well established, multicultural education will continue to fan the diversity among students.

Some educators feel the neighborhood elementary school is really too small a unit to function effectively in the future. As students become increasingly diverse and technology continues to expand, it may be wise to consider creating campus and community schools. Some school districts already have such environments, which they often keep open into the evening for adult education programs.

The campus school is not yet well established, but, quite probably, elementary schools will not continue to be single buildings that house 500 to 600 pupils; they will likely be arranged on campuses accommodating as many as 2000 pupils. Small classes will still exist, because greater numbers of students in one locale to share interests will permit a greater diversity of program offerings.

When school buildings are arranged on campuses and schools begin to use technology more effectively, it is likely the construction of the buildings will change. Some may be geodesic domes, to allow for uncluttered spaces; others will be created from pressurized skins and reinforced concrete shells; and probably others will be created from yet-to-be-developed materials.

These directions are not science fiction; but whether they continue and whether educators take advantage of and assume some management of them is a decision that requires action today. If educators do not assume a leading role in creating and managing these changes, others will. If this happens, social studies educators may have lost a major chance to influence the nature of social studies education now and in the future.

Educators must respond to these directions, anticipate some, and initiate others to lead to effective social studies education. Teachers and teachers-to-be need to relate these trends to social studies content and instructional strategies.

Future Content and Instructional Strategies

Current educational programs are designed for these times; as times change, educators must adjust curricula and, at times, lead in social change. In what specific directions are our programs likely to go? Despite the push for going back to the basics, curricula will increase in diversity and range of offerings. The rate of new program development will increase. New content organizations, new curriculum designs, and even new associations among disciplined and nondisciplined knowledge will accompany this heightened pace of curriculum growth. Social studies in the elementary schools will include the topics, or even mini-courses, in the psychology of art, group dynamics, the morality of politics, and the politics of schooling.

There will be a continued push to make curricular activities relevant to the times, and teachers will more often experiment with content and instructional designs. Elementary educators will become more involved with research and development activities to assure that potential programs will be relevant and productive for the diverse student populations. The creation and testing of programs will link some schools to regional labs, universities, and even to publishers, and teachers will asume new professional relationships in generating new content and educational experiences. Schools will also have closer connections with state offices of education in creating new contents and programs.

We can probably expect a massive reorganization of social studies, as you might guess from the mention of a topic such as the psychology of art. But we can talk, too, about entirely new blends of social studies content—universe studies, for example, encompassing the geography of the moon, the evolution of planets, and the climate of Venus. With the help of computers, teachers could generate unique combinations of content in response to a particular student interest. The press of a button will deliver information about what different subjects might be combined to answer a question. For example, if a gifted student wants to explore the ways people view their environments and what effects their perceptions have on their behavior, the question could be written into a computer's processing system. The computer would deliver a printout detailing the several content areas that alone or in combination might provide answers to this question. We might ask the computer, "How do people view their environments and what effects do such views have on their behavior?" and the computer might respond this way:

> I like your question. It has lots of possibilities. Some standard content areas that might help you deal with the question are:
>> geography
>> psychology
>> sociology
>> history
>> anthropology
>
> Some new areas of content for you to consider are:
>> environmental psychology
>> architecture
>> urban planning
>> force-field analysis
>> group dynamics
>> social medicine

380

human ecology
interior design

Now, let's try some topic combinations for your question.

The sociology of space
The geographic distribution of spatial structures in urban settings
Persons' reactions to architectural forms
Psychosomatic behaviors in artificial environments
The morality of good space

Now, write down some of your reactions to my suggestions. Do you like
your computer's ideas? If not, please reword your original question.

This kind of printout might seem far-fetched today, but the time when such communication will occur is not distant. On the other hand, we do not mean to imply that teachers in the future will not maintain standard social studies curriculum offerings. Indeed, much from today's programs will remain, but we can expect the content and manner of treatment to change greatly.

In the future, we will deal not only with new social studies content, but with new formats as well. New instructional organization patterns will integrate contents, experiences, instructional media, and instructional personnel in the most effective way. There will probably be different shapes of space and varying time allotments to promote more effective and efficient learning encounters. The traditional 45-minute period or unvarying daily schedule may change drastically; in the future, we may have two-week periods in which social studies is the only subject covered. Realistic simulations such as role playing and intensive reasearch may fill extended periods of time. It is also possible that pupils will work on personalized programs tailor-made to their abilities and interests.

Educators will probably schedule many more opportunities for students to interact with other agencies that deal with areas stressed in the school's curriculum. If students are studying law in the community, they may have active dialogue with a law firm and visit a courtroom during a trial; they may even have opportunities to work with law professors. Currently, many students, usually of junior high age, gain social studies knowledge through participation in community agencies. Others learn about economics and the marketplace by participating in Junior Achievement programs. Still others gain some understanding of psychology and sociology as members of community counseling centers that offer a type of ongoing internship. Many businesses have relationships with schools whereby students interested in that line of work can visit, ask questions, and observe.

Working in the community is one facet of the expanded range of experiences we can expect to find an integral part of future school programs. This expansion will be in all directions, and we believe this expansion of experiences will affect not only elementary-age children but adults as well. Many social studies offerings will be redesigned for adult participation.

381

This projection has major implications for elementary teachers—they may come to be social studies specialists, instructing individuals from elementary to adult levels.

In the near future, field experiences will not be the one-day, once-a-year variety common today. We presently have a "foot in the door" with this type of school activity; many curricula include an outdoor-education segment in which students spend several days or a week living at a camp. This environment allows intensive investigations relating to biology, climatology, geography, geology, and earth science that are impossible in the regular classroom. Total emersion in the topic also heightens interest in the content. These outdoor programs are known by a variety of names: outdoor education, survival education, earth science education, or community education. But whatever the name, social studies teachers will undoubtedly be designing more of these kinds of educational experiences.

New concepts will bring novel strategies and educational activities. Education is presently a labor-intensive activity; the future will find it more technology-intensive. Certainly, computers will figure more prominently in the teaching-learning process. CAI will become an integral part of curricular experience, allowing greater personalization of content. The computer will also handle more of the burden of classroom management. Teachers of the future will be relieved of a great deal of record keeping and reporting; the computer will have this responsibility. Teachers will be able to get an instant readout each day on each pupil, to help them individualize plans for a day or even a week. Social studies progress reports may well be jointly written by the teacher and the computer.

We spoke earlier of the use of lasers to extend the capabilities of computers; in fact, the day of the self-programming computer is now. We already have prototypes of the talking computer. Educators will have available in their classrooms computers with the capacity to learn from their experiences and specific training. Perhaps the greatest boon to social studies will be that lasers will allow computers to store vast amounts of information on a square-inch of photographic film. With this capacity, a 20,000-volume library can be reduced to an 8×10-inch piece of nickel foil; the same amount of information presently requires ten miles of magnetic tape. Not only can the laser increase the storage capacity, but it can do so at a major savings in cost. Think of the information that social studies students will have at hand in the near future!

Holography was mentioned under possible new directions. Such technology will be used in the schools—the issue is not if, but when. Holography, with or without lasers, will have a major impact on reproduction of the visual image. Holographics will allow students to "see" three-dimensional images. Students will be able to visit distant museums and "visually" handle artifacts without ever leaving the classroom. The level of student learning will be much more sophisticated as a result of such interaction with materials. Students will be able to make copies of holographs to use later for more detailed analysis. The only restraints on a teacher's potential instructional strategies will be the narrowness of his views and the limits of his creativity and daring. If teachers truly believe they can manage the future, they can bring many of these fringe developments into the mainstream of classroom instruction.

New Roles for Teachers and Students

The greatest promise for improved instruction lies not within organized national efforts to reconstruct or create curricula, but rather lies within the realm of imaginative teaching that stimulates in students academic excitement.

(Hunkins, 1972)

Social studies educators need to realize that as they change programs, school space, schedules, and relationships with the community, they must also adjust their roles. If they envision a future in which students are actively involved with legions of materials in numerous environments, they cannot perpetuate the current role of teacher as presenter of material. We discussed the need to assume new roles in chapter 2, but it may be productive to review some of that discussion. It seems plausible that the teacher of the future will play three major roles: specialist, executive, and professional (Frazier, 1968).

Teachers will be specialists in some aspect of the social sciences as well as general education, but even within this specialist role, they will have to go

In creating, piloting, and teaching educational programs, team decision making by teachers will become commonplace.

383

beyond merely presenting information. They will also be diagnosticians and prescribers, skilled in observation of student performance and able to determine avenues for further learning—but no longer in isolation; they will work collectively with colleagues and professionals outside the school. Already, in creating educational plans for handicapped students, teachers are required to plan cooperatively with parents, students, administrators, psychologists, and sometimes legal counsel. Team decision making will become commonplace.

Teachers will not merely teach programs created by a team; they will also be responsible to a greater degree for creating and piloting programs, thus filling an executive role. As of now, most teachers do not create social studies curricula. They occasionally serve on curriculum advisory committees, but in most cases content has already been determined. Teachers and other professionals will have to determine what is the most productive content for students at any given time, using diagnostic skills to determine the appropriate types of social studies learnings. Teachers will often work in teams to test new programs. As executives, teachers will be involved in materials selection and perhaps, in some instances, in materials creation, although materials creation will still fall mainly to publishers and regional educational laboratories. It is highly probable that some teachers will be members of teams associated with at least the regional educational labs or university research and development centers.

In the role of executive, teachers may consider themselves directors of instruction or curriculum managers, responsible for enabling students in social studies to achieve the greatest range and depth of learnings, and managing educational environments to facilitate learning. Special groups of educators and specialists from the community will form committees responsible for guaranteeing quality social studies programs; students will sometimes be integral members of these committees.

The majority of social studies teachers today just teach. They cannot really do much else; the structure of the school and the expectations of the community are such that teachers must spend all their time presenting information. Rarely are teachers allowed to function as educational professionals, in the sense of being students of education. Classroom teachers and school curriculum specialists today are not responsible for advancing the field of education. They do not, for example, have time during the regular school day to design educational experiments, and they have little time to write about topics relevant to the social studies. Most readers of this book will not yet have taught, but it is not too early to begin planning the roles you expect to play in the future.

Future Social Studies Environments

Inside the Schools

In chapter 11, we discussed educational environments in a somewhat global manner. Anyone who adopts a futuristic stance will realize that as curricula and roles change, the spaces for working with social studies must necessarily change as well. A futuristic curriculum housed in a traditional, past-oriented school structure is a paradox.

One expectation for the future is that classrooms and curricula will become adaptive rather than selective. Glasser (1975) notes that, currently, most school environments and programs say to students, "to succeed, you *must* adjust. The mode of education and the physical space are not going to vary. The ways to success are limited. It is you, the student, who must change."

With the selective mode, the curriculum was designed not to change; the instructional methods were set, and the pathways available for students were well established and unalterable. Students who could not adapt to the establishment were sometimes outcasts; those who did adjust were "successful" students.

While we realize there are common social studies learnings that all students should know, we feel strongly that the social studies classroom should utilize the adaptive mode. The adaptive mode is based on the premise that the educational environment can support many and various instructional methods and opportunities for success. Indeed, it is the challenge of social studies educators to diagnose students' current levels of understanding and prior exprience and then adapt the curriculum, the experiences, and even the materials and space to promote essential social studies learnings. The adaptive mode does not omit crucial social studies knowledge; instead, it ensures that all students will learn some social studies content because the curriculum, experiences, and spaces are adapted to guarantee success.

In an adaptive school environment, social studies educators will consider individual learning styles and abilities. Teachers will, often in cooperation with the students, plan personalized pathways for acquiring social studies content. As educators gain additional information about the students, they can modify content arrangement, planned activities, and the design of the educational space. Future classroom environments will be created and managed on the assumption that students are active inquirers. The classroom will have places for inquiry, for quiet reflection, for student interaction, for experimentation, for challenging, and for additional reading.

Pupils are highly responsive to the conditions around them; as teachers and pupils adjust conditions, they will find themselves changing as well. In the future—near and distant—one role of social studies educators will be to design adaptive environments and to make environments sensitive to learners' performances. Instructors will also find pupils developing skills at modifying their own classroom environments to enhance learning and skill development.

Outside the Schools

We have stated that students often learn more effectively outside the regular classroom. We have noted that technology has already made some homes potential information centers; teachers have to decide how much education they want to occur directly in the home. The degree of home involvement is or can be largely under the teacher's control.

The technology exists to tie homes into educational networks. Many television specials are aired for which educational materials have been prepared for teacher use in integrating the viewing experience with the regular school program. Educational television has long been used in schools, and parents have been urged to watch at home so they can continue discussions begun in school. The future possibilities are endless.

Considering the Future

It is easy to say that educators can manage their futures, but just how do they do that? What strategies can one use to project the future and to control it to some degree? Have you ever daydreamed? In a real sense, daydreaming is a futuristic procedure. Do you have feelings or views about what will or should happen next week? Next year? Most people do. This is what futurists call intuitive forecasting, a technique everyone can perfect to some degree. One imagines the future and how he wants to exist in it, then maps the specifications he must accomplish today in order to materialize the images of tomorrow. At some point, all educators decided to become teachers; they saw themselves in a future in which they were teachers. Most of them did something to increase the likelihood they would have this future—they took certain courses required for college, then took other courses necessary for certification. Taking this course in social studies methods or reading this book has been part of your plan to increase the probability that you will be a successful social studies teacher—not today, but in the near future.

The major technique of futuristics is forecasting, a means of creating windows through which one can survey potential happenings, both good and bad (Joseph, 1974). Looking through these windows provides direction as to what to avoid, what to modify, and what to maintain. Making short-range forecasts in social studies is easier than making long-range forecasts. For instance, forecasting what will occur in social studies class next month is much easier than forecasting about a potential class five years from now. This does not mean that teachers should avoid mid- or long-range forecasts. Indeed, if programs are to be responsive to future students, educators will need to have generated some long-range forecasts or projections. Remember, however, that these are projections, not predictions. What is the difference? Predictions state what *will happen* in the future; projections state what *is likely to happen* in the future if certain things continue to happen or if some other events occur.

Although most people do not recognize it as such, one futuristics procedure is often used today—that of brainstorming. It allows thinking about the future and generating schemes for achieving "dreams." Social studies teachers need to dream a little; frequently, they get too bogged down in everyday reality, saying, "I can't do that; there is no time, and besides my principal or supervising teacher would not let me do it." If you really think an idea is good, don't cancel it out too soon.

Another means of forecasting is the scenario, a story or description about the future that draws its basis from current trends and happenings. The scenario writer uses current realities to show how a particular future state might evolve if such events continue. An attractive feature of the scenario is that one need not be an expert futurist to understand it. Scenarios allow one to look at potential alternatives, to speculate as to how realistic they are, and to determine whether or not they are desirable. Scenarios project the future consequences of current technological and social and educational policies. But they are not science fiction, which is based on someone's imagination; they are based on fact.

Activity 15:1

Projection—Social Studies Content

Using one of the procedures mentioned, make a projection of social studies content in the time periods 1985, 1990, 1995. Provide some basis for these projections.

Activity 15:2

Projection—Social Studies Teachers' Roles

Make a projection about teachers' roles in 1985, 1990, and 1995. Provide some support for your projection. What are your current feelings about these projected roles? Explain your feelings.

Activity 15:3

Projection—The Elementary School

Make a projection about elementary schools in 1990 and 1995. Share your future view with a colleague and record his reactions.

Some other procedures futurists can employ are based on mathematical probability models and used in computer simulations. For those readers who want more information about these procedures, many books on the market deal with futuristics in great detail. More important for the present, however, is not that teachers have great skill in forecasting techniques, but rather that they have a futuristic frame of mind. Armed with the attitude that the future can be studied, anticipated, and managed, teachers use their wealth of information about social studies in the elementary school to make curricula and educational experiences relevant for today's students, and to assure relevance in the future.

Discussion

Individuals and societies have always influenced their futures through the choices they have made, but the choices, for the most part, have been random. Today we can influence our futures more systematically with the principles of "futuristics," which teaches us to identify possible, probable, and preferable futures. Educators are beginning to apply its methods and techniques for managing their various fields, and social studies teachers must consider the future when they plan curricula.

Social studies teachers must be prepared to address student and community needs as they arise; those needs must be anticipated and programs must be at the ready to deal with them. To cope effectively in the future, teachers must understand current trends, identify which trends are likely to persist, and plan ways to manage the social trends that will affect education. The goal in social studies is to make teaching and programs consistently responsive to the times.

Teachers can anticipate and manage the future by acting in ways that make certain events likely to occur and other events less likely to occur. Some trends for which we can now plan are the increasing use of technology, the use of new kinds of educational structures and environments, new types of educational goods and services, increasingly diverse student bodies, and the probability of campus and community schools.

As the times change, so must the social studies curriculum, and we will see much greater diversity and a wider range of course offerings. Teachers will be more likely to experiment with content and instructional designs, and will engage more actively in program planning with other professionals. More extensive use of computers will help us generate whole new content areas and blends of study. We can also expect much more active involvement with agencies and environments outside the schools.

We discussed earlier the roles of today's social studies teacher; in the future, we can expect to see him as specialist, executive, and professional, as programs and curricula expand. We can also expect the environments for social studies to become more adaptive to student needs, with the student, at the same time, acquiring skills for modifying his classroom environment to enhance his own performance.

Just as those who become teachers must at some point *plan* to become teachers, so may they plan for the future. Planning may begin with as common an activity as daydreaming, or the more formal activities of brainstorming and scenario writing. The most important factor, however, is nothing more than a forward-looking attitude—a sense of expectation and a desire to influence the future, rather than to be a passive victim of time.

References

Frazier, Alexander. "The New Elementary School Teacher." In *The New Elementary School*, edited by Alexander Frazier. Washington, D.C.: Association for Supervision and Curriculum Development, 1968.

Glasser, Robert. "The School of the Future: Adaptive Environments for Learning." In *The Future of Education: Perspectives on Tomorrow's Schooling,* edited by Louis Rubin. Boston: Allyn and Bacon, 1975.

Hunkins, Francis P. "New Identities for New Tasks." *Educational Leadership* 29 (1972): 503–506.

Joseph, Earl C. "An Introduction to Studying the Future." In *Futurism in Education,* edited by Stephen P. Hencley and James R. Yates. Berkeley, Calif.: McCutchan, 1974.

Knezevich, Stephen J. *Administration of Public Education.* New York: Harper and Row, 1975.

Lindaman, Edward B., and Lippitt, Ronald O. *Choosing the Future You Prefer.* Ann Arbor, Mich.: Human Resource Development Associates of Ann Arbor, Inc., 1979.

Rubin, Louis. "Observations on Future Schooling." In *The Future of Education: Perspectives on Tomorrow's Schooling,* edited by Louis Rubin. Boston: Allyn and Bacon, 1975.

Strudler, Harold L. "Educational Futurism: Perspective or Discipline?" In *Learning for Tomorrow, The Role of the Future in Education,* edited by Alvin Toffler. New York: Vintage Books, 1974.

APPENDIX A
Resources for the Educational Use of Evening Television Programs

Even within the limited scope of evening programming for educational use (i.e., excluding the in-school use of television programs such as those on ITV), the number of organizations that are developing materials seems to grow daily. This listing contains the major ones that are distributing on a national basis. Educators should also contact state departments of education, as well as local education associations, commercial and public television stations, and community groups, for additional materials.

Guides to Television Programs

Probably the first television programs to be utilized were the specials—programs like *Roots, Masterpiece Theatre, Jacques Cousteau, Eleanor and Franklin, The Autobiography of Miss Jane Pitman, The Belle of Amherst,* and *The Long Search.* These programs generally air once, though some are repeated. Eventually, some also become available for rental or purchase from film and video distributors. The programs range in subject, and may be used in a wide variety of disciplines.

A number of groups develop and distribute study guides for broadcasts on commercial and public networks. These guides generally include a synopsis of the program, a wide range of student activities, and suggested resources.

From Linda Kahn, "Criteria for TV Viewing Skills," *Media & Methods* (October 1979): 34, 90. Reprinted with permission.

Organizations

- Prime Time School Television (120 South LaSalle St., Suite 810, Chicago, IL 60603), produces program guides for three to five specials or series specials each month, plus periodic curriculum projects which contain lesson ideas and student activities that focus on a particular television-related issue.
- Public TV stations such as WGBH (125 Western Ave., Allston, MA 02134), WNET (356 West 58th St., New York, NY 10019), and WQED (4802 Fifth Ave., Pittsburgh, PA 15213) produce study guides for specials. Contact the stations directly for costs and information regarding distribution.
- Teachers Guides to Television (Television Information Office, 699 Madison Ave., New York, NY 10021) publishes two guides a year. Each includes approximately twelve programs, plus articles about current television-related topics. Its Parent Participation Workshops (see article, page 70) involve teachers, parents and students in active discussions about specific TV programs.

Publications

- *American Educator* (The American Federation of Teachers, 11 Dupont Circle, N.W., Washington, DC 20036) is a quarterly magazine that includes a sixteen-page supplement which covers eight to twelve programs and includes general articles about television.
- *Audiovisual Instruction* (AECT, 1126 Sixteenth St., N.W., Washington, DC 20036) periodically includes materials from Teachers Guides to Television. Television.
- *Cultural Information Service* (P.O. Box 92, New York, NY 10016) is a bi-weekly publication which carries reviews of TV programs and viewer guides to specials and series programs.
- *Media & Methods* (401 North Broad St., Philadelphia, PA 19108) is published nine times a year, and regularly carries the Prime Time School Television study guides, as well as articles which deal with the impact of television and video on education.
- *Scholastic Magazines* (50 West 44th St., New York, NY 10036) publishes their *Teacher's Editions of Scholastic Magazine* which provides "Tele-guides," lesson plans designed to incorporate discussion of specific TV programs into classroom activity, and a periodic television review column. The student magazines *(Scope, Voice, Sr. Scholastic, Search, Jr. Scholastic,* and *Science World)* reprint excerpts from scripts and feature articles about television programs. Scholastic also develops learning kits on selected programs.
- *Today's Education* (National Education Association, 1201 Sixteenth St., N.W., Washington, DC 20036) is a bi-monthly journal which features articles about television, and will include selected Prime Time School Television program guides. NEA recommended programs are detailed in the *NEA Reporter.*

Television and Reading

Materials are available in three basic areas. The first is television scripts. These are from popular programs or specials and are used as the basis for reading skill development exercises and for discussions of program content. Accompanying teacher guides contain comprehensive classroom activities. For information, contact:

- Dr. Michael McAndrew, Director of Educative Services. Television Reading Program, Capitol Cities Communications, Inc., 4100 City Line Ave., Philadelphia, PA 19131.
- John P. Blessington, Director of Educational Relations, CBS Television Reading Program, 51 West 52nd St., New York, NY 10019.
- Scholastic Magazines, 50 West 44th St. New York, NY 10036.

The second area is TV tie-in books. Most paperback publishing companies are distributing books that are related to specific TV programs. They are available in local book stores, or directly from the paperback publishers.

The third area is skill development. Skills such as inference, scanning, sequencing, classifying, and cause and effect analysis are necessary for comprehension of reading materials as well as TV programs. *Channel*, a color/sound filmstrip developed by Rosemary Lee Potter, Camille Faith, and Lynne Brenner Ganek, is intended for use with TV and reading skill development in grades 4-12, and is available from Educational Activities, Inc., Freeport, NY 11520. It sells for $39.95, and includes resource cards and a teacher's manual.

Critical Viewing Skills

Increased emphasis is being placed on the development of critical television viewing skills, and along these lines, there are numerous projects and resources.

Projects

The U.S. Office of Education has funded four projects for grades K-5, 6-8, 9-12, and post-secondary. The K-12 projects included a component for family use as well as a teacher booklet and printed student materials. The projects will be available for general distribution in 1980. For information, contact:

- (K-5) Charles Corder-Bolz, Project Director, Southwest Educational Development Laboratory, 211 East 7th St., Austin, TX 78701.
- (6-8) Debbi Bilowit, Education Dept., WNET, 356 West 58th St., New York, NY 10019.

- (9-12) Donna Lloyd-Kolkin, Project Director, Far West Laboratory, 1855 Folsom St., San Francisco, CA 94103.
- (post-secondary) Donis Dondis, Project Director, Boston University, School of Public Communication, 640 Commonwealth Ave., Boston, MA 02215.

Resources

- *The Way We See It* (teacher handbook, $12.50) and *Television and You* (student handbook, $3.00) are comprehensive materials that were developed by James A. Anderson of the University of Utah, and Milton E. Ploghoft of Ohio University. Though intended for use in grades 3-6, they contain many ideas which may be adapted for secondary school use. Included is information on the uses of television, on entertainment programs, on commercials, and on new programs. Contact: James A. Anderson, Dept. of Communication, University of Utah, Salt Lake City, UT 84112.
- *TVision* is a monthly newsletter published by the Television Commission of the Journalism Education Association. It's the only current publication providing three-week advance information on the plots of weekly series programs, along with suggestions for classroom use. Subscription is $4.50 a year, and an examination copy is available. Contact: Jim Matthews, 1101 Arlington Ave., LaGrange, IL 60525. The JEA also publishes *Me and My TV* ($4.00) which details an experiment in which popular TV programs were used in high school English and social studies classes. There are suggestions for curriculum planning with television, as well as a readable summary of research in vocabulary development and adult-teen dialogue using TV as a catalyst. (The book was reviewed in *Media & Methods*, April 1978, pg. 8.) For a copy or information, write: JEA Books, Tomahawk Trail, Shabbona, IL 60550.
- "Reading TV" consists of developmental lesson plans and videotapes for use with existing programs. Emphasis is on building analytical viewing skills, with special attention paid to program openings. "Reading TV" is geared to grades 5-12. For more information, contact: Barbara Stecconi Koven, Watertown Public Schools, 30 Common St., Watertown, MA 02172.
- "Television and Values" by Jeffrey Schrank is a multimedia kit containing a sound filmstrip which examines commercial TV as a system of values. TV addiction, passivity vs. violence, models and heroes, TV drug advertising, and instant solutions to conflict—all are explored. The kit also includes a teacher's guide, project cards, forms for monitoring TV, the *TV Action Book* (an excellent collection of essays and TV activities for use with high school students), the *TV Sponsors Directory*, and a simulation game called "TV on Trial." Contact: Jeffrey Schrank, The Learning Seed Company, 145 Brentwood Dr., Palatine, IL 60067.
- Drs. Dorothy Singer and Jerome Singer have developed a series of lessons for critical viewing skill development, a student workbook, and a videotape. Intended for use in grades 3-6, it could also be of interest as a

resource for higher grades. Contact the Singers at: The Family Television
Research Center, Yale University, 405 Temple St., New Haven, CT 06511.
- The PTA is currently developing and field testing a critical viewing skills
curriculum. For more information, write: PTA TV Action Center, 700 N.
Rush St., Chicago, IL 60611.

Curriculum Units

Prime Time School Television has developed three curriculum units which
link evening television programming to the broad subject areas of law, economics, and values. Intended as supplemental instruction, they include lesson
plans, background readings and resource listings for students and teachers, as
well as such materials for the students as TV viewing logs, newspaper and
magazine articles, literary works, concept guides, charts and graphs.

- "Television, Police and the Law" is a springboard to discussion on the role
of police in the society, duties and responsibilities of police, constitutional
guidelines for law enforcement, and the impact of TV police shows on students' law enforcement expectations. It's aimed at grades 6-12, for use in
social studies, language arts, law, and communication classes. A starter kit
is available for $4.50 from Argus Communications, 7440 Natchez Ave.,
Niles, IL 60648. It includes a teacher's guide, one student book, and six
spirit masters; additional student books are available separately.
- "Television & Economics: From the Medium to the Marketplace" uses
programs and commercials to explore the workings of the American economy, and to examine basic economic concepts. Planned for use in social
studies, economics, business, and consumer education classes, grades 8-12, it
is available for $20.00 from Prime Time School Television, 120 S. LaSalle
St., Suite 810, Chicago, IL 60603.
- "Televised Values" focuses on heroes and role models, family relationships,
discriminatory stereotypes, and moral dilemmas. It's for use in language
arts, social studies, and media classes, grades 7-12, and will be available
from PTST in spring, 1980.

Networks

The commercial and public television networks are recognizing the importance of the instructional use of evening television. ABC has funded TV
study guides for programs like *Roots: The Next Generations, Friendly Fire*, and,
most recently (it's in this issue of M&M), *Making the News*, an analytical
new curriculum project. The CBS Reading Program works with local stations, foundations, corporations, educators, and newspapers, duplicate scripts
and prepare teaching guides for selected television dramas. CBS has also
funded TV study guides for *Joey and Redhawk*, the CBS Festival of Lively

395

Arts for Young People, and the CBS News Program for Young People. NBC is developing viewing guides for selected programs, which can be obtained through local affiliates. In addition, the network also funded the Parent Participation Workshops. Many local PBS stations have educational liaisons, and some produce and distribute study guides or make available guides from other sources. For more information on network materials, contact:

- Pam Warford, Director of Community Relations, ABC-TV, 1330 Avenue of the Americas, New York, NY 10019.
- John P. Blessington, Director of Educational Relations, CBS-TV, 51 West 52nd St., New York, NY 10019.
- Betty Hudson, Vice President of Corporate Projects, NBC-TV, 30 Rockefeller Plaza, New York, NY 10020.
- Grace Cavalieri, Director of Educational Services, PBS, 475 L'Enfant Plaza, S.W., Washington, D.C. 20024.

Organizations and Media Interest Groups

Many organizations are concerned with the quality of television broadcasting and its influence on young people. Among them are:

- Action for Children's Television, 46 Austin St., Newtonville, MA 02160.
- American Council for Better Broadcasts, 120 E. Wilson St., Madison, WI 53703.
- National Association for Better Broadcasting, P.O. Box 43640, Los Angeles, CA 90043.
- National Citizens Committee for Broadcasting, 1028 Connecticut Ave., N.W., Washington, D.C. 20036.
- National Council for Children and Television, 20 Nassau St., Suite 215, Princeton, NJ 08540.
- Committee on Impact of TV on Children, National Council of Teachers of English, 1111 Kenyon Rd., Urbana, IL 61801.
- TV for Learning, PBS, 475 L'Enfant Plaza, S.W., Washington, D.C. 20024.

APPENDIX B
Simulation Games for Elementary Social Studies

Each entry includes the title, recommended grade levels, amount of time needed to play, number of players, and the cost as of the summer of 1979. The initial entry is followed by a brief description of the activity and its source for acquisition. Complete addresses for each source appear at the end of the games list. Sources range from commercial distributors to professional journals and private individuals. If game directions appear in an out-of-print book, the book is included since it could likely be obtained through inter-library loan services. Prices range from free to $50. Most of the games are recommended for use in grades four and above, although five are designed for the early primary grades. Only one is specifically noted for educable mentally retarded students.

A code preceding each entry indicates the social science discipline(s) with which the activity is associated:

AS = Anthropology-Sociology including Careers
E = Economics
G = Geography
H = History
PS = Political Science, including Ecology

AS ACCESS, grs. 5–12, 1½ hours, 8–40 players, $5. Explores questions about the role of women on issues such as affirmative action, marriage, and equal employment opportunities. Simile II; SSSS.

AS ADAPT, grs. 5–7, 5 class periods, entire class, $15. Each student receives
G   one of 5 maps (climate, vegetation, landforms, wildlife, minerals) of a

Excerpted from Sharon Pray Muir, "Simulation Games for Elementary Social Studies," *Social Education* (January 1980): 35–39. Reprinted by permission.

newly discovered continent. Working alone, the students select a locale suitable for a hunting-gathering society. Later, groups of 5 consider all geographic factors. Interact; EMI.

AS   AGENCY, grs. 5–8, 1 week, entire class, $15. Students examine advertising from various media and analyze the language and visuals. In agencies of 6–8 members, teams compete to promote 4 new products through ad campaigns to be presented to the whole class. Interact.

G   ANDESIA, grs. 5–6, 2–5 hours, 20–30 players, in $12.95 book. Partici-
PS   pants assume roles of politicians, mine workers, mine owners, farm workers, farm owners, and middle class in an imaginary Andean nation of South America. Reese, pp. 31–38.

E   AUCTION OFF APATHY, grs. 4–6, 3 days, entire class, free. An auction illustrates the concepts of supply and demand, how prices are determined, how personal wants are influenced by the ability to pay, and how value judgments influence buying and selling. *Teacher* magazine, September, 1972, pp. 80, 82, 86, and 88.

PS   BALANCE OF POWER, grs. 6–8, 1–2 hours, entire class, in $12.95 book. Students are leaders of 4 imaginary nations. They try to keep peace while bringing as many small nations as possible under their influence. Reese, pp. 67–71.

E   BLUE WODJET COMPANY, grs. 6–10, 4–7 hours, 25–30 players, in $12.95 book. Players are stockholders, managers, and the work force of an imaginary manufacturing concern. Others are residents in the city where the company is located. Reese, pp. 74–85.

E   BOXCARS, grs. 5–8, 4 class periods, entire class, $11. Simulates competing trading companies in Western Europe, explores economics of trade as well as geography of the continent. Interact; SSSS; EMI.

AS   BRONZE AXES, grs. 4–6, 1–2 class periods, entire class, in $2.45 book.
E   Based on methods of an archaeologist, groups of Arkwarks, Bankoos, and Zuhogs barter for food, tin, or copper with other tribes. Youngers & Aceti, pp. 15–20.

E   CANADA'S PRAIRIE WHEAT GAME, grs. 4–7, 1–2 hours, 4–7 +
G   players, $3.05. Farmers experience wheat sales using banking system. Each one begins with bank balance of $3,000 and may borrow up to $7,000 at 5% interest. They keep records of the amount of land under cultivation, how many bushels of wheat are grown, and payment price for them. Alberta School.

G   CENTRAL AMERICAN SUMMIT, grs. 6–12, 1–2 hours, entire class,
PS   in $12.95 book. As government leaders of Central American nations, Mexico, and the United States, students hold a "summit meeting" to discuss possible union into one nation as well as other problems. Reese, pp. 38–41.

E   CLASSROOM STOCK MARKET, grs. 5–9, 3–4 days, up to 30 players, in $12.95 book. Students buy stock in corporations based on *Monopoly* properties, elect officers, and collect dividends. A stock market board lists stocks and current market values. Reese, pp. 103–108.

E   COCOA BEAN GAME, grs. 5–9, 1–2 hours, entire class, $22.50. Buyers and sellers trade cocoa beans, with each round representing a year. Chance factors are given which influence the supply and demand. Directions in 6th grade teacher's edition, *Inquiring About Technology*, pp. 170–178. Holt.

AS   CODE, grs. 5–8, 4–8 days, entire class, $11. Students explore means of written language and codes. Teams develop and trade messages and decipher codes. Interact: SSSS.

AS   DESIGN, grs. 5–8, 15–25 hours, 18–35 players, $22. Examines American housing today. Considers advantages and disadvantages of single family homes, condominiums, apartments, and mobile homes, as well as features such as number of bathrooms, bedrooms, fireplace, air conditioning, and swimming pools. Culminates by designing house, buying and arranging furniture. Interact; SSSS.

AS   DIG, grs. 6–12, 3 weeks, 14–36 players, $15. Deals with archeological reconstruction of a vanished civilization. Competing teams create 2 cultures, including economics, government, family, language, religion, and recreation. They create and collect artifacts and bury them. Each team scientifically excavates, restores, analyzes, and reconstructs the other team's artifacts and culture. Interact; SSSS; EMI.

H   DISCOVERY, grs. 4–9, 3 weeks, 25–35 players, $15. Simulates early American colonization including problems faced in the 17th century. Roles assigned are leaders, bankers, mappers, traders, recorders, and generals. They decide why they are colonizing and what supplies and how much must be taken to New World, as well as the selection of site, establishment of the colony, and daily economic, political, and military decisions. Interact; SSSS; EMI.

H
PS   ECOPOLIS, grs. 4–8, 3 weeks, 25–35 players, $15. A community struggles to solve ecological problems. Players enact lower animals, Indians living in harmony with environment, and settlers. Simulation covers 150-year period from original settlement to growth of a city of over 225,000. Interact; SSSS.

E
PS   ENERGY X, grs. 5–12, entire class, $19.95. 9 committees study natural resources location and production, and plan their allocation. Includes maps, graphs, cassette and filmstrip. EMI.

PS   EQUALITY, grs. 5–12, 3 weeks, 25–35 players, $15. Students play members of 6 ethnic groups in a mythical city as tension develops between minority groups. Interact; SSSS.

399

E   FAMILY BUDGET, grs. 3–6, 1–2 days, entire class, $2.45. Students form families of 5 and establish budget of no more than $500 based on list of "wants" of family. Youngers & Aceti, pp. 30–34.

H   FAMILY TREE, grs. 4–7, varying time length, entire class, $23.50. Students role-play historians as they interview and record information on ancestral charts and time lines. Interact.

AS   FLAME, grs. K–1, 3 class periods, entire class, $5. Firetrucks Leaving
PS   and Meeting Emergencies (F.L.A.M.E.) concerns a hypothetical fire at the residence of the Jones family. The family first tries to extinguish the fire, fails, and calls the fire department. Cohen.

E   GALACTICA, grs. 5–7, several 5-minute rounds, 20 + players, in $12.95 book. Students are traders from various planets with specialized goods to exchange and specific goods to obtain in a limited time. They have money, but it is worthless; so bartering ensues. Reese, pp. 97–103.

AS   HELP!, grs. 3–6, variable time length, entire class, $19.50. Students act out responses to common household emergencies. Kit includes 32 crisis cards and a toy telephone. Uses local directory. Games Central.

E   HOLIDAY CARD FACTORY, grs. 3–6, 1 to 2 class periods, entire class, in $14.95 book. Students explore advantages and disadvantages of mass production techniques. Welton and Mallan, pp. 298–300.

PS   HOW A BILL BECOMES A LAW, grs. 4–6, 1 class period, entire class, free. Class members take roles of President, Vice President, Speaker of House, Senators, and Congressmen. Bills are introduced, discussed, voted upon, sometimes vetoed and overridden. Muir.

E   IMPORT, grs. 4–5, 2–4 weeks, 18–35 players, $10. Simulates activities of 6 importing firms in various parts of world. Each firm buys from several countries. To win, a firm must buy 8 products from 3 countries and sell them at a profit. Simile II; SSSS; EMI.

E   MERCHANT, grs. 5–8, 2 weeks, 18–35 players, $23.50. Simulates
H   small town businesses competing in a free market in 4 different Western communities at the turn of the century. Also explores changes from agrarian to industrial society. Interact; SSSS.

E   MONEX, grs. 4–7, 1–2 class periods, entire class, in $14.95 book. Students explore the advantages and disadvantages of barter systems while acquiring materials to be used in making a group collage. Jarolimek, pp. 337–339.

H   NEIGHBORHOOD, grs. 3–7, 3–5 hours, 4–12 players, $21.50. Players
PS   represent 4 different ethnic groups modeled after historical transitions of Boston's North End. They plan, locate, and relocate housing units, industrial units, commercial units, and cultural facilities on a tabletop map in a re-enactment of 200 years in the unidentified city's history. Games Central.

PS PARENT-SATELLITE NATIONS, grs. 5–8, 1–2 class periods. 24–30 players, free. Students explore trade negotiations and advantages which parent nations hold over their satellite nations. *Teacher*, October 1967, pp. 116–120.

AS RAFÁ RAFÁ, grs. 4–8, 80 minutes, 12–40 players, $15. Players divide into Alpha and Beta cultures. Each culture sends groups to the other culture to observe and interact as a means of gathering data without asking questions. Groups form and test hypotheses about the other culture. Directions for cultures are on a cassette tape. This is the elementary version of Bafa Bafa. Simile II; SSSS.

G   REMOTE ISLAND, grs. 4–10, 3–5 hours, 12+ players, $5. The game concerns a hypothetical island which the U.S. gained from Japan after World War II. It has remained virtually uninhabited since the time of its discovery by the crew of a shipwrecked sailing vessel. Players apply knowledge of map symbols, learn physical characteristics of the island, and then solve problems based on that information. There is also a version for the educable mentally retarded; specify it when ordering. Cohen.

E   STORES AND SHOPPERS, grs. 1–3, 1–2 class periods, entire class, free. Explores prices, income, expenses, profits, and buying preferences of both store owners and shoppers. *Instructor*, March 1970, pp. 96–97.

E   SUPERMARKET, grs. 4–7, 1+ hours, 2–32 players, $39. Shopkeepers mark prices, arrange displays, and check out shopper's groceries while other participants shop with tokens. Shoppers receive randomly chosen shopping lists which present at least one problem involving a tradeoff in cost, quality, or quantity. Revised 1977. Games Central; SSSS.

PS WORLD, grs. 6–9, 5 weeks, 20–35 players, $23.50. A simulation of how nations develop and become involved in power struggles. Groups create their own country, select a name, draw what the country looks like, and develop a form of government. Leaders, diplomats, and spies are selected. Each country competes to complete projects. Interact; SSSS.

APPENDIX C
Resource Materials

Documentary Photo Aids

These are a collection of photographs depicting historical events. Information regarding each picture is on the photograph. These aids are very good for getting children to investigate primary source materials.

> Documentary Photo Aids
> P.O. Box 2237
> Phoenix, AZ 85002

Free and Inexpensive Materials

Informative materials are often available from large business companies. Check your local telephone directory for the addresses of major businesses in your area. See also the *Thomas Register of Manufacturers.*

The U.S. Government Printing Office provides a huge number of materials at very low cost.

> U.S. Government Printing Office
> Division of Public Documents
> Washington, DC 20402

Other free and inexpensive materials include:

Catalogue of Free Teaching Aids	G. S. Salisbury and R. H. Sheridan Box 1075 Ventura, CA 91401
Choosing Free Materials for Use in the Schools	American Association of School Administrators Washington, DC 20036
Elementary Teachers Guide to Free Curriculum Materials	Educators Progressive Service Randolph, WI 53956
Inexpensive bulletins concerning teaching materials and sources of teaching materials	Bureau of Educational Research Ohio State University Columbus, OH 43210

Guides to Commercially Prepared Materials
Learning Directory (Westinghouse Learning Corporation)
New Educational Materials (Citation Press)

Guides to Social Studies Reading Materials
Basic Book Collection for Elementary Grades
Subject Index to Books for Primary Grades
Subject Index to Books for Intermediate Grades

These publications, published annually by the American Library Association, offer a comprehensive listing of materials available.

Jackdaw Kits
These kits contain collections of authentic reproductions of historical documents, prints, paintings, letters, and maps. Children can use the kits to gain experience in dealing with primary source materials. Documents difficult to read in the original are translated. These kits contain a great many items and cover many topics. Topic areas covered are U.S. colonization and independence, U.S. growth and expansion, world history from the Middle Ages to current times, and cultural history. There are also some kits dealing with Canadian history.

> Jackdaw Publications Ltd.
> 30 Bedford Square
> London, WC 1, England
> *in association with*
> Grossman Publishers, Inc.
> 125 East 19th Street
> New York, NY 10003

Sound Filmstrips and Sound Films
See the catalogue of the Social Studies School Service for listings of sound filmstrips and films dealing with the various social sciences as well as map and globe skills.

> Social Studies School Service
> 10000 Culver Blvd.
> P.O. Box 802
> Culver City, CA 90230

Periodicals Useful to Elementary Social Studies Teachers
Bulletin of the Center for Children's Books
Grade Teacher
Booklist

Instructor
Library Journal
Social Education
Audiovisual Instruction

Teacher Materials

National Council for the Social Studies
3615 Wisconsin Ave., N.W.
Washington, DC 20016

National Council for Geographic Education
University of Houston
Houston, TX 77004

Curriculum Associates
5 Esquire Road
North Billerica, MA 08162

The Social Science Education Consortium produces the *Social Studies Curriculum Materials Data Book*. This reference provides analyses of recently published curriculum materials appropriate for social studies classes.

Social Science Education Consortium
855 Broadway
Boulder, CO 80302

Excellent suggestions for potentially useful materials can also be found in catalogues, lists of resources, and curriculum guides available from the curriculum offices of local school districts, the state department of education, and the curriculum materials section in university and college libraries.

Name Index

Subject Index